# Scientific Realism and Human Emancipation

Following on from Roy Bhaskar's first two books, *A Realist Theory of Science* and *The Possibility of Naturalism*, *Scientific Realism and Human Emancipation* establishes the conception of social science as explanatory — and thence emancipatory — critique.

*Scientific Realism and Human Emancipation* starts from an assessment of the impasse of contemporary accounts of science as stemming from an incomplete critique of positivism. It then proceeds to a systematic exposition of scientific realism in the form of transcendental realism, highlighting a conception of science as explanatory of a structured, differentiated and changing world.

Turning to the social domain, the book argues for a view of the social order as conditioned by, and emergent from, nature. Advocating a critical naturalism, the author shows how the transformational model of social activity, together with the conception of social science as explanatory critique which it entails, resolves the divisions and dualisms besetting orthodox social and normative theory: between society and the individual, structure and agency, meaning and behaviour, mind and body, reason and cause, fact and value, and theory and practice. The book then goes on to discuss the emancipatory implications of social science and sketches the nature of the depth investigation characteristically entailed.

In the highly innovative third part of the book, Roy Bhaskar completes his critique of positivism by developing a theory of philosophical discourse and ideology, on the basis of the transcendental realism and critical naturalism already developed, showing how positivism functions as a restrictive ideology of, and for, science and other social practices.

**Roy Bhaskar** is the originator of the philosophy of critical realism, and the author of many acclaimed and influential works including *A Realist Theory of Science*, *The Possibility of Naturalism*, *Reclaiming Reality* and *Dialectic: The Pulse of Freedom*. He is an editor of the recently published *Critical Realism: Essential Readings* and is currently chair of the Centre for Critical Realism

**Key Texts in Critical Realism**
Other books in the Series:

**Dialectic**
*The pulse of freedom*
By Roy Bhaskar

**Reclaiming Reality**
*A critical introduction to contemporary philosophy*
By Roy Bhaskar

**Plato Etc**
*Problems of philosophy and their resolution*
By Roy Bhaskar

**A Realist Theory of Science**
By Roy Bhaskar

# Scientific Realism and Human Emancipation

## Roy Bhaskar

**Routledge**
Taylor & Francis Group

LONDON AND NEW YORK

First published 1986 by Verso

Published 2009
by Routledge
2 Park Square, Milton Park, Abingdon, Oxon, OX14 4RN

Simultaneously published in the USA and Canada
by Routledge
711 Third Avenue, New York, NY 10017

*Routledge is an imprint of the Taylor & Francis Group, an informa business*

© 2009 Roy Bhaskar

Typeset by RefineCatch Limited, Bungay,
Suffolk

*British Library Cataloguing in Publication Data*
A catalogue record for this book is available from the British Library

ISBN13: 978-0-415-45495-7 (pbk)
ISBN13: 978-0-203-87984-9 (ebk)

ISBN10: 0-415-45495-6 (pbk)
ISBN10: 0-203-87984-8 (ebk)

For
Andrew Wainwright

# Contents

# Preface

The essays which comprise this book are designed to justify and develop scientific realism, critical naturalism, and a certain, characteristically Marxian, approach to the analysis and criticism of philosophical ideas. The first two chapters consolidate and develop the theories outlined in *A Realist Theory of Science* and *The Possibility of Naturalism*, as well as in a number of other recent publications of mine. The third is more experimental in approach: it is essentially an exercise in the analysis and explication of philosophical ideologies, focussed on one specific, historically crucial, case.

The origins of this book lie in a draft of the first three chapters to a much larger book that I was writing in 1982-83. Together they constitute a kind of extended introduction to a book on *Dialectic and Materialism*, which I hope to be in a position to publish shortly. Insofar as this book concentrates its fire on 'analytical' philosophy, *Dialectic and Materialism* will redress the balance by tackling the varieties of dialectical, idealist and specifically Marxist philosophical thought.

I am too indebted to too many people to be able to begin to compile a list of them. But I must express my special thanks to Ted Benton, Andrew Collier and William Outhwaite for some most stimulating conversations in April 1985; to the participants at the 1st Conference of the Standing Conference on Realism in the Human Sciences, held in Sussex in December 1985; to

Andrew Collier, Peter Dews, Joe McCarney and William Outhwaite for detailed comments on the body of the text; and to Sue Kelly, William Outhwaite and, above all, Hilary Wainwright, without whose help and encouragement this text would not have seen the light of day.

Roy Bhaskar
October 1985/July 1986

# Introduction

Like the theory of the logic of scientific development it reprises, in which the concept of ontological depth reconciles 'the Janus faces ... of growth and change' (p. 63), *Scientific Realism and Human Emancipation* [*Scientific Realism*] is oriented both backwards and forwards in the dialectically developing system of critical realism. While this must of course be the case up to a point in respect of any moment other than the first and last in such a system, in which the later moments are implicit in and constellationally contain the earlier, *Scientific Realism*, along with *From East to West*, arguably occupies a peculiarly transitional status within the system — and precisely for that reason is of peculiar relevance to an understanding of its evolution, as well as of great interest in its own right. In this respect it stands to *Dialectic*[1] as Marx's *Grundrisse* stands to his *Capital*. One can see the concepts in motion.

On the one hand *Scientific Realism* embraces all three parts of the triplex project Roy Bhaskar set himself as a postgraduate student at Oxford in the late 1960s: the elaboration of an adequate realist philosophy of science, philosophy of social science and explanatory critique, both theoretical and substantive, of the existing orthodoxies in these fields. Bhaskar had

---

1.     R. Bhaskar, *Dialectic: The Pulse of Freedom* [*DPF*], with an introduction by M. Hartwig, London and New York: Routledge, [1993] 2008.

already in 1971 attempted to cover the entire terrain of this project in a PhD thesis he submitted called *Some Problems about Explanation in the Social Sciences*. The name he gave a development of it — *Empiricism and the Meta-Theory of the Social Sciences* — shortly afterwards better describes what it is about. The first part of this triptych was published as *A Realist Theory of Science* in 1975, the second as *The Possibility of Naturalism* in 1979. The theory of the third was sketched in broad outline on the terrain of philosophy in the latter book but is given much fuller treatment and applied substantively on the terrain of ideology-critique in Chapter 3 of the present work. On the other hand, *Scientific Realism* looks forward to the project carried through in *Dialectic* a decade later: the dialectical enrichment and deepening of the earlier project (already implicitly dialectical), the 'emancipation of dialectic for (the dialectic of) emancipation',[2] and the elaboration of a metacritique of western (irrealist) philosophy. In so doing it constitutes, in Bhaskar's own words, 'a kind of extended introduction to a book on *Dialectic and Materialism*' (Preface), a book he had been working on since 1979–80 that was destined to be published as *Dialectic* in 1993. It may thus be viewed as a prolegomenon to *Dialectic* — or, better, a *prodrome* in the literal sense, a running towards it, a working through of some of the main issues in that direction. But it is also a consolidation, refinement and elaboration at a higher level of abstraction of what went before, a marshalling and stoking up of energies and resources that 'concentrates its fire' on analytical rather than dialectical philosophy (Preface) while its author seeks the key to transposing and elaborating his overall project in a fully dialectical register.

This transitional quality of the book is registered in its presentational structure. The fundamental goal of philosophy for Bhaskar had always been 'the nature of, and prospects for, human emancipation', and this is now explicitly made 'the organising theme' of the book as a whole (pp. 103–4). Abstracting from overlap, its three chapters justify and develop transcendental or scientific realism (TR), critical naturalism (CN) and explanatory critique (EC), in that order — an order determined by the fact that EC > CN > TR (see below). Whether considered in terms of its primary focus or subsidiary thematics, each of the first two

---

2.    Ibid., 40.

prepares the ground for its successor chapter(s). All three both reprise and develop the elements of the earlier project and will in turn be reprised and developed in *Dialectic*, as illustrated in Table 1.

*Table 1* The architectonic of Bhaskar's philosophical project, 1967–94[3]

| Ontological–axiological chain | 1M Non-identity | 2E Negativity | 3L Totality | 4D Transformative agency |
|---|---|---|---|---|
| | *transcendental realism* | *critical naturalism* | *the theory of explanatory critique* | *explanatory critique of philosophical ideologies* |
| 1967-79 | *PES, EMS* *RTS* | *PES, EMS* *PN* | *PN* | *PES, EMS* [*PI*] |
| 1980-90 | [*DM; DMHE*] *SRHE* Ch 1 *RR* Ch 2 | [*DM; DMHE*] *SRHE* Ch 2 *RR* Ch. 5 | [*DM; DMHE*] *SRHE* Chs 2.5–2.7 *RR* Ch 6 | [*PI; DM; DMHE*] *SRHE* Ch. 3 *RR* Chs 3, 4 |
| 1991-94 | [*DMHE*] *DPF* Ch 1 | [*DMHE*] *DPF* Ch 2 | [*DMHE*] *DPF* Ch 3 | [*DMHE; PI*] *PIF; DPF* Ch 4 |

*Note.* Square brackets indicate planned books or chapters of books. Periodisation is in terms of (1) the formation of basic critical realism; (2) the transition from (1) to dialectical critical realism; and (3) the breakthrough to dialectical critical realism and the writing of *Dialectic* and *Plato Etc.* Note that, while the development of the theory of EC belongs at 3L, the transformative work of its application belongs at 4D.

| | |
|---|---|
| *DM* | [*Dialectic and Materialism*] (evolved into [*DMHE*]) |
| *DMHE* | [*Dialectics, Materialism and Human Emancipation*] (evolved into *DPF*) |
| *DPF* | *Dialectic: The Pulse of Freedom* |
| *EMS* | *Empiricism and the Meta-Theory of the Social Sciences* (evolved into *RTS, PN, SRHE*) |
| *PI* | *Philosophical Ideologies* |
| *PIF* | *Philosophy and the Idea of Freedom* |
| *PN* | *The Possibility of Naturalism* |
| *PES* | [*Some Problems about Explanation in the Social Sciences*] (evolved into [*EMS*]) |
| *RR* | *Reclaiming Reality* |
| *RTS* | *A Realist Theory of Science* |
| *SRHE* | *Scientific Realism and Human Emancipation* |

---

3.    This table was originally devised, in consultation with Bhaskar, for R. Bhaskar with M. Hartwig, *The Formation of Critical Realism: A Personal Perspective* (*FCR*) (London: Routledge, forthcoming, 2009), Ch. 5.

Because its most important contribution to the overall development of the system is arguably the development of the theory of explanatory critique (3L), the place of *Scientific Realism* in the system may be registered in terms of EC. Where 'PMR' stands for 'the philosophy of meta-Reality', 'TDCR' for 'transcendental dialectical critical realism', 'DCR' for 'dialectical critical realism', 'EC' for 'explanatory critique', 'CN' for 'critical naturalism', 'TR' for 'transcendental realism' and '>' for 'constellationally contains' or 'preservatively sublates', the place of EC within the system can be written as: PMR > TDCR > DCR > EC > CN > TR.[4] This schema can also be written in terms of (the main emphasis of) the key works that articulate each moment: *MR* > *EW* > *DPF* > *SRHE* > *PN* > *RTS*. These six moments arguably comprise three larger phases of the system: the philosophy of meta-Reality, dialectical critical realism (DCR + TDCR) and critical realism (EC + CN + TR), where PMR > DCR > CR.[5] A perspectival switch from moments to phases highlights the transitional status of EC and the book that first systematically articulates it, along with that of TDCR. An embryonic explanatory critique is already a vital component of critical realism, it is greatly developed in *Scientific Realism*, and receives its deepest and widest articulation in *Dialectic* — a movement reflecting the more general one from the implicitly to the fully dialectical via the intermediate stage of the present work.

The system is also articulated in terms of seven dimensions of being (comprising the ontological-axiological chain) that I normally designate 'stadia' — that is, its dialectic is a seven-termed one — as follows (where '7A' [seventh awakening] stands for non-duality, '6R' [sixth realm] for (re-)enchantment, '5A' [fifth aspect] for reflexivity understood as spirituality, '4D' [fourth dimension] for human transformative praxis, '3L' [third level] for totality, '2E' [second edge] for negativity, '1M' [first moment] for non-identity):

7A > 6R > 5A > 4D > 3L > 2E > 1M[6]

---

4.  For a fuller elaboration of the overall dynamics of the system and some reflections on system-building in philosophy, see my 'Introduction' to Bhaskar, *DPF*; Bhaskar with Hartwig, *FCR*.

5.  See ibid.; Seo MinGyu, 'Bhaskar's philosophy as anti-anthropism: a comparative study of Eastern and Western thought', *Journal of Critical Realism* 7(1) (2008): 5–28.

6.  Allowing for the fact that 7A and 6R are both elaborated by PMR, it will be

Or conversely, and chronologically (omitting the numerals): MELDARA.[7] This is by no means a purely mnemonic device, as I have noted elsewhere: '*Moment* signifies something finished, behind us, determinate — a *product*: *transfactual* (structural) *causality*, pertaining to *non-identity*; *first* is for *founding*. *Edge* speaks of the point of transition or becoming, the exercise of causal powers in *rhythmic* (*processual*) *causality*, pertaining to *negativity*. *Level* announces an emergent whole with its own specific determinations, capable of reacting back on the materials from which it is formed — *process-in-product*: *holistic causality*, pertaining to *totality*. *Dimension* singles out a geo-historically recent form of causality — *product-in-process*: human *intentional causality*, transformative agency or praxis.'[8] To complete the series: *Aspect* is for the sake of euphony, signifying the *spirituality* presupposed by emancipatory projects; *Realm* is for realms of *enchantment* that the shedding of disenchantment discloses; *Awakening* is to understanding *non-duality* and the experience of *being being*, rather than thinking being, when, as the saying goes, we are 'in the *Zone*'.

The bare bones of the stadia and moments in their articulation are displayed in Table 2.[9] The ultimate concern of EC is with thinking being as totality, understood as including values, at 3L, but, as is the way with the developmental moments of a dialectical system, it also brings its own particular emphasis to the thinking of the 'earlier' stadia. Thus, whereas at 2E CN thinks negativity as contradiction and emergence (social relationism, transformationalism), EC thinks it also as absenting ills conceived as constraints. And whereas at 1M TR thinks being as structured and differentiated, and CN thinks it as also containing mind and concepts, EC thinks it as also intrinsically valuable.

---

seen that the stadia of this schema correspond to the (main emphasis of) the developing moments of the system.

7.   7A is also designated 7Z (seventh zone), in which case the acronym is MELDARZ.
8.   M. Hartwig, 'MELD', in Hartwig, ed., *Dictionary of Critical Realism*, (London and New York: Routledge, 2007), 295.
9.   Considered diachronically, both the stadia and the moments of the system are less than fully preservative sublations of their predecessors because they enrich and deepen (or, if you prefer, add something) to them; formally, they are *essentially preservative* sublations. Considered synchronically, they are fully or *totally preservative*, because 1M is 'already' enriched or added to by 7A, TR by PMR, and so on. See M. Hartwig, 'Sublation', in Hartwig, ed., *Dictionary of Critical Realism*, 449.

*Table 2* The moments of the philosophy of critical realism and meta-Reality mapped to the stadia of the ontological-axiological chain[10]

| Stadion/phase | 1M NON-IDENTITY | 2E NEGATIVITY | 3L TOTALITY | 4D TRANS-FORMATIVE AGENCY | 5A SPIRITUALITY | 6R (RE-) ENCHANTMENT | 7A/Z NON-DUALITY |
|---|---|---|---|---|---|---|---|
| CRITICAL REALISM as a whole: thinking being | as such and in general | processually + as for 1M | as a totality + as for 2E | as incorporating human praxis and reflexivity + as for 3 | as incorporating spirituality + as for 4D | as incorporating enchantment + as for 5A | as incorporating non-duality + as for 6R |
| Form of reflexivity — immanent critique of | philosophical discourse of modernity (PDM) | PDM + 1M | PDM + 1M, 2E | PDM + 1M-3L | PDM + 1M-4D | PDM + 1M-5A | PDM + 1M-6R |
| TRANSCENDENTAL REALISM: thinking being as | structured and differentiated | | | | | | |
| CRITICAL NATURALISM inflection: thinking being as | containing mind and concepts | negativity as contradiction, emergence (social relationism, trans-formationalism) | | | | | |

| | | | | | | | |
|---|---|---|---|---|---|---|---|
| **EXPLANATORY CRITIQUE inflection: thinking being as** | intrinsically valuable | negativity as absenting constraints (ills) | totality, understood as including values (retotalisation) | | | | |
| **DCR inflection: thinking being as** | alethic truth (reality principle, axiological necessity) | negativity as (determinate) absence, generalised to the whole of being as real and essential to change | totality, understood as maximised by praxis (which absents incompleteness) | transformative praxis and reflexivity (emancipatory axiology) | | | |
| **TDCR inflection: thinking being as** | underlying non-duality (God, transcendentally real self) | co-presence transcendence creativity | totality, understood as including unconditional love | spontaneous right-action | spiritual | | |
| **PMR inflection: thinking being as** | underlying non-duality (cosmic envelope, ground-state) | co-presence transcendence creativity | totality, understood as including unconditional love | spontaneous right-action | spiritual | enchanted | non-dual |

---

10. M. Hartwig, 'Introduction' to Bhaskar, *DPF*, pp. xvi–xvii (Table 1).

After the publication of *The Possibility of Naturalism* in 1979 Bhaskar set himself two main philosophical objectives: to bring the tripartite project he had initiated in the 1960s to a satisfactory conclusion by the publication of a book on *Philosophical Ideologies*, on the one hand, and to develop and deepen critical realism dialectically, on the other. He soon encountered serious obstacles to the achievement of each of these goals. In presenting seminars in the area of ideology-critique (a species of totalising explanatory critique or metacritque$_2$ [see below]), he met with a somewhat disheartening response — people seemed more interested in the story of how a philosophical tradition had arisen than in its structural explanation and critique — and his own daemon, spurred by the full onset of the neo-liberal counter-revolution, was impatient to move explanatory critique forward into the more constructive domain of what he was soon to call emancipatory axiology or the dialectics of freedom. His dialectical work had meanwhile run up against the problem of absence and its reality — how to arrive at an adequate understanding of all the categories and concepts we have for the negative — a problem of a similar order to that of isolating the epistemic fallacy. Unable to feel happy until he had solved the problem and brought intellectual order to the field of dialectics in a manner analogous to what he had accomplished in the philosophy of science and social science, Bhaskar increasingly felt the need to devote all his energies to the dialectical project. He therefore decided to limit ideology-critique qua sociology of knowledge to positivism for the time being, and to publish it, along with two other pieces reprising and developing the original triptych, as the first three chapters of the book on dialectic. These were written in 1983. Two years later, since he was not making much headway on the problem of absence but considered the three chapters to be important in their own right, he decided to publish them as the book you have before you, which appeared in 1986.[11]

---

11.   See Bhaskar with Hartwig, *FCR*. The desire to put the house of dialectic in order was in considerable degree realised by a series of dictionary entries Bhaskar wrote at this time, but he was not entirely happy with this work because of the unresolved problem of absence. See R. Bhaskar, 'Contradiction', 'Determinism', 'Dialectics' (reprinted with corrections in R. Bhaskar, *Reclaiming Reality: A Critical Introduction to Contemporary Philosophy* [*RR*], London: Verso, 1999), 'Empiricism', 'Idealism', 'Theory of knowledge (reprinted with corrections in ibid.), 'Materialism' (reprinted with corrections in ibid.), 'Realism', 'Science', and 'Truth' in T. Bottomore, ed., *A Dictionary of Marxist Thought*, Oxford: Blackwell, [1983] 1991.

The chief areas in which *Scientific Realism* registers significant advances over first-level or basic critical realism[12] are (1) the meta-philosophical justification of transcendental realism; (2) the situation of the problem of naturalism in relation to the biological sciences, and the development of dialectical concepts centring on processuality and geo-historicity; (3) the theory of explanatory critique, including ideology-critique, leading on to what was soon to be designated emancipatory axiology; and (4) the substantive application of the theory of ideology-critique. These correspond roughly to 1M–4D, as indicated in Table 1, but for convenience of exposition the theory of ideology-critique will be treated under (4). In what follows I comment on them seriatim. For ease of identification and to highlight the extent of conceptual space mapped in this remarkable work, new concepts, that is, concepts not (to the best of my knowledge) used by Bhaskar in his previous books, hereafter appear in **bold italics** when first mentioned.[13]

1. As Bhaskar had noted in 1978, one of the chief lacks in his earlier account of transcendental realism was the absence of an explicit meta-philosophical justification of its transcendental procedure.[14] This is now made good, in the context of the fullest account of his approach to philosophy anywhere in the Bhaskarian oeuvre (see especially Chapter 1, §3). It is preceded by an account, finessing that provided by *A Realist Theory of Science* (§1), of how, although the fundamental assumptions of the positivist account of science as monistic in development and deductive in structure had radically been called into question, 'the ensuing accounts of science have been unable to sustain the coherence of precisely those features of science which they have placed to the fore of the philosophical agenda, namely scientific change and the non-deductive aspects of theory' (p. 1) — aporiai attributable to 'the supervention of new epistemological insights upon old (empiricist or idealist) ontologies, more

---

12. 'Basic critical realism' or 'first-level critical realism' is Bhaskar's recent term of art for the first main stage of his system: transcendental realism + critical naturalism + explanatory critique; but it can also refer to the first two of these only, and this is the sense in which it is used here. See especially Bhaskar with Hartwig, *FCR*.
13. The list of new concepts so identified is by no means exhaustive.
14. R. Bhaskar, *A Realist Theory of Science [RTS]*, fourth edition, with an introduction by M. Hartwig (London: Routledge, 2008), 259 (Postscript).

or less materially incompatible with them' and absentable by a new transcendental realist ontology and corresponding account of science that comprise 'a Copernican revolution in the strict sense . . . of a de-anthropocentric shift in our metaphysical conception of the place of (wo)man in nature' (p. 4).

This is followed by a definitive dissection of the different forms these (implicit) ontologies take, that is, the different forms of realism that are presupposed by the various philosophies of science on offer (§2), as set out in Table 3. It furnishes the basic taxonomy for Bhaskar's developing metacritique of *irrealism*, which will culminate in *Plato Etc.* but the 'first steps' towards which are taken in *Scientific Realism* (§7). Transcendental realism, like ontology, which it vindicates, is argued to be more or less axiologically necessary: ' "When the company breaks up . . ." we are all practising (transcendental) realists' (p. 33). While it entails two other basic forms of realism that are not displayed in the table — predicative and perceptual realism, which inform the categorial framework of our commonsense understandings of the world — it is by no means reducible to them.

Philosophy proceeds for Bhaskar fundamentally by a combination of transcendental argument and immanent critique: transcendental critique. In *Scientific Realism* Bhaskar distinguishes between *metaphysics α* and *metaphysics β*, which Kant had illicitly conflated, thereby breaking the necessary connection postulated by Kant between accepting that philosophy is heteronomous or possible only in relation to practices other than itself and transcendental idealism. Metaphysics α is purely formal; it investigates what some social practice as conceptualised in experience (for example, science) presupposes about the general contours or forms of the world. Metaphysics β is descriptive and critical; it identifies theory–practice inconsistencies and other aporiai in existing accounts of social practices in order to arrive at a more adequate account conceptually. If metaphysics α is the philosophy of science and other social practices, metaphysics β is the philosophy of the philosophy of science and other social practices. The former shows what the world must be like given the relevant social practice, the latter demonstrates that an account cannot sustain the intelligibility of important features of a social practice that it itself calls attention to, and shows how transcendental realism can. This procedure is 'essentially post-critical in form, but pre-critical in function'; it exploits post-critical insights but 'plays characteristically Lockean and Leibnizian roles', that is, it underlabours for the sciences by generating a philosophical ontology and by the immanent critique of conceptual formations (p. 22). By taking its departure from existing social practices as conceptualised in experience, it both eschews all pretense of foundationalism, absolutism and first philosophy and avoids the 'bad circularity' or arbitrariness of external criteria; it is 'necessarily heteronomous — soiled in life' (p. 16). While not reducible to other social practices (its conditional *a priori* procedure confers relatively autonomy), it is relative to them in that its arguments are praxis-dependent and both its results and claims about itself are susceptible to the findings of science. It thus avoids the Scylla of the *speculative illusion* — the reduction of science to philosophy — and the Charybdis of the converse *positivistic illusion* — the reduction of philosophy to science. Moreover, it is necessarily conditioned by *axiological standpoints* or interests outside philosophy, which 'it can no more justify than boots can climb mountains'. Here, Bhaskar suggests, philosophy encounters an immanent barrier to immanent critique, and one's only recourse in the final analysis is to 'openly take one's stand with science' — not as the only way of knowing but at any rate one with excellent historical credentials (pp. 18–19). This in no way makes transcendental realism a form of scientism. It takes its stand, not with shoddy or reductive or techno- science, which it relentlessly critiques, but with the concept of science arrived at by reflection on the achievements of the great scientists of modernity, such as Copernicus, Darwin, Marx, Freud and Einstein.

Philosophy, like any other body of thought, has both an *intrinsic* or normative *aspect* (IA) in that it is intentional, aspiring to achieve goals, and an *extrinsic* or causally conditioned *aspect* (EA) in that it is imbricated in human social being and the geo-historical process. Under the former aspect, consciousness is regarded judgementally in terms of validity, under the latter historically and contextually, in terms of credibility. These are distinctions within the transitive dimension of any cognitive process. Corresponding to the IA, Bhaskar now identifies, in addition to transitive (TD) and intransitive dimensions (ID), a *metacritical dimension* of philosophical discourse, and within that distinguishes between *metacritique₁* (the main form of which is immanent critique — it 'typically aims to identify the presence of causally significant absences in thought' (p. 25), that is, theory–practice inconsistencies and the like) and *metacritique₂* (totalising

*Table 3* Forms of realism/irrealism in the philosophy of science

| Form of realism/ irrealism | TRANSCENDENTAL OR SCIENTIFIC REALISM (reality-knowable non-identity theory) | IRREALISM (non-transcendental realism) | | | | |
|---|---|---|---|---|---|---|
| | | *anthroporealism* or *subject–object identity theory* (immanent) | | | | *transcencent realism* |
| | | *empirical realism* | *subjective conceptual realism* | *objective conceptual realism* | *intuitive realism* | |
| **Definition of the real objects of science in terms of** | relative or absolute independence from human thought | human experience | human thought (explicitly anthropomorphic) | thought or reason (implicitly anthropomorphic) | human intuition, sensibility or affect | inaccessibility to humans (ineffability) |
| **Exemplified by** | any science that makes real discoveries | empiricism, positivism (Hume); transcendental idealism (Kant) | *superidealism* (Kuhn); some forms of neo-Kantianism, sociology of knowledge, social constructionism and poststructuralism | pre-critical rationalism (Plato, Descartes) | romanticism | the noumenal realm (Kant), absolute idealism |

| | | | [Beautiful Souls] | other-worldliness (Jenseitigkeit) |
|---|---|---|---|---|
| **Characteristic ideological effect** | **destratification and dehistoricisation** of being and science | voluntarism | hypostatisation of conceptual forms | [Beautiful Souls] | other-worldliness (Jenseitigkeit) |
| **Real basis in our spontaneous consciousness in science** | **axiological necessity**: referential detachment of generative mechanisms; the **fact form**; the **constant conjunction form** | experience of ideas coming 'out of the blue' | experience of discovery; regulative ideal that 'God is sophisticated but not malicious' | **enchantment**; aesthetic pleasure in a beautiful theory if true | experience of the sublime |

*Note.* The immanent and transcendent poles of irrealism — anthroporealism and transcendent realism — are *dialectical complements* or *counterparts*, which mutually presuppose each other.[15]

15. Later also called dialectical antagonists, contraries, couples or pairs. See M. Hartwig, 'Dialectical antagonists' in Hartwig, ed., *Dictionary of Critical Realism*, 128–9.

explanatory critique which, in virtue of the historically conditioned nature of thought, includes substantive sociology of knowledge or *ideology-critique*). To this I return in §4, below, in relation to Chapter 3.

Throughout the first two chapters Bhaskar deploys meta-critique₁ brilliantly to refute various irrealist tendencies in the philosophy of science and social science. Most of these resume and finesse earlier accounts, but the critique of *subjective super-idealism* — the Kuhn-inspired view that when our theories change the world changes with them — is new and definitive, demonstrating that the superidealists cannot sustain the intelligibility of the phenomena of paradigm change and incommensurability that they themselves call attention to. This critique can be generalised to tendencies within poststructuralism, postmodernism and social constructionism. One of the weaknesses of *Scientific Realism* is that it does not do this. Bhaskar was critiquing these tendencies in his public engagements in the 1980s, but because he had not yet adequately meta-theorised some of the relevant issues, such as power and change/difference, felt that it would be premature to do so in print.[16]

Bhaskar had previously shown that transcendental realism entails the necessity of ontological realism (in the ID), and the actuality of epistemic relativity (in the TD). He now deploys the IA/EA distinction to show that ontological realism and epistemic relativity also entail the possibility of *judgemental rationality*[17] (in the IA), which will in general depend also on ethical reflexivity and responsibility. In this way all three members of the subsequently named 'holy trinity' of critical realism are present in *Scientific Realism*, as displayed in Table 4. Bhaskar refers to the theory of judgemental rationality as *intrinsics* (p. 37).

2. The attentive reader will have noticed that reference was made above to the pivotal 2E category of absence as 'causally significant'. While Bhaskar deploys this concept frequently in his work from the outset, and necessarily so in that, *inter alia*, he is engaging in immanent critique, *Scientific Realism* is the first of his

---

16. Bhaskar with Hartwig, *FCR*, Ch. 5.
17. This concept is already implicitly present in R. Bhaskar, *The Possibility of Naturalism: A Philosophical Critique of the Contemporary Human Sciences* [*PN*] (Brighton, Sussex: Harvester, 1979), p. 57.

Table 4 The holy trinity of critical realism, with key correspondences[18]

| [HOLY TRINITY] of critical realism | Transcend-entally | Dimensions of any cognitive process | Dimensions of philosophical discourse | Key categories | Distinctions within being | Human being in being | Specifically human being | [UNHOLY TRINITY] of irrealism |
|---|---|---|---|---|---|---|---|---|
| judgemental rationalism | possible | transitive dimension — intrinsic aspect | metacritical dimension | historical reason [i.e. dialectical reason] | ethics | intentionality, self-conscious subjectivity, historicity | rational nature | judgemental relativism, entrained by [primal squeeze] on natural necessity and empirical science on the Platonic–Aristotelian fault-line |
| epistemic relativism | actual | transitive dimension — extrinsic aspect | transitive dimension | work (on) or praxis absence change historicity | epistemology | sociality | social nature | epistemic absolutism, entrained by the epistemic–ontic fallacy |
| ontological realism | necessary | intransitive dimension | intransitive dimension | 1M–4D: non-identity, process, totality, transformative praxis | ontology | being | biological nature | ontological irrealism, entrained by [ontological monovalence] |

*Note.* Concepts in square brackets were developed or named after *Scientific Realism*. Note that all the moments of the four-termed dialectic of *Dialectic* are present as key ontological categories, except that the concept of process stands in for absence, which has not yet been developed as the unifying logical infrastructure of the ontological–axiological chain. Bhaskar normally refers to the members of the unholy trinity of irrealism as primal squeeze, the epistemic fallacy and ontological monovalence, that is, in terms of the main categorial error(s) underlying judgemental relativism, epistemic absolutism and ontological irrealism.

18. Adapted from Hartwig, ed., *Dictionary of Critical Realism*, p. 238 (Table 24).

books to refer to it explicitly as causally efficacious (pp. 25, 291).[19] However, he is as yet unable to give an adequate account of how this can be, and when he turns to the ideology-critique of positivism in Chapter 3 dramatically illustrates the point by leaving a blank space under the section heading 'Ideology in the Metacritical Dimension: Presence of an Absence' (p. 292). If positivism lacks a concept of itself in a metacritical dimension, *Scientific Realism* lacks a metatheory of absence. This will be made good in *Dialectic*. However, the key that will unlock that metatheory, unchaining reference from positive existence,[20] is already at least demi-present in *Scientific Realism* when it argues, anticipating the later concept of 'the tropic', that fictional beings are causally efficacious: 'The imaginary, when imagined, is inscribed within the real; and no other kind of imaginary exists' (p. 43).

In the meantime *Scientific Realism* deploys a bevy of related concepts at level 2E of the chain of being. Basic critical realism had already emphasised the category of change, along with those of structure and differentiation at 1M, in both the ID and the TD.[21] Change is now argued to be on a par ontologically with structure and differentiation (difference) — a position that will be developed further in *Dialectic*[22] — as a transcendentally necessary condition of science: 'Understanding science as part of being' — which is not denied but presupposed by affirmation of the TD/ID distinction — 'yet rejecting the *ontic fallacy* . . . means . . . comprehending ontological emergence, presupposing qualitative complexity and change, as equally necessary conditions for science' (p. 53, n. 92).

Basic critical realism had correspondingly emphasised process, in particular in relation to the transitive dimension of science. It is now given a definition as an ontological category: process is 'where structure meets events; that is, . . . the mode of becoming, bestaying and begoing of a structure or thing, i.e. of its genesis in, distantiation over and transformation across space-time'. It is not

---

19. Cf. p. 63, where 'the notion of scientific activity as labour' and 'the concept of ontological depth' are deemed to be 'critical absence[s]' that 'underpin' orthodox accounts of ontology and epistemology, respectively [emphasis changed]).

20. See Bhaskar, *DPF*, 40; Bhaskar with Hartwig, *FCR*, Ch. 6.

21. Bhaskar, *PN*, Postscript, 178.

22. Bhaskar, *DPF*, 45.

a category 'apart from structure and event; it just is structure (or thing), considered under the aspect of its story — of formation, reformation and transformation — in time' (p. 215).

*Scientific Realism* highlights the emergence of the social realm, arguing that social objects are 'taxonomically and causally *irreducible*, but *dependent*, modes of matter' and, further, that it is only if an emergent powers materialism of this kind can be upheld that emancipation is possible: 'It is only if social phenomena are genuinely *emergent* that realist *explanations* in the human sciences are justified; and it is only if these conditions are satisfied that there is any possibility of human self-*emancipation* worthy of the name' (pp. 103–4). Contrary to a common view, such metaphysical materialism, espousing a differentiated and differentiating monism, is not a position that is fundamentally resiled from in the spiritual turn, which sees consciousness as implicitly enfolded within matter.[23]

Closely related to emergence, and also to totality (3L), are the concepts of **integrative pluralism** (IP) and **developing integrative pluralism** (DIP) as descriptors of the critical realist ontology. They lead into and convey much the same idea as the concept of a structured and differentiated totality articulated in *Dialectic*, which is expanded in the philosophy of meta-Reality to embrace the constellational containment of layers of duality and demi-reality within non-duality. While Bhaskar has accordingly not much used IP and DIP since *Scientific Realism*, they are sound concepts that, as he has subsequently pointed out,[24] possess one advantage over the notion of a structured and differentiated totality: the element of (differentiating) monism, a theme that is taken up again in the philosophy of meta-Reality in terms of the theses of the priority of unity over conflict and of identity over difference.

In basic critical realism, the specific emergent properties of the social sphere, which make a *sui generis* science of society possible, are specified by the transformational model of social activity (TMSA). A lapidary formulation (one of many) now highlights its cardinal features: it makes human intentional agency 'criterial for the social, as distinct from the purely natural, sphere' in that it expresses the 'onto-logical structure of human activity or praxis

---

23. See Bhaskar with Hartwig, *FCR*, Chs 2, 3, 4, 8.
24. Ibid., Ch. 6.

as essentially transformative or poietic, as consisting in the transformation of pre-given material (natural and social) causes by
efficient (intentional) human agency' (p. 122). It thus calls for
'the geo-historicisation of social theory' (p. 213). Although it
recognises a reproductive moment,[25] its emphasis is on the power
of human agency to tranformatively negate the given (produce
change). This one-sidedness is corrected in the later philosophy,
which puts the reproductive moment, broadened to included the
notions of caring, nurturing and sustaining, on a par with the
transformative power of agency.[26] The transformational model of
social activity is now developed into that of the *social cube*
(p. 130, Diagram 2.10; p. 155, Diagram 2.13). This is a concept
Bhaskar deploys in *Scientific Realism* to refer to what he later
normally calls four-planar social being;[27] it is more fully developed
in *Dialectic*. It generalises the TMSA, a 1M concept in dialectical
terms, to the other stadia of the chain of being, and its four
planes correspond also to the moments of the *concrete universal*
and to the components of *human nature*, as displayed in Table 5.

It will be seen that the concept of four-planar social being lends
greater specificity to each of 'the components of human nature'.
Indeed, it is a theory of the (changing) nature of human being in
geo-history, and Bhaskar often uses the two terms interchange-
ably; but he also prefers to keep them distinct so that in its universal aspect human nature can function as a norm for judging
social institutions and practices.[28] Some view of human nature
will characteristically form the basis of the ethical ingredient in
explanatory critique, so a philosophical ontology is necessary
for its theorisation. Although social being has only four named
planes, it is a cube because, diachronically considered, it is a

---

25. However, while 'no transformation is total . . . all reproduction is transform-
    ation' (p. 152). The passage goes on to put change 'on a par' with lack of
    change in a context critiquing the notion that lack of change is epistemically,
    logically and ontologically prior to change.
26. Bhaskar with Hartwig, *FCR*, Ch. 6.
27. In *Dialectic* and subsequently, Bhaskar usually employs 'social cube' to refer
    to a sub-cube of four-planar social being comprising power$_2$, discursive/
    communicative and normative/moral relations, intersecting in ideology. See
    M. Hartwig, 'Human nature' and 'Social cube' in Hartwig, ed., *Dictionary of
    Critical Realism*.
28. Bhaskar, *DPF*, 283n; Hartwig, 'Human nature', in Hartwig, ed., *Dictionary
    of Critical Realism*, 244.

*Table 5* Four-planar social being and the social cube[29]

| [Ontological–Axiological Chain] | 1M Non-Identity | 2E Negativity | 3L Totality | 4D Transformative Agency |
|---|---|---|---|---|
| **Concrete universal** | universality | processuality | mediation | (concrete) singularity |
| **Components of human nature** | (1) core universal | (4) changing | (2) historically specific | (3) unique individuality |
| **[Four-planar social being] or human nature [social tetrapolity]** | d. (intra)subjectivity (the stratified person) | c. social relations (concept-dependent, site of social oppositionality) | b. inter-/intra-subjective (personal) relations — transactions with ourselves and others | a. material transactions with nature (making) |
| **Social cube** | | (1) power$_2$ (2) discursive (3) normative relations $\underline{\text{intersecting in}}$ | (1) power$_2$ (2) communicative (3) moral relations (4) $\underline{\text{ideology}}$ | |

*Note.* Concepts in square brackets were coined after the publication of *Scientific Realism.*

29  Adapted from Hartwig, ed., *Dictionary of Critical Realism*, 243 (Table 25).

'*space-time flow*' or '*rhythm*[ic]'[30] open at either end, giving it two additional unnamed planes, denoting the not-yet and the intransitive determined (pp. 213, 220).

Just as the social cube corrects and deepens the TMSA, so consideration of the analogies and disanalogies of the social sciences with the biological sciences in *Scientific Realism* corrects and deepens the resolution of the problem of naturalism in basic critical realism. Any deduction of the possibility of (non-reductionist) naturalism must proceed in two stages: (1) the independent derivation of an adequate account of science, and (2) the independent analysis of the subject matter of the various social sciences designed to establish the extent to which their knowledges can and do fall under (1). (1) is accomplished in Chapter 1 and in *A Realist Theory of Science* on the basis of physics and chemistry, because those sciences have traditionally been regarded as paradigmatic in the philosophy of science. (2) is accomplished in *The Possibility of Naturalism* on the basis of sociology and psychology. However, as Bhaskar acknowledges, full specification of the possibility of naturalism would involve consideration of the entire array of the sciences and also of the social sciences and humanities and the arts, which would then 'cross-confirm, modify, enrich or amend the results achieved in (1)' (p. 119). While this is probably beyond the powers of a single person, *Scientific Realism* does consider an impressive array of sciences, both natural and social, under the rubric of a rough typology in terms of degrees of abstractness/concreteness and whether a science is social and/or natural in content and form. In this context a distinction is drawn between natural (A-type), social (C-type), and mixed (B-type) determinations, and it is stressed that those in the sociosphere will in general be mixed, such that purely biological or psychological or social explanations are illicit. However, the main emphasis is on analogies and disanalogies with biology, thereby remedying a major absence in the earlier derivation of critical naturalism. The emphasis on biology is fitting also in that Bhaskar's intent is to perform for the social and historical sciences the kind of ground-breaking

---

30. Bhaskar uses the concept of 'rhythm' in *Scientific Realism* to mean very much what 'rhythmic' means in *Dialectic* and subsequent works. On rhythmic, see M. Hartwig, 'Process', in Hartwig, ed., *Dictionary of Critical Realism*, 387–8. A rhythmic is a more concrete form of process.

conceptual and classificatory work that Aristotle accomplished for biology.[31] His overall argument is that 'a modified evolutionary schema [derived from biology] furnishes one useful, if limited, framework for situating social change, on the condition that it is understood as presupposing the TMSA and provided that basic ambiguities in key terms such as "adaptation", "function", etc., are resolved'; and that the disanalogies confirm the conceptual and practical character of the *sociosphere* (p. 137).

In the course of developing this argument Bhaskar conceptualises a number of major asymmetries in being that are entailed by its depth-openness (while higher-order entities can have feedback effects on lower-order [more fundamental] ones, they could not exist without them, but not vice versa): the *ecological asymmetry* (environment over organism, more generally totality over its aspects), and its methodogical twin, the *primacy of the pathological*; the *temporal asymmetry* (the determinacy of the past over the indeterminacy of the future, 'marking the real irreversibility of time'); the *axiological asymmetry* (constraints on human action over enablements); 'the binding of the present by the *massive presence of the past*', and 'the pervasiveness of social quasi-entropic processes in time, i.e. the conversion of free (open) possibilities into bound products'.[32] Corresponding to the temporal asymmetry, the bogus asymmetry between the fatalism of the past and the freedom of the future is despatched: 'freedom is irrespective of the arrow's flight, no regarder of the river's flow'; it is circumscribed, but was real in the past, is real in the present and will be real tomorrow — '*things could have been* (just as they might be) *different*' (pp. 140, 142).

The discussion of biological analogies and disanalogies also issues in a magisterial account of consequence and functional explanation (explaining something in terms of its effects and in terms of its beneficial effects for its own continued existence, respectively). This demonstrates that, when causal laws are construed as tendencies and powers rather than empirical regularities, consequence and functional explanations are perfectly valid explanation forms, albeit with limited applicability in the sociosphere. In the important zone of intentional activity,

---

31. Cf. R. Bhaskar with M. Hartwig, 'The philosophy of meta-reality, part 2: agency, perfectibility, novelty', *Journal of Critical Realism* 1(1) (2002): 82.
32. See Hartwig, 'Ecological asymmetry' and 'Primacy (priority)', in Hartwig, ed., *Dictionary of Critical Realism*, 152, 376–7.

however, explanations can always be cast in teleological form: in the social realm, teleology is thus 'an indispensable condition and a part-cause of adaptive changes' (p. 152). The valorisation of consequence explanation clears the ground for ideology-critique, which explains the persistence of theoretical and practical ideology partly or largely in terms of the effects they have on their own reproduction. Relatedly, one of the disanalogies Bhaskar draws attention to is positive for the sociosphere: only there does functionality become a socio-political project and *historicity* (the self-reflexive consciousness of history as a process of change) 'enter, as a material force with an efficacy of its own, into history' (p. 149).

3. An indispensable part of any such project is explanatory critique. By bringing to consciousness hidden or unsuspected sources of determination of false or inadequate beliefs about social objects, explanatory critique facilitates action directed at removing them: 'When unreflected processes are rendered amenable to conscious control, we are free to fulfil our natures' (p. 153). This presupposes the refutation of 'Hume's law', which asserts a logical gulf between facts and values, theory and practice. This had already been accomplished in *The Possibility of Naturalism*, which arrived at the conclusion that values are not science-free. This position is much disputed within critical realism. But Hume's dichotomy is refuted every time we criticise a belief, for to criticise a belief is implicitly to criticise any actions informed by it, CP (pp. 179, 183). The wonder is that this is commonly not seen. That it is not suggests that the reason for the persistence of a false belief in philosophy lies largely or wholly outside philosophy — which is one of the main contentions of ideology-critique. *Scientific Realism* is at pains to answer the critics in some detail[33] in the course of further developing the theory of explanatory critique, together with the notion of transformative *depth-praxis* that it logically entails. This is accompanied by a typology and critique of major errors concerning the relation between facts and values, theory and practice.

In its basic form an explanatory critique demonstrates that, if we can show a belief to be both false and necessary, that is, explain it in terms of underlying social causes, then inference to

---

33. For a summary statement of the kind of response it gives, see Hartwig, 'Critical naturalism', in Hartwig, ed., *Dictionary of Critical Realism*, 94–6.

the negative evaluation of its sources and the positive evaluation of action oriented to removing them is mandatory. It thus unites criticism of beliefs with analysis of the social causes of their inadequacy (***depth-explanation***). It is the internal relationality of the social sciences and their subject-matter, that is, the concept-dependence of social forms, that renders critical explanatory theory in general possible, for it entails that criticality is '*intrinsic* to {their} explanatory function ... If criticism without explanation is impotent, explanation without criticism will often just be simply false' (pp. 193–4). Social science itself is accordingly conceptualised *as* explanatory critique. Explanatory critique is a transcendentally necessary, not an optional, explanation-form — a condition of every rational praxis: for there can be no action without judgements as to the truth or falsity of beliefs and no rational adjustment of beliefs without explanation. But its social situatedness further entails that it is *conditioned critique* — that it is itself subject to 'the same possibilities of unreflected determination and historical supersession it situates. Hence continuing self-reflexive *auto-critique* is the *sine qua non* of any critical explanatory theory' (p. 210).

On this theory, which 'dissolves the rigid dichotomies – between fact and value, theory and practice, explanation and emancipation, science and critique – structuring traditional normative discourse', issuing in a modified ***ethical naturalism***, social science has 'an essentially emancipatory impulse' (p. 169). Not only is explanatory knowledge a necessary condition for any act of rational self-emancipation, but the critique of cognitive ills can be extended to cover the non-fulfilment of axiological needs, wants[34] and interests besides truth, including those that are effectively necessary conditions for truth, such as basic health and education. However, although the knowledge generated by explanatory critical social science is necessary for freedom, it is insufficient, for to be free is not only to know one's real interests but to possess the means, opportunity and disposition to realise them. While the 'special qualitative kind of becoming free' that is emancipation – which 'consists in the *transformation,* in self-emancipation by the agents concerned, *from an unwanted and unneeded to a wanted and needed source of determination*' – is 'both causally presaged and logically entailed by explanatory

---

34. Wants are rationally assessable because grounded in beliefs (p. 174; cf. *PN*, 95–6).

theory, . . . it can only be effected in *practice*' (p. 171). This potentially sets up a rational or progressively developing emancipatory spiral or helix in which science informs the values and practice of emancipatory movements/politics, which in turn motivate science — a notion that links in to the elaboration of the dialectics of freedom in *Dialectic*. It is potentially a spiral rather than a vicious circle because, whereas in favourable epistemic conditions facts and theories logically entail value and practical commitments, CP, these commitments do not non-trivially entail facts and theories. It provides the basis of Bhaskar's provisional answer to the Kantian problem of the survival of the human species: while the possibility of explanatory critique 'constitutes the kernel of the emancipatory potential of the human sciences', the possibility of its 'effectivity . . . in human history comprises perhaps the only chance of non-barbaric, i.e. civilised, survival for the human species'; indeed, of 'survival, non-extinction' as such, given that we are in the grip of 'the infantile fantasy' that, contrary to what the ecological asymmetry shows, the world was made for us to manipulate and control (pp. 180, 221–2).

Bhaskar illustrates these possibilities by developing the argument in relation to levels of historical rationality. Seven levels in all are identified, then grouped into four: (1) instrumental; (2) critical (including explanatory critical); (3) emancipatory; and (4) historical reason (later, geo-historical rational directionality).[35] Even at level (1) explanatory knowledge has emancipatory implications by increasing the range of possibilities open to humans and as a condition for rational self-emancipation. From level (2) on, the argument is encapsulated in a remarkable array of subtly different types of inference schema. The base schema for cognitive ills allows for the following notionally distinct stages: (i) theoretical critique (demonstrating the falsity of some belief P); (ii) explanatory critique (identifying the structural source of P); (iii) value judgement (negative evaluation, CP, of the structural source of P); (iv) practical judgement (positive evaluation, CP, of action rationally directed at removing the source of P); (v) *concrete axiological judgement* (bridging the logical gap between [iv] and a particular course of action: this is what we should do in this context to remove the source of P); (vi) transformation in the

---

35. These are set out alongside slight modifications to them made in *Dialectic* and *Plato Etc.* in Hartwig, ed., *Dictionary of Critical Realism*, 398 (Table 36).

agent's praxis (bridging the logical gap between [v] and actually performing the action, that is, resolving the problem of akrasia); (vii) emancipatory action (praxis oriented to emancipation); (viii) transformative praxis (transformation of the source of P); and (ix) emancipated (free) action. Of course, a decision not to act at (v) or failure to act at (vi) is always possible, in which case the dialectic would stop there. Note that, while theory demonstrates that the transition from theory to practice is logically possible, it does not itself effect the transition. 'Only practice itself can do that. It is in this sense that the explanatory critique is always *conditioned* critique' (p. 188). The base schema is then generalised in adapted form to non-cognitive ills, psychological rationalisation, and ideological mystification (discussed in §4, below).

At level (3) explanatory critique in the form of **depth-enquiry** or **depth-investigation**[36] is introduced. A depth-investigation is the practical application of the theory of explanatory critique to particular cases in the social world, whether historically reconstructed or living, and thence iteratively to the empirical confirmation, correction and further development of that theory, the objective of the whole exercise being to replace unwanted, unnecessary and oppressive sources of determination with rationally wanted and empowering ones. If successful it thus initiates a theory-practice helix. What constitutes well-being and rationality cannot of course be stipulated in advance of DI; it is discovered during its course. This is captured in the concepts of **depth-explanatory critical rationality** and **depth-rationality** (later, dialectical reason or the unity of theory and practice in practice), which together constitute level (3), emancipatory reason, and **depth-praxis**.

In relation to level (4), historical reason, Bhaskar has in mind something like the geo-historical rational directionality that he calls in *Dialectic* the pulse of freedom, which is a directional tendency$_b$ at the level of the real, established by 'relatively *a priori*' argument from human praxis.[37] However, there would seem to be actualist residues in the earlier discussion, which rules out

---

36. See also H. Lacey, 'Explanatory critique', in ibid.; T. Rogers, 'The doing of a depth-investigation: implications for the emancipatory aims of critical naturalism', *Journal of Critical Realism* 3(2) (2004): 238–69.
37. Bhaskar with Hartwig, *FCR*, Ch. 5. 'Relatively a priori' is used by Bhaskar to refer to the fact that transcendental arguments from human intentionality take some data on board in their premises (ibid., Ch. 9).

a priori argument for what it calls 'the emancipatory drive' on the grounds that, although it is a necessary truth that people always act on their wants, it is false 'that they always act on their interests and needs' (p. 203). But in an open world a tendency at the level of the real does not require that people *always* act on their interests and needs. On the other hand, this is clearly recognised by *Scientific Realism*'s thematisation of the emancipatory drive as a 'historical tendency$_2$' (p. 214).[38]

4. *Scientific Realism* arguably provides the most adequate philosophical account we have of the Marxian theory of ideology as false consciousness. I have already indicated that ideology-critique is a species of metacritique$_2$ (totalising explanatory critique). The basic form of explanatory critique provides the minimal necessary formal criteria for designating a belief or theory as ideological: it demonstrates, as we have seen, both the *falsity* or inadequacy of a theory and its *necessity*, issuing in a mandate to change the social causes of falsity, CP.[39] Ideology-critique shows in addition (1) that the theory–practice ensemble within which a belief or theory is embedded is (characteristically categorially) false or misleading; that is, it shows that falsity pertains to social forms (which are quasi-propositional), not just to the theory of them; for example, the wage form, which collapses powers to their exercise, or the **constant conjunction form** and the **fact form** which, together with the concept of a fact, *Scientific Realism* definitively dissects. In such a case, it is not so much that the subject deceives herself (makes cognitive mistakes) but that the structure of social reality produces the deception in her, analogously to the effect of a mirage or of a brilliant actor in the role of a real historical character. (2) It explains the falsity as a necessary misrepresentation of the essential structures (social relations) generating it, to which it is internally related and which it therefore functions to conceal in a quasi-self-reproducing way, such that a consequence explanatory framework is appropriate.

---

38. A tendency$_2$ is a power ready or predisposed to be exercised. The concept derives from *A Realist Theory of Science* (pp. 230–31). Bhaskar did not distinguish between the closely related tendency$_2$ and tendency$_b$ (expressing the directionality of a process) until *Dialectic*. See also B. Pinkstone and M. Hartwig, 'Tendency', in Hartwig, ed., *Dictionary of Critical Realism*, 458–60.

39. Full criteria are set out at pp. 243–4.

(1) and (2) together constitute a dialectical contradiction of a specific kind already identified in *The Possibility of Naturalism*,[40] a Colletti contradiction or false necessity: 'the necessary co-existence in social reality of an object and a (categorially) false presentation of it, where it is the inner (or essential) structure of the object which generates the categorially false presentation (or appearance)' (p. 195). Ideology-critique, and more generally explanatory critique, may thus ground a three-fold criticism, (1) of theories (*theoretical ideologies*), (2) of social practices (*practical ideologies*) and (3) of the generative social structures that underpin them, issuing in a mandate to change them, CP. A remarkable passage pinpoints its relation to other kinds of philosophical critique. In identifying 'forms which structure and inebriate experience', Bhaskar writes, it is akin to *Kantian* critique, but differs from it

in that it understands these forms as objective systems of con-straints, historically produced, reproduced and potentially trans-formable. It is analogous to *Hegelian* critique in that it sees reflection on the conditions of possible knowledge as at once reflection on a system of humanly produced constraints, but it differs from it, in that the medium of this reflection is explanatory theory, the form of the constraints are transcendentally real and historically defined, and the agency of their dissolution is trans-formative (e.g. class) praxis rather than speculative experience. It anticipates too the great insight of *Nietzschean* 'critique' that 'among the conditions of life might be error', but locates the source of error in structural causes, neither fated nor fixed. (p. 199)

Such a conception lays the groundwork for the more fully developed theory of ideology/alienation in Bhaskar's later work, and within that the theory of the demi-real. Demi-reality is in effect the compounding of Tina *compromise formation* on Tina compromise formation, the basic elements of which are already theorised in *Scientific Realism* (without the name 'Tina', though not without the idea it signifies, that 'there is no alternative'). A compromise formation is entrained when, as Bhaskar later put it,

---

40. Bhaskar, *PN*, 71

'a falsity in theory [is] held in tension with a truth in practice',[41] that is, when a theory that contravenes *axiological necessity* (epistemologically mediated natural necessity that asserts itself in practice) is persisted with, resulting in an internally contradictory or *duplicitous* and *plastic* ensemble of irrealist and realist elements.

The theory of the compromise formation provides the fundamental scaffolding, forged largely on site, for the substantive application of the theory of ideology-critique to positivism in Chapter 3. Although this critique is restricted to positivism, it should be borne in mind that at the time of penning it Bhaskar still planned to critique all the main irrealist approaches to philosophy of science and social science in the modern epoch in detail in *Philosophical Ideologies*.[42] The chapter elaborates a structural analysis and explanation of the production and reproduction of positivism as an abstract cognitive structure or 'stratified conceptual totality' (p. 291), focusing on the cognitive rather than non-cognitive conditions for this. It demonstrates that the cardinal axiological necessities positivism flouts are the transitivity of science and the intransitivity of its objects. This flouting is enshrined in the epistemic fundamentalism and cognitive anthroporealism of its problem field, which together engender 'the great *anthroporealist exchange*' that is common to all subject–object identity-theory, in which 'a naturalised (and so incorrigibly *eternalised*) science is purchased at the price of a humanised nature' (p. 23). These are the fundamental terms of Bhaskar's account of the synchronic production of the ideology of positivism. Its reproduction is shown to be largely a function of the ways in which it 'mystifies or otherwise rationalises scientific and other social practices' (p. 235). This is supported by a meta-theorem inverting Kurt Gödel's incompleteness theorems: 'the determinant outcomes of internally inconsistent (and so formally indeterminate) systems can only be explained by reference to factors, uses or principles not contained within the system' (p. 262). A real definition ensues: positivism is, 'one might

---

41. R. Bhaskar, *Reflections on Meta-Reality: Transcendence, Emancipation and Everyday Life* [RMR] (New Delhi, Thousand Oaks, and London: Sage, 2002), 84–5.

42. He was still working on this book (and close to finishing it) in 1994, at which stage he put it aside in order to pursue the spiritual turn (see Bhaskar with Hartwig, *FCR*, Ch. 7). It would be an intriguing exercise in Bhaskar exegesis to compare the 1971 manuscript with *Scientific Realism*.

say, the house-philosophy of the bourgeoisie', an 'anti-scientific scientism', 'anti-historical historicism' and 'anti-philosophical ... philosophy' that naturalises and normalises the capitalist social order by the reification of facts and the fetishism of constant conjunctions and 'reflects in an endless hall of mirrors the self-image of Bourgeois Man' (pp. 270, 289–90, 307–8).

*Scientific Realism and Human Emancipation* is an epistemic halfway house between transcendental realism and critical naturalism, on the one hand, and dialectical critical realism on the other. In the basement of this house there is a laboratory in which Bhaskar is working at transmuting his analytic of analytical and dialectical reason into a dialectic of dialectical and analytical reason. He is mixing the new in with the old, attempting to work his way to a new transcending concept that will reconcile negativity, totality and transformative praxis with non-identity and difference at a fundamental logical level. But he is missing a key ingredient. Although he regularly deploys the concept of absence and is aware that it will play a vital role in the dialectical deepening and development of his system, there is an absence of an *adequate* concept of absence in his work, constituting an aporia or practice–theory contradiction: he speaks and writes of the negative but cannot yet say what the negative is about in the intransitive dimension. In terms of the epistemological dialectic he later adapted from Hegel and from his own work on the logic of scientific discovery, he is at the stage of the $\sigma$ (sigma) transform, which is always an attempt to move to a more adequate conceptual formation via the synthesis of positive contraries (aporiai, anomalies, and so on) that the supervention of new upon old insights tends to bring in its train. He has not yet reached the stage of the $\tau$ (tau) transform, at which a vital clue arrives permitting transcendence of the contraries (the restoration of totality) in a new and more complete conceptual formation that transmutes positive contraries into negative subcontraries: in the case in point, where R = 'reference to' and N = 'the negative or non-being, the absent', (R–/–>N) will become, in dialectical critical realism, (–(R–/–>N)). But we can see in retrospect and from the vantage point of the epistemological dialectic that the synthesising work of the $\sigma$ transform is necessary for the dialectical leap effected at the $\tau$ transform. For that reason, when he later wanted to reconcile West with East, duality with non-duality, in the transition from dialectic to the spiritual turn, it was a synthesis that Bhaskar attempted in *From East to West* before moving on to transcendence of the opposing elements in the philosophy of meta-Reality. If, then, a great book is defined with Marcel Proust as 'not just the sum of existing masterpieces; it is particular and unforseeable, being made out of something which, because it lies somewhere beyond the existing sum, cannot be deduced simply from acquaintance with it, however close',[43] *Scientific Realism and Human Emancipation* falls just short of greatness. (Proust's criterion for greatness matches Bhaskar's own account of creativity and the moment of absolute transcendence at the τ transform.) But it prepares the way for a great book, which could not have been written without it.

Bhaskar's work since the publication of *The Possibility of Naturalism* has moved forward on two main fronts: the deepening of ontology from 1M to the other six stadia of the ontological–axiological chain, and the metacritique of irrealism on the terrain of philosophy. *Scientific Realism* makes a major contribution to both, and to the sociology of knowledge to boot. The deepening of ontology has unquestionably been the main thrust, and *Scientific Realism*'s most important contribution by common consent is in the area of explanatory critique and emancipatory axiology. Yet in Bhaskar's own estimation in the early 1970s the most important part of his triptych, which as we know *Scientific Realism* resumes and develops, was one particular kind of metacritique: ideology-critique, in particular because of its demonstration of resonance effects with the prevailing social order.[44] While there is no gainsaying the weight and power of the deepening of ontology, and while ideology-critique presupposes that deepening (and vice versa), there is a sense in which the intuition of the young Bhaskar might well stand the test of time, at least in relation to his output down to and including the present work. *Scientific Realism* will perhaps come to be remembered above all as the crucible in which the fundamental elements of the theory of the demi-real, including the metacritique of irrealism, were forged, a theory that presupposes the unity that underlies conflict and the identity underlying difference articulated in the philosophy of meta-Reality. In the last sentence of the book 'the positivist illusion' is likened to a spider's web. The web or maze of

---

43. M. Proust, *In Search of Lost Time, Volume 2, In the Shadow of Young Girls in Flower* (London: Penguin), 235.
44. Bhaskar with Hartwig, *FCR*, Ch. 2.

*maya* (illusion) and *avidya* (ignorance) in *From East to West*, which constitutes the demi-real, and in which we are all caught up, is this same spider's web compounded many times over in four dimensions. In Samuel Beckett's *Waiting for Godot*, the slave Lucky is profoundly convinced that he is caught in an invisible net, presumably along with every other slave. While it does not yet have a concept of generalised master–slave-type or power$_2$ relations, *Scientific Realism and Human Emancipation* demonstrates that this invisible net is real and ensnares us all; that, if we are to survive as a species, let alone flourish, it is imperative that we break free; and that explanatory critical philosophy and social science are indispensable, though not the only, means to accomplish this.

Mervyn Hartwig
September 2008

# 1

# Scientific Realism and the Aporias of Contemporary Philosophy

*'All social life is essentially practical. All mysteries which lead theory to mysticism find their rational solution in human practice and in the comprehension of this practice'.[1]*

## 1. Rifts in recent philosophy

Of late the philosophy of science has appeared a prisoner of paradox. The fundamental assumptions of the positivist world-view, dominant for over a century, that science is *monistic* in its development and *deductive* in its structure, lie shattered. But the ensuing accounts of science have been unable to sustain the coherence of precisely those features of science which they have placed to the fore of the philosophical agenda, namely scientific change and the non-deductive aspects of theory.

Consider first the anti-monistic tendency, exemplified most notably perhaps by the work of Bachelard, Canguilhem, Koyré, Popper, Kuhn, Lakatos, Feyerabend, Stegmüller and Laudan. Both Bachelard and Kuhn, in attempting to do justice to the phenomena of scientific change, veer very close to the position, which is in effect a collectivist variant of what I shall call '*sub-*

---

1.   K. Marx '8th Thesis on Feuerbach', *Early Writings*, Harmondsworth 1975, p. 423.

*jective super-idealism'*, that we create and change the world, along with our theories[2] — a position which renders change in either unintelligible. Neither Kuhn nor Feyerabend have managed to explain how there can be a clash between incommensurable descriptions, or to say over what such descriptions clash. Popper has not demonstrated how the refutation of a conjecture could be rational, unless nature were uniform; and he has apportioned no ground for assuming that it is, in the face of standard sceptical (Humean, Goodmanesque[3], etc.) scenarios. For what is there to prevent nature altering so that our most decisively rejected theories turn out true and our most cherished falsifiers, implicitly universal, false? This is of course nothing other than that old 'scandal of philosophy'[4]: the Humean problem of induction. Similarly Lakatos has not shown how, unless nature were uniform, it would be rational to work on progressive rather than degenerating programmes; or, for that matter, to pay any attention to the history of science. For almost all the philosophers within this corps there is a tension between (ontological) realism and (epistemological) relativism. And generally they have encountered some difficulty in squaring their emphasis on scientific discontinuities with the seemingly progressive character of scientific development, in which there is growth as well as — and in — change. Parallel problems beset the anti-deductivist camp, typified by the work of Kneale, Waismann, Hanson, Scriven, Polanyi, Toulmin, Hesse and Harré. Such philosophers have reacted sharply against the standard Humean and positivist account of science on which, in the last instance, there can be no ground for divaricating a necessary from a merely accidental sequence of events, for expecting emeralds to be green rather than grue[5] or for supposing that water might not freeze rather than boil when it is

---

2. See e.g. G. Bachelard, *La dialectique de la durée*, Paris 1936, pp. 63-64, and T.S. Kuhn, *The Structure of Scientific Revolutions*, 2nd Edition, Chicago 1970, p. 121. Cf. also P.K. Feyerabend, *Science in a Free Society*, London 1978, p. 70.
3. N. Goodman, *Fact, Fiction and Forecast*, 2nd Ed., New York 1959, pp 73-80.
4. Cf. C.D. Broad, *The Philosophy of Francis Bacon*, Cambridge 1926.
5. 'Grue' is an artificial predicate (introduced by Goodman in *Fact, Fiction and Forecast* (2nd ed. New York 1959, p. 74)) with a time-dependence condition such that things, e.g. emeralds, which appear green when examined before time t, appear blue when examined after time t, where t is

heated. These philosophers, writing under the initial pull of Wittgenstein but also self-consciously recuperating the arguments of Kant, Whewell, Peirce and Campbell (and, to an extent, Aristotle and Locke), have sought to show how scientific practice yields cognitive items — whether dressed as models, paradigms, heuristics, conceptual schemata or regulative ideals — which are irreducible to syntactical operations upon sense-experience and yet indispensable for the intelligibility and empirical extension of theory. In this way such items function as it were, as social surrogates for natural necessity.[6] However, so long as it retains an empiricist ontology, three stark problems straight away confront this school. First, to the extent that the surrogate can be empirically described, its independent cognitive role disappears (as the necessity of the connection, analogical character of the model, ideality of the order, etc. evaporate); conversely, to the extent that its cognitive role is preserved, its epistemic warrant crumbles (since it now ceases to designate real phenomena).[7] Second, as the analysis presents natural necessity as a product or mediation of human mind, it scarcely seems adequate to explicate the sense in which science presumes to discover necessities in mind-independent things. Third, an evident tension exists between the principles (of coherence, intelligibility and structure) invoked to make sense of science and the properties (of atomicity, fragmentation and flatness) tacitly attributed to being. Together, these problems comprise a homologue of the old Kantian problem of the synthetic *a priori* in science: that is, the problem of sustaining the necessity and universality apparently accruing to scientific judgments, when such judgements are supposedly about a world of loose and disconnected events. The anti-deductivist faction then is immediately assailed by an antinomy between the cognitive function of the surrogate and its epistemic title, a discrepancy between philosophical analysis and its intended object and a rift

---

some arbitrary date in the more or less immediate future. (Thus if t is 2000 AD, or midnight tomorrow, all existing evidence for emeralds being green is equally evidence for their being 'grue', i.e. green up to 2000 AD, or midnight tomorrow, and blue thereafter). This is an epistemological variant of Hume's original problem of induction.

6.  Cf. R. Harré, 'Surrogates for Necessity', *Mind 1973*, pp. 350-80.
7.  Cf. C.G. Hempel, 'The Theoretician's Dilemma', *Aspects of Scientific Explanation*, New York 1963, Chapter 8.

between epistemological principles and ontological presuppositions. And these are as evident in their Kantian prototype as in its contemporary avatars. For patently there is no way in which, even if the Kantian principles were all demonstrably valid, they could be used to justify any particular inductive inference (any more than Aristotelian 'nous', or more precisely active intellect, could prohibit the inference to grue): that the world will 'carry on', under the descriptions in terms of which it is currently known to us, remains an article of faith.[8] More generally, writers within this tradition have not always succeeded in blending their stress on the synthesising activity of the scientific imagination with the messy practicalities of science's causal transactions with nature — the nuts and bolts, so to speak, of scientific life.

I have tried to show elsewhere[9] how the antinomic constitution of contemporary philosophy of science, betraying its historical station as an *incomplete critique of positivism* and reflected in these and a plethora of related aporias, can be traced to the supervention of new epistemological insights upon old (empiricist or idealist) ontologies, more or less materially incompatible with them. My primary aim in this chapter is to demonstrate why and how, if the rational gains of both the anti-monistic and anti-deductivist movements are to be saved, a new ontology, and corresponding account of science, must be cultivated to accommodate them. This new ontology comprises a Copernican revolution in the strict sense (of Copernicus, not Kant) of a de-anthropocentric shift in our metaphysical conception of the place of (wo)man in nature, in which the umbilical cord uniquely tying thought to things in traditional philosophy is snapped (the significance of discontinuism) and ontological structure, diversity and change emerge as conditions of the practical cognitive activity of science (the significance of non-deductivism). My secondary aim is to locate the impasse in contemporary philosophy of science in terms of its foundational structural, historical and aporetic parameters. For we shall see that positivism, discredited but not dissolved, is merely the dominant historical attractor position in a plate with deeper

---

8.  That is to say, in Kantian terms, this supposition must renounce the proud title of an analytic of the understanding, or that of a transcendentally necessary condition of experience, and assume instead the more modest status of a mere idea of reason, or regulative ideal.

9.  *A Realist Theory of Science*, 2nd Ed., Brighton 1978.

alethic roots. I want also to prepare the ground here for the specification of the logic of distinctively social scientific enquiry and so to set the scene for an 'explanatory critique' of positivim and its current progeny. Such a critique aims to demonstrate not just why an idea or system is false, but how it comes to be believed and acted upon, i.e. reproduced, or more or less transformed, in some or other historically determinate society.[10]

## 2. Forms of realism

The account of science I wish to commend to the reader is a realist one. In its broadest sense in philosophy any position can be nominated 'realist' which asserts the existence of some disputed kind of entity (universals, material objects, causal laws, numbers, probabilities, propositions, etc.). But for my story the most historically significant types of realism are: *predicative realism*, asserting the existence of universals independently (Plato) or as the properties (Aristotle) of particular material things; *perceptual realism*, asserting the existence of material objects in space and time independently of their perception; and *scientific realism*, asserting the existence and activity of the objects of scientific enquiry absolutely or relatively independently of the enquiry of which they are the objects or more generally of all human activity. (The different grades of strength of scientific realism need not detain us at present.) It is scientific realism with which I am directly concerned here, although of course it reduces to predicative or perceptual realism if the objects of scientific knowledge just are Platonic (or Aristotelian) forms or material objects.

Scientific realism, then, is the theory that the objects of scientific enquiry exist and act, for the most part, quite independently of scientists and their activity. So defined, it might be supposed that the question of whether or not natural science is 'realist' can only be settled empirically, viz. by determining whether or not scientists believe, or behave as if, the theoretical terms they employ possess real referents independently of their theorising.[11] This issue is obviously important. But I intend to

10. Cf. my *The Possibility of Naturalism*, Brighton 1979, p. 154.
11. Cf. H. Putnam, 'Realism and Reason', *Meaning and the Moral Sciences*, London 1978, pp. 123-140.

argue the case for a metaphysical realism, consisting in an elaboration of what the world must be like *prior* to any empirical investigation of it and *for* any scientific attitudes or activities to be possible — a realism which neither endorses nor presupposes a realistic interpretation of any particular theory.

It is clear that such a metaphysical realism, in contrast to a merely first order or 'internal'[12] realism, depends upon the feasibility of a philosophy, as distinct from a sociology or history, of science; and, within philosophy, of an ontology as well as an epistemology. For realism is not a theory of knowledge or truth, but of *being* — although as such it is bound to posses epistemological implications. Accordingly, a realist position in the philosophy of (natural) science will consist, first and foremost, of a theory about the nature of the being, rather than the knowledge, of the objects investigated by the sciences — to the effect that they endure and operate independently of human activity, and hence of both sense-experience and thought. So realism is immediately opposed to both empiricism and rationalism, wherein being is defined in terms of the human attributes of experience and reason. And it repudiates, from the beginning, that dogmatic canon of post-Humean philosophy (which I have styled the '*epistemic fallacy*'[13]) decreeing that ontological questions can always be transposed into an epistemological key, i.e. that statements about being either just are or may always be parsed as statements about knowledge.

Acceptance of Hume's canon characterises the analytical and dialectical traditions in modern philosophy alike. For it was ratified by Kant, objectified by Schelling and beatified by Hegel as the criterion of philosophy, understood as the unfolding consummation in thought of the primal Parmenidean postulate of the identity of being and thought. This is a postulate from which contemporary scientific realism registers a complete, but reasoned, break.

Now any theory of the knowledge of objects entails some theory of the objects of knowledge; that is, every theory of scientific knowledge logically presupposes a theory of what the world must be like for knowledge, under the descriptions given it by the theory, to be possible. Thus suppose a philosopher analyses scientific laws as, or as dependent upon, constant con-

---

12. Such as that of Putnam, *loc cit.*
13. *A Realist Theory of Science*, pp. 37-38.

junctions of events — as, for instance, Kant did in the Second Analogy, in maintaining that for every event there is a condition upon which it invariably (and necessarily) follows.[14] S/he is then committed to the view that there are such conjunctions; that, in Mill's words, 'there are such things in nature as parallel cases: that what happens once will, under a sufficient degree of similarity of circumstance, happen again'.[15] In this way, then, as Bachelard recognised, 'all philosophy, explicitly or tacitly, honestly or surreptitiously ... deposits, projects or presupposes a reality'.[16] Hence, to invert and circumscribe Hegel's famous dictum about idealism: every philosophy, inasmuch as it takes science for its topic, is essentially a realism, or at least has realism for its principle, the pertinent questions being only *how far* and *in what form* this principle is actually implemented.[17]

Thus the mainstream in the philosophy of science, in both its classical empiricist (Humean) and transcendental idealist (Kantian) currents, presupposes an implicit *empirical realism* according to which the real objects of scientific investigation are defined in terms of actual or possible experience. More recently, the super-idealist party has secreted an implicit *subjective conceptual realism*, according to which the real objects are envisaged as the product of thought, i.e. of the spontaneous play of the human mind (or its socialised form, the scientific community), unconstrained by sense-experience. The remoter ancestry of this position includes Vico's *Facimus* and Fichte's *Tathandlung* as well as Nietzsche's perspectivism. But it is nowadays usually approached by the simple shedding (e.g. in a historically relativised neo-Kantianism[18]), rather than by the

---

14. I. Kant, *Critique of Pure Reason*, trans. M. Kemp Smith, London 1970, B246.
15. J.S. Mill, *A System of Logic*, 8th edition, London 1961, Book 111 chapter 3, Section 1.
16. G. Bachelard, *Le matérialisme rationnel*, Paris 1953, p. 141.
17. G.W.F. Hegel, *The Science of Logic*, trans. A, Miller, London 1969, pp. 154-5: 'Every philosophy is essentialy an idealism or at least has idealism for its principle, and the question then is only how far this principle is actually carried out.'
18. This position is thus vulnerable to what I will call the antinomy of transcendental pragmatism. Cf. T. McCarthy, *The Critical Theory of Jürgen Habermas*, London 1978, p. 111. To paraphrase (and expand) McCarthy's criticism of Habermas, if nature has the transcendental (cf. Habermas) or merely *soi-disant* (cf. e.g. Rorty) or constructed (cf. e.g. van Fraassen) status of a constituted objectivity, then it cannot yield the historical or empirical ground of the constituting subjectivity or knowledge; conversely,

reconstruction of a practical or subjective genealogy, of the idea of an independent reality. Both these kinds of implicit ontology are explicitly anthropomorphic. In contrast, the older pre-critical rationalism of Platonic and Cartesian provenance, positing an explicit *objective conceptual realism*, is implicitly anthropomorphic. For the real objects it entertains, although presented as independent of finite, human minds, are divined as quintessentially rational, as, in effect, reason in the (dis)guise of being: that is, as constituted by and/or causally or teleologically dependent upon what is known to us only as an attribute of *human* being, namely thought or reason. The philosophy of science also contains a persistent romantic strain, nurturing an *intuitional realism*, incubating real objects identified wholly or partially in terms of human intuition, sensibility or affect. In each case we have an anthropomorphic definition of being, based on some anthropocentric (which need not always be an epistemo-centric) view of the world, with the human attribute in question (e.g. knowledge) being in turn reciprocally — in the momentous anthroporealist exchange of subject-object identity theory — defined by the presumed character of the world. In rejecting this anthroporealist array, whose constituents may be combined in more or less subtle ways, I am going to contend that only a realism fully consonant with the principle of scientific realism enunciated above — a *transcendental realism* — can uphold and display the intelligibility and rationale of science.

But in addition to those anthroporealisms, transcendental realism is also and equally opposed to any non-immanent or transcendent realism, which posits a sphere of pure uncog-nisable other-being, defined in terms of its *inaccessibility* to human being (as are Kantian noumena). A realm of 'ineffibilia', e.g. held in contrast or conjunction with the sensibilia or intel-ligibilia of empirical or conceptual realism, is certainly con-ceivable, but it is something *about* and *for* which nothing (or at any rate very little) can be said. In other words, transcendental realism is occupied, at least in the first place, with the being of

---

if nature is the historical ground of subjectivity and/or an empirical ground of knowledge, it cannot be regarded solely as a constituted or posited objectivity: it must be essentially *in-itself* (and only, so to speak, contin-gently a possible object of knowledge for us).

the objects of science. Now I am going to argue here, and show in more detail in Chapter 3, that any non-transcendental realism, i.e. any incomplete, inexplicit or ineffable realism, any '*irrealism*'[19] — such as an empirical, conceptual, intuitional and/or transcendent realism — must in practice presuppose its contrary, thus generating a contradictory complex, which acts as a vibrant source of mystifying power. In fact, to be more specific, two things must be true in the case of any actually historically efficacious irrealist (non-transcendental realist) philosophy. First an anthroporealism always presupposes a transcendent realism and vice versa — neither a purely transcendent nor a purely immanent analysis is sustainable,[20] so that what results is always a *compromise formation*, an inconsistent ensemble constituted by a normally asymmetrically weighted mix of achieved and unachieved identity theory, of a more or less immanent (e.g. empiricist) anthroporealism and a more or less transcendent idealism.[21] Second, this compromise formation itself presupposes (redescribed and/or re-enacted) sui generis transcendental realist elements in practice. For transcendental realism, understood as involoving *inter alia* the idea that knowledge of objects is possible and (contingently) historically actualised but that such knowledge and their objects cannot be inter-identified (that is to say, as involving what we might call a 'reality-knowable, non-identity theory'), is not, I shall be arguing, merely a theoretical option: it is transcendentally necessary and axiologically, practically irreducible too.

In this way, then, any irrealist philosophy of science will constitute a doubly — once internally, once externally —

---

19. This is not intended to have any connection with Goodman's or Husserl's concepts of the same name.
20. Cf. in this respect the acute analysis of R.G. Collingwood, *The Idea of Nature*, Oxford 1945, Part 1, chapter 2.
21. These constitute a kind of duplicitous unity of bad dialectical (individually and jointly refuted) complements or counterparts. The tacit complicity and mutual practical presupposition of both anthroporealist and transcendent realist forms of irrealism stem from the impossibility of a completely achieved and the impotence of a completely unachieved identity theory. Thus we shall see, in Section 4 below, how the officially immanent Humean analysis of laws necessitates either an internal cleavage within the world of phenomena into Humean and non-Humean parts and/or the projection of the Humean ideal, as an external duplicate, onto a trancendent beyond.

determined compromise formation. Moreover it will be seen that while transcendental realism entails, but is irreducible to, those modified forms of Aristotelian predicate and Lockean perceptual realism which undergird the categorical framework of everyday life, it is this very same framework, supporting the *Lebenswelt* of common-sense and routine mutual understanding inside and outside science, which shapes the trellis for the most alluring irrealist figures in the contemporary social world.

## 3. Metaphysics and Method

How is a metaphysics of science, more especially transcendental realism, possible?

Traditional metaphysics set out to elaborate a comprehensive, ideally apodeictic, account of reality (including the place of our knowledge in it). Thus it busied itself with what and how many kinds of things existed, and in what modes and relations (of dependency, etc.). Do abstract entities, such as forms or universals or minds, exist in addition to or perhaps instead of particular material things? Is the universe monistic, as Spinoza maintained, or a pluralistic monadology, in which each individual reflects the whole, as Leibniz urged? Are things, events or processes fundamental? Are space and time real? Is the finite more real than the infinite, as the Greeks believed, or the reverse, as Christianity postulated?

Speculative enquiries of this sort received near-fatal blows from Hume and Kant who argued that, purveying 'news from nowhere',[22] they envitably generated nonsense (Hume) or antinomies (Kant). But Kant also initiated two metaphysical programmes:

($\alpha$) a programme of purely immanent metaphysics — in his own terms, transcendental rather than transcendent[23] — and
($\beta$) a programme of merely descriptive (or only mildly 'revisionary'[24]) metaphysics.

---

22.  W.H. Walsh, *Metaphysics*, London 1963, Chapter 3.
23.  *Critique of Pure Reason*, A296/B352.
24.  P.F. Strawson, *Individuals*, London 1959, p. 9: 'Descriptive metaphysics is

In so doing, he took himself to be exchanging the fantasy of a disclosure of the nature of being *per se*[25] for (a) the project of an investigation of the presuppositions of our knowledge of being. This task he then identified — in his doctrine of transcendental idealism — with that of (b) the elucidation of the conceptual structures in terms of which any knowable being must be thought. It is evident that (a) and (b) are *in principle* distinct. And it is Kant's illicit conflation of them (and, growing from this, his inosculation of ($\alpha$) and ($\beta$)) which, *inter alia* accounts for the intractable Kantian problems of the status and scope of the critical philosophy itself. For my present purposes, however, the important thing is to disengage them conceptually.

If this is done, and a trancendental enquiry is identified as an enquiry into the conditions of the possibilty of $\phi$, where $\phi$ is some especially significant, central or pervasive feature of our experience, then it must be recognised that:

(i) such an enquiry is intelligible only as an instance of the wider class of enquiries into the necessary conditions of social activities as conceptualised in the experience of agents (or in a hermeneutically grounded theoretical redescription or critique of them);

(ii) generalised transcendental reflection of this kind is in turn merely a species of the wider genus of retroductive argument[26] characteristic, as I shall show in Section 5 below, of scientific activity generally and is not distinguished by any social logic or innate certainty of its own;

(iii) the pattern, order or form of such arguments do not necessarily reflect, are not normally homologous with, seldom constitute and never determine the structure, order or nature of their subject-matters;

(iv) the activity analysed may depend upon the powers (and liabilities) people possess as material (physical and biological), causal, social and/or historical agents;

(v) activity, conceptualisation and analysis may each be nor-

---

content to describe the actual structure of our thoughts about the world, revisionary metaphysics is concerned to produce a better structure.'

25. Cf. Kant's very 'Feuerbachian' *Dreams of a Spirit-Seer* (1766), London 1900.

26. A retroductive argument moves from a description of some phenomenon to a description of something which produces it or is a condition for it.

matively corrigible, socially contested, spatially localised and
temporally transient;
(vi) the analysis may yield, in the case of science, ontological,
realist, epistemically relativist (rather than absolutist — or
irrationalist) and domain-specific results; and
(vii) such results must always be construed as conditional
(praxis-dependent) and expressed in hypothetical not assertoric
form.

This is to say that there is no necessary connection between
acceptance of the central methodological insight of the critical
philosophy, namely that philosophy is possible but only in
relation to a practice or object *other than itself* (science,
morality, art, etc.), i.e. as *heteronomous*,[27] and Kant's particular
idealist premises, presuppositions, arguments and conclusions.
On the contrary, Kantian idealism, inasmuch as it fails to sustain
the intelligibility of its own practice and, as we shall see in
Section 4, grounds all knowledge (and a fortiori both knowable
being and the being of knowing) in a fiction,[28] raises the
conundrum of its own (epistemic and ontic) standing.

On my conception, there can be no philosophy as such or in
general, but only the philosophy of particular, historically
determinate, social forms. It is philosophy's other, its *topic*,
securing premises for its arguments and potential referents for
its conclusions, which both historically *roots* it and establishes
its *syncategorematic* and *this-worldly* character, so that it ceases
to consider itself privileged by some special (high) subject-
matter or (superior) mode of truth. Thus, for example, the
province of philosophy (or metaphysics) is no longer co-
extensive with the domain of the necessary. And henceforth
philosophy neither subsists apart from the various sciences (and
other social practices) nor contemplates a distinct, transcendent
realm of its own. On the contrary, philosophy treats the self-
same world as the sciences, but *transcendentally*, i.e. from the
perspective of what such practices presuppose about the world.
In this respect it pursues a line of questioning with contingent
historical origins and definite social conditions, but which can

---

27. In the same way, Kant's crucial substantive insight is that human intelli-
    gence is possible but only as *discursive*, operating on materials which it
    does not itself supply, but are rather given '*from without*'.
28. Cf. also G.W.F. Hegel, *The Science of Logic*, pp. 46-7.

always be (re-)opened and never foreclosed. Kant's great meta-philosophical significance is that, in investigating the possibility of grounding metaphysics in the contingent actuality of social practices, he illumined a third way between the uncontrolled hypostases of traditional metaphysics and the self-nullifying reductionism of positivism. However, transcendental realism, but not idealism, builds a double first order *constraint* into this third way. For in the long run philosophy must be consistent with the findings of science – both in respect of its claims about the world (because what is philosophically demonstrable is also potentially scientifically comprehensible) and in respect of its claims about itself (because philosophy, understood as a branch of a division, human knowing, of being, is fully susceptible to substantive socio-historical research). On this approach, then, philosophy is dependent upon the *form* of scientific practices, but irreducible to (although ultimately constrained by) the *content* of scientific beliefs. Thus philosophy can mark the condition that if experimental activity is to be possible, the world must be structured and open. But it cannot anticipate what structures the world contains or the ways in which they are intricated, which remain entirely within the jurisdiction of primary scientific investigations.

So conceived, critical philosophy clearly encompasses itself among its objects. This does not mean that the conclusion of some piece of philosophical reasoning can simultaneously appear as its premise, so that philosophy, as it were, swallows its own tail. It is rather that, although every philosophical discussion must take some specific social form (a scientific practice, philosophical theory, cultural tradition, etc.) for its topic, there is no particular topic,[29] at which philosophy, so to speak, stops. And because there is no topic immune from the possibility of further philosophical analysis, this convers-contest-ation is in principle an *open-ended* one. Philosophical argumentation thus assumes the logical aspect of an endlessly recursive unbounded step-function, such that, as new premises

29. Such as the Cartesian, Kantian, Fichtean or Husserlian Ego's; the Par-menidian one, Platonic form of the good, Aristotelean self-thinking thought, Hegelian absolute; or Locke's ideas, Russell's sense data, Moore's moral or Austin's ordinary language intuitions, Winch's self-interpreting life-forms, Wittgenstein's language-games — or, if you like, Popperian falsifiers, Lakatosian research programmes, etc.

(forms of social practice) arise, new modes of philosophical reflection become possible (and necessary); at the same time it acquires the historical meaning of a particular conjunctural intervention. This rooted recursivity which organises it, combines and unites, in binomial form, dialogue and self-reflection, reflexivity and critique. In sum, then, a philosophical discourse is: (1) a real, historically determinate, object; (2) characterised by a distinctive and open-ended line of enquiry; (3) about the same world as the sciences; but (4) reflexively subject to substantive scientific investigations (in virtue of (1)) and control (in virtue of (3)), plus potential analysis as the topic of a fresh or deepening movement of philosophical thought (in virtue of (2)).

However, at this juncture we immediately come upon a difficulty. How are the premises of our transcendental enquiries to be selected without already implying an unvalidated commitment to the epistemic (moral, aesthetic, etc.) significance of the activities analysed? How, that is to say, are we to avoid that bad circularity implicit in recourse to arbitrary and external criteria of knowledge with which Hegel so trenchantly charged traditional (Cartesian-Kantian) non-phenomenological epistemology?[30] (For would it not be as gross an *ignoratio elenchi* to attempt to refute Plato by appealing to the criteria of say, Popper or Mach, as to test the theory of caloric by balloting the members of the Paris Academy of Sciences?). This snare can be eluded only if philosophical enquiry assumes the form of immanent critique, so that transcendental arguments paradigmatically become, or at the very least are always supplemented by, transcendental refutations of pre-existing, and more generally alternative, accounts.[31] Thus, in the case of science, by focusing on activities which non-realists have historically picked on as of paramount importance, we shall see how they supply the criteria for their own refutation, pulling the rug from under their own feet and placing it very conveniently for the realist.

But the conception proposed here differs from that of a Hegelian dialectical phenomenology in at least two major respects. First, it explicitly disavows what Hegel, backsliding in the direction of Cartesian First Philosophy, was occasionally

30. G.W.F. Hegel, *Phenomenology of Spirit*, trans. A. Miller, Oxford 1977, pp. 46-57.
31. Cf. *A Realist Theory of Science*, Postscript to the 2nd edition, pp. 251-262.

prone to suggest: namely that one could begin with the simplest form of consciousness (or category)[32] and then, with the phenomenological process thus initiated, just 'look on' as the dialectic, comprehended as the indwelling movement of the concept,[33] unwound. In other words, transcendental realism eschews any notion of the simplicity of beginnings, self-evidence of arguments or passivity (or innocence) of observers. Philosophical traditions evolve unkempt; and their reception, interpretation and rejection is the work of men and women, each generation, in situated and interested (i.e. guilty) dialogue and disputation. It is important to remember that all cognitive claims, including claims to knowledge of necessities in *any* mode (whether logical, mathematical, transcendental, conceptual, natural, conventional, psychological, historical, etc.) are fallible; and that discourse, and perhaps especially philosophical discourse (from the Sophists and Socrates on), is typically dialogical or conversational in structure, i.e. proximately or mediately *ad hominem et feminam* — not only about a topic and at a place in a time, but oriented to others, communicative in intent. These considerations are easily obscured in that smug and sanitised self-celebration of the present implicit in the Whiggish *Histoire Sanctionnée*[34] of most post-Kantian philosophy.[35] Second, the conception advocated here repudiates outright the pivotal Hegelian assumptions of the continuity and autonomy (or final self-sufficiency) of philosophy. In this respect it endorses *ab initio* the Marxian critique of what I shall term the '*speculative illusion*', viz. the sublimation of social life, including science, in philosophy. This critique breaks into the parthenogenetic self-development of the conceptual world by treating philosophy as merely a (subordinated) moment in a practical ensemble, thereby restoring to it an ample — but now historically charged — measure of heteronomy. I am arguing for the principle of immanent critique without parthenogenesis, and for the non-absolutist deployment of transcendental arguments,

---

32. Notwithstanding his comments on the immediate and the mediate in 'With What Must the Science begin'?, *The Science of Logic*, p. 67 ff.
33. Cf. *Phenomenology of Spirit*, p. 34
34. G. Bachelard, *L'activité rationaliste de la physique contemporaine*, Paris 1951.
35 Cf. R. Rorty, *Philosophy and the Mirror of Nature*, Oxford 1980, p. 391; and J. Rée, 'Philosophy and the History of Philosophy', *Philosophy and its Past*, J. Rée *et al.*, Hassocks 1978.

viz. as typically turning on the isolation of practico-epistemological or more generally axiological inconsistencies.[36] I shall argue in a moment that, *contra* positivism, philosophy is necessary; just as, *contra* Hegel, it is heteronomous; and, *contra* 'philosophical hyper-professionalism' it is necessarily heteronomous — soiled in life.

Philosophy has an irreducibly normative character. For any investigation of consciousness or self-reflective trajectory of thought is bound to consider it (-self) under two related aspects:

(i) as something which it is or aspires to be; that is, as something which, inasmuch as it is intentional, aims at or succeeds or fails in being (e.g. an adequate explication of a topic, a true description of a state of affairs, a kind or courageous act, a just or prudent decision, etc.); and
(ii) as something shaped and conditioned, which has been historically produced or formed and which it seeks to understand or explain.

(i) is the *intrinsic* or normative aspect (IA), presupposed by the applicability of some or other intentional description to the act in question — though not necessarily that under which the action is performed — provided only it is intentional under some description. (ii) is the *extrinsic,* caused or historical aspect (EA) of any cognitive process (philosophical, scientific, moral or whatever). Under the intrinsic aspect consciousness is regarded *judgementally,* under the extrinsic aspect *historically.* The IA is concerned with questions of *validity,* the EA with questions of *credibility.* From the first perspective, an act, state or performance (whether imagined,

---

36. If, unlike Kant but with P.F. Strawson (*The Bounds of Sense,* London 1966) and e.g. R. Walker (*Kant,* London 1980), one differentiates transcendental arguments from their subject-specific results (whether realist, idealist, constructivist or whatever), two consequences immediately follow. First, it must be conceded that the central theses of transcendental realism - the implicit (or 'diurnal' in Bachelard's sense — see *The Philosophy of No,* New York 1968) philosophy underlying the practice of the sciences — could be arrived at (chanced upon or accepted) without recourse to any characteristically philosophical or transcendental mode of argument. Second, the possibility opens up of arguing for say a transcendental idealist or quasi-conventionalist account of some specific topic area (e.g. the nature of propositional identity) within an overall transcendental realist perspective.

planned or completed) is assessed or evaluated in terms of the criteria for acts etc. of the relevant type; from the second perspective, both the acts etc. and the criteriologies are situated and explained. Note that although it is epistemologically relevant considerations that are adduced in the IA or the EA, these considerations are not (or need not be) just modes of apprehending consciousness; they are (or may become) features of the apprehending consciouness itself, and, as such, real. It would be as wrong to identify the judgemental and the practical as to extrude the former from the latter. The extent and ways in which normative considerations may become causally efficacious (and so real) in the generative matrix in which human action occurs cannot be settled by philosophical fiat in abstraction from consideration of specific cases. (Between the conduct of a premeditated deliberate strategy and the habitus of everyday routines lie a host of intermediate cases.) The distinction between the intrinsic and extrinsic aspects is not to be associated with distinctions (whether well-grounded or not) between the present-future and the past, self and others, private and public, inner and outer, mental and corporeal, freedom and determination or philosophy and science; nor is it to be identified with Sartre's distinction between non-positional and positional consciousness[37] or with Kant's distinction between noumenal and phenomenal selves. At its grandest, the IA may be viewed as or as describing a real, if circumscribed, possible and contingently actualised moment in cognition, established by the capacity to reflexively monitor and initiate conduct (and therefore presupposing the causal efficacy of reasons), situating the possibility *inter alia* of deliberation and/or assessment in the light of norms, standards and more broadly-reasoned considerations.[38]

---

37. For Sartre, following Husserl, all consciousness is intentional, i.e. of something; more specifically, in every cognitive act, consciousness posits an object of which it is conscious, and among such objects may be states and acts of consciousness itself. But in all such positional(ised) consciousness, a distinct non-positional(ised) consciousness, namely the consciousness which is conscious of consciousness, is presupposed.

38. Of course, when it is efficacious, the IA is contained within, and presupposes, the object of the EA, just as thought generally is contained within, describes a real part of, and presupposes, being. As such, it might be thought that the relationship between the IA and EA is thus contingently asymmetrically inclusive. However, equally, when historical con-

It is also worth emphasising at this point the *practical* and *practically conditioned* character of philosophy. For philosophy, as understood here, does not dispense with the need for, but rather iteratively depends upon extra-philosophical *axiological standpoints* and interests, such as might be inclined by a particular class, gender, occupation, generational etc. experience and excited by involvement in a particular activity (e.g. science or a popular campaign) or concern about a specific issue (e.g. personal or species survival). Such standpoints are necessary: (i) logically, for the transformation of the conditional propositions of philosophy into subjectively warranted beliefs about the world; (ii) biographically, for the agent's engagement in the particular discourse in question; and (iii) historically, for the emergence, development and persistence of those discourses (as 'language-games'). Patently, such commitments can no more be justified by philosophy, or by philosophy alone, than boots can climb mountains; they must instead be grounded in the wider horizon of historical experience. Moreover the philosopher will have to draw upon this experience in appraising the weight to be placed on arguments from science as against arguments from other historically materialised practices (magic, religion, etc.) where the activities and/or their presuppositions are incompatible. Clearly at this point we appear to have reached an immanent barrier to immanent critique. In the final resort this is indeed so; and there is no alternative but to openly take one's stand with science. However, it would be impossible, or at any

---

siderations are adduced as a ground for action they are assessed in the light of criteria (for adequate explanation etc.) under their IA. So the asymmetry disappears. The 'objectivist' error of attempting to reduce the IA to the EA is affined to the *naturalistic fallacy*. The converse 'subjectivist' mistake comes in a variety of forms (rationalist, existentialist, spiritualist, etc.), depending upon the particular philosophical declension of intentionality informing the position. Both fallacies are prevalent, and often interdependent. Thus if existentialism is consciousness unsure of anything outside itself, positivism is consciousness aware of everything but itself. Yet positivism must rely on a solipsistic mode of access to its exterior, and existentialism on sheer givens to define the situation of its interior. Later we shall see that the casuality of reasons; the dual practico-epistemological intentionality of agency (trained at once on objects and objectives); the intransitivity of referents; the rationality of judgement (collapsed in positivism and absolute idealism alike); and the historicity of social life are all systematically interconnected.

rate unreasonable, to deny the historical significance of science (and *a fortiori* of results based on its analysis), especially in view of the considerations that cluster around what has come to be known as the 'Big Ditch Argument',[39] and in particular the fact that almost everywhere, within the span of a generation or two, agents come to accept modern natural science in the Galilean style as superior in its explanatory power to its pre-modern and/or non-scientific rivals and to prefer — by and large, for better or worse — natural-science based technologies. Allowing Big Ditch to procure a *prima facie*, standing case for science (and hence for the axiological transform required to speak, in philosophy, assertorically, about the world) does not of course imply assent to all that passes for science in any particular society, or to the notion that science is, in some historical or evaluative sense, the most important or worthy kind of social activity.

The formal, immanent metaphysics — which I shall designate as *metaphysics* $\alpha$ — of the type mooted here is still properly entitled a 'metaphysics' inasmuch as it arises out of but 'goes beyond' first order scientific enquiries. At the same time it may play a vital defensive, or even offensive, role for them: either as a plain Lockean cognitive underlabourer[40] or as a Bachelardian-Leninist partisan in the *Kampfplatz*[41] of cultural struggles in and around them or as a component of a more or less fully elaborated critique of the ideologies at work in and about them i.e. as, in one or more of these ways, in effect a philosophy *for* science.[42] Here the rooted recursivity of philosophy is matched by the *methodological susceptivity* of science. For just as there can be no discourse on method in abstraction from the sciences, so there can be no science in abstraction from the possibility of a critical discussion of its method. This is the *methodological circle*, twinscrewing philosophy and science.

But contemporary philosophical reflection on the sciences also yields another concept of metaphysics — *Metaphysics* $\beta$ —

39. E. Gellner, 'Options of Belief', *Spectacles and Predicaments*, Cambridge 1979. Cf. S. Lukes, 'Relativism in its Place', *Rationality and Relativism*, ed. M. Hollis and S. Lukes, Oxford 1982, p. 298.
40. J. Locke, Epistle to the Reader, *Essay Concerning Human Understanding, Volume 1*, New York 1909, p. 14.
41. Cf. L. Althusser, *Lenin and Philosophy*, London 1971, p. 57.
42. Cf. *A Realist Theory of Science*, p. 10

deriving from the second strand of the Kantian programme. For it is now generally (although by no means universally[43]) appreciated, in the wake of the anti-positivist crusades, that any developing scientific research programme depends upon one or more substantive metaphysics — categorial frameworks, general conceptual schemata, calculi or matrices which are not directly testable in experience because they provide the terms in which any test must be posed. Metaphysics β concerns the highest order or most fundamental categories and principles of the contents, rather than the methodological character of the activities, of the various sciences. The metaphysician is typically engaged in the Leibnizian art of unravelling the fabrics of conceptual systems — or in the parlance of Derrida and Habermas respectively — of deconstructing and/or reconstructing them. This is a craft which, as we know since Marx (and Wittgenstein), in principle embraces and in practice usually necessitates some excavation of the institutional matrices within which such systems are set, including the possibility of a depth-critique of them. Here intellectual integrity may demand of philosophy that it adopts a Socratic-Nietzschean stance, as the bad conscience of its age, 'a gadfly on the neck of man'[44] or, more likely, of the all-too-mundane powers-that-be. Metaphysics β, unlike metaphysics α, picks out cognitive features of science itself, rather than merely practical presuppositions of it. But as such, it is susceptible to a meta-conceptual transcendental enquiry, viz. into the presuppositions of the conceptual scheme to hand, just as any transcendental enquiry is liable to a meta-transcendental conceptual analysis, viz. into its more or less recondite conceptual articulation — activities which could be referred to as 'metaphysics α (β)' (the metaphysics α of some metaphysics β) and 'metaphysics β (α)' (the metaphysics β of some metaphysics α) respectively.

The issue now arises as to whether a purely formal metaphysics can licence the deduction of categorial principles at the level of specificity at which they nucleate the hard-cores of

---

43. E.g. where there is a heavy commitment to a programmatic total extensionalism (i.e. to the idea that the sentences of artificial and/or natural languages can be explicated as truth-functional complexes of predicates defined in completely non-intensional terms). Cf. e.g. D. Davidson, 'On the Very Idea of a Conceptual Scheme', *Proceedings and Addresses of the American Philosophical Association*, 47 (1973-74), pp. 5-20.

44. F. Nietzsche, *Gesammelte Werke, Volume 2*, Munich 1920, p. 11.

research programmes (e.g. the Newtonian laws of motion together with an appropriate, e.g. Boscovitchian, cosmological model). Both Kant and Whewell tried, like their rationalist predecessors, to square this epistemic circle by attempting to deduce a fully developed and schematised set of synthetic a priori principles, corresponding to empirically grounded laws, from purely formal considerations.[45] But if, on pain of a relapse into rationalism or a slide into Schellingian or Coleridgean *Naturphilosophie*, this cannot be done,[46] then the two aspects of the Kantian programme must be prised apart, and a place found, alongside a formal metaphysics α, for a purely descriptive (or critical) metaphysics β, of science. The former explicates the presuppositions of practical activities, the latter elucidates the structures of conceptual fields; both must now be regarded as historically relative but rationally appraisable.[47] The irreducibility of descriptive to formal metaphysics does however imply that an *epistemic indeterminacy*[48] and a *conservative bias*

---

45. See I. Kant, *Metaphysical Foundations of the Natural Sciences*, (1786), New York 1970 and *Opus Postumum* (1795-1804), Berlin 1955 and W.H. Whewell, *The Philosophy of the Indictive Sciences*, London 1840. While the deduction in the *Foundations* depends on the empirical concept of matter, that in the *Opus Postumum* precedes in an altogether a priori way.

46. It is Kant's elision of the critical distinction between (a) an investigation of the presuppositions of our knowledge of being and (b) the elucidation of the conceptual structures in terms of which knowable being is thought (see page 11 above), indicated by the precarious status of the thing-in-itself, in his transcendental idealism which (1) presages his late epistemological neo-rationalism (as the thing-in-itself is discreetly dropped or tacitly returned as an object of purely intellectual intuition, in a form very close to that of Fichtean constructivism) and (2) underlies his conflation of (α) and (β) as he increasingly comes to associate transcendental argumentation as such with the identification of particular historically specific conceptual forms — notoriously Aristotelean logic, Euclidean geometry and Newtonian mechanics (not to mention Pietist morality) — knowable by man only insofar as and because imposed by man. On Kant's relation to rationalism, see J.M. Findlay, *Kant and the Trancendental Object*, Oxford 1981; on Whewell see R.G. Butt, 'Necessary Truth in Whewell's Philosophy of Science', *American Philosophical Quarterly*, 1965, pp. 161-181.

47. *Contra* e.g., R. Collingwod, *An Essay on Metaphysics*, Oxford 1940.

48. This is just a special case of that general underdetermination of 'higher-order' by 'lower-order' beliefs (as indeed phenomena generally), of which so much has been made in recent years. The obverse of this is the irreducibility of practical (applied) judgements (phenomena etc.) to the subsumption of 'lower-order' cases under 'higher-order' principles. N.B.: For transcendental realism underdetermination is a feature of the world, not just of beliefs.

lie at the fulcrum of every scientific enterprise. For conceptual schema are neither a priori demonstrable nor empirically refutable and so can only be assessed indirectly — in terms of their developmental potential, empirical fertility, heuristic plausibility, synoptic power, etc.[49] At the same time the consideration that the linguistic and conceptual forms in which primary data are couched themselves embody world-views helps to explain, if not always excuse, the notorious difficulty of so much revisionary — or revolutionary — metaphysics $\beta$. For such a metaphysician is forced to ply his or her refutations, to a greater or lesser extent, in the terms of the very categories s/he deigns to oppose (just as any radical metaphysics $\alpha$ must comprise an immanent critique), inducing an ineluctable element of conceptual excentricity (necessitating perhaps only a merely developmental consistency) in any authentically subversive work.[50]

Let us take stock. The conception of philosophy I am advocating is essentially post-critical in form, but pre-critical in function. Philosophy exploits Kantian, Hegelian and Marxian insights and plays characteristically Lockean and Leibnizian roles. Its standard pattern of reflection is transcendental, but the critique it affords is an immanent one, and it is comprehended as only a component in a practical ensemble. It can ($\alpha$) act as methodological underlabourer for, and occasional midwife to, science and other (e.g. putatively emancipatory) social practices — an activity which may be radicalised to include ideology-critique; and ($\beta$) decode and decipher the conceptual schemes informing those practices — an activity which must be contextualised to incorporate analysis of the forms of social life in which the schemes act.

An adequate account of science will engage arguments at four main levels (besides that of the topic sciences themselves): (a) ontology; (b) epistemology; (c) metaphysics generally; and (d) substantive historical sociology of knowledge. The crucial distinctions between (a) and (b) and (a)-(c) and (d) themselves hinge upon the isolation of a pair of twinned metaphysical mistakes:-

---

49. Cf. I. Latakos, 'Falsification and the Methodology of Scientific Research Programmes', *Philosophical Papers Volume 1*, Cambridge 1975.
50. Cf. e.g., T. Adorno, *Negative Dialectics*, London 1973.

(i) the reduction of being to knowledge — the *epistemic fallacy* — characteristic of post-Humean analytical and dialectical thought alike, but with far deeper and longer historical roots on what I shall call the '*Platonic-Aristotelian fault line*' which structures our philosophical tradition. This goes together with its converse, the *ontic fallacy*, involving the reduction of knowledge to being;

(ii) the reduction of science to, or its incorporation within, philosophy — the *speculative illusion* — endemic to absolute idealism together with its converse, the typically *positivistic illusion*, involving the reduction of philosophy to, or its abnegation in exclusive favour of, science.

On the epistemic fallacy, being either just is (constituted by) knowledge or is analysable in terms of the knowledge (of objects). On the ontic fallacy, knowledge either just is being *simpliciter* or is analysable in terms of the being of its objects. In post-Fregean philosophy, the epistemic fallacy is often packaged in a linguistic form[51] and it possesses, as we shall see in Chapter 2 Section 7 below, important ethical and substantive analogues. Typically, the quest for certain foundations of knowledge from Plato on (or the recoil from change, including epistemic change, which manifests itself in the normative guise of the fear of error) results in a de-socialised account of science and a de-realised account of being. Thus in what I will call the great 'anthroporealist exchange' a naturalised (and so incorrigibly eternalised) science is purchased at the price of a humanised nature. In this way is revealed the tacit complicity of the epistemic and ontic fallacies, the duplicity implicit in any indentity theory [thought $\frac{EF}{OF}$ things], in respect of both particular and general knowledge, and irrespective of the degree and manner of its achievement. If the speculative illusion is ultimately science-, and more generally alter-, subversive, the positivistic one, is intentionally philosophy-, and thereby unwittingly auto-, subversive.[52] Thus if absolute idealism (or more generally, the

---

51. See *The Possibility of Naturalism*, pp. 170-171 & 188-189.
52. Humean meta-philosophical injunctions to consign any book containing neither 'abstract reasoning concerning quantity and matter' nor 'experimental reasoning concerning matters of fact and existence' to the flames (D. Hume, *An Equiry concerning Human Understanding*, ed. L.A. Selby-Bigge, Oxford 1962, p. 165), like the Vienna Circle's principle that the meaning of a proposition is its method of verification, shares a family

representative at the transcendent pole of the irrealist immanent-transcendent couple) gradually loses its topics, as these are progressively transmogrified into a notional disciplinary monism infused by philosophy alone, positivism immediately (or, more generally, the immanent pole of the couple, tendentially) undermines itself, depositing a meta-theoretical and conceptual vacuum in its place. In this vacuum a general epistemological dogmatism and/or scepticism and an unprincipled disciplinary totalitarianism and/or eclecticism can flourish. The twinned fallacies are by no means mutually exclusive; rather they characteristically presuppose each other.

The distinction between (a) and (b) (on p. 22 above), ontology and epistemology, implies a distinction between the *intransitive*, normally knowledge-independent, real objects of scientific knowledge and the *transitive*, socio-historical, processes of the production of the knowledge of such objects, and accordingly between what I have termed the intransitive dimension [ID] and the transitive dimension [TD] in the philosophy of science.[53] The relation between the intrinsic features, transitive process and intransitive object of some determinate scientific investigation can be schematically represented as in diagram 1.1. opposite, which reflects the theorem that critical deliberation is part of science, is part of reality.

The three curves represent, as it were, the planes of self-conscious subjectivity, sociality and (knowable) being (and in the domain of specifically human being, people's rational, social and finite biological natures respectively). Transcendental realism entails the necessity of *ontological realism* (in the ID), the actuality of *epistemic relativity* (in the TD) and the possibility of *judgemental rationality* (in the IA). However, judgemental rationality in cognition depends not only upon the recognition of ontological realism and epistemic relativity, but upon meta-epistemic reflexivity and ethical (moral, social and

---

resemblance to the Epimenidean ('I am lying') group of paradoxes, exhibiting that self-deracinating quality that lurks in wait for all monotypical, unilateral and atemporal thought. Thus Hume's injunction implies that it should be ignored; and Schlick's principle, if true, is meaningless and therefore false. Wittgenstein was wiser to compare the propositional scaffolding of the *Tractatus* to a ladder one throws way after climbing it. See L. Wittgenstein, *Tractatus Logico-Philosophicus*, London 1961, 6.54.

53.   See *A Realist Theory of Science*, pp. 21-4 & passim.

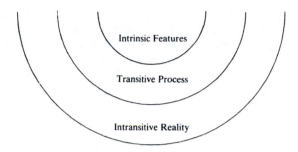

Diagram 1.1: *The cognitive situation in science*

political) responsibility on the part of the cognitive agents concerned.

Besides the intransitive and transitive dimensions, the philosophy of science needs a third dimension — which I shall call the '*metacritical dimension*' (MD) of discourse, in which the philosophical and sociological presuppositions of accounts of science are critically, and self-reflexively, scrutinised. The requirement for this stems, on the one hand, (*contra* e.g. positivism) from the irreducibility (implied by the methodological circle) and inherent recursivity of philosophical discourse, and, on the other, (*contra* e.g. absolute idealism) from its socially conditioned and practical character, so that the MD essentially incorporates propositions in substantive historical sociology of knowledge, i.e. (d) above.[54]

In its most general sense, a 'metacritique' typically aims to identify the presence of causally significant absences in thought, seeking to elicit, for instance, what cannot be said or done *in* a particular language or conceptual system about what is said,

---

54. Hence if (c) (metaphysics generally) is understood as spanning (a) (ontology) and (b) (epistemology) — where (d) is substantive historical sociology of knowledge, we could write as a rough mnemonic: MD $\approx$ c+d, TD $\approx$ (b), ID $\approx$ (a). The three trios (1), intrinsic features, transitive process, intransitive reality (depicted in Diagram 1.1), (2) IA (TD), EA (TD), ID and (3) MD, TD, ID should not be identified. For (1) designates features of the cognitive situation in science, (2) aspects of its philosophical reconstruction and (3) demensions of philosophical discourse.

done, known, implied or presupposed *by means of* it[55]; or, more broadly, what cannot be *said* in a scheme about what is *done* in the practice into which the scheme is connected. (Here we need of course to distinguish what is necessarily inexpressible within the scheme from what is merely unknown to (and/or merely tacit knowledge of) the agents employing it.) A metacritique is a type, component or precursor of explanatory critique generally. For in the metacritical movement of thought, as we press against the limits of conceptual forms, we are continually impelled to explain — and if needs be transform — the practical activities they indue and by which they are in turn sustained. Clearly not every metacritique in this sense is in what I have called the metacritical dimension [of philosophical accounts of science]. Equally patently, not all discourse in this dimension takes the form of that deep and totalising explanatory discourse which constitutes a metacritique. Where necessary, I shall refer to a metacritique in the strict sense as 'MC$_1$' and use 'MC$_2$' to refer to a critique in the metacritical dimension, whether or not it takes the form of a metacritique.

In the balance of this chapter, I propose to put this philosophical apparatus to work on science and its empiricist and idealist reconstructions, in order to motivate a transcendental realist ontology, account of science and critique of empirical and conceptual realism. This necessitates the deployment of transcendental arguments at two levels: in the philosophy of science, where my premises are practical activities; and in the philosophy of the philosophy of science, where my premises are conceptual forms (so that, in the terminology introduced earlier, I shall be engaged in the metaphysics $\alpha$ of metaphysics $\beta$ — or metaphysics $\alpha$ ($\beta$ ($\alpha$)). In the following sections my principal premises will be scientific experiment and structure, advertised by empiricist and neo-Kantians respectively as quintessential to science, and conceptual transformations, championed by super-idealists. My argumentative strategy is designed to show that the sponsoring theory cannot sustain the intelligibility of the sponsored activity, but that a transcendental realist analysis can render the activity, once it is properly conceptualised, readily intelligible. The reader should be cautioned that I am not claim-

---

55. Cf. my 'Scientific Explanation and Human Emancipation', *Radical Philosophy* 26 (1980), p. 20.

ing certainty or uniqueness for my analyses, merely that they are demonstrably superior to the irrealist accounts currently or lately in vogue. Moreover, this realism possesses the advantage of offering a clear and consistent alternative to positivism which preserves the cumulative character of science without restoring a monism, and rescues a 'surplus-element' in scientific theory without plunging into subjectivism; while the metacritique of positivism it permits goes some way to explaining its perennial appeal.

## 4. Praxis and Ontology

Empirical realists have seized on the (1) experimental establish-ment, (2) knowledge and (3) practical application of laws as of prime epistemic significance in science. For this tradition empirical regularities or instrumental successes are at least necessary (transcendental idealism) and perhaps sufficient (classical empiricism) conditions for causal laws and other items of general or instrumental, i.e. implicitly general, knowledge; and causal laws etc. are analysed as dependent upon, or just as, constant conjunctions of events (or states of affairs) perceived or perceptions. By contrast, for transcendental realism an ontological distinction between causal laws and patterns of events is a condition of the intelligibility of (1)-(3). If this can be shown, then an immanent refutation of the Humean and Kantian orthodoxies and a transcendental revindication of ontology will have been obtained.

I start by registering some pertinent features of our phenomenal experience of science, and by formulating a pair of crucial distinctions. Constant conjunctions are in fact both extremely rare and spatio-temporally restricted (cf. (2) and (3)) and must normally be artifically produced (cf. (1)); on the other hand, law-like knowledge appears to be both available and use-ful (cf. (2) and (3)) and some of it experimentally corroborated (cf. (1)). I distinguish: (a) between *closed systems*, where con-stant conjunctions obtain, and *open systems* where they do not; and (b) between *structures*, generative mechanisms and so forth (which comprise the real bases of causal laws) and the *events* which they — normally, conjuncturally — generate. (a) evinces the *differentiation*, (b) the *stratification* of reality. Turning now to the considerations (1)-(3) highlighted by empirical realism, it will be seen that in each instance the Humean-based account distintegrates into metaphysical absurdity, disclosing the way to a more satisfactory, realist alternative.

(i) Constant conjunctions are praxis-dependent, but causal laws are not. Experimentation is deliberate intervention in the course of nature. It is *practically necessary* to the extent that the experimentally designed, produced and controlled sequence would not have occured without it. It is *epistemically significant* to the extent that the causal law it enables us to identify and test holds outside and independently of the experiment. Conversely, reducing laws to constant conjunctions, as in the doctrine I have characterised as 'actualism',[56] commits the empiricist either to the absurdity that scientists actually produce, i.e. create, the laws of nature (on which it passes over into a voluntaristic super-idealism) or to the self-immolation of denying either our causal agency or its significance in science (on which it transmutes into a reductionistic and/or deterministic hyper-rationalism). Patently, however, what scientists produce in laboratories are not the laws of nature, but their empirical grounds; and it is upon the elision of the ontological distinction between them that the empirical realist account tactily depends.

(ii) Constant conjunctions are empirical, but causal laws are not. Once the scarcity of spontaneously occurring constant conjunctions, and hence the prevalance of open systems in nature, is admitted, empiricists are again impaled on the dilemma of abandoning either their phenomena or their analysis. For since in open systems the instantiation of the antecedent of a lawish statement is by defintion not invariably accompanied by the realisation of the consequent, known laws cannot be *both empirical and universal.* Conversely, conceptually tying laws to closed systems, e.g. by treating the satisfaction of a *ceteris paribus* clause (indicating the stability or absence of circumambient context) as a condition for them, saddles the Humean with the embarrassment of explaining what governs phenomena in the vast majority of cases where this condition is not satisfied. She or he can either opt for the position that nothing governs phenomena in these cases, so that nature becomes radically and

---

56. *A Realist Theory of Science*, p. 64.

capriciously indeterministic (weak actualism), or elect that science has as yet discovered no laws — the heroic 'strong actualist' line promulgated by Mill in his official doctrine of laws as 'unconditional sequences' and more recently by Lakatos[57] but implicit in the Hempelian tale about 'explanation sketches'[58] and the Davidsonian credo of homonomic and heteronomic generalisations.[59] The strong actualist saves the Humean analysis only at the cost of its premise, namely knowledge (2), by projecting it onto a scientific *Jenseits* (or beyond) as a regulative ideal, expressing the 'unhappy consciousness'[60] of modern empiricism — the epistemologically postulated, but cognitively unachieved, Humean causal laws. There are three main objections to this strategem. First, it lacks both empirical and transcendental support — for just as there are no known laws conforming to Humean desiderata, there is no reason to suppose that the world is ultimately Humean (either in-itself or for-us), so that, as an ideal, it is irrational. Second, were it to be justified, it would still serve neither to vindicate our present (non-Humean) knowledge nor to direct our current enquires — for, as an elementary generalisation of the 'Second Best theorem' as first formulated in Welfare Economics[61] shows, it cannot license movement in a particular direction; so that, as a norm, it is useless. Third, were it to be realised, all scientific activity, including the experimental establishment, knowledge of and practical application of laws (viz. (1)-(3) above), would (on Humean theory) become otiose. From this it may be plausibly conjectured that the skills that constitute science would atrophy, and that learning, and hence the reproduction of Humean knowledge over time, would gradually grind to a halt; so that, as an

---

57. e.g., I. Lakatos, 'Necessity, Kneale and Popper', *Philosophical Papers Volume 2*, Cambridge 1978.
58. See, e.g., C.G. Hempel, *Aspects of Scientific Explanation*, pp. 423-424.
59. See, e.g., D. Davidson, 'Mental Events', *Essays on Actions and Events*, Oxford 1980, p. 219. For Davidson, heteronomic, as distinct from homonomic generalisations, '... may give us reason to believe there is a precise law at work, but one that can be stated only by shifting to a different vocabulary.' For an explication and critique of the Davidsonian defence of Humean theory, see *A Realist Theory of Science*, pp. 140-141.
60. Cf. G.W.F. Hegel, *Phenomenology of Spirit*, pp. 126-128.
61. R.G. Lipsey and K. Lancaster, 'The General Theory of Second Best', *Review of Economics Studies*, December 1956.

achievement, it would be Pyrrhic. Contrariwise, if the universality of *known* laws is to be sustained, they must be analysed as dynamic and non-empirical properties (powers) of structures, not as conjunctions of events.

Recognition of the pervasiveness of openness in nature also discloses the forgotten or repressed dual of the problem of induction, not systematically formulable within the empirical realist conceptual frame, in virtue of that frame's tacit presumption of closure. This is Poincaré's problem[62] of what I shall call, coining a necessary neologism, '*transduction*': the problem of what justifies our supposing that the laws of nature continue to hold outside the laboratory or closed systems generally (in the future as in the past, and whether identified or not). Distinguishing between real and universal (more precisely, transfactually efficacious) but non-empirical laws and their real and empirical but contextually localised grounds, the transductive/inductive/eductive problem matrix is rationally resolved. It is the real stratification of nature which supplies our transductive, and hence inductive, warrant in the case of each specific law (and transcendentally there is no further or more general justification for either than the recognition that such stratification is the condition of science), while eduction, or inference to particular instances, is only warranted in closed systems.[63]

(iii) Given that knowledge of constant conjunctions is not in general available, it can hardly be practically indispensable. On

---

62. H. Poincare, *Science and Hypothesis*, New York 1903, p. 98.
63. Cf. *A Realist Theory of Science*, pp. 115-128. Note that there are circumstances in which transduction, but not induction, is legitimate, e.g. where there are grounds for supposing a transformation in the backing mechanism. There is an important sense in which the problem of transduction is more basic than the traditional problem of induction. For it is only if our knowledge already possesses transductive credentials, i.e. if we are justified in assuming transfactual and a-temporal generality that the questions of cross-temporal generality and counterfactual licence can plausibly be posed. And in this respect it would perhaps be more apposite to regard the problem of transduction as a progressive generalisation (revealed by transcendental realism) than as the occluded dual (repressed by empirical realism) of the old Humean tease. The problem of transduction [and hence induction and eduction] can be further generalised both in respect of the question of the stability of non-cognitive social structures; and in respect of the question of the stability or continuity of non-cognitive moments or aspects of or influences on action.

the other hand, knowledge of causal laws, understood as specifying the tendencies of mechanisms rather than as licensing the deduction of events, is practically useful in the cognitive, conative and affective (plus various specifiable second-order self-reflective) orientations of intentionality,[64] and in the retrospective, prospective and contemporaneous orientations to, as well as the three characteristic modi of, time. But once more the empirical realist must cede either datum or account. S/he may elect either to include the pactical activity within, or to exclude it from, the relevant state description. In the former case, inside a closed system, practically transformative activity under the presumptively enclosing state-descriptions cannot occur; but, outside it, it cannot be justified. In the latter case, which presupposes the ejection of the agent from the context of her or his action and a purely instrumental view of knowledge, there is now no problem about action within a closed system. Within an open system, law-like knowledge, if interpreted actualistically, can at best be construed *counterfactually*, i.e. as a fictional counterpart to reality (conceived as empirical). Knowledge of this sort warns us what would have happened if certain conditions, which did not in fact happen, had done so. As such, manifestly, it cannot cast any direct light on what actually transpired. But equally, any indirect illumination it affords must be given some other, non-Humean grounding. In contrast, from the transcendental realist perspective, knowledge of laws is transfactual knowledge of the *modus operandi* of generative mechanisms (not counterfactual knowledge of the concommitances of events). And such knowledge tells us immediately, when there are grounds for supposing the mechanism to be operative, something about what is really going on, whether or not it happens to be manifest in a particular outcome. That is a circumstance, in open systems, which will always be co-determined by the operations of other mechanisms too.

The paradox of counterfactual analysis puts paid to weak actualism. But what of the strong actualist persuasion here? Is

---

64. In the first, our beliefs are shaped in accord with the world. In the second, the world is shaped in accord with our desires. In the third, our beliefs and desires, or the world and sentiment, seem mutually shaped to accord with one another. They can then come to (cognitively or otherwise) effect the cognitive, conative, affective, dynamic and circumstantial components of action.

there a sense in which non-Humean knowledge is practically necessary? Or could the steadfast Humean adopt a pose of practical scepticism, abstaining from activity until the Laplacean day dawns and all-enclosing atomistic state-descriptions lie numinously to hand? No. For two reasons. In the first place, because an abstention at one level is itself an action (within, moreover, an open system) at a higher-order level, so that a consistent general policy of abstentionism is logically impossible. This is the moral of Hegel's discussion of the 'Beautiful Soul',[65] as well as of Artistotle's diatribe against Heraclitus. One can no more abstain from activity than from life. Secondly, because there are some levels at, or respects in, which it is practically (and ultimately, biologically) imperative to act. The idea that scepticism — in the sense of suspension of commitment to some idea of an independent reality, known under some or other description of a particular type — is not a tenable or 'serious' position is of course a prominent theme of Hegel's *Phenomenology*, where it figures both as a general methological disposition and in the refutation of a specific attitude (although for Hegel the independence is always ultimately only phasic and apparent). Thus: '[scepticism] pronounces an absolute vanishing, but this pronouncement *is*, and this consciousness is the vanishing that is pronounced. It affirms the nullity of seeing, hearing, etc., yet it itself is seeing, hearing, etc. It affirms the nullity of ethical principles, and lets its conduct be governed by those very principles. Its words and deeds always belie one another'.[66] Aristotle was even more disdainful of the practical sceptic. 'It is evident', he remarks, 'that no-one — neither those who state the thesis nor anyone else — is actually in that condition. For why does anyone walk to Megara rather than stay where he is when he thinks he should walk there? Why doesn't he walk into a well or over a cliff in the morning if there is one about?'[67] But the most poignant rebuttal of practical scepticism comes from the pen of Hume himself: 'Whether your scepticism be as absolute and sincere as you pretend we shall learn by and by, when the company breaks up; we shall then see whether you go out at the door or the window, and whether you doubt if your body has gravity or can be injured by its fall,

---

65. *Phenomenology of Spirit*, pp. 400 ff.
66. *Ibid*, p. 125.
67. Aristotle, *Metaphysics* IV. 1008B 12-16.

according to popular opinion, derived from our senses and more fallacious experience'.[68] When the company breaks up ... we are all practicing (transcendental) realists. Realism, considered as commitment to the idea of an absolutely or relatively independently law-governed (transfactually efficacious) reality, contingently, partially and fallibly known by us, appears then to be more or less *axiologically necessary*. It is implied by our deeds, whatever our words, and then of course by our words, once we understand them too as deeds.[69] The contingent questions which remain are of course how adequately, consistently and self-consciously it has been, is and can be comprehended and acted upon in particular instances and fields.

Discussion of the empiricist-sponsored features (1)-(3) exposes the existence of an *ontological gap* between causal laws and patterns of events, which the empirical realist cannot bridge, because the existence of the gap is the condition of the very activities to which s/he calls attention. The principle underlying my critique of what may be called the *antinomy of reductive analysis* may be expressed abstractly as follows: [1]: x cannot be reduced to or analysed or defined in terms of y, where x but not y is (i) praxis-dependent, (ii) universal and (iii) effective in open systems, where x = causal laws and y = constant conjunctions of events.

The antinomy displays an internally destructive dilemma between the empirical realist premises and analyses as, on the empirical realist gloss on laws, the empirical establishment, knowledge and practical application of laws successively become impossible, mandatory or void of the significance analytically attributed to them — with the gloss saved only by its expedient projection onto a beyond, but as a normatively idle and epistemically ungrounded ideal. From the transcendental realist vantage point, the antinomy is rationally resolved in the recognition that constant conjunctions, but not laws, are activity-dependent, empirical and only locally or sporadically applic-

---

68. D. Hume, *Dialogues Concerning Natural Religion*, New York 1948, p. 7. This line of argument which appeals to how we *must act* is formally far superior to Moore's notorious ostensive refutation of scepticism, which appeals to what we would *usually infer* in perception, and better than Dr. Johnson's robust rejoinder to Bishop Berkeley, which relies upon what we would *normally feel* upon contact.

69. This is an implication which idealism can avoid only insofar as it tacitly treats deeds as (human or super-human) words.

able. Laws are analysed as the tendencies of mechanisms which may be possessed unexercised, exercised unrealised and realised undetected (or unperceived) by science; and the satisfaction of the CP clause is treated as a condition for the empirical identification or (dis)confirmation and the event-predictive or instrumental use of law-like knowledge in effectively closed systems (viz. where only a single mechanism or complex of mechanisms is operating), but not for the causal efficacy of laws. A sequence A.B is necessary if and only if there is natural mechanism M such that when stimulated or released by A, B tends to be produced; (i)-(iii) presuppose that such mechanisms exist and act, as the intransitive objects of enquiry, independently of their identification, knowledge and use by science; and it is in their transfactual activity — described in 'normic' statements[70] — that the real ground for our attributions of natural ncessity, and *a fortiori* for the 'surplus-element' in the analysis of laws, lies. From this perspective the prima facie plausibility of the Humean account can be seen, in retrospect, to have stemmed from the illicit conflation of three quite distinct phenomena: (i) the emergence and consolidation, in the seventeenth and nineteenth centuries respectively, of an experimental natural science, embellished on both occasions by an overblown experimentalist rhetoric; (ii) the successful mapping, under epistemically significant descriptions, of some closed or quasi-closed systems in nature (from the spectacular celestial cartography of Newtonian mechanics to the more mundane descriptions of the life-cycles of organisms achieved by nineteenth and twentieth century naturalists); and (iii) the cosmological zonal stability, rough-hewn ecological regularities, biological limits, natural and quasi-natural human competences, and functional and stylised routines underpinning everyday social existence.

Deferring further discussion of applied science, I want to elaborate briefly upon experimentation, because of its central importance for all but the most rationalist or romantic philosophies of science, before reviewing the genealogy, differentiae and implications of the transcendental realist theory of laws.

A scientific experiment, in contradistinction from a mere

---

70. See *A Realist Theory of Science*, pp. 91-104.

experience, is a designed practical intervention in, and theoretical interrogation of, nature, conducted under artificially produced and deliberately controlled, normally reproducible, conditions, issuing in a socially contrived set of observations, measurements, traces, etc. At its core is the notion that the conditions for the production of a given type of effect can be separated into factors which can be varied independently of one another, so as to reveal the way the factors behave in their natural, i.e. non-experimental, state. The key assumption here is that the entities under study retain their identities (and dispositional powers), whether or not their circumambient conditions are held constant, as in the laboratory, or vary freely, as in extra-experimental reality. This is the assumption of *transfactual identity* or invariance under empirical conditions, divulging the ontological stratification or depth required to reconcile the causal agency of scientists and the transfactual efficacy of laws, and to square the practical necessity and epistemic significance (fusing the interventionary and interrogatory aspects) of experiment. An experiment may now be understood, quite simply, as an attempt to trigger or unleash a single kind of mechanism or process in relative isolation, free from the interfering flux of the open world, so as to observe its detailed workings or record its characteristic mode of effect and/or to test some hypothesis about it. As such it involves the activities of experimental design, production, control and perception. Aside from the pivotal assumption of transfactual identity, there are a number of other major assumptions underlying the classical experimental method, including those of essential independence, actual separability, physical reproducibility, spatio-temporal generality and plasticity of context to human manipulation and control. Many of these assumptions are of restricted generality. Some of the consequence of their breakdown in the social domain in particular will be adumbrated later.

An experiment almost always presupposes both an antecedently conjectured theory and one or more auxiliary theories. The former serves to designate the focus of enquiry and to differentiate causes from conditions (antecedent from context) and necessary from purely accidental or *de facto* sequences. The latter may inform the design of the experiment, construction of the equipment and interpretation of the results. However, that experimental results are theory-dependent does not mean, as some recent neo-rationalists have rashly concluded, that they are theory-determined. Theory limits the range of possible experimental outcomes but, provided the experiment is well-designed, it does not pre-select an outcome within the range. It is equally important to repudiate empiricist hyperbole here. Francis Bacon, for instance, was well aware (but in his doctrine of 'prerogative instances' failed to make it clear) that an experiment can be truly crucial, absolutely decisive, only if it is inconsistent with every hypothesis save one. It was nearly three centuries later before the crucial point was made by Duhem that this condition can *never* be satisfied[71]: that an experiment is always (a) consistent with a (generally infinite) plurality of further sets of hypotheses; (b) a test of a multiplicity of hypotheses, any one of which may in principle be saved; and (c) subject to the possibility of revision, redescription or outright rejection in the subsequent history of science. For example, Copernicus's celebrated arguments for the curvature of the earth presuppose the rectilinear motion of light. If it is assumed, as it *is* in general relativity, that light traces a curved path, then the hypothesis that the earth is flat can be retained! As we shall see in Sections 5 and 6, (a) subsequently became the logical lynchpin of Popper's fallibilism; (b) constituted the basis of Quine's holism[72]; while (c) in part motivated Lakatos's insistence that the proper units of normative appraisal in science were not isolated theories, but sequences of theories, rationally connected in research programmes.

I now want to introduce some terminological stipulations. First, I distinguish between *philosophical* and *scientific* ontologies; that is, between the kind of world presupposed by a philosophical account of science and the particular types of entities and processes postulated by some substantive scientific theory. This distinction follows straightforwardly from the argument of sections 2 and 3. In this chapter I am principally concerned with philosophical ontologies. Second, I use 'ontology' ('ontological', etc.) to refer to (1) propositions in the general (philosophical) theory of being, or what pertains to it, *ontology*₁

---

71. P. Duhem, *The Aim and Structure of Physical Theory* (2nd ed. 1914), New York 1962, Part 2, especially chapters IV and VI.
72. See, e.g., W.V.O. Quine, 'Two Dogmas of Empiricism', *From a Logical Point of View*, Cambridge Mass. 1953.

and, within that rubric, to (2) propositions in the transcendental theory constituted by reflection on the presuppositions of scientific activities, or what pertains to it, *ontology₂*. An $ontology_1$ may be explicit or implicit, self-consciously under-stood as such or not. In the former case I shall write it as '$ontology_1$*'. Third, I differentiate the 'ontic' ('ontical' etc.) from the 'ontological'. I employ the former to refer to (1) what-ever pertains to being generally, rather than some distinctively philosophical (or scientific) theory of it (ontology), so that in this sense, that of the $ontic_1$, we can speak of the ontic pre-suppositions of a work of art, a joke or a strike as much as a theory of knowledge; and, within this rubric, to (2) the intran-sitive objects of some specific, historically determinate, scientific investigation (or set of such investigations), the $ontic_2$. The $ontic_2$ is always specified, and only identified, by its relation, as the intransitive object(s) of some or other (denumerable set of) particular transitive process(es) of enquiry. It is cognitive process- and level-specific; whereas the $ontological_2$ (like the $ontic_1$) is not. Thus a world without human beings would have an $ontology_2$ (although obviously there would be no one in such a world to articulate it) but not an $ontic_2$; the $ontological_2$, but not the $ontic_2$, compasses the intransitive objects of non-actualised (and perhaps humanly impossible) scientific enquiries; and the $ontological_2$ includes, while the $ontic_2$ excludes, the processes of scientific enquiry of which the $ontic_2$ in question is the $ontic_2$.[73] 'Epistemology' pairs with 'ontology', and the 'epistemic' with the 'ontic'. Consequently an $epistemic_2$ process or product falls within the $ontological_2$ (and $ontic_1$), but not within *its* $ontic_2$, though it may of course become the $ontic_2$ of a higher-order, or reflexive, enquiry. If the neologism '*intrinsics*' is coined for the theory of judgemental rationality, a distinction parallel to that between the $ontic_1$ and $ontic_2$ can be drawn within the intrinsic features of cognition, with the '$intrinsic_2$' indicating those features in some specific ($epistemic_2$) enquiry. The point of these seemingly cumbersome

---

73. My concepts of the 'ontological' and the 'ontic' are not equivalent (or theoretically indebted) to Heidegger's. But Heidegger's 'ontological', the realm of everyday pre-understood being, is encompassed within my umbrella '$ontic_1$'; and Heidegger's 'ontic', having to do with entities, over-laps with my '$ontic_2$', the specific intransitive objects of particular scientific, more or less empirically-based, enquires.

distinctions, which — to avoid pedantry — will only be invoked when absoutely necessary, will emerge in due course.

I turn now to the metatheory of laws. It is worth remarking that the term 'law' in ordinary usage is systematically ambiguous between statements and their intransitive objects — e.g. 'Ohm's law' stands for both a proposition and the relationship that proposition decribes. Normally this ambiguity is anodyne, but where there is any risk of confusion I shall explicitly discriminate laws and law (or lawish) statements. Note, however, that in the absence of an explicit ontology in the empirical realist tradition there is a definite tendency for the two senses to be casually conflated.

Two issues have dominated philosophical controversy about laws. These can be unfurled by divaricating:

(i) analyses which seek to preserve an ontological distinction between necessary and accidental sequences (which I shall dub 'necessitarian') from those which do not ('accidentalist'); and
(ii) analyses which regard necessary connections in nature as knowable by science ('immanent') and those which do not ('transcendent').

An *immanent necessitarian* analysis of the type commended here will attempt to sustain an ontologically irreducible necessary/accidental distinction as falling within the existing cognitive competence of science. Clearly an immanent necessitarian need not hold the distinction fixed, or law-like statements immune from revision, nor that all necessary connections are actually known or even potentially knowable.

Most discussions of the concept of law take as their point of departure Hume's account of the causal modality in science and everyday life. In opposition to Descartes, and in contrast with Leibniz's optimistic rationalism, Locke had concluded that although there were indeed necessary connections in nature, human beings could not aspire to knowledge of them. Building on epistemic ground prepared by Berkeley, and invoking a radicalised version of Locke's own principle of empiricism, namely that all knowledge of 'matters of fact and existence' hails from sense-experience alone, Hume challenged the Lockean to *produce* empirical grounds for his notion of natural necessity. Palpably, Hume claimed, the idea of necessary connection cannot be drawn from our observation of the external world, but must instead be a projection onto it, originating from our repeated experiences of the regular associations of events. Whence he arrived at his famous analysis of that idea as empirical invariance plus subjective habit of mind. Two assumptions coordinate Hume's account: (α) a *reductionist epistemology*, crystallised in the principle that all (non-analytic) knowledge must be derived from and justified by sense-experience alone, subsequently contested by Kant; and (β) an *empiricist ontology*, encapsulated in the notion that the objects of sense-experience are atomistic events constantly conjoined in determinate ways, tacitly presupposed by Kant but disputed by modern scientific realism. Depending upon their attitude to these assumptions, most philosophers (of science) since Hume can be divided very broadly into three camps: empiricism, transcendental idealism and transcendental realism.

Thus empiricists from Mill to Mackie have swallowed both Hume's premises, tendering at most refinements of his analysis — usually, when less radical than Hume, by locating the 'surplus-element' in the analysis of laws (that is, that element over and above the presumed constant conjunction of events) in their systematic interconnection as deductively organised theories. A second group of philosophers have bought Hume's ontological, but not his epistemological premise, striving to ground the idea of necessary connection in more or less rational operations of mind irreducible to sense-experience. This has naturally come in a variety of historical guises. Thus Kant and Whewell discerned the necessity attached to laws in synthetic a priori principles acting as fixed form to the essentially Humean contents or data conveyed by the senses; some recent anti-monists have portrayed scientific history as a procession of necessity-endowing conceptual schemata imposed upon or directing experience; while some contemporary anti-deductivists, most notably Harré, stressing the stratification of science, have located the necessity of laws in the models, depicting generative mechanisms or structures, at the heart of the theories explaining them. If such mechanisms, initally entertained as hypotheses, can come in the course of scientific development to be established, via the satisfaction of direct (pereptual) or indirect (causal) criteria, as real, then an objective basis for our ascriptions of natural necessity is found — not at the level of events and their conjunctions, but at the level of the mechanisms generating them. And the way is accordingly paved for the third, transcendental realist, view of laws.

In general, transcendental idealists subscribe to a '*bicameral*' theory of laws, on which the Humean condition, viz. empirical invariance, is treated as necessary but insufficient, with the second conjointly sufficient condition, tier or chamber, the surplus-element, bestowed by the distinctively Kantian epistemological ingredient (a priori framework, conceptual scheme, plausible model or whatever). But transcendental realists call into question the necessity and underlying ontology, as well as the sufficiency and overt epistemology of the Humean account. While the Kantian critique fastens on the Humean failure to sustain the necessity of laws, in virtue of its assumption of the contingency of the causal connection, the transcendental realist metacritique pinpoints their common failure to sustain the universality (qua transfactual efficacy) of laws, in virtue of their shared presumption of the actuality of that connection — the empiricist ontology (β above). Transcendental realism comprehends the sciences as developing in an open world. Understanding the sciences as developing confers a vertical carriage and depth to realism, as the remote hypotheses of yesterday become the validated existents of today and the comprehensively explained (and redescribed) phenomena of tomorrow. Conceiving the world as open imparts a horiztonal span and breadth to realism, as the ground of natural necessity is discovered in the transfactual efficacy of mechanisms, i.e. in their activity irrespective of the closure or otherwise of the systems within which the events they generate occur. Moreover, the realism is dynamic in both respects. Science is (vertically) in motion in a world (horizontally) in motion. This is the world from which science arises, of which it composes a part, which it endeavours to understand and to which it is destined to return.

The Kantian critique of the Humean base-line turns essentially on three points: (a) its *insufficiency*, in that empirical invariance requires supplementation by additional criteria (e.g. simplicity) for the identification of laws; (b) its *fragility* or non-robustness, in that any scientifically well-established law can be readily discredited in the light of a host of counter-intuitive and seemingly ineluctable considerations (e.g. the problem of induction); and (c) its *torpor*, in that it affords no rationale for scientific development, or even effort (cf. points (a) — (c) on page 36 above). The transcedental realist metacritique of the

Kantian critique is similarly modulated, viz. around *its* (a) insufficiency, (b) fragility and (c) inadequately dynamic character.

(a) Transcendental idealist reconstructions of the concept of law are subject to all the aporias of empiricist ontology; and in particular the antinomy of reductive analysis in pure, modified and/or displaced form. In pure form, to the extent that the world is conceived as simply Humean; in modified form, to the extent that the world, as experienced, is pervaded with the Kantian epistemological ingredient; in displaced form, to the extent that the world, so pervaded, is rationally characterised by essential ontological attributes (such as structure, diversity and change) yet confined, and so involuted, within a sentient intelligence or community consubstantially characterised as the ground of those attributes. (Prototypes of these forms may be descried in Kant's own 'perception', 'experience' and (synthetic a posteriori) 'judgement' respectively[74]). On the paradox of pervasion, intellectual conformity appears as a condition of natural uniformity[75] and so of induction. But on the greater paradox of involution, the natural order as such appears as the product of man. In both cases it becomes impossible to discriminate the non-Humean attributes in their grounding (social, inter-subjective) and grounded (natural, objective) modes; and hence to maintain the intelligibility of either. Moreover, in all three versions, the transcendental idealist can still offer no ground, independent of human activity, for natural necessity; whence s/he can at best speak of a nomically necessary statement, but not of a nomically necessary sequence, tendency or power.

(b) What is the ontological (1) commitment and (2) standing of the neo-Kantian surplus-element? (1) Does it possess a referent other than events and their conjunctions in space and time yet is also susceptible to *a posteriori* scientific investigation? If it does, transcendental idealism surges on towards transcendental realism; but if it does not, it leaves itself very exposed to empiricist counter-attack. Hence we could say, echoing Jacobi's lucid diagnosis of the central impasse of the critical philosophy: 'without real generative mechanisms, no entry into the world of

---

74. On Kant's own changing and somewhat confused doctrines in this area, see W.H. Walsh, *Kant's Criticism of Metaphysics*, Edinburgh 1975.
75. Cf. *A Realist Theory of Science*, p. 163.

models (or whatever); with real generative mechanisms, no staying there'.[76] Transcendental idealism is an uneasy halfway-house in the philosophy of science, which is caught in a metaphysical cleft stick: subjectively, it is unwilling to retreat with its newly-won epistemological purview; objectively, it is unable to advance with its old, unreflected ontological legacy. Moreover, without a matching ontology furnishing an intransitive referent for the neo-Kantian surplus-element, the principle of discursivity for the object level collapses. For what exactly is there to talk *about*? Suppose this point is countered with the suggestion that the world is constituted by talk. Then, if the principle of discursivity for this (language) level is to be preserved, it must be possible to talk about it. That is to say, it must be possible to talk about talk or, if one prefers, for talk to talk about itself. In other words, the object of such talk must be susceptible of reference and a possible topic for investigation: that is, it must be real (talk), not talk (as opposed to what is real) or talk (period). Here, as elsewhere, the slogans 'no discursivity without ontology' and 'no transitive without an intransitive dimension' hold.

The consideration that the discursive 'itself' must be real leads on to (2), the question of the surplus-element's own ontological credentials. Is the model (or whatever) itself real or merely a construction? If it is real, then the ontological dyke has been breached and some non-Humean ontological features are knowable. If, on the other hand, it is regarded as merely imaginary, then natural necessity becomes a fiction of a fiction, which seems altogether too counterfactual for epistemological credibility. Further, just as every counterfactual statement logically presupposes at least one factual statement (and hence the possibility of a transfactual or normic statement grounding the counterfactual), any fiction presupposes a range of fictionalising facts. For as talk must have objects, fiction must have authors (or copiers, re-tellers, repeaters, sustainers and listeners), media and content. And in each of these respects for a claim that some x (or that there is some x which) is a fiction to be upheld, an ontological cheque will sooner or later need to be presented and

---

76. Cf. 'Without the thing-in-itself, no entry into the *Critique of Pure Reason*; with the thing-in-itself, no staying there'. The problem of the surplus-element both parallels (at the level of ontological commitment) and exemplifies (at the level of ontological standing) that of the thing-in-itself.

cashed. The 'imaginary' or 'as if' is not only ontically$_2$ opposed (in its assertoric content) to, but also ontologically$_2$ a part (in its semantic — and psycho-social — identity) of, reality. To imagine an 'as if' without an 'as iffer', an 'as iffing' or an 'as iffed' is as absurd as to envisage a faceless smile. The imaginary, when imagined, is inscribed within the real; and no other kind of imaginary exists.

(c) The diversity of beliefs, both over time and at any one time, generates dilemmas of change and communication for the transcendental idealist, who tends to be torn between absolutism and uniformism, on the one had, and irrationalism and (collective) solipsism, on the other. For in the absence of grounds for the surplus-element independent of human activity, it becomes difficult to sustain judgemental rationality without sacrificing epistemic relativity or vice-versa. In effect, the neo-Kantian tends to be driven either into a more or less dogmatic a priorism and consequent non-dynamic epistemic absolutism, rendering scientific change impossible; or into a more or less arbitrary conventionalism, leaving it irrational. Moreover whilst on the conventionalist-relativist horn of neo-Kantianism, communication between agents or communities inhabiting different conceptual schemes, possessing qualitatively different surpluses, ultimately becomes impossible; on the absolutist-rationalist horn, it ultimately becomes unnecessary, as difference reveals itself merely as an isotope of identity, with the variety of surpluses comprising so many expressions of the same archetype, episteme or form.

Suppose, however, that the vertical axis of realism is conceded, as many modern neo-Kantians undoubtedly would do. Are there now plausible grounds for witholding assent to the horizontal axis? Would it not be a very strange world indeed in which natural mechanisms existed, *but did not act*, independently of the social conditions for their discovery? Moreover, to revert for a moment to (a), only a horizontal as well as a vertical realism can do justice to the experimental establishment, knowledge of, and practical application of laws ((1)-(3) on p. 27), which are as precious for most contemporary neo-Kantians, as for diehard Baconian inductivists. But once both axes are admitted, rational criteria for theory change are (or become, as we shall see in the next section) readily available.

Two other influential metatheories of laws may be summarily considered. Instrumentalists and pragmatists do not spin a story genuinely independent of empirical or transcendental realism. For their conception of laws as policies or inference tickets invites the comment that either the ticket is valid only so long as some corresponding empirical generalisation is true, in which case it presupposes empirical realism; or else it is a ticket to a different order of station, not specifiable at the level of events but at that of the mechanisms generating them, whereupon it transmutes to transcendental realism. But because almost all instrumentalists have been empirical, not transcendental realists, it is worth emphasising that event-predictive (or eductive) success is only a plausible criterion in closed systems. Moreover, were science preoccupied with it, there would be no reason for scientists to instigate a decision procedure designed to select between equally successful theories, or to reject as falsified a theory still instrumentally effective in a particular field.

These considerations suggest that science is more concerned with explanation and representative adequacy or truth than with prediction or instrumental success.

Rationalists, on the other hand, purveying a distinct — conceptual realist — ontology do offer an alternative to empicial and transcendental realism. However, rationalist and absolute idealist analyses of natural laws as a species of logical necessity seem vulnerable to the obvious objection that scientific laws are established by a process which incorporates a non-redundant appeal to nature (in experiment or an analogue) or at least some *a posteriori* component, as well as reason or thought. Moreover, the problems the empirical realist faces in sustaining the notion of natural necessity are mirrored in the embarrassment the conceptual realist suffers in accommodating a notion of natural accident or contingency. For both alike, the world is actual and undifferentiated. Similarly, as we shall see in Section 5, neither can satisfactorily handle scientific change, in virtue of the iso-morphisation of being and knowledge consequent upon any anthroporealism. Other internal difficulties in rationalist and absolute idealist programmes will materialise later.

I now want to return to the subject of ontology and to resume my critical discussion of empirical realism. Analyses of (1)-(3), i.e. the experimental establishment, knowledge and practical application of laws has ontologically uncoupled causal laws from patterns of events. But (1)-(3) all depend upon sense-perception as well as causal agency. And reflection on two forms of scientific discontinuity, viz. (i) the discontinuity of the sciences over time, manifesting the ever-present possibility of scientific change; and (ii) the discontinuity between the sciences and everyday life, commonsense and experience and mutual understanding and belief, manifest in the normal requirement for a scientific education or training, ontologically dissociates events from experiences. The Humean-Kantian concept of causal laws as, or as dependent upon, empirical regularities thus embodies a double reduction: of causal laws to constant conjunctions of events, and of the conjoined events to experiences. This double reduction incorporates two interdependent category mistakes: the actualist (reductive, uniformitarian) and epistemic fallacies, expressed most starkly in the ideas of the actuality of causal laws (presupposing the ubiquity and spontaneity of closed systems) and of the empirical world. Their combined effect is to make an ontology appear superfluous. And that makes a philosophical self-conscious discursive science, and so a critique of a self-styled scientific practice or theory, impossible.

Underlying the critique of the reduction of events to experiences are two general principles which may be expressed abstractly as

[II]: x cannot be the sole source, or completely explained in terms, of y, if x is relatively unchanging and y is not.

[II]′: y cannot be fully justified or comprehensively criticised in terms of x, if x is relatively unchanging and y is not.

[II] and [II]′ pinpoint the *explanatory genetic* and *transhistorical justificationist* fallacies respectively. The general point is of course that in a world characterised by inconsistency, diversity or change (or, in the normative mood, error, evil, unhappiness, etc.), the invocation of alleged or real invariants (such as the given, human nature, sense-experience, reason, or God) can neither adequately explain the occurence nor underwrite the rationality of one rather than another set of historically actualised (or possible) practices. It is as easy to abuse as to ignore this principle. Here the two forms of scientific discontinuity merely establish the differentiation of ontological domains, namely the domain of events, states of affairs and so forth and the domain of human experiences (of them).

In fact the mistakes isolated by [II] and [II]′ have normally been illicitly combined and condensed in practice — to such an extent that it will be convenient to refer to the condensate just as the *'genetic fallacy'*. Thus there is a systematic descriptive-

normative ambiguity in most forms of a-historical epistemological essentialism, including Lockean empiricism,
Cartesian rationalism and Kantian transcendental idealism.
Take the case of empiricism. Consider the ensemble of theories
of explanation, definition and justification to the effect that our
concepts and knowledge are derived from and to be explicated
and assessed in terms of sense-experience. It is important to
appreciate that, as a condition of its possessing any normative
(or plausible explanatory) force, the 'sense-experience' in terms
of which our ideas are to be explained (and which·is levied in
the denial of innate ideas) cannot be the same as the 'sense-
experience' to which we are enjoined to submit our cognitive
claims (and which is invoked in the rejection of the possibility of
(non-analytic) a priori knowledge). These distinct senses,
naturalistically and descriptively fused in most empiricist
epistemologies, may be separated out as (i) our sensuous social
activity — *sense-experience*$_1$ — in terms of which all ideas, irrespective of cognitive status (i.e. whether analytic, false,
meaningless, ill-grounded, moral, religious, aesthetic, flippant,
etc.) are ultimately to be explained; and (ii) experimentally-
controlled observation — *sense-experience*$_2$ — in terms of which
all non-analytic cognitive claims, however arrived at, are to be
tested.[77] Exactly the same explanatory-justificatory duplicity is
at play in rationalist epistemology in the confounding of innate
ideas or capacities and a priori concepts or knowledge; and in
Kant where the transcendental unity of apperception and the
application of the schematised categories to the sensory manifold are enrolled both as constitutive conditions of any experience and as discriminating criteria for the differentiation of
objective and subjective (or illusory) forms of it.

A world without human beings would contain no (human)
experiences and far fewer constant conjunctions of events. For

---

77. Enlisting this distinction a contemporary empiricist might then, for
instance, be prepared to concede the force of Mill's naturalistic claim that
mathematical truths do not have 'a different origin from the rest of our
knowledge' (*A System of Logic*, Book 2, chapter 5, Section 4), so that they
are 'empirical' in the first sense, while resisting the suggestion that they can
be *validated* in the same way as say physical and chemical laws, i.e. according to Mill by induction from 'experience' in the second sense (*loc cit.*,
Book 2, chapter 6, Section 1). Of course, any normatively plausible contemporary explanatory empiricism would need to pay much more heed to
innate structures and social forms than historically empiricism, with its strong
behaviourist and individualist proclivities, has normally been willing to do.

experiences always and essentially, and epistemically significant invariances normally, if contingently, depend upon human activity. But the generative mechanisms, structures, processes, relations, forces and fields of nature do not. Thus in a world without (wo)men the causal laws that sciences have hitherto managed to discover would prevail, despite the paucity of conjunctions and the absence of experiences to mark them. The analysis of (1)-(3) shows that the assertion of a causal law entails the (contingently counterfactual) possibility of a non-human world: that is, that it would operate (transfactually) even if it were unknown, just as it continues to operate (transfactually) outside the closed conditions that permit its empirical identification in science. It follows immediately from this that the epistemic fallacy *is* a fallacy, i.e. that statements about being cannot be reduced to or analysed in .terms of statements about knowledge, so that a philosophical ontology$_1$* is both possible and indeed (descriptively) necessary, with some propositions in ontology$_2$ now already established. But I have already argued (in section 2) that theories of knowledge presuppose theories of being, so that an ontology$_1$ is not only possible, but inevitable in the philosophy of science. So if ontology as a subject is not consciously thematised, some or other ontology will be, willy-nilly, unconsciously imbibed.

In this way the epistemic fallacy has served to screen from the analytical mainstream in the philosophy of science the generation and persistence of an implicit ontology, structured on the concept of experience, and an implicit realism, endowed with the presumed characteristics of the objects of experience, atomistic events, and their (presumed) relations, invariant coexistence in space and succession over time. These presumptions are in turn only intelligible in relation to the idea of knowledge they subserve and sustain. From Hume's hour onwards, empiricist-inclined philosophers have thus more or less unwittingly allowed, in order to preserve their ontological innocence, his particular account of our knowledge of reality (his reductionist epistemology (α) identified on p. 39 above) — which they may explicitly reject — to infuse and implicitly define their notion of the reality known by science (his empiricist ontology (β)). The outcome has been a pervasive 'ontological tension', the proximate source of the rifts recorded in section 1, induced by the conflicts between the rational intuitions of philosophers about science and the constraints imposed upon their articulation by their unreflected inherited ontology. This is turn has produced a nexus of interminably insoluble problems (within that ontology), the anthropocentric (and increasingly convoluted) displacement of those intuitions and the generation of a fissure between the irrealist implications of philosophy and the more or less realist practice of science, uprooting philosophy and breaking the methodological circle to the immediate impoverishment of philosophy and the ultimate detriment of science. For Hume's sceptical turn in philosophy holds out only a dogmatic moral for science. Thus, in the first place, current knowledge (mediated via its reduction to or mapping onto sense-experience) comes, in empirical realism, quite literally to define the world, thereby naturalistically immunising itself against the possibility of rational criticism (the effect of the collapse of the I.D. to the T.D.). Then, in the second, such already naturalised knowledge is further consolidated by the prestige attached to the normative concept of sense-experience, misconceived as given or implied by the empirical data (the effect of the collapse of the I.A. to the E.A.), generating what I will characterise in Chapter 3 as a 'descriptivist prescriptivism', complementing the implicit ontology already achieved. The result of this double denegation — first of being, then of judgemental responsibility — is a double reinforcement of the natural spontaneous dogmatism of the theoretical status quo in any cognitively robust — or institutionally well-entrenched — programme. So science is left bereft of the possibility of critical purchase on, within or about the sciences (or 'science').

In this section, I have shown how the dominant tradition in the philosophy of science, in both its classical empiricist and transcendental idealist avatars, has uncritically accepted the doctrine, implicit in the empirical realist dissolution of ontology, of the actuality of causal laws, and how it has interpreted these, following Hume, as empirical regularities. In this way, by spawning an ontology constituted by the category of experience, three domains of reality — the domains of the real, the actual and the empirical, which may be represented by $D_e \subset D_a \subset D_r$ or alternatively by $D_r ((D_a (D_e))$ and from a particular cognitive perspective by $D_r \geq D_a \geq D_e$ — are illicitly squashed into one, the empirical. The effect of this double compression in ontology is to conceal from the empirical realist the crucial metacritical question of the conditions under which experience is *in fact* significant in science. In general this depends upon the anterior transformation of both human beings (including their conceptual and technical capacities) and nature, so that the percipient is suitably skilled and the system in which the phenomena occur is effectively closed. But it is only when the non-identity of the domains are registered and the possibility of their disjuncture thereby disclosed, that we can recognise the enormous effort — in scientific research, including experiment and training — required to *make* human experience (that is, *before* it can become) an epistemically significant conduit or index of nature in science.

It should be already evident that a central absence in empirical realist construals of science is the notion of scientific activity or labour as *work*; and that the complement of the anthropocentricity in any Humean-based analysis of laws (or nature generally), and necessary for it, is neglect of the self-conscious human transformative activity or praxis required for our knowledge of them.[78] Subsequently, I shall return to the nodal question of the extent to which there is a more general connection between the absence of a transformational sociology of practices and a realist ontology of structures, on the one hand; and reified accounts of science (and more generally social life) and anthropomorphic (or more generally idealist) theories of being, on the other. In the meantime, the ontological upshot of the immanent critique of empirical realism presented here may be summarised in the formula $D_r \geq D_a \geq D_e$, where (i) the special case $D_r = D_a = D_e$, assumed in the double (empirio-actualist) reduction of empirical realism to be spontaneously satisfied, has in fact to be *socially produced* in the arduous, tantalising, untidy business of science[79]; and where (ii) the typical situation $D_r > D_a > D_e$

---

78. In the constitution in Humean empiricism of empiricist ontology, the double compression in the I.D. ($D_r \rightarrow D_a \rightarrow D_e$) presupposes two orders of reduction in the T.D.: (i) of the social process of cognition to individual moments of sense-perception, i.e. (solipsistic) methodological individualism; and (ii) of judgement to causal impact in such moments of perception, so that theory can appear as quasi-mechanical effects of, or behavioural responses to, the stimuli of the (unreflective) given, thus of the I.A. to the E.A. At the foundational, world-constitutive level, there is then neither work nor judgement. Transcendental idealist and conventionalist theories restore these moments in their accounts of science but leave the basic form of ontology, predicated on the presence of the absence of work and judgment in world-constitution, intact.

79. Note that the irreducibility of the I.D./T.D. distinction includes the irre-

embraces (α) the *ontological irreducibility* of the domains, (β) the *normal disjuncture* or mismatch of their objects, and (γ) the *conceptual stretching* or distanciation and transformation (including the possibility of semantic opposition) usually necessary for adequate comprehension of these objects as we cognitively cross domains. In shifting from the critique of empirical to that of contemporary conceptual realism, our spotlight will switch from the practical to the conceptual aspects of the labour of alignment, attunement or phasing — of skilled human receptivity to the deep structures and inner workings of nature — upon which the very fragile, contingent accomplishments of the sciences ultimately *wholly* depends.

## 5. Epistemology, Explanation and Scientific Change

Before the publication in 1934 of Bachelard's *Le nouvel esprit scientifique*[80] and Popper's *Logik der Forschung*,[81] few philosophers would have demurred at the cosy picture of science growing remorselessly, sedately accumulating knowledge in a serenely monistic manner, leaving truth-values and meanings undisturbed, on soil nurtured by common experience. Meyerson had undertaken to deduce Einstein's theory of relativity from Newtonian principles,[82] and it was commonly agreed that the concepts of classical physics were, in turn, merely refinements of those of daily life.[83] In the subsequent half-century there has been a gradual percolation into the general philosophical consciousness (which includes the 'nocturnal'[84] philosophical meta-reflections of scientists upon their 'diurnal', everyday scientific work) of the actuality of scientific discontinuities with respect to commonsense or experience and over time, i.e. of the phenomena of scientific education and change — a seepage powerfully assisted by Kuhn's *The Structure of Scientific Revo-*

---

ducibility of the $D_r$ to $D_a{}^*$, where $D_a{}^*$ is experimentally produced and controlled; and of $D_a$ to $D_e{}^*$, where $D_e{}^*$ is theoretically-informed, experienced (sic) and skilled.

80. Translated as *The Philosophy of the New Scientific Mind*, New York 1968.
81. Translated as *The Logic of Scientific Discovery*, London 1959.
82. E. Meyerson, *La déduction relativiste*, Paris 1925.
83. See e.g. W. Heisenberg, *Physics and Philosophy*, London 1955.
84. G. Bachelard, *Le rationalisme appliqué*, Paris 1949.

*lutions*[85] and Feyerabend's *Against Method*.[86] During this
period, philosophy's erstwhile complacency about science — in
which it was characteristically treated as a simple substitution
instance of an 'indeterminately abstract',[87] generic and homogeneous knowledge — has been swept aside by a growing sense
of epistemological malaise. For although the anti-monistic
movement has vigorously promoted the ideas of scientific discontinuity and change, it has been unable to successfully
assimilate them.

Why do these phenomena portend such disquiet for philosophy? Their acknowledgement sunders the constitutive
relation of classical philosophy between subject and object,
humans and their universe which interlocks, intertwines and
interdefines thought and things. It shatters, in a single double-
edged stroke, the isomorphism classical philosophy would
establish, in an (empirical or conceptual) anthroporealism,
between knowledge and being, as social cognitions and natural
phenomena are coupled, drawn together and finally fused in the
concepts of the empirical or rational worlds. *No longer can
thought be conceived as a mechanical function of given things,
as in empiricism; nor can the activity of creative subjects continue to be seen as constituting a world of objects, as in idealism;
nor is some combination of the two possible.* In short, it becomes
mandatory to make the distinction between the (relatively)
unchanging real objects which exist outside and perdure independently of the scientific process and the changing (and
theoretically-imbued) cognitive objects which are produced
within science as a function and result of its practice; that is,
between the intransitive and transitive objects of scientific
knowledge, and accordingly between the intransitive and transitive dimensions in the philosophy of science. But if, as will be
elaborated in a moment, an intransitive dimension (ID) is a condition of the intelligibility of scientific discontinuity and change,
the necessity for a transitive dimension (TD) is an immediate
corollary of the ontological realism developed in § 4. For if the
(intransitive) objects of scientific knowledge exist and act independently of the knowledge of which they are the objects, then
such knowledge as we actually possess cannot be identical,

85. 2nd ed., Chicago 1970.
86. London 1975.
87. G. Della Volpe, *Logic as a Positive Science*, London 1980.

equivalent or reducible to these objects, or any function of them.[88] Rather such knowledge must consist in an element materially irreducible to these objects — that is to say, in more or less historically specific, symbolically mediated and expressed, praxis-dependent, ineradicably social forms. Thus without a TD or philosophical sociology to complement the ID or ontology legitimated, any attempt to sustain the irreducibility of knowable being — the only kind of being of concern to science — to thought, and hence the discursivity (and thence the rationality) of science must ultimately come to grief. For without an ID things become a mere manifestation, expression, externalisation or embodiment of thought, devoid of extra-discursive conditions and empirical controls; and without a TD thought becomes a mere impress, effluxion, internalisation or *Doppelgänger* of things, bereft of intra-discursive conditions and rational controls.

Once an ID, more especially an ID/TD distinction, is established, both specifically scientific change and ontological change generally, including both scientific (epistemic$_2$) and ontic$_2$ change, become readily intelligible. That is, we can allow both new and changing knowledge (scientific discovery and change), at both the collective and individual levels, of relatively unchanging (independently existing and acting) objects, and new and changing objects (ontological emergence and change), whether comprising particular entities or natural kinds, independently of any knowledge, thought or description of them. Transitive knowledge[89] and intransitive objects, beliefs and beings, thought and things, descriptions and referents, can each now change without a corresponding change (as must happen in any consistent anthroporealism) in the correlative term on the other side of the TD/ID divide. Moreover, the non-identity of the correlatives in any particular case, i.e. of the epistemic$_2$ and

---

88. This indeed is the ontic fallacy (noted on p. 23 above). The ontic fallacy is complicitly covered by, as it is esoteric effect of, the epistemic fallacy in foundational empiricism, and (although occasionally in more nuanced forms) epistemology generally.

89. As Althusser, among others, has noticed, the singularised concept, 'knowledge', carries unfortunate Spinozist-Parmenidean connotations, so that it would be preferable to speak, without encumbrance, of 'knowledges' or *cognitions* (or perhaps cognemes), in the sense of the German *Erkenntnisse*. Of course Althusser's own concept of knowledge itself suffers heavily from Parmenidean residues.

the ontic$_2$, is a condition of the accommodation of change in either (and so both).[90] Unless knowledges and their objects possessed relatively distinct beings and histories, scientific change would be impossible and ontic$_2$ change could not be reported. For to change, e.g. to correct or revise (as to substantiate or confirm) a description, the previously designated object must still be (adequately) susceptible of reference; and to refer to a change in an object (as to attest its stasis), its former descriptions must still be (sufficiently) available to apply a tense operator[91] to its negation or more properly to use 'true' of it in both a tensed (token reflexive) and untensed way. The heterogeneity of thought and things is thus a condition of knowledge of change (and stability, and hence of course, once the possibility of change is recognised, of *any* knowledge) in both domains alike.[92]

Appreciating the necessity and irreducibility of both dimensions in the philosophy of science enables us to make sound sense of Kuhn's notorious and enigmatic claim that 'we must

---

90. A parallel theorem applies to the relation between cognitive and linguistic change: change in beliefs and change in meanings cannot be equivalent, if either of them is to be possible.

91. Tense operators are sentence-forming operators on sentences, changing the tense of the sentence. See e.g., A.N. Prior, *Past, Present and Future*, Oxford 1967.

92. Note that to affirm the distinct identity of thought and intransitive object, or of the epistemic$_2$ and the ontic$_2$, is not to deny, but on the contrary presupposes not just that thought is (ontologically$_2$) part of being, but also the possibility of causal relations between the being of a knowledge and the distinct being of its object — in both the cognitive and conative 'directions of fit'. This holds both in particular cases, e.g. in the causal efficacy of an object in the process of its cognition (e.g. in experiment) and in the possible reciprocal efficacy of knowledge, once achieved, on its object (e.g. in the mining of a mineral, once its presence has been detected); and as between knowledge and being generally, e.g. in emergence and technology respectively. In §4 I argued that ontological struture and diversity are transcendentally necessary conditions of science. Is change on a par? Understanding science as part of being, i.e.refusing to hypostatise it, yet rejecting the ontic fallacy in both its empiricist-behaviourist and reductive-materialist forms, means (as we shall see later) comprehending ontological emergence, presupposing qualitative complexity and change, as equally necessary conditions for science. Scientific structure, diversity and change, then, at once instance and are contained within ontological$_2$ structure, diversity and change, while being distinct and emergent from ontic$_2$ structure, diversity and change. (On 'direction of fit' see, e.g., G.E.M. Anscombe, *Intention*, 2nd ed., Oxford 1963 and J.R. Searle, 'What is an Intentional State?', *Mind 1979*, pp. 74-92.)

learn to make sense' of sentences like 'though the world does not change with a change of paradigm, the scientist afterwards works in a different world'.[93] For this sentence can now be strainlessly transcribed as 'though the [natural, *intransitive*, $ontic_2$] world does not change with a change of paradigm, the scientist afterwards works in a different [social, *transitive*, $epistemic_2$] world'. Furthermore, once Kuhnian paradigms are understood as bearing on (approximately) the same world, rational criteria for choosing between different theoretical perspectives can be disinterred, without too much difficulty, from his own writings[94]; so that the judgementally relativist, as well as the ontologically idealist implications of his thesis, and *mutatis mutandis* of the diversity of beliefs stressed by the sociology of knowledge generally, are very largely dispelled.

Now if we are to avoid the absurdity of the supposition of the production of (new and changing) knowledge *ex nihilo* (on which more anon) and to sustain the material continuity of the process of cognitive transformation, this process must be conceived as iteratively dependent upon the employment of antecedently existing cognitive resources, taken from the same or some other domain (Bachelard's 'scientific loans').[95] These resources comprise the transitive objects of knowledge; their transformation is the transitive process of knowledge-production; and its product, knowledge (of an intransitive object or topic), in turn supplies resources for further rounds of inquiry. This imparts to the cognitive process a quasi-autopoietic character, with the production of knowledges accomplished by means of (anterior) knowledges. And it immediately suggests the possibility of provisionally characterising, or modelling, science in essentially Aristotelian terms (though this

---

93. *The structure of scientific revolutions*, p. 121.
94. Thus Kuhn in a number of places formulates criteria, including accuracy of predictions, number of problems resolved, etc., which he says would enable an observer 'to tell which [of two theories] was the older' ('Reflections on my Critics', *Criticism and the Growth of Knowledge*, eds. I. Lakatos and A. Musgrave, Cambridge 1970, p. 264. Cf also 'Postscript', *The Structure of Scientific Revolutions*, p. 206). In fact these are [not very good] criteria for rational choice. Kuhn's objectivistic reduction of the intrinsic to the extrinsic aspect of science not only obscures this from him, but leads him to overlook the important possibility of historical regression. 'Newer' is not necessarily (or always) 'better'.
95. *Op. cit.*

was not in fact the way in which Aristotle most characteristically viewed science). Its material causes (or transitive objects) would then consist in pre-existing cognitions used as *models*; its efficient causes in the theoretically-guided *research activity* of (wo)men; its final causes in the achievement of adequate *explanations* and its formal causes in *knowledge* of the intransitive objects of inquiry. On such a model, science is a social process, possessing material causes of its own kind, anterior and irreducible to any individual acquisition, oriented to the production, via the dynamic exploitation of whatever cognitive resources lie at its disposal, of the knowledge of the mechanisms of the production of phenomena in nature.

Two cardinal properties of this conception should be stressed: ($\alpha$) transitive continuity of process; and ($\beta$) transitive/intransitive difference or non-identity of being. It is the assumption of material continuity of process which underpins and enables the assimilation of discontinuity and transformation of content in the TD; while the postulate of TD/ID difference and in particular epistemic$_2$/ontic$_2$ non-isomorphism marks the decisive break with any form of anthroporealism. On this view, the already known is the indispensable means for the production of the unknown; models, analogies and so forth provide the only type of craft a science can set sail in as it embarks on its voyages of discovery, the only kind of resource it can bend and shape as it labours on its work of transformation. Engels grasped this point well when, in speaking of 'modern socialism', he remarked that 'like every new theory, it had first to link itself onto the intellectual material which lay ready to its hands, however deep its roots lay in economic facts'.[96] Theories, then, develop by analogies with already established explanations, and scientific languages and conceptual fields grow by the metaphorical (or metonymic) extension, stretching or distanciation, decomposition, rejigging and recomposition of existing (or earlier) scientific or natural usages and forms (Cf. ($\gamma$) on p. 50 above). In this continuing process of *transformation*, cognitive claims at both the theoretical and observational levels of any cycle of inquiry may display inconsistency and meaning-variance (and indeed paradox) at any and over time. For observational predicates are not, contra empiricism, isomorphs of

---

96.  F. Engels, *Anti-Dühring*, Moscow 1969, p. 25.

physical or sensual objects or operations but more like 'knots' attaching a developing body of beliefs and comitments to experience in a theory-dependent and mutable way[97]; and theoretical predicates are not, *contra* rationalism, isomorphs of essences but distanciated and multiply-connected metaphors embedded in experience-dependent and mutable interpretations of more or less formalised structures designed to grasp the mechanisms generating some particular range of phenomena, their intransitive objects of inquiry.

The possibility of *change* is inherent in the central idea of the model of science as a process of *transformation*. Before considering the way in which change has been mishandled by the anti-monistic movment and in particular by its super-idealist wing, I want to look briefly at the metatheory of the 'final' and 'material causes' of science, namely explanations and models, as a prelude to the presentation of a rational account of the logic of scientific development capable of fulfilling the frustrated insights of both the anti-monistic and anti-deductivist schools in contemporary philosophy of science.

At the heart of the scientific enterprise is the project of explanation. An explanation may be understood as the process or account (the 'explanans') by which something (the 'explanandum') is made intelligible. Broadly speaking, modern theories of explanation, like theories of law, can be divided into three main kinds: deductivist, contextualist (and/or neo-Kantian) and realist.

For deductivists, to be able to explain an event is to be able to deduce it from a statement of initial (and boundary) conditions plus universal laws; and the explanation of laws, theories and sciences likewise proceeds by deductive subsumption. Although the explanatory virtues of deduction were celebrated by both Aristotle and Descartes, contemporary deductivism derives immediately from the theory of explanation implicit in Hume's analysis of causality. This theory was expressly articulated by Mill and Jevons and has been fully elaborated by Popper, Braithwaite, Nagel and, most exhaustively, Hempel.[98] Hempel's deductive-nomological (D-N) and inductive-probabilistic (I-P) schema

---

97. See, e.g., the plausible 'network' model proposed by M. Hesse, *The Structure of Scientific Inference*, London 1974.
98. See C.G. Hempel, *Aspects of Scientific Explanation*, New York, 1965.

and their critical reception are well-known.[99] It is sufficient here merely to note that criticism of the basic D-N model has revolved chiefly around the following points:

(a)   Conformity to its requirements cannot be sufficient for explanation, because in general an infinite number of sets of explanantes (including false and ridiculous ones) will entail any explanandum. For instance, 'all wooden objects are conductors and all metal objects are wooden' plus 'this is a metal' entails 'this conducts electricity'. So we must add the epistemic requirement that the explanans is true or independently confirmed or at least not refuted.

(b)   It is doubtful if any D-N arguments are explanatory per se. For to say 'this X $\phi$s because all X's do' merely generalises the initial query in the form 'why does any X $\phi$?'. An explanation of a question of this type will normally require the (non-redundant) introduction of new concepts *not already contained* in the explanandum or inital conditions — as, for example, in Drude's theory of electrical conductivity, where it is the idea of metals possessing free electrons, behaving analogously to gas molecules in the kinetic theory, which explains why any (and thence this) metal conducts electricity. Any explanation worthy of the name involves, that is to say, conceptual work (just as experiment involves practical activity). In fact, the deductive scheme secures explanation only by *redescription*, for which the covering law requirement is dispensable or at best only a backgrounding condition. ('What is this?' — 'A metal'.).

(c)   The deducibility and covering law requirements may each be significantly satisfied independently of one another, and neither independently nor jointly do they seem compelling. On the contrary, if the argument of § 4 is correct, laws may be empirical or universal but not both. The explanation of events is not in general deductive (although the deducibility of laws, such as the Wiedemann-Franz law relating electrical and thermal conductivity, from theories, such as Drude's, may serve as a criterion for our know-

---

99.   See, e.g., my entry on 'Explanation' in *Dictionary of the History of Science*, eds. W. Bynum, E. Browne and R. Porter, London 1981.

ledge of natural necessity); while the deductively justified prediction of events, when and where it is possible, is not in general nomological (because of the transient validity of the assumption of closure). Moreover, the deducibility requirement may be violated in the development of science (relativity theory corrected, as well as explained, classical theory), even though all the statements involved may be strictly universal (transfactual).

For contemporary contextualism, taking off from the philosophy of the later Wittgenstein, Austin and Ryle, an explanation consists essentially in a social exchange, paradigmatically in speech interaction between an explainor (A) and an explainee (B), in which B's puzzlement about something is dissolved.[100] The typical contextualist view is that explanation depends upon semantic considerations of familiarity, plausibility, coherence, etc., together with pragmatic considerations of relevance, etc., *as well as*, and/or perhaps *instead of*, the syntactical ones associated with the D-N model. While some contextualists have latched onto the pragmatic features or social form of the explanatory episode, others have concentrated on the imaginative or heuristic content of the explanatory account. Philosophically contextualism, like neo-Kantianism generally, tends to get squeezed between the epistemological counter-critique of radical (Humean) empiricism and the ontological meta-critique of transcendental realism, which pitches into contextualism's residual empiricism, i.e. its 'as well as', and queries its entitlement to help itself to an 'instead of'.

Pragmatic contextualism will be treated in its hermeneutic version in the next chapter. The mediate sources of semantic contextualism lie in the neo-Kantianism associated with model theory, already abstractly touched on in the previous section. On the standard deductivist position, as propounded by Mill, Duhem and Hempel, a theory just consists in a deductively organised structure of empirical laws. It does indeed 'bind' laws together, but only in virtue of that deductive structure. Hence,

---

100. See, e.g., M. Scriven, 'Explanation, Prediction and Laws', *Minnesota Studies in the Philosophy of Science Vol III*, eds. M. Feigl and G. Maxwell. Minneapolis 1962, and 'Truisms as the Grounds for Historical Explanation', *Theories of History*, ed. P. Gardiner, New York 1959.

any model associated with it is logically and epistemologically quite redundant, and in particular cannot be held to explain phenomena by representing a reality purporting to underlie them. On the normal contextualist response, as expounded by Whewell, Campbell and Hesse, a theoretical model is an interpretation of a formal or partially formalised cognitive structure or complex, whence phenomena are indeed deducible, but it is semantically dependent upon some other cognitive structure epistemically prior to it, and indispensable for both the intelligibility and empirical extension of the theory.

Thus on Whewell's seminal account, knowledge consists in the 'colligation' or binding together of facts (established results) by 'ideas', which are added to or 'superinduced' upon the facts in explanation of them — as when, for instance, Kepler added the new organizing idea of an ellipse to the recognised facts of planetary motion. Science, on Whewell's picture, develops by conceptual integration, achieved via such acts of creative insight, in a process he called the 'consilience of inductions'. For Campbell, a theory, to be intellectually satisfying or capable of growth, must involve a (non-deductive) relation of analogy with some already known field of phenomena. Thus, according to Campbell, it is not merely the fact that the gas laws are all deductive consequences of the kinetic theory, but the corpuscularian model animating that theory — by virtue of which gas molecules are imagined to be, in certain respects (the positive analogy), like billard balls bouncing off each other and exchanging their momenta by impact — which secures our intellectual assent to it.[101] In the theory the respects in which gas molecules are unlike billiard balls, e.g. colour size (the negative analogy), are just ignored; while the respects in which we are undecided as to whether or not gas molecules are indeed like billiard balls (the neutral analogy) are used, as a source of 'surplus (or unbound) meaning', to suggest ways in which the theory can be modified and refined. However Campbell's implicit notion of explanation — as the reduction of the strange or unknown to the familiar — is suspect on both rational and historical grounds. For the intellectually satisfying nature of an explanation can hardly justify the choice of any particular one; and scientific revolutions, possibily mediated, *ex ante*, by paradox, may

---

101. See N.R. Campbell, *Physics, The Elements*, Cambridge 1919.

entrain transformations in what we find satisfying or plausible. At the root of these difficulties lies Campbell's acceptance of the restrictive ontology of empirical realism, and in particular his unwillingness to admit models as hypothetical descriptions of an unknown but knowable reality. From a realist stand-point the significance of models lies not in their reduction of the unknown to the known, but in their use of the already known in the exploration of the potentially knowable but currently unknown. Recent writers in model theory, such as Hesse, mostly concede what I earlier characterised as the vertical axis of realism. But full, transcendental realism sees deducibility as neither sufficient nor necessary for explanation (thereby adding a horizontal axis to the ID); and acknowledges that in the scientific process even the positive analogy may be overturned (thereby necessitating, within the 'transitional' or 'bridge' concept of 'vertical realism' (discussed on p. 40 above), a rigorous differentiation between scientific and ontological stratification or depth, i.e. between stratification in the TD and ID respectively).

For transcendental realism, explanations are quintessentially socially produced and fallible causal accounts of the unknown mode of production of phenomena, or the episodes in which such accounts are furnished. In theoretical science, explanation is accomplished by an account of the formerly unknown generative mechanism; in practical (applied and concrete) science, by an account of the formerly unknown mode of combination or interarticulation, in some specific 'conjuncture', of ante-cedently known mechanisms. Realism attempts to incorporate the situated strengths of both deductivism and contextualism. But, for it (to repeat), deducibility under covering-laws is neither necessary nor sufficient for adequate explanation; satis-fying models may stupify instead of stimulate; and consensually negotiated explanatory exchanges may mystify rather than enlighten (or emancipate).

The cumulative character of scientific development forcefully indicates that theories are *fallible* attempts to describe the real structures of nature, as they complement, succeed and situate one another in offering fuller, deeper, more comprehensive accounts of reality. Manifestly, such a position does not entail what Popper calls 'essentialism ',[102] i.e. the thesis that there are

---

102. K.R. Popper, *Conjectures and Refutations*, London 1963, pp. 103-7.

'ultimate explanations' neither requiring nor permitting explanation themselves. To the contrary, the true moral of Feyerabend's polemic is, as I have argued elsewhere,[103] that without realism, fallibilism collapses into dadaism — into an epistemological displacement of Humean ontological scepticism ('anything may happen'). And scepticism here ('anything goes'), as elsewhere, means in practice tacit acquiescence in the status quo, i.e. more or less, 'everything stays'.[104] Irrespective of the author's intentions, scepticism (as anarchism) is invariably dogmatic (and conservative) in effect [if not indeed often in intent also!].

On the other hand, once the transcendental realist ontology of structures and differences is, as in § 4, substantiated, then a rational account of scientific discovery and development quickly follows. Typically, the construction of an explanation for — the production of the knowledge of the mechanisms of the production of — some newly identified phenomena will necessitate the building of a model of the mechanism which, *if* it were to exist and act in the postulated way, would account for the phenomena concerned. This movement of thought, which may be characterised as 'analogical-retroductive'[105] must always prompt existential questions. For whether or not the postulated mechanism acts in the postulated way cannot of course be decided by theory alone, since in general a plurality of possible explanations will be consistent with the phenomena, reflecting the general underdetermination of theory by experience. So the reality of the conjectured mechanism must be empirically ascertained, and the variety of plausible alternative explanations sorted, elaborated and eliminated until the explanatory mechanism at work has been, in the fallible judgement of the scientists concerned, successfully identified and adequately described. Whereupon it now becomes the phenomenon to be explained. And so science displays a four-phase pattern of development, in which it identifies a range of epistemically sig-

103. See my 'Feyerabend and Bachelard', *New Left Review* 94, November 1975, pp. 31-55.
104. Cf. J. Krige, *Science, Revolution and Discontinuity*, Brighton 1980, p. 142; and A. Chalmers, *What is this thing called science?*, 2nd ed., Queensland 1982 chapter 12.
105. Retroduction or abduction after Aristotle, Peirce and Hanson. See N.R. Hanson, *Patterns of Discovery*, Cambridge 1963, pp. 85 ff. (Cf. p. 11, footnote 26 above).

nificant phenomena; constructs explanations for them; empirically tests its explanations; leading to the identification of the responsible generative mechanism; which now moves centre stage as the newly-identified phenomena to be explained. Note that the model-building of the second phase must normally draw upon cognitive resources not already employed in the description of the object (mechanism) in question — if it is to count as an 'explanation'. And that such work is seldom simply 'the free creation of our minds, the result of an almost poetic intuition',[106] but proceeds under definite protocols of analogical and metaphorical reasoning[107] and is subject to the contextually variable weight imposed by considerations of consistency, coherence, plausibility, relevance, non-redundancy, independence (novelty), comprehensiveness, depth, fertility, empirical testability, formalisability, geometric or iconic representability, as well as others of a semi-aesthetic kind, such as elegance.[108]

If the classical empiricist tradition halts at the first phase of this dialectic, the neo-Kantian tradition sees the need for the second but refrains from drawing the full implications of the third (and so fourth) and, in addition, characteristically denies either the need for or the possibility of the fourth. Transcendental realism differentiates itself from empirical realism in interpreting the first phase as the invariance of a result rather than a regularity; and from transcendental idealism in allowing that what is imagined at the second need not be imaginary but

106. K.R. Popper, *op. cit.*, p. 192.
107. See R. Harré, *Principles of Scientific Thinking*, London 1970, Chapter 2 and M.B. Hesse, *The Structure of Scientific Inference*, chapters 9-11. Note that criteria for the aptness of analogical links include not just antecendently known similarities but the capacity of a model to generate existential hypotheses, predict novel or surprising facts (cf. Herschel), facilitate conceptual integration or economy and permit extensive theoretical elaboration and/or empirical application.
108. However, if a voluntaristic account of the genesis of scientific explanation is mistaken, it is equally erroneous to suppose that one can eliminate the practical tacit-intuitive, affective-expressive and unconscious elements at play in the scientific imagination of the skilled craft-innovator in favour of some purely discursive organon of discovery. Cf. e.g. M. Polanyi, *Personal Knowledge*, London 1957, J.R. Ravetz, *Scientific Knowledge and its Social Problems*, Oxford 1971, and J. Ziman, *Reliable Knowledge*, Cambridge 1975.

may be real and come to be known as such.[109] It differentiates itself from super-idealism, as we shall shortly see, in maintaining the continuity of science as a process of cognitive and practical transformation (cf. (α) on p. 55 above) and the discursivity of our intelligence in it (cf. (β)). In the continuing process of science, as deeper shores and wider reaches of reality are progressively disclosed, the various sciences must compose and evaluate their explanations with the cognitive resources, symbolic media and physical machinery available to them, the 'transmits'[110] from the scientific generations preceding them which, in their own explanatory work, they then reproduce, transform, augment, deplete, modify and refine as their legacy to the generations succeeding them.

On the transcendental realist view of science, then, its essence lies in the *movement* at any one level from knowledge of manifest phenomena to knowledge, produced by means of antecedent knowledge, of the structures which generate them. As deeper levels of reality are successively identified, described and explained, knowledge at more superficial levels is typically revised, corrected or more or less drastically recast, issuing in a characteristic pattern of description, explanation and redescription for the phenomena understood at any one level of reality. If the critical absence underpinning orthodox ontologies (or accounts of the ID) is the notion of scientific activity as *labour*, the critical absence shared by rival philosophical sociologies (or accounts of the TD) is the concept of *ontological depth*, i.e. the idea of the real stratification of being apart from our knowledge of being. This concept is required in order:

(i)   to reconcile the Janus faces of scientific development, growth and change, so overcoming both the hypernaturalist monism of positivism (all growth and no change) and the self-specifying theoretical solipsism of super-idealism (all

---

109. The (correct) Kantian doctrine that existence is not a predicate must not obscure or detract from the central importance of existential judgements in science. For although to say truly of some X that it exists (or of the concept 'X' that it has instances) adds nothing to the concept of X, it may add immeasurably to our *knowledge* and so precipitate an expansion or transformation in our existing *conceptual stock* (including the original concept X).

110. S. Toulmin, *Human Understanding Volume I*. Oxford 1972, p. 158.

change and no growth), as well as the onesidedness of more moderate continuists, such as Nagel, and discontinuists, such as Popper, alike;

(ii)   to acknowledge the historicity of science without espousing relativism, that is, to avoid the Scylla of epistemic absolution without succumbing to the Charybdis of judgemental irrationalism, i.e. to preserve a moment of judgemental rationality within an overarching epistemic relativity and so spare, in contra-distinction from Feyerabend and Kuhn, the propriety of at least some scientific transformations;

(iii)  to discern the rationale of the actual historical stratification of the sciences in the multi-tiered stratification of reality, and so display the consequent logic of discovery which that stratification imparts to science.

This logic must be sited in the movement or transition from the identification of invariances to the classification of the structures or mechanisms which generate them. Characteristically, in every transition of this type, knowledge corresponding to the differing Humean, Kantian, Lockean and Leibnizian levels of natural necessity is progressively obtained. At the first, *Humean* level, there is just the bare invariance of an experimentally produced (or naturally striking) result. Given such a 'protolaw', science sets to work on the construction and testing of possible explanations for it at the second, *Kantian* level. If there is an explanation, located in the nature of the thing or the structure of the system of which the thing forms a part, then there is a *reason* for its behaviour, *independent* of its actual behaviour. Such a reason may be empirically established. And if the thing's normic (really transfactual/actually tendential) behaviour can be deduced, then the most stringent possible or *Lockean* criterion for our knowledge of natural necessity is satisfied. Accordingly if, for instance, the dispositional properties of copper can be deduced from an empirically determined statement of its structure, we may be said to possess *a posteriori* knowledge of natural necessity.

Finally, at the fourth, *Leibnizian* level, we may seek to express our discovery of its structure in an attempted real definition of the substance, process or thing, so obtaining (not synthetic a priori) but analytic *a posteriori* knowledge. This is not to put an end to inquiry, but merely a stepping stone to a new cycle of discovery in which science seeks to fathom the mechanisms explaining that level of reality. At any one level, causal laws now appear as the tendencies of natural kinds, realised under closed conditions; and knowledge of them as historically produced, empirically established and normatively corrigible.

For an adequate account of scientific development both the concepts of (1) ontological depth (in the ID) and (2) knowledge as a produced means of production (in the TD) must be sustained. Scientific work appears as doubly articulated, using pre-existing social materials to apprehend and express independently existing natural matter (to borrow an old Thomist locution). At any level, its essential movement is from knowledge of manifest phenomena (in the ID) to knowledge, produced by means of antecedent knowledge (in the TD), of the structures which generate them (in the ID), discovery of the new (growth) proceeding *pari passu* with criticism and correction of the old (change). And science develops by iterative reapplication of this triad, organised around the distinction between manifest phenomena and their structural explanation: that is, from the identification of empirical invariances to the construction and testing of possible explanations for them, from which ideally normic statements will be deducible, leading on to the identification, description and classification of novel kinds of entities and processes in a continuing dialectic of explanatory and taxonomic knowledge. However, on this vista, the fundamental theoretical principles or real definitions of a science (including its axiomatic base, if any) are achieved, *contra* Leibniz, as part of an irreducibly empirical and irreducibly historical process of inquiry, so that they are both *a posteriori* and potential explananda of further cycles of scientific work, in the course of which they may come to be re-described as well as explained. Indeed, in a moment we shall see how change can be at once empirically rational and historically inevitable (for indeed the question is never *whether*, but *what* change is to occur).

A critique of empiricism and transcendental idealism is secured by showing how knowledge at the Lockean level, namely of real essences, is possible, thus resolving the aporias of empirical realism. But a complementary critique of rationalism and super-idealism is achieved by demonstrating how such knowledge is produced in the transitive, discursive and continuous (i.e. empirical and historical) process of science, so resolving the aporias of conceptual realism. Can either species of anthroporealism sustain the desiderata for the adequacy of an account of scientific development, namely (1) and (2) above? No. I have already noted that neither empirical nor conceptual realism can assimilate scientific change, in virtue of their common indigenous isomorphising anthroporealism, tying the world to man — so both patently fail the transitive requirement (1). But the condition of such an *isomorphism* is an *ontological destratification*, the actualist collapse of the tied world to man — so both fail the intransitive requirement (2). The intelligibility of scientific development necessitates an independently structured world, presently at least partially unknown to us; the presupposition of an anthroporealism is a flat world already (implicity or explicitly) completely known to man, as knowledge (in as much as it is not transcendent — a possibility, as remarked in § 2 above, of no immediate concern to us here) comes to define being. But *the meaning of the epistemological definition of being*, in an anthroporealism, *is the ontologisation*, and thus naturalisation (and eternalisation and so also consolidation, defence and a priori guarantee), *of existing* (current, contemporary) *knowledge* — or, at any rate, some privileged sector of it, identified through the particular concept of knowledge employed.

Naturally within this global characterisation, there are significant generic and specific differences. In the case of empirical realism the immediate problem facing it is that it cannot satisfactorily accommodate the notion of natural necessity (or account for the 'surplus-element' in theory), in virtue of its palpably unstratified, collapsed ontology. The immediate difficulty for conceptual realism is its incapacity satisfactorily to cope with the notion of natural contingency (or account for the 'empirical moment' in theory), in virtue of its manifestly undifferentiated, uniform ontology. But § 4 demonstrated that empirical realism cannot sustain the intelligibility of experimental activity or of insignificant experiences; while non-transcendent conceptual realism actualistically collapses any surplus to human subjectivity and reduces natural to logical or conventional necessity. Whereas empirical realism presupposes an atomistic ontology and normally an individualist sociology, conceptual realism comes in both atomistic and holistic and both individualist and collectivist forms. Restricting our attention to atomistic ontologies, let us look briefly at these familiar and epistemologically inter-dependent sites of philosophical aporias. In the inductivist problem-field any true or well-confirmed law is logically *consistent with any other* (i.e. non-equivalent) proposition whatsoever, while in the deductivist problem-field any falsehood or self-contradictory statement logically *implies every other* proposition whatsoever. These consequences, and the paradoxes associated with them, flow inexorably from an atomistic ontology underpinning the notion of the complete independence and absolute parity of all predicates. This licenses, in the inductivist case, *unrestricted conjunctive suppositioning* to absurd and arbitrary (ungrounded) possibilities (as in e.g. Goodman's and Hempel's paradoxes) and, in the deductivist case, *unconstrained disjunctive syllogizing* to ridiculous and irrelevant implications (as in e.g. the paradoxes of material and strict implication).[111] In science these paradoxes do not normally arise, once it is recognised that the logical subject of, for instance, a law of nature is a natural kind of thing — the locus of a real generative mechanism, grounding some but not other possibilities. This confers upon its discourse a topic, which prevents the unconstrained use of the disjunctive syllogism; and the inbuilt assymmetry between the thing and its properties prohibits such manoeuvres as contraposition.[112] There are no grounds for supposing, in the light of the stratification of our knowledge and of being, that this acorn might turn into a frog rather than an oak; and there is no way of inferring, in the light of the differentiation of our knowledge and of being, from the falsity of Berzelian electrochemistry that I am wearing purple socks. Predicates are not independent of one another and on a par in science because there are necessary connections in nature and

---

111. Indeed, we could say that if the metacritique of empiricist inductivism is signposted in its incapacity to sustain the idea of insignificant (or, even more basically, impossible) experiences, in virtue of its undifferentiated ontology, the metacritique of empiricist or rationalist deductivism is signposted in its incapacity to sustain the idea of *irrelevant* (or even more basically, naturally necessary) *implications*, in virtue of its destratification and dedifferentiation of discursive contextx. Cf. A.R. Anderson and N. Belnap 'Tautological Entailments', *Philosophical Studies 13*, (1961) pp. 9-24; and, for a discussion of the consequences of their argument, S. Haack, *Philosophies of Logics*, Cambridge 1978, pp. 197-203.

112. Cf. the argument of *A Realist Theory of Science*, Chap 3, Section 6, especially pp. 224-5.

things fall into natural kinds.

It is because some things collect into natural kinds that taxonomy is possible and a rationale exists, based on the assumption of real deep identities, for the stratification of science. It is because some natural phenomena are necessarily connected that explanatory theory is possible and a rationale exists, based on the assumption of transfactually active tendencies (grounded in those identities), for the experimental and applied activity of science. But scientifically significant generality does not lie exposed on the face of the world prone to the gaze of the casual observer. Rather it is, for the most part, hidden encrusted in things, needing to be excavated in theoretical and practical labours of the most arduous kinds. Thus the transcendental complement of the real universals posited and unearthed by science are the singularities of the world of our everyday experience, where caprice, resemblance and mere regularity hold sway.

On the structured and differentiated ontology of transcendental realism, then, two basic models of explanation come to the fore. Theoretical explanations are *analogical-retroductive*, exhibiting what I shall label the DREI schema: i.e. *description* of law-like behaviour; *retroduction*, exploiting analogies with already known phenomena, to possible explanations of the behaviour; *elaboration* and elimination of alternative explanations; issuing (ideally) in the empirically-controlled *identification* of the causal mechanism(s) at work. Practical explanations, i.e. explanations of particular concrete phenomena, are especially tailored to open systems, the normal condition of things. They are *decompositiory-retroductive* in struture, exhibiting the RRRE schema: viz. *resolution* of a complex event (situation, etc.) into its components; *redescription* of these components in theoretically significant terms; *retrodiction*, via independently validated normic or tendency statements, to possible antecedents of the components; and *elimination* of alternative possible causes. It is with the dynamics of theoretical explanation that I have been principally concerned here. Practical explanations will be considered in more detail in Chapter 2.

I now return to the situation of scientific change. At the centre of conceptual work in creative science is, as we have seen, modelling. Typically a model involves an analogy, i.e. a relation between two (or more) objects, which allows inferences to or understanding of one on the basis of the other. Any model of some subject must possess a source (which may itself be a model); and models may be conveniently classified (following Harré)[113] into those in which the subject is the same as its source, *homoeomorphs* (e.g. replicas, idealisations, class-representatives) and those in which it is different, *paramorphs*. It is clearly paramorphic model-building, i.e. the construction of a model for an unknown subject (nominally identified in some other way), but whose reality can potentially be (eventually) empirically ascertained, which is most important in knowledge-extending science. *Ex post* a paramorph may reveal an identity of subject and source processes (in which event it is a homologue) or an identity or similarity between their respective structural states or a more or less radical discrepancy between states and/or processes. But *ex ante* we only know a paramorph's relation to its sources. And here it may be based on one, more than one, or just an aspect of a source, as in the case of the kinetic, Darwinian and Freudian theories, exemplifying singly-, multiply- and semi-connected paramorphs respectively. Multiply-connected paramorphs must lead to the postulation of strange or unfamiliar types of entities or processes, such as wave particles or natural selection.

In the paramorphic case, there is a double conceptual uncoupling, at the core of the creative moment, in a developing explanatory theory, as Diagram 1.2. below indicates. In as much as the theory is dynamically dependent upon its model(s), it displays split sense $(T_a/T_b)$ and disjoint reference $(O_a/O_b)$. But in as much as the theory is a purported explanation of a range of phenomena, there will also be dissociation of both sense and reference as between the theoretical and observational levels. Because, in such a paramorph the hypothetical entities imagined for the purposes of theory-construction must initally derive at least part of their meaning from some other source (here $T_a$), theories must be already understood (along the ($\alpha$) connection) before correspondence rules are laid down for them (along the ($\beta$) connection). By the same token this means that the descriptive terms used in their ostensive or operational (nominal) definition must already have possessed a meaning independent of the theory. When these two connections are brought into

---

113. R. Harré, *The Principles of Scientific Thinking*, chapter 2.

relation in the theory, semantic work is done (the more so, of course, when first independent access to the subject (along $(\gamma)$) and then eventually identification of the explanatory link (along $(\delta)$) is obtained). Thus, on the transformational (quasi-autopoietic, analogical-metaphorical) conception of science, meaning-change is not only possible but *inevitable*, in the course of scientific development.

Now, is it possible, as Feyerabend and Kuhn have claimed, that no meanings might come to be shared between conflicting scientific theories in this process? And if this — or something like it — were indeed the case could we then still retain the notion of a rational choice between such 'incommensurable' theories? If the answer to the second question is 'yes', then epistemic relativity (in the EA), even in this radical form, gives no grounds for judgemental relativism (in the IA). But if the answer to the first question is 'no', it might still be important and relevant to have demonstrated this.

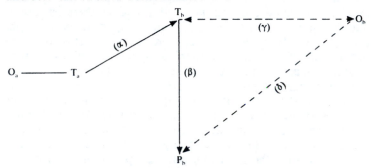

Diagram 1.2: *Dissociation of Meaning in Explanatory Theory Development*

$T_a$ = source theory; $O_a$ = source object; $T_b$ = subject theory; $O_b$ = subject matter (object) of subject theory; $P_b$ = phenomena to be explained by $T_b$. $\alpha$ = subject/source (model) connection; $\beta$ = theory/observation (explanatory) connection; $\gamma$ = theory/object (representative adequacy) connection; $\delta$ = object/phenomena (generative) connection.

## 6. Incommensurability and the Refutation of Superidealism

I want to begin by more or less dogmatically affirming certain distinctions which are commonly overlooked or insufficiently attended to in discussions of incommensurability (henceforth usually abbreviated to 'inc') and meaning-variance in science. The significance and import of these distinctions will, I trust, become clear in the following discussion.

(1) It is important to differentiate the theses of incommensurability, meaning-variance, meaning-filiation and meaning-uniformity (or-invariance). The strong thesis of *incommensurability* posits a situation in which there is no mutuality of meaning; the weaker position of *meaning-variance* holds merely that radical or quite wide variations in meaning do (or at least may) occur. The strong anti-incommensurabilist thesis of *meaning-uniformity* asserts that there is not (and perhaps cannot be) any meaning-variance at all, or at least any of a kind liable seriously to jeopardise translation, mutual comprehensibility or the possibility of rational choice; the weaker position of *meaning-filiation* claims merely that sufficient mutuality (identity or kinship) in meaning normally, or at any rate frequently, occurs so as to permit successful and correct translation, etc. Inc. and meaning-variance are inconsistent with general meaning-uniformity; while meaning-filiation and meaning-variance are consistent with particular instances of inc. My argument in § 5 evidently commits me to both meaning-variance and meaning-filiation in the course of scientific development, with the possibility of meaning-uniformity and inc. as limiting special cases.[114]

(2) Inc. may be partial or complete; in the former event, some sentences of the (two or more) schemes are non-intertranslatable; in the latter event, no sentences of the schemes are. One can thus distinguish the inc. of sentences or of expressions; of more or less integrally coherent blocs of sentences, i.e. sectors; and of schemes, or ways of life. Non-reciprocal, i.e. one- rather than two-way, partial, sectoral or complete inc. is conceivable. The distinction between (a) inc. and meaning-diversity between cultures (a-temporal inter-societal inc. and meaning variance) and

---

114. In *The Possibility of Naturalism*, Brighton 1979, chapter 4, I adduced arguments indicating that the supposition of complete meaning-uniformity is as nonsensical as that of complete incommensurability.

(b) inc. and meaning-change over time (intra-societal and a-temporal inc. and meaning-variance) is a familiar one. (a) raises the problems of the possibility of communicative (and so explanatory) failure and of the rationality of forms of life within anthropology, (b) those of the possibility of interpretative (and so explanatory) failure and of the rationality of change within history. I will be principally concerned with the inter-temporal inc. and meaning-variance within the specific historical culture of modern science. But here it is vital to separate ($\alpha$) historical, ($\beta$) logical and ($\gamma$) psychological or socio-psychological inc., as we shall shortly see.

(3) I discriminate between: (a) the meaning of an expression or sentence (the intransitive object or target of a possible hermeneutic mediation or translation exercise); (b) its translatability into (or mensurability within) some other language or meaning-frame; and (c) its actual translation to the satisfaction (or in the opinion) of the translator and/or translatee. Inc. and meaning-variance both allow that (c) may sometimes occur without (b), so that one or both of the communicants may be engaged in unwitting, possibly corroborated and/or reciprocated, misunderstanding.

(4) I discriminate between the sense, reference and referent of an expression. Reference if an *act*, typically for others, *to* objects etc. within ontogeny; referents *are objects* etc., only contingently related to communicatively and denotationally successful acts of reference, within ontology. Reference may be simple, i.e. to particulars or kinds (denotation), or composite, i.e. to particulars or kinds characterised in a certain way — that is, to states of affairs, tendencies and so forth (designation). The composite referent of a sentence is what makes a sentence true when it is.

(5) I attach considerable importance to the distinction between ($\alpha$) the principle of *epistemic relativity*, viz that all beliefs are socially produced, so that knowledge is transient and neither truth-values nor criteria of rationality exist outside historical time and ($\beta$) the doctrine of *judgmental relativism*, which maintains that all beliefs are equally valid in the sense that there are no rational grounds for preferring one to another. I accept ($\alpha$), so disavowing any form of epistemic absolutism, but reject ($\beta$),

so upholding judemental rationality against a- (and/or ir-) rationalism. It will be seen that epistemic relativism is as necessary for judgmental rationality as ontological realism is for epistemic relativity. Relativists have mistakenly inferred ($\beta$) from ($\alpha$),[115] while anti-relativists have wrongly taken the unacceptability of ($\beta$) as a reductio of ($\alpha$).[116]

(6) Finally, I discriminate sharply between the largely illusory *philosophical* problems of inc. and the *superidealism* which sponsors it (which can be shown to be incoherent) and the real and often acute substantial problems of translation, understanding and rationality as occasioned by meaning-variance both in the social world generally and within the specific ambit of modern science. These problems cannot be wished away by epistemological fiat or dissolved in any easy philosophical solution. Accordingly I propose first to discuss the philosophical problems of inc. as posed by superidealism, and then to pass on to consider the more general problems of meaning-variance in science.

Suppose it is the case that no meanings are shared between conflicting theories. Can we still retain the notion of the possibility of a rational choice between them? The superidealist answers 'no' in sceptical (e.g. Feyerabend) or voluntaristic (e.g. Kuhn) temper. I suggest the answer is 'yes' — provided we are prepared to distinguish clearly between the sense (in the TD) and reference (to the ID) of expressions and to admit that difference of meaning does not preclude identity (or at least commonality) of reference. For we can then submit, as a first approximation to a criterion of rational choice (in the general vein of Lakatos), that

[L]: a theory $T_c$ is preferable to a theory $T_d$, even if they are inc., provided that $T_c$ can explain *under its descriptions*, almost all the phenomena that $T_d$ can explain under its descriptions, plus some significant phenomena that $T_d$ cannot explain.

---

115. See, e.g., T.S. Kuhn, 'Reflections on my Critics', *Criticism and the Growth of Knowledge*, eds. I. Lakatos and A. Musgrave, pp. 264-265.
116. See, e.g., K.R. Popper, *Objective Knowledge*, Oxford 1972, p. 308.

This criterion will not, however, do as it stands, since it makes no mention of a subject who is to adjudicate and choose between the rival theories (without which L is, so to speak, running normatively idle). So L must be reformulated subject to the condition

[S]:     there is a subject capable of applying L.

Now it is straightaway evident that the acceptability of L and S depend upon (i) the explicit recognition of a philosophical ontology (in the ID) and (ii) the possibility of a subject capable of engaging (e.g. in virtue of their bitheoretic-linguality) in the comparison of the explanatory results (in the TD). But are not (i) and (ii) precisely what the superidealist denies? Quite so. But such an ontology and sociology are already implicit in this formulation of the problem, or definition of the phenomenon, of inc. For, in the first regard, to say of two theories that they are inc. (that they clash) is to suppose that they share an area of referential overlap (so satisfying the condition of L). And, in the second, to say of two theories that they are inc. (that they possess no meanings in common) is to presuppose that the theories have been sufficiently identified — by a subject — to substantiate that judgement. This goes some, albeit only some, way to satisfying the condition for S. For it is conceivable that a subject might have grounds for supposing that two theories (or forms of life) were inc. without being able to demonstrate this in an enumerative proof, that is, in the absence of an exhaustive knowledge of both sets of meanings.

Note that I am not debarring the possibility of two or more theories with no referential overlap. On the contrary such circumstances are commonplace. But then the theories do not clash and they are therefore not deemed 'incommensurable'. Nor am I secluding the possibility of two epistemic communities travelling on, so to speak, semantic world-lines which never meet and know nothing of each other. Such communities could in principle be sufficiently identified by a third party to warrant the judgement of their (conflictual) inc. without that party having sufficient information to apply L, and so satisfy S. But it is not such a remote scenario that animates our incommensurabilist. For she or he is fired by the alleged inc. between different mundane, i.e. historically realised, human cultures at or over time, especially within science. Moreover the choice situation which excites him or her is not the 'external' one open to a prospective third party, but that actually confronted from within by the communities concerned. Can they come to a rational agreement about *their* theories? So S must be reformulated as

[I-S]: the adherents of rival (including inc.) theories are capable of consensually applying L;

or, more especially as

[I-S]′: the adherents of rival (including inc.) theories are (historically, socio-psychologically) capable of consensually applying L.

My argument against superidealism is that a philosophical ontology sufficient for the putative applicability of L is implicit in it; but that if such an ontology is explicitly shunned, the principles of material continuity and discursivity — cf. ($\alpha$) and ($\beta$) on p. 55 above — (i.e. of historicity and spontaneity) fail, and a solipsism of such vertiginous propositions ensues, as will be shown in a moment, that no judgement of inc. can be made. This does not secure the satisfaction of I-S, let alone I-S′, in history, anymore than the refutation of empiricism ensures the discovery of natural necessities in science. But it does mean, as we shall see, that no agents could ever find themselves in the situation described by the superidealist, so that the philosophical fancy of inc. must cede to appreciation of the real difficulties of meaning-variance-in-filiation in and around science. These are difficulties which superidealism, no less than the meaning-monism against which it reacts, serves only to obscure.

So long as two prerequisites are fulfilled, namely (1) that the relationship between the theories is one of conflict rather than mere difference, so that they are *alternatives*, and (2) that such alternatives are *of* the same world, then two theories (whether or not they are inc.) must share a part-world in common, i.e. possess some commonality of reference, so that the ontological condition for the applicability of L is satified. On the other hand, if the theories do not share an area of referential overlap, i.e. if the phenomenon of 'Kuhn-loss (or difference)' is total, then, as I shall show, no sense can be attached to the notion of a clash or competition between the theories, and hence to the concept of a change from one, $T_c$, to the other, $T_d$, (let alone criticism of $T_c$ by $T_d$) or of communication between them. They now *ipso facto* cease to be alternatives, either ($\alpha$) for the same community over time or ($\beta$) for different communities at the same time. In the single community inter-temporal case, such total replacement scouts both material continuity and discursive intellection, conjuring up the spectre of an archetypal intuitive understanding constructing its world *de novo* in a single synthetic act.[117] Such an understanding is locked, narcissistically, into its own immediate self-particularising conceptual sphere, and has no way of referring to its origins or to anything outside its world-constituting, panenthizing, self. Possessing no past, it has no memory or sense of its own (transformative) achievement. Hence, it would seem that it must lack a way of saying *what* it is inc. with (which of course makes it doubtful whether it could say what *it* is). How does $T_c$ indicate $T_d$? Abstractly, there appear four possibilities here: (1) it could point to it; (2) it could refer to its referent; (3) it could refer to its sense; or (4) it could know it as its own creation. (1) is palpably insufficient for any judgement. (2), that is, referring to $T_d$ by way of referring to the referent of $T_d$ is precisely what, on the hypothesis of no referential overlap, it cannot do. (3) must therefore involve a way of referring to the sense of $T_d$ without referring to its referents. Thus $T_c$, say relativity theory, now becomes a theory of the behaviour of scientists in $T_d$, say Newtonian theory, rather than an alternative theory of its subject matter — that is, a (completely behaviourist) sociology, not a physics! But only option (4) is fully consistent with the idea of a self-particularising understanding. $T_c$ is now seen as constituting the social world of $T_d$ — on which vista, Einstein procreates his progenitors! Note, by contrast, that when cases of suspected inc., or widely divergent meaning actually arise, what typically happens is that the scientists of $T_d$ follow line (2). They use their capacity to refer, under their own descriptions, to the referent of $T_c$ (the possibly inc. system) to report and repair this situation, thus employing a referential route to the sense of $T_c$.

Similar aporias beseige the a-temporal multiple community

---

117. See I. Kant, *Critique of Judgement*, New York 1972, pp. 249-258. It is significant that even Feyerabend has shied away from this scenario. Thus note the tell-tale overlapping domain, marked D, demarcating an area of clash, in the second diagram in *Against Method*, p. 178.

case, with the absence of any referential overlap entailing a complete (and inexplicable) solipsism for each community. It is unclear why such a solipsism should be supposed to have any significance for *us*. More pertinently perhaps, what is clear is that the superidealist can never apply judgements of incommensurability internally, from within a form of life, because there is no referential 'outside', nothing for the 'within' to be 'outwith'. Conversely, if the superidealist is content to fall back on an external judgment of inc., as in S rather than I-S, such a judgement could never come to be known within one or more of the competing life-forms (because, for them, there are still no 'outsides', only the concave surfaces bounding the insides of their self-worlds). And so the superidealists' judgement is quite literally devoid of possible significance for *them*. The superidealist must end in mere gesture.

Moreover it would seem that an external judgement that two systems are inc. entails that they are commensurable at least in respect of their possession of meanings (so comprising conceptual fields). But in virtue of what (what common factor or features) do we attribute meanings to both? Are there criteria for the concept? If there are, then the incommensurabilist must identify the common (meaning-endowing, meaningful) feature(s); and if there are such features then the systems are not 'inc.' (externally). But if there are no criteria for the concept of meaning (or systematicity) then why call the X's 'inc.'? We might just as well say of them anything we chose, e.g. that they are (or are not) both 'blue', 'Jack', 'zot' or $\sqrt{-2}$. This is of course absurd, but it reflects the absurdity of a position which entertains the possibility of a conversation with a single voice, a possibility as incoherent as the sound of one hand clapping. Conversely, to say of a community that it possesses meanings is to say that it is a community of beings with commonality of being, presupposing a world for the beings to 'mean things' in. Admitting this much, we can then readily allow the possibility of meaning-change and -diversity of more and less radical kinds, of misunderstanding both within and between communities, and of the identification (and misidentification) of such misunderstanding, internally, mutually and 'externally'. But to speak of such an external identification is already to situate oneself in community, in possible meaning-filiation, with the community or communities concerned, and that is already to presuppose a zone or margin of referential overlap with them.[118]

Here again, as in the case of the empirical realist tradition in §4, an immanent refutation has been obtained (subject to the fulfilment of provisos (1) and (2) on pp. 75 above), as it transpires that superidealism cannot sustain the intelligibility of precisely that feature of science, viz major conceptual transformations (more specifically of a radically inc. sort — whether this notion is tenable or not, and whether the phenomenon it purports to describe is real, exaggerated or altogether imaginary), to which it draws attention. But perhaps conditions (1) and (2) are, or need not be, met? Perhaps the superidealist has a way out here?

(1) Incommensurable is not the same as 'different'. Whereas 'different' is an unicategorial three-place predicate, in as much as two things differ in a respect they both contain, 'incommensurable' is a bicategorial four-place predicate, in as much as two or more objects, specifically here theories, are always 'inc.' with respect to something outside or other than themselves, specifically here a domain (which may be characterised in the meta-language of philosophy by the syncategorematic notion of 'same being') over or about which the difference (conflict) occurs (such as Feyerabend's 'D'[119]). Paradigmatically in science this is a realm of real objects and/or relations existing and acting (relatively or absolutely) independently of that clash. To confirm this, try to imagine a situation in which two parties agreed that their theories disagreed or clashed without also agreeing that there was something in respect of, or about which, they clashed, whether or not they could also agree (or even individually specify) what this was. Or remember that in the case of simple Gestalt switch figures, such as Wittgenstein's Duck-Rabbit or Hanson's Bird-Antelope[120], the different aspects are

---

118. Is it coincidental that Feyerabend does not doubt that *he* can score the differences between the archaic and non-archaic modes of life, or between the rhetorics of Galileo and Bellarmine? Or that Kuhn never supposes that he cannot tell the difference between Lavoisier and Priestley, or identify the incommensurabilities between Einsteinian and Newtonian theory? Once more 'words and deeds belie one another'.

119. See footnote 117 above.

120. L. Wittgenstein, *Philosophical Investigations*, II.xi, 2nd ed., Oxford 1958, p. 194; and N.R. Hanson, *Patterns of Discovery*, Cambridge 1965, p. 13.

of a single (one and the same) figure.[121] Note that it is not the notion of inc. qua mere difference, but that of a conflicting, clashing inc. which gives the ontological game away. Special relativity is in conflict with Newtonian mechanics, but not the Battle of Hastings, Lymeswold cheese or the rules of chess, although these are all undeniably different.

Suppose, however, that the superidealist stipulates that inc. is to be understood only as mere difference, then it now becomes at most a purely negative limiting concept devoid of descriptive interest or regulative import, save against only the most draconian Parmenidean theories of science. Moreover she or he is now left bereft of any way of discriminating what I shall nominate the 'ω factor', namely the difference between e.g. chemical and sociological theories, on the one hand, and between rival (putatively inc.) chemical theories (e.g. Lavoisier's and Priestley's on the other; that is, between differentiation within scientific activity and its discontinuity over time. But without the 'ω factor', the superidealist's premise crumbles, so that her or his attempted rehabilitation of inc. as difference fails, by undermining the very phenomena to which superidealism appeals.

(2) It might be objected that my presumption that alternative descriptions are of the same world overlooks the possibility that the clash involved in inc. theoretical perspectives is, so to speak, *for* a subject rather than *of* an object. However, *any* mutually incompatible modes of experience or expenditure of time are potentially axiologically conflictual. Thus in switching from playing tennis to writing a letter a transformation occurs in an agent's activity such that he or she cannot normally do both. Such 'incommensurability' is the fate and predicament of any conscious subject who must discriminate in time.

Once more, however, if the superidealist legislates that this is the way inc. is to be taken, she or he loses her or his premise. For if, to simplify (supposing that, as one well-known ex-President said of another, a person cannot both walk and chew gum at the same time), time is discrete and consciousness unitary, everything becomes inc. with everything else. So that

---

121. That there are often criteria for *choosing* between the aspects of a figure shows that the paradigm does not necessarily carry judgementally relativist implications. Cf. C. Dilworth, *Scientific Progress*, Dordrecht 1981, Chapters 8-9.

this line culminates in a Heraclitian subjectivity as unacceptable as the Parmenidean objectivity against which the first defence seemed to be directed. And, here again, the vital '$\omega$ factor', the superidealist's point of departure, fades from view.[122]

The implosion of philosophical superidealism, and its subjective conceptual realist ontology, of course resolves nothing in actual science. For I want to maintain against philosophical 'disillusionists' that problems of inc. and meaning-variance can raise important practical issues. Translation, for instance, is a skilled, and frequently unsuccessful, accomplishment, no more a priori guaranteed (or *de facto* legitimated by an existing consensus) than a good experimental design. There are no free riders in science.

Consider first a very simple case. Two theoretical parties, X and Y, may agree, in a convenient meta-language (such as natural English) or a shared scientific register, that two theories (C), initally sponsored by X, and (D), sponsored by Y, can explain a range of phenomena, $P_1 \ldots P_{1,000}$ equally well under their own descriptions $Cp_1 \ldots Cp_{1000}$ and $Dp_1 \ldots Dp_{1000}$, but that there is some further range of phenomena, say $P_{1000}$ to $P_{1009}$, which C does and D does not (at least at present) appear to be able to adequately explain in their own terms; where e.g. C may be relativity and D classical theory.

Normally, however, matters will be more complicated than this, as the following diagram indicates:

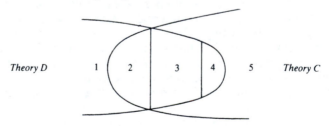

*Theory D*    1    2    3    4    5    *Theory C*

Diagram 1.3: Kuhn-Loss and Referential Overlap in Theory Conflict

---

122. The allocation of scientific labour time is of course a vital issue. But it arises quite independently of the superidealist problem of inc.. However it is worth nothing that, in the absence of an explicit ontology (or ID), the two problems of inc. are bound, for the superidealist, to become more or less confused — just as the empirical realist will tend to confuse our two quotidian senses of 'laws'. (See page 38 above.)

(2)-(4) comprise the area of referential overlap. (1) represents what is forgotten or ineffable in, i.e. the 'Kuhn-loss' for, C — for new theories often say nothing at all about, i.e. forget (repress), often indefinitely, not just contradict or redescribe some previously known phenomena. (5) represents what cannot be said in D. (3) specifies the domain adequately explained by both A and B in their own terms, which may to a greater or lesser extent be meaning-variant. (4) consists in the anomalies for D successfully resolved by C; whereas (2) demarcates the new anomalies emerging for C, phenomena which had been successfully handled by D, denoting the 'mopping-up' operations which a new theory rarely, if ever, completes.

Diagram 1.3 itself represents a major over-simplification in that: 1) it does not indicate the significance of either the phenomena explained, or their explanations; 2) it does not severalise distinct modes of inter-theoretical conflict; 3) it does not budget for suspended commitment; 4) it is non-dynamic; and 5) it does not allow for the possibility of conflicting assessments by the theoretical protagonists. (The consideration that theory comparison always in principle, and often in practice, involves more than theories complicates matters further, but raises no new issues of substance).

1. Phenomena cannot be counted and/or aggregated. For a start, if the theories are in competition only over a very small domain and/or the area of difference is very small in relation to the area of agreement, but Kuhn-loss operates both ways, the appropriate direction of scientific work will be determined as much by the significance, as the 'quantity', of phenomena explained or problems resolved in (4) + (5) v. (1) + (2). But in any evaluation of the theories, even more important than the quality or significance of the phenomena explained, and often directly determining it, will be the significance of their *explanations*. And the most important of these considerations will relate to the *ontological depth* and/or *comprehensiveness* of the conflicting theories. What makes one theory qualitatively better than another is its capacity to identify, describe and (ideally) successfully explain a deeper level of reality and/or to conceptually and explanatorily unify formerly disparate sectors or fragments of our knowledge of the world. Such considerations will bear directly on our evaluations of the calibre of the explanations C and D proffered at (3). Diagram 1.3 is seriously misleading in that it does not indicate the *n + 1 tiered* and/or the *n*

+ *1 segmented* character of actual historical choice situations in science. *A fortiori* any criterion such as L must be reformulated in order to include a qualitative clause such as

[Q]: especially, or even only, if it can either (a) identify and/ or describe and/or explain a deeper level of reality; and/or (b) achieve a new order of epistemic (explanatory and/or taxonomic) integration, or at least show grounded promise of being able to do so.

2. Discussion of scientific change has often been vitiated by a failure to differentiate (a) inconsistency and/or theory-replacement generally from incommensurability or meaning-variance generally (all of which presuppose referential overlap); (b) partial, sectoral and total inc. and *mutatis mutandis* meaning-variance; and (c) (α) historical,(β) logical or semantic and (γ) psychological or socio-psychological inc. or meaning variance. Since inconsistency and incommensurability (or even meaning-variance) are logically incompatible modes of scientific incompatibility, they must characterise staggered phases (or reconstructed aspects) of scientific development. Understanding science as a diachronic process of transformation allows a gradual transition (mediated by the straining, stretching, severing and sundering of meanings) to the semantic inc. of fully-developed scientific theories. Such theories may, when rigorously axiomatized, operationally defined and fideistically-conventionally interpreted, show the semblance of total inc. with their predecessors and/or rivals and reveal only the faintest patina of 'open texture'.[123] But such logical or semantic inc. — which patently holds between contemporary and classical physics, or between, say, Marxian political economy and neo-classical economic theory — does not preclude psychological bi-(or multi-) theoretic-linguality any more than the perspectival inc. of two aspects of a Gestalt switch figure inhibits our ability to move from one to the other. It is also worth pointing out that such semantic inc. does not entail the inc. of all the implications of the theories; nor is it normally complete; and that when it appears to be so, this is the illusion of a 'snap shot' (or text-book) view of theory, an illusion readily dissolved when the theory is seen at work dealing with disturbing anomalies, when

---

123. Waismann, 'Verifiability', *How I See Philosophy*, London 1968.

the full weight of its hidden semantic resources will be remorse-lessly summoned to its assistance.

The practical recognition of situations of inter-theoretical conflict, where theories are characterised by greater or lesser meaning-variation (including the possibility of some order of inc.), may be facilitated by the ability of the agents X and Y to participate in, or at least, understand, some of the differential implications of both theoretical discourses and (i) to weigh the area of (dis)agreement in both (bi-theoretically) or in a rela-tively neutral meta-language or (ii) to effectively mensurate the critical implications of the conflicting theories C and D in a third, neutral (auxiliary, common-or-garden or theoretically impoverished) language or (iii) to point to, or actually produce, the object of reference, or some causal index of it, via a pro-cedure which does not prejudge the issue between the theories.[124]

3. The typically three-valued logic of scientific discourse,[125] viz. true/false/undecided; yes/no/maybe: positive/negative/ neutral, highlights the importance of indecision or suspension of commitment as a logical mode. This should not be confused with either psychological ambivalence or ontological indeterminacy. The hypothetical stance to a proposition, theory, etc., or the interrogative attitude to a natural structure, tendency, etc., are temporal pre-requisites for the identification of phenomena, the determination of truth values and the development of theories (e.g. in the exploitation of the neutral analogy of a paramorph).

4. Needless to say, all commitment is revocable. And the quasi-autopoietic conception of scientific activity, sketched in section 5, implies that science is a continuous process of pro-duction, dependent on the imaginative and disciplined research (productive) and educational (reproductive) transformative

---

124. Cf. T. Benton, *Philosophical Foundations of the Three Sociologies*, London 1977, p. 197. It is an (intellectualist) error to suppose that grounded choice between theoretical schemes necessarily presupposes understanding them. On the contrary, while a striking explanatory, instru-mental or political success for a theory may provide a contingently necessary motive for the effort to understand it; more usually a (ground-able) choice has to be made without the time, need or facilities (resources) to do so. Thus consider, for example, the generic disposition of con-temporary agents to accept the cognitive authority of modern science (rather than, e.g., religion or magic).

125. See, e.g., S. Körner, *Experience and Theory*, London 1966.

activity of (wo)men. It is a great merit of Lakatos's philosophy of science to have stressed the *continuity* of the transitive process of scientific development. But, because he never broke from empirical realism or explicitly thematised ontology, he was unable to sustain the other indispensable parameter for a rational account of it — the notion of intransitive *ontological depth* (see page 65 above). And without such a notion, the methodology of scientific research programmes is entirely at the mercy of two modalities of scepticism — a primary ontological and a secondary, and distinct, epistemological form. Working within a fallibilist framework, Lakatos saw that the basic Popperian model, constructed around the notion of a dyadic confrontation between conjectured theory and refuting (or corroborating) fact, could account for neither the complexities of actual history nor the genesis, persistence and development of particular research lines. Reformulating the problem of rational choice as tantamount to the problem of allocating scientific labour time, distributing research funds, accepting papers for publication, etc., Lakatos argued that the dynamic profile of a sequence of theories in a research programme is, or should be, a major consideration in such decisions. A preferable cognitive project will then be one which is not only capable of explaining as much as, and then some more than, its rivals (as in L), but will be progressive in time in the sense of continually generating corroborated excess empirical content (anticipating novel facts), and open-ended.

Now, obviously from a Lakatosian standpoint the decisive factor here should be the dynamic or *future potential* of theories, not their *past performance*. But, equally obviously, any such judgement must be made at some particular time, and we know that the event-sequential past will not always be a reliable guide to the future (any more than it has always, or even typically, been so in the past). Thus the sequence $Tc_i \ldots Tc_n$ may stagnate, even deteriorate, over $t_1 \ldots t_j$, but flourish and soar triumphantly over the (now degenerating) $Td_1 \ldots Td_n$ after tj. For, as Feyerabend has pointed out, Copernicus was in the tradition of the demented Pythagorian, Philolaos, not that of the great Aristotle and Ptolemy: 'the butterfly emerges when the caterpillar has reached its lowest stage of degeneration'.[126]

---

126. P.K. Feyerabend, *Against Method*, p. 183.

Lakatos's dynamic falliblism is thus vulnerable to two orders of inductive problem. For it is clear that, on the one hand, we must be able to project the past, as historically described by our theories, and constituting the existing stock of accumulated cognitive values, as the past *of* our future (Hume's original problem); and that, on the other, (assuming the uniformity of nature) we must be able to project the past dynamic profiles of programmes, describing their cognitive successes and failures and constituting the apparent measure of their comparative rates of accumulation (of cognitive values), as a reliable index of their future potential — i.e. we must be able to project our epistemic past as a past *for* a still-to-be-made future (Feyerabend's epistemological displacement of the original Humean problem).[127] In fact, the projection of undifferentiated instances is valid at neither level. But recognition of the stratification of nature, revealing invariance as a predicate of structures not events, resolves the primary sceptical problem. And recognition of the stratification of our knowledge of nature, necessitating the modification of a Lakatosian criteria by some qualifying clause such as Q (on page 59 above), allays the severity of the secondary problem. For once we are in possession of a good theory of electronic structure, we really need not dally with the theory of chemical bonding and valency,[128] just as once we know about atoms we do not need to overtax ourselves concerning the fine structures of tables and chairs. Science is, indeed, a continuous process; but it is a continuous process with a point: deepening knowledge of the ever deeper transfactually active mechanisms of nature. It is the dialectic of discovery and development, pivoting on the notion of ontological depth, which gives the transitive transformative process of science its rationale and supplies the most significant reference points for the development of any rational criteriology of scientific knowledge or praxiology of scientific work.

5. Hitherto I have argued that meaning-variance, including the possibility of some order of inc., gives no support to judgemental relativism, i.e. for rejecting the notion of the *possibility* of rational choice (in the IA), in accordance with a criterion

---

127. Cf. my 'Feyerabend and Bachelard', especially pp. 46-7.
128. Unless of course there are special reasons to think it important to elaborate a theory of it, distancing it from our knowledge of electronic structure. Such level retracing may sometimes be necessary.

such as L or better, L + Q. The logic of scientific explanation, plotted in section 5, gives, in as much as it is substantiated by detailed historiographical work, grounds for supposing some degree of the *actualisation*, i.e. the practical effectivity, of such criteria in the history of science. But is there any reason to suppose that the proponents of conflicting scientific theories, such as X and Y can (or perhaps even must) come to a *rational consensus* about their theories (as postulated in I-S or I-S' on page 75 above), a position which rationalistic philosophers have always wanted to maintain? Or must we conclude that the apparent realisation of reason in scientific history is a fortuitous coincidence of proof and persuasion, or in Robespierre's terms, 'of virtue and terror'? Or is some different kind of explanation in order?

I noted earlier that a groundable choice between two theories (and a fortiori a groundable agreement about them) does not necessarily presuppose (and may indeed often precede) understanding them (or both of them). But it is a clear presupposition of the idea of a rational consenus in I-S (and perhaps also implicit in L or L + Q) that bi-theoretic-linguality and/or mutual understanding on the part of X and Y should be possible. Now, once we accept both the possibility of meaning-variance, i.e. once we reject meaning-uniformity[129] and the intransitivity of meanings (as urged on page 72 above), then we must allow that a translation or interpretation of C by Y may be correct, even if it is unacceptable to X; or acceptable to X, even if it is incorrect.[130] A rational consensus evidently presupposes that translations of C by Y and of D by X should be both acceptable and broadly correct. Implicit in this condition is the quasi-reflexive requirement that X should correctly identify C

---

129. Total meaning-uniformity is only really plausible if one supposes a completely extensionalist theory of meaning plus a reductively truth-functional theory of theories; i.e. if meanings are effectively identified with the objects actually meant, and these objects are conceived as atomistic simples. But as a theory committed to total meaning-uniformity cannot even, as indicated on p. 53 footnote 90 above, cater for the simple case of a change of beliefs with unchanged meanings; and further, inasmuch as a contradiction implies any, and so every, statement whatsoever, such a theory cannot really be accorded serious consideration in post-Bachelardian and post-Popperian philosophy of science.

130. In general of course these are transcendental features of all speech acts which are intended to be both cognitive and communicative.

and Y correctly identify D. Corresponding to this quasi-reflexive requirement on the correct identification of meanings by the agents of the speech communities concerned, is a quasi-reflexive requirement on any consensus the agents establish, namely that it should be understood as such by the agents forming the consensus. This situates the more general possibility of two forms of consensually-oriented communicative (C.O.C.) failure (or more generally of speaker-hearer non-mutuality or misunderstanding). Primary C.O.C. failure consists in the failure to agree about something e. Secondary C.O.C. failure consists in the failure to agree about whether or not they agree about e. (Between primary and secondary C.O.C. failure, lies, as always in the case of any intransitive object, the possibility of mis-identification — thus one or other of the parties to the prospective consensus may not see that they disagree about e). A rational consensus (about meanings) between X and Y pre-supposes then: (1) descriptive-hermeneutic adequacy (correctnes); and (2) inter-locutionary acceptability (communi-cative success), jointly establishing the *reciprocity* of primary C.O.C. achievement; plus (3) consensual acknowledgement (or recognition), securing secondary C.O.C. achievement, so con-jointly establishing the *mutuality* of meaning, standardly pre-supposed in any living speech community. It is this mutuality which may (but need not) break down in meaning-variance. Its restoration, perhaps over the course of several generations, re-establishes *meaning-filiation.*

Thus let us suppose that a definite meaning-variation (whether of an inc. sort or not) exists between C and D. We cannot infer from this that X and Y will be able to (a) agree that C and D differ in meaning, or differ in meaning in the way that they do (they may seem variant to X but not Y, or Y but not X may misidentify the difference); (b) (i) agree about the domain over which their theories referentially overlap (e.g. (2)-(4) in diagram 1.3 on page 70 above) or whether their overlap clashes (3) or (ii) recognise this agreement and/or formulate or express it effectively bilinguistically; (c) agree about a mutually accept-able decision procedure, such as one based on L or L + Q, for testing and/or deciding between the theories; (d) agree upon the results, and/or their interpretation and significance, of such an arbitrating procedure. In short, the achievement of a rational consensus, which presupposes, but is not entailed by, the achievement of a consensus about meanings, even of a temporary and/or retrospective (backward-looking) kind, is often actually and always potentially problematic in the sciences.

In this respect, the position outlined here differs markedly from standard anti-incommensurabilist responses. These tend to gainsay the phenomena of conceptual diversity and change, and so obscure the problematicity of communicative and cognitive consensus, both within science and between cultures, as much as the superidealists, by hyperbole, unwittingly do. Thus the rationalist, by positing a fixed innate core of essentially human knowledge, the positivist, by invoking an allegedly infallible algorithm for uniquely fixing meanings and assessing beliefs, the conventionalist, by resting on the bedrock of established usage and the hermeneuticist, by appealing to the *de facto* successes of actual translations all revert to some species of epistemological fundamentalism — a position chronically antiquated by the actuality of scientific change. Nor can the scientistically-minded profess to settle the issue by protesting, in an undifferentiated way, the cognitive power of scientific theory without begging the question: *which* scientific theory? This is not to say, as we shall see in a moment, that such responses are entirely beside the point. But they need careful philosophical and historical elaboration, if they are not to insinuate an obscurantism as disenlightening as their superidealist foil. Thus whereas superidealists short-change meaning-filiation, positivists and rationalists, with their fixed procedures and universal essences, scorn meaning-variance, while the hermeneutic and conventionalist brigade, for their part, scout the intransitivity of meanings. As superidealists (such as Feyerabend and Kuhn, in their superidealist moods) tend to a judgemental relativism by implicitly reducing the composite reference (see page 72 above) to sense, their extensionalist (e.g. Davidsonian) opponents tend to restore an epistemic absolutism by reducing sense to the composite reference, thus yielding meaning-change as impossible, as the superidealists leave it unintelligible. In their turn, the intensionalist anti-incommensurabilists collapse the referent of a hermeneutic enquiry (the sense of a semantic community) to its sense for an interpreter, thereby effectively rendering the interpreted and interpreting meaning-frames indistinguishable (by the reduction of the former to the latter); so that what is a skilled, and only contingently successful (if and when, indeed, it is) achievement disappears in the very move designed to underwrite the necessity of its success.[131] It is as erroneous to suppose that hermeneutics automatically and correctly commensurates meanings, as it is to rely on a truth-functional, truth-conditional theory of meaning to secure uniform and naturalistically (ontically) defined meanings for the difficult and changing thought of science.

What makes the problems of meaning, and cognitive (which is also always practical), diversity and change and of the (formal) underdetermination of rational choice appear less pressing and to be so uniquely (if not painlessly) resolved, within the span of a generation or two, in the province of natural science and technology are: (1) the existence of a common world (ontological realism); (2) certain very general shared human interests in it, stemming from our nature as biologically constituted beings with a certain innate endowment, interests which always acquire their specificity in, and rarely manifest themselves save through, some or other historically determined social form; (3) the world-historical existence and spread of capitalism as the bearer (or carrier) of certain specific forms of natural science and technology; (4) the existence of a continuous scientific tradition incorporating a distinctively post-Galilean 'style of reason-

---

131. The hermeneuticist's argument is that no-one could ever actually be in the situation of being able to specify from within a particular cognitive milieu that some other cognitive set-up was inc., or even significantly meaning-variant, from it, without already having succeeded in effecting a translation of it (see e.g. H Putnam, *Reason Truth and History*, Cambridge 1981, p. 116). In fact, as I have already noted, one may have good grounds for supposing a wide variation in meaning without being able to specify what that variation is. (Translation is an achievement). The argument leapfrogs immediately from the existence of communicatively-oriented activity to that of meaning-mutuality, a jump whose ubiquity and ease the super-idealist can legitimately question. By failing to distinguish philosophical and scientific ontologies, an ID distinct from a TD (here in the shape of a hermeneutic variant of the epistemic fallacy, covering the collapse of the identity of meanings in the social world of a community to their [attempted] identification by an interpreter or translator), the internalist engenders a self-certifying solipsism, reverberating with the superidealist's self-specifying solipsism of the theoretical community and indued by the self-same mistake. But whereas Kuhn and Feyerabend commit the mistake unwittingly and externally, Putnam posits it as a methological point of order and commits it from within. The internalist is thus as incapable of seeing the problem as the superidealist is of becoming philosophically self-conscious about the contingently realised conditions for its solution.

ing',[132] oriented to augmenting explanatory power and characterised by a measure of consensus on the general character of
decision procedures (e.g. recourse to empirical, and wherever
possible experimental, test). It is (1) and (2) which jointly
facilitate the establishment of a '*bridgehead*'[133] between
cultures, composed mainly of beliefs about the everyday world,
geared largely to sustaining a viable mode of material human
being at the level of what Horton has called 'primary theory'[134];
and furnish the setting for the constitution, in a practical
mediation of meanings (in embodied and engaged dialogue) of
(sufficient elements of) a *mensurating material object language*,
a language in which Aristotle, Aquinas and Locke are naturally
at home and in which deictic, indexical and spatio-temporal
individuating expressions are strainlessly employed. This
language acts at once: (a) as a common or garden a-theoretic
intra-scientific auxiliary, in terms of which the conflicting
implications of synchronically inc. or widely meaning-divergent
theories can, in the last resort, be spelt out, in the event that the
scientific communities or generations are not sufficiently bi-
theoretically-lingual; (b) as a medium for the expression of
(always socialised but historically specific or transhistorically
generic) human needs, wants and interests, in terms of which
the explanatory power of modern natural science and the instrumental utility of science-based and/or characteristically capitalist technology can be motivated in comparison with alternative modes of cognition and appropriation of nature (the 'Big
Ditch' argument already mentioned[135]); and (c) as a means of
the initiation of the neophyte into the scientific mysteries and

---

132. I. Hacking, 'Language, Truth and Reason', *Rationality and Relativism*, ed.
    M. Hollis and S. Lukes.
133. M. Hollis, 'The Limits of Irrationality', *Rationality*, ed. B. Wilson, Oxford
    1970.
134. R. Horton, 'Tradition and Modernity Revisited', ed. M. Hollis and S.
    Lukes, *op. cit.*
135. See references page 19 footnote 39 above. Note C. Taylor's cautionary essay
    in the same volume reminding us that the Big Ditch (associated as it is with
    the peculiar capitalist form of modernity) had and has costs, and that, if we
    are disposed to forget it, science is not the only human value. I would add
    the thought that if, as I claimed earlier, capitalism is the world-historical
    bearer of natural science, in the contemporary world socialist thought and
    struggles, considered as the putative bearer of a possible social science, may
    now provide the more effective motivation for a scientific *natural* science.
    (In Angola, under Portuguese rule, it was the revolutionaries who became
    doctors.)

virtues, enabling agents everywhere to participate in its own esoteric rights and practices, including its apostasies, splits and schisms, under the sign of a supreme excellence: explanatory power. Note that the bridgehead enabling the identification of beliefs is not fixed; and primary theory is neither Russell's 'metaphysics of the stone age' nor a Strawsonian 'massive central core of human thinking which has no history'[136] — it is theory, and it changes more or less slowly under the impact of changes in secondary theory (including science) and the mode of organisation of social life and contact with other cultural orders. Note that it is because we are material beings, with a position in space and a point of view in time, that a material object language forms the only possible meta-language for science conceived as the study of the enduring and trans-factually efficacious mechanisms of nature. For our criteria for ascribing reality to things can ultimately only turn on their capacity to affect changes in changes in ... material things affecting material beings such as ourselves; that is, ultimately in virtue of *our* perception of *their* affects. [Cf Marx: 'to be sensuous is to suffer']. The humanity (and specific historicity) of our criteriology in science is the necessary complement of the transcendental reality (that is, the non-anthropocentricity but knowability) of our claims.

If epistemic relativity (diversity and change) presupposes (as I argued on page 51) ontological realism, judgemental rationality presupposes epistemic relativity, and especially historicity. This is so both in the constitutive respect that we can only know the world under particular, historically specific, descriptions and in the historical respect that questions of normativity, rationality and choice only arise within, and are unintelligble save in relation to, a changing historical environment. The questions: what should I believe?, how ought we to act?, what is to be done? (or the Cartesian, what, if anything, can I know?, plus the other members of the Kantian tetrarchy: what ought I to do?, what may I hope for?, and above all else, what is man?[137]) only make sense in the context of the emergence of historical alternatives. The great obelisks of philosophical thought (Plato, Descartes) themselves strikingly attest this phenomena. If it is true, as

---

136. P.F. Strawson, *Individuals*, London 1959, p. 10.
137. *Critique of Pure Reason*, A805/B833. (The fourth question is pronounced the key to the others only in the later *Logic*).

Kierkegaard said, that 'concepts like individuals, have their histories and are just as incapable of withstanding the ravages of time as individuals',[138] this itself is a profoundly historical thought, one unavailable to, say, Aquinas or even Aristotle or then again, Hume. At the same time, I want to argue that just as an ontological realism presupposes the possibility of epistemic relativity, epistemic relativity presupposes, through its commitment to ontological realism, the possibility of a historically situationally specific judgemental rationality. How? Recall the two essential theorems of the transcendental realist account of science, viz. (1) the social production of knowledge (TD continuity) and (2) the intransitive nature of its object (ID/TD difference); and set these in the context of (3), the dialectic of discovery and development as outlined in §5. We now have a picture of a traveller on a particular epistemic world-line, marshalling and transforming the historical materials and media at its disposal, aspiring to assess and express claims in the only way open to it, that is, using these historically generated, transmitted and transformable (so transient) materials and media, about how the world is, independently of these claims (and the materials and media and more generally the conditions that make these claims possible), in a continually iterative process of the identification, description, explanation and redescription of deeper strata of reality. In the ongoing process of science, as deeper levels and wider shores of reality come to be known and reknown, historically *situated subjects* make *ontic* (being-expressive) *claims* about a reality which transcends their situation, in a dialectic which affords *objective grounds* for their inevitably *local choices*.

Let us take provisional stock. I have attempted to show that although the anti-monistic and anti-deductivist schools *promote* the ideas of scientific change (historicity) and discontinuity and structure respectively they cannot, for the most part, sustain their intelligibility or reveal their rationale; i.e. they cannot

---

138. S. Kierkegaard. *The Concept of Irony*, London 1966, Introduction §2. Once the implications of historicity are accepted then it becomes clear that, as Toulmin has put it, expressing exactly the standpoint espoused here, 'a man demonstrates his rationality not by a commitment to fixed ideas, stereotyped procedures or immutable concepts, but by the manner in which, and the occasions on which, he changes these ideas, procedures and concepts', S. Toulmin, *Human Understanding Vol. 1*, p. vi.

successfully *assimilate* these phenomena. Moreover, although both schools are responsible for major insights, unless they are taken together and given a new ontology, they fall into familiar aporetic minefields. Thus the anti-monistic tendency does not resolve but merely epistemologiclly generalises and displaces the Humean ontological problem of induction; while the anti-deductivists do not overcome the difficulties surrounding the Kantian thing-in-itself or synthetic a priori, but merely repeat them, albeit in an historicised and displaced (and partially — 'vertically' — realised) form. I have argued with Kant against Hume that necessity and universality are properly applied in our ascriptions of laws to nature; but against Kant that the ground for such ascriptions lie in the enduring mechanisms of nature, not the synthesising activity of man. For such ascriptions to be possible three transcendental conditions must be satisfied: the world must be composed of mechanisms existing and acting independently of (wo)men; knowledge of them must be pro- duced in the social activity of science; and human beings must be free in the specific sense of being able to act according to a plan, e.g. in the experimental testing of a scientific hypothesis and to come to reasonable decisions, e.g. about its likelihood.

## 7. First Steps Towards the Metacritique of Irrealism

In §§4-6, I ventured transcendental analyses of scientific experiment and stratification, the premises of classical (including positivistic) empiricism and of anti-deductivist neo-Kantianism, and of scientific discontinuity and change, the premises of anti-monistic (including quasi-and/or neo-rationalist) neo-Kantianism and super-idealism (which sponsors in particular incommensurable conceptual switches and situ- ations), obtaining immanent refutations of empirical and sub- jective conceptual realist ontologies and epistemologies of science. I pass now, in partial anticipation of the more detailed discussion in Chapter 3, to the metaphysics $\alpha$ of the tran- scendentally refuted positions or conceptual forms (metaphysics $\alpha$ ($\beta$ ($\alpha$)) in the nomenclature of §3); that is, to a consideration of the meta-conceptual transcendental question as to what *their* necessary conditions or presuppositions are, in what I earlier characterised as the metacritical dimension of the philosophy of science — which includes, it will be remembered, the historical sociology as well as the philosophy of the philosophy of science.

In §4, I argued that constant conjunctions are not in general spontaneously available in nature, but rather need to be worked for in the laboratories of science; so that causal laws, together with the other objects in the lexicon of scientific investigation, must, if that investigative activity is to be rendered intelligible, be regarded as ontologically irreducible to the patterns of events and the activities of human beings alike. And in §5 I argued that, conversely, if *inter alia*, scientific discovery and development is to be possible, the concepts and descriptions under which we bring such objects must be comprehended as part of the irreducibly social process of science. Thus experiences and the facts that they ground, and the constant conjunctions that form the empirical grounds for causal laws, are social products. But the objects to which they afford us access, such as causal laws, exist and act quite independently of (wo)men.

Now, empiricism can sustain neither the idea of an independent reality, nor that of a socially-produced science. Rather, what happens is in a way quite extraordinary. These ideas become, as it were, *crossed,* in a momentous exchange, so that a *naturalised science* comes to be purchased at the price of a *humanised nature*, as the concept of the *empirical world* finds its counterpart and condition in a *reified* account of science. For the necessary dual of the anthropocentricity implicit in the empirical realist analysis of laws, is the denegation of the conscious human transformative activity or praxis required for our knowledge of them. Thus the Humean theory depends (at the level at which the distinction between the domains of the real and the actual becomes relevant) upon a view of conjunctions existing quite independently of the human activity necessary for them, and hence upon the *fetishism* of the systems within which the conjoined events occur. And it depends (at the level at which the distinction between the domains of the actual and the empirical becomes relevant) upon what is apprehended in immediate sense-experience as a fact constituting an atomistic event or state of affairs, existing quite independently of the human activity necessary for it; and hence upon the *reification* of atomised facts, apprehended by autonomised minds. When the conjuctions of such facts are reified and identified with causal laws, science becomes an epiphenomenon of nature. And so it comes about that, in the practico-intellectual grid within which philosophical ideas are produced, the man-dependence of knowledge (its social nature) and the activity-independence of the world (its transcendentally real character) are transformed, in the crucible of empirical realism, into the mandependence of the world (its empirical nature and the activity-independence of knowledge (its a-social character). In this equilibrating equation of mystification, categories are preserved and predicates exchanged: so that the sociality of knowledge and transcendental reality of the world separate out as the empirical world and human knowledge (i.e. knowledge as a purely individual attribute).

The consequences of this transubstantiation are striking. The positivistic concept of a fact as what is more or less immediately apprehended in sense-perception generates, as we shall see in Chapter 3, characteristic ideologies *for* and *of* science — the former rationalising the practice of what Kuhn has called 'normal science',[139] the latter secreting mystiques of common-sense and/or expertise. Similarly, reductively descriptivist, instrumentalist and fictionalist interpretations of theories, by reducing their ontological import to a given self-validating experience, serve to exempt our current claims to theoretical knowledge from criticism. More broadly, the Humean theory of causality, in as much as it presupposes a conception of the world as atomistic, closed and completely described, encourages the notion of the social world as unstructured (and so obvious), undifferentiated and unchanging, constituted by human atoms and their constant connections (or conventions). Earlier (page 39) I noted that two operations rivet the Humean or classical empiricist account of science, in relation to (or reaction against) which others, since then, have been very largely formed: a fusion of the world and experience, encapsulated in the doctrine of empirical realism (empiricist ontology); and a reduction of our knowledge to the level of experience which, as constitutive of the nature of reality itself, is held to be certain (reductionist epistemology). This fusion depends on the absence of the idea of scientific activity as work, or at least (when as, in transcendental idealism, intellectual work is accredited), as practical labour, in causal exchange with nature. In consequence, the empirical realist cannot see knowledge, or at least the achievement of a closure, as a transient social product. This isomor-

---

139. *The Structure of Scientific Revolutions*, Chapter II.

phising fusion of anthroporealism in its empiricist form thus establishes at once the *destratification* of being in ontology and the *dehistoricisation* of knowledge in epistemology. But underpinning the undifferentiated ontology of empirical realism is an individualist sociology, in which people are regarded as passively sensing (or else as conventionally deciding upon) given facts and their constant conjunctions, that is, as passive spectators, absorbers (and accumulators) of a given world rather than as active agents, always in debt to the past, in a complex and multi-faceted one. In the gensis of empirical realism, in the operation empiricist ontology ⇌ individualist sociology, it is sociology and the model of (implicity gendered) man at the centre of it, characterised by his essential epistemic predicate, knowledge, which calls the tune. For it is the need felt by the philosophy of science (and more generally, epistemology), conceiving its role as the guarantor of justified belief, rather than as the analyst of intelligble activities, for *certain foundations for knowledge*, which determines the atomicity of experiences and thence of their ontological counterparts. This in turn necessitates the constancy of their conjunctions and the closure of the systems within which the conjoined events occur. And an undifferentiated reality implies an unstratified one — and, if any knowledge is to be possible, an unchanging one too. So the world appears flat, fixed and fortuitous.[140]

If empirical realism presupposes reification and rationalises normal science, the superidealist ontology of subjective conceptual realism presupposes a voluntarism, in which theory is unconstrained by either nature or history, which readily lends itself to the rationalisation of so-called 'revolutionary science'. Of course, both ideologies possess a measure of practical adequacy, in that they accord with aspects of our spontaneous consciousness in science. Thus we do tend to read the world as if it were constituted by facts, rather than composed of particulars (and kinds); we do tend to see it under certain descriptions in everyday and epistemic perception; and in moments of creativity we experience ideas as coming unmade,

---

140. My argument against empirical realism is that this is precisely how science, in its experimental and theoretical labour, must *presuppose* the world *not* to be. Need I add that it is also precisely how science, in the fruits of that labour, *knows* the world *not to be*?

'out of the blue' or, as we say, in defiance of Kant's First Analogy, 'from nowhere'.

For its part, the rationalist ontology of objective conceptual realism involves *hypostatisation*, i.e. the illicit substantification of conceptual forms. As a general position it belongs to an historically eclipsed moment in our experience of science. We can no longer believe that the world is the work of reason or even that reason is at work in the world (that is, that it is there for us to discern, or perhaps for the sake of being discerned by us for it). Rather, since Darwin (and Feuerbach), instead of supposing that the world is the work of reason, we assume that reason is the work of the world; and we invoke natural adaptation, or alienation, or specific sets of socio-historical co-ordinates to account for the transcendentist illusions of rationality and of teleology (whether of a divinely, logically, historically or biologically based sort). But if rationalism is no longer intellectually credible as a general metaphysic, it may still possess force for us in the phenomenology of, or as a regulative ideal for, science. In the former respect it corresponds perhaps to the moment of *discovery*, the 'Eureka!' that every scientist knows; in the more absolutist forms of such experience the scientist may even come to feel him or herself a kind of conduit of being. As a regulative ideal, rationalism is captured best by Einstein's aphorism that 'God is sophisticated but not malicious'.

Intuitional realism belongs with a world seemingly even more lost, the world of *enchantment*, in which man is at home and one with nature. This world, if it ever really existed, has vanished in the wake of post-Galilean science, enlightenment culture, capitalist production, and modern technological forms. In the disenchanted world, nature appears *only* as an object to be probed and not also cultivated, to be seen but not listened to, a resource to be exploited yet not preserved, as the contradictory other and unremittingly hostile adversary of man,[141] at best to be tamed, dominated and used. And re-enchantment seems a romantic dream. But it may even so be a necessary one. Phenomenologically, it accords perhaps with the aesthetic pleasure in science that a beautiful theory, if true, affords us. Scientific elegance is often confused with simplicity. Truth in

---

141. Cf, e.g., R. Williams, *Problems in Materialism and Culture*, London 1980.

science is sometimes beautiful, but it is always profound.

Finally, to consider the case of the transcendent realist mode of irrealism, if this is combined, as it normally must be, with some or other species of anthroporealism, this may be regarded, in as much as it has a phenomenological counterpart, as corresponding to our experience of the sublime, rather than the beautiful, to invoke the Kantian (more generally eighteenth century) contrast. And in particular to that moment in science in which we comprehend the awesome aspects of our ignorance; which is at the same time a recognition of our finitude, projected outwards and reflected back on to us.

In Chapter 3, where I essay a more thorough investigation of irrealism in its positivist and post-positivist modes, and elsewhere, where I examine the case of Hegelian absolute idealism in some depth and turn explicitly to the topic of materialism in its Marxist sense (that is, as opposed to 'idealism'),[142] we shall see that the varieties of realism are neither historically nor logically independent of one another, and that they repeat, reinforce and rescue one another in a plenitude of more and less subtle ways.

## 8. Some Implications of Realism

In the concluding section of this chapter I want to briefly indicate some of the consequences of adopting the new realist ontology and account of science. I suggest that transcendental realism is characterised by the absence of strain between philosophy and science, realism and relativism, relativity and rationality, science and freedom, the natural and the human sciences and the theory and practice of science, whereas these couples typically mark the site of tension, ambivalence or antinomy for irrealist theories.

By making the possibility of philosophical discourse contingent upon the historical actuality of social practices such as science, transcendental realism presents a way of integrating philosophical and sociological and historical studies of these

---

142. See my forthcoming *Dialectic and Materialism*, anticipated to an extent in my articles (see especially 'Dialectics', 'Knowledge, Theory of' and 'Materialism') in *A Dictionary of Marxist Thought*, ed. T. Bottomore et al, Oxford 1983.

practices. In particular there is now neither opposition nor any question of a unilinear reduction (such as in the positivistic or speculative illusions) between philosophy and science. Rather they infuse and are mutually susceptive to each other. On the conception set forth here philosophy is not something onto-logically unreal which somehow stands outside or dissociated from the realm of causal connections studied by science, escaping explanation by it; nor is it epistemologically sovereign, standing in a position of unqualified judgement upon it. Instead philosophy may be seen as a contingently emergent possibility of science, as science is ultimately a (more) contingently emergent possibility of being. (In the philosophy/science case, the intrinsic enabling conditions for the emergent features are present *ab initio.*)

Trancendental realism avers the non-identity of the objects of the transitive and intransitive dimensions, i.e. between thought (*qua* epistemic$_2$, transitive process) and things (*qua* ontic$_2$, intransitive objects of that transitive process). And it relegates the notion of a correspondence between them to the status of a metaphor for the goal of an adequating practice, in which cognitive matter is fashioned into a matching representation of a non-cognitive object. For transcendental realism ($\alpha$) there is no way of knowing the world except under particular more or less historically transient descriptions and ($\beta$) what is known exists and acts independently of those desciptions. Both ($\alpha$) and ($\beta$), epistemic relativity and ontological realism, must be accepted; and, as I argued in §5, they presuppose each other in science. If ($\alpha$) expresses the truth, ($\beta$) expresses the limitations of a histori-cal Kantianism. Together, ($\alpha$) and ($\beta$) capture the two aspects — epistemic and ontic — of what I shall call the '*duality of truth*'.

This duality turns on the condition that we must use human mediations in cognitive discourse to *express* extra-human states of affairs. In its epistemic aspect, the concept of truth is used in the context of reporting judgements, assigning values and expressing states of affairs; in its ontic aspect, it is used in the context of designating the states of affairs expressed and in virtue of which judgements are assigned the value 'true'. But the duality has an asymmetry or tilt to it, which stems from the fact that, rejecting both an immediate and an ultimate hypostatisation of truth, *truth* (unlike being per se) *is always tied to the possibility of language, theory and human practice.* However, within this trancendental horizon, truth effectively functions *bivocally* — to designate, on the one hand, claims, judgements and values (truth-claims, truth-judgements and truth-values) which are, or could be, made or avowed within social activity; and, on the other, conditions, states of affairs and what I earlier (page 72) termed composite referents (truth-conditions or more simply truths) which exist quite independently of us. (Thus, although truths are not things, laws, natural kinds, etc., it would be misleading to deny that the latter were, in some sense, truths.) Truth thus has a genuinely ontological and not just an (e.g. heuristic or regulative) ontogenetic use (i.e. circumscribed within the ambit of some determinate scientific investigation); but its ontological use depends upon the *possibility* of ontogeny (and hence human practice) in a way in which the concept of a natural law, for instance, does not. 'Truth' in its ontic aspect may be regarded as standing to, e.g., the concept of natural laws in roughly the way in which 'object of knowledge' (understood intransitively) stands to generative mechanism.[143] Indeed the duality of truth reflects the duality of the notion of an object of knowledge across the TD/ID divide. Philosophers have misinterpreted the duality of truth, flowing from the *being-expressive* (or representative) and assertoric character of cognitive discourse, with the idea of a relation of correspondence between constituents which are supposed to be at once substantive and separately identifiable in the cognitive moment itself. Expression (as representation or description) is not identity and only metaphorically correspondence. Speaking of 'expression' reminds us that there are different (and better and worse) ways of expressing something — i.e. it reminds us of the connections between ontological realism, epistemic relativity and judgemental rationality. And it reminds us that the expression can never be reduced (as in the ontic fallacy) to what it expresses and that what is expressed can never be reduced (as in the epistemic fallacy) to its expression. In this way the expressive theory of truth sustains the *duality* of the terms or poles of a categorial distinction in place of the *duplicity* implicit in the

---

143. That is to say, if we know that the world contains objects of knowledge and that those objects are generative mechanisms and so forth, we should speak of the world (to avoid residual anthropomorphism) as composed of generative mechanisms, rather than objects of knowledge, although these mechanisms are, as it so happens, also possible objects of knowledge for us.

ambivalence consequent upon the epistemological definition of being, and the concomitant ontologisation of knowledge characteristic of anthroporealism.

I have already argued against the notion that judgemental rationality and epistemic relativity are opposed, and against the characteristic reductionist fallacies here. I postpone further discussion of this now until after the fuller discussion of rationality in the next chapter.

Through the resolution of the problems generated by the notion of the contingency of the causal connection and the critique of the deductivist (and deterministic) theories generated by the notion of its actuality, the scene is set for a philosophy which will once more act as a Lockean underlabourer and occasional Leibnizian midwife to the various sciences.[144] On the new, integrative-pluralistic world-view which emerges, both nature and the sciences (and the sciences in nature) appear as stratified and differentiated, interconnected and developing. And the possibility now arises that the behaviour of higher-order (biological) entities, such as human beings, might be both explanatorily irreducible to (i.e. emergent from) and yet entirely consistent with lower-order physical laws.

It is clearly in the human sciences that the propaedeutic work of philosophy is most needed and likely to be most rewarding — if only by allowing a clearer contrast and fairer comparison to be drawn between the conditions and possibilities of the natural and human sciences. Thus the unavailability of spontaneously occuring, and the impossibility of experimentally establishing, closed systems means that criteria for the rational development and assessment of theories in the human sciences cannot be predictive and so must be explanatory. Again, as we shall see in the following chapter, the concept-, activity- and time-space-dependence of social forms means that any social science must incorporate a historically situated hermeneutics; while the condition that the social sciences are part of their own field of enquiry means that they must be self-reflexive, critical and totalising in a way in which the natural sciences typically are not. But there is neither antinomy nor unbridgeable chasm nor the possibility of mutual exclusion between the sciences of nature and of (wo)man.

---

144. See pp. 19-22 above.

But realism, of the sort adumbrated here, also has implications for the day-to-day practice of the natural sciences. For although my argument implies that scientists, when they are engaged in experimental or theoretical activity, are implicitly acting on transcendental realism, it does not imply that they realise that they are, or that transcendental realism is the only, or at any moment of time the dominant perspective informing their work. Of course the possibility of a realist description at any particular level or reach of reality may be bounded in practice by semi-permanent conceptual, technical or even socioeconomic problems, or by the domain assumptions of the particular science, or by the fact that reality is itself bounded for us there. These possibilities limit internal, but do not refute transcendental, realism. For this says nothing about how much there is to know, or how much of that can actually be known by existing men and women.

Three main positions characterise the history of philosophical reflection upon the sciences. For empiricism, the natural order is what is given in experience; for idealism, it is what we make or construct; for realism, it is recognised as a presupposition of our causal investigations of nature, but our knowledge of it is socially produced with the cognitive resources at our disposal, on the grounds of the effect of those investigations. For realism, it is the nature of the world that determines its cognitive possibilities for us; it is humankind that is the contingent phenomena in nature and human knowledge which is, on a cosmic scale, accidental. In science (wo)man comes to know (wo)man-independent nature, fallibly and variously. This cognitive relation is both the theme of philosophy and a topic for science. But only transcendental realism by setting (wo)man in nature is consistent with the historical emergence and the causal investigation of the sciences and philosophy themselves. Now any such investigation will already presuppose an intransitive (and so non-anthropocentric) ontology of transfactually potent and active structures. This ontology is realism. And it is a necessary condition of science. But it remains entirely open how far, in what forms and with what effects it will be realised in the laboratories and classrooms, journals and colloquia, seminars and contest-convers-ations of our actual, historically determinate sciences.

# 2

# Critical Naturalism and the Dialectic of Human Emancipation

*It is the mark of an educated mind to seek in each inquiry the sort of precision the nature of the subject permits.*[1]

In this chapter, I turn from the nature of science as such to the specific timbre of the social sciences. In it I want to consider the forms of explanation appropriate to their ontological circumstances; to outline a heuristic for the understanding of social phenomena; to calibrate the differentiae of the social, as distinct from the natural, sciences and the specificity, if any, of history; to gauge the applicability of evolutionary and functional concepts to human history and to assess the significance of the conceptualised and norm-imbued (norm-alised) character of social life. The resulting *critical naturalism*, which is grounded in the scientific realism advanced in chapter 1, permits a situation of conflicting schools in contemporary social thought; a generalised critique of fundamentalist 'First Philosophy'; a re-evaluation of the problem of the value and a reappraisal of the character of historical rationality. But my main concern is to relate this perspective to the organising theme of this inquiry: the nature of, and prospects for, human emancipation. My overall contention can be summarily stated. It is only if social

---

1.　Aristotle, *Nicomachean Ethics*, Book 1.1094b25.

phenomena are genuinely *emergent*[1a] that realist *explanations* in the human sciences are justified; and it is only if these conditions are satisfied that there is any possibility of human self-*emancipation* worthy of the name. But, conversely, emergent phenomena require realist explanations and realist explanations possess emancipatory implications. Emancipation depends upon explanation depends upon emergence. Given the phenomena of emergence, an emancipatory politics (or more generally transformative or therapeutic practice) depends upon a realist science. But, if and only if emergence is real, the development of both science and politics are up to us.[2] This chapter is intended then as a kind of abbreviated prolegomenon to a natural history of the human species.

## 1. Scientific Realism and the Emergence of the Social Order

*The fundamental methodological problem of any human science lies in the division [découpage] of the object of study ... Once this decision has been made and accepted, the results will be practicaly predictable.*[3]

Probably the most significant type of event in the history of any science is that in which it comes to define — or rather redefine — its object of enquiry. Normally such redefinition of *object-constitution* is bipolar in structure, reflecting the dual articulation of science (TD/ID), resulting in the reorganisation of knowledge, on the basis of some newly discovered feature of *being*, most characteristically the causal structure explaining the phenomena organising (or disorganising!) the previous level of inquiry. Typically this process will necessitate some scientists breaking free, perhaps under the stimulus of 'crisis', of the 'tissue of tenacious truisms' currently congealed in their field. Creatively exploiting their cognitive and technical legacy, they

---

1a.  In its most general sense, a property possessed by an entity at a certain level of organisation may be said to be emergent from some lower level insofar as it is not predictable from the properties found at that level. More specifically, I shall be arguing below that, although social phenomena are conditioned by and dependent upon and only materially manifest in natural phenomena, they are nevertheless not only taxonomically, but causally, and so ontologically (as well as epistemologically), irreducible to them.

2.  Cf. my 'Emergence, Explanation and Emancipation', *Explaining Human Behaviour*, ed. P. Secord, London 1982.

3.  L. Goldmann, *Marxism and the Human Sciences*, Paris 1970, p. 251.

may succeed in identifying a hitherto unknown kind of generative mechanism, so for the first time elucidating a pattern of determination already efficacious in the world. Such an achievement will often require a more or less drastic 'recasting' of their science, the transformation of their 'transmit', the very legacy they used: a scientific revolution.

Post-Humean philosophy, in virtue of its flat and uniform ontology, cannot think this process of object-constitution. This metaphysical failure reflects and reinforces a methodological one, as the human sciences appear, on empirical realist reconstructions, chronically beset by interconnected problems of definition, verification and application. Thus, on this ontology, undifferentiated events become the object of only conventionally differentiated sciences, every theory finds confirming and disconfirming instances with equal ease and there seems neither principled distinction nor non-arbitrary connection between pure and applied science (or, more generally, theory and practice). The ensuing crises of definitions and boundaries and problems of the criteria for the appraisal of theories and their imbrication with practice amount to the kenosis and draining of historical reason, reflected in the absence of a defensible organon for either social theory or political practice. Clearly if headway is to be made on the problem of object-constitution in the human sciences, we must start afresh on the basis of a new, non-empiricist ontology.[4]

As was seen in chapter 1.4, transcendental analysis of experi-

---

4. From this perspective, Smith's exchange-value/use-value distinction (at least on Marx's interpretation of it), Saussure's langue/parole distinction, Chomsky's competence/performance distinction — and perhaps Durkheimian facts, Paretian residues and Weberian types (together with their respective contrasts) — may all be seen as so many attempts at '*découpage*': that is, to conceptualise in opposition to the empirical *melange*, a non-empirical but real (stratified) subject of enquiry, designating the proper focus of scientific thought. Outhwaite has usefully distinguished epistemic and ontological object-constitution in the human sciences (W. Outhwaite, *Concept Formation in Social Science*, London 1983, especially chapter 3). In my terminology, the former relates to the transitive and the latter to the intransitive dimensions. It is clear that epistemic constitution — the constitution in thought, of some appropriate object of knowledge, in the human sciences — must always be grounded in some conception of the constitution, in social reality, of the intransitive object of that knowledge; and that such a *découpage* will normally precede a '*coupure*' in the sense of Bachelard and Althusser.

mental and applied activity in the natural sciences shows that the objects of scientific investigation are structures, not events; and that such structures exist and act independently of the conditions of their identification, and in particular in open and closed systems alike. These structures are non-empirical but empirically identifiable, transfactually efficacious but only contingently manifest in particular outcomes and they form the real ground for causal laws. Moreover it follows from this analysis that the world, *as we historically know it* (i.e. under the descriptions in terms of which it is actually known to science), is characterised by situations of dual and multiple control and by the phenomenon of emergence.[5] On this conception, reality consists of partially interconnected hierarchies of levels, in which any element e at a level L is in principle subject to the possibilities of causal determination by and of higher-order, lower-order and extra-order (extraneous) effects, besides those defining it as an element of L (including those individuating it as an e).

Such an *integrative* or structured *pluralism*[6] (IP), which must also be seen dynamically, as a developing integrative pluralism (DIP), recognises both (α) *distinctions* and (β) *connections* between the various objects of scientific inquiry. In so doing, it differentiates itself from, on the one hand, ontological monism (or holism) and epistemological reductionism (e.g. physicalism, biologism, individualism) and, on the other, ontological (monadic) pluralism (or atomism) and epistemological meta-empiricism, 'separatism' or 'eclecticism'. Metaphilosophically, it dissociates itself from both Hegelian autonomy and Kantian system. Monism/holism spurns distinctions and is typical of positivistic philosophies of science. In the human sciences it readily lends itself to reification and more generally neglect of the subjective aspects of social life (including denial of the intrinsic aspect of consciousness). Pluralism/atomism scorns the possibility or significance of interconnections between the sciences and is characteristic of romantic and idealist philosophies. In the human sciences it encourages hypostatisation and more generally neglect of the interdependencies between, and in particular the material grounding of, the various facets of

5. See my *A Realist Theory of Science*, 2nd ed., Brighton 1978, especially chapter 2.5.

6. Cf M. Bunge, *Method, Model and Matter*, Dordrecht 1973, chapter 9.

human existence (including denial of the extrinsic aspect of consciousness), sometimes tending to a solipsistic repudiation of any alterity or other-being. Metaphysically, it is most importantly manifest in the varieties of post-Cartesian dualism and immaterialism (e.g. vitalism, Alexander's 'emergentism', Bergsonian 'intuitionism'), but epistemologically its result is an eclectic empiricism of effects. The most plausible form integrative pluralism takes in the human sciences is that of a *synchronic emergent powers materialism* (SEPM).[7]

## Scientific Explanation and 'The Concrete'

The impossibility of artificially procuring, and the nonexistence of spontaneously occurring, epistemically significant empirical invariances, and hence of closed systems in the human sciences, means that social phenomena always only happen in open systems. And it follows directly from this that:

(i)   Criteria for the assessment and development of theory in the human sciences cannot be predictive, and so must be exclusively *explanatory*; and,

(ii)  Social phenomena must be seen, in general, as the product of a multiplicity of causes, i.e. social events as '*conjunctures*' and social things as (metaphysically) '*compounds*'.

However these considerations do not *per se* imply any differentiation in the structure of human and natural scientific explanation. Thus if, as I argued in 1.5, to explain something is neither to deduce nor induce nor familiarise it, but paradigmatically to 'collect' it under a new scheme of concepts, designating the structures, agents or whatever producing it, both the characteristic modalities of explanation may apply equally well within the social sphere. Theoretical explanations typically assume, it will be recalled, an iteratively analogical-retroductive form, exemplifying the DREI (description, retroduction, elaboration-elimination, identification) pattern (identified on p. 68 above), in which antecedently available cognitive resources are used to make plausible models of the unknown mechanisms

---

7.   See my *The Possibility of Naturalism*, Brighton 1979, especially chapter 3.4.

generating identified patterns of phenomena, which are then empirically checked out and, if and when deemed adequate, in turn explained, in a continually unfolding dialectic of explanatory and taxonomic knowledge. Practical or applied explanations are standardly decompository-retrodictive, exemplifying the RRRE (resolution, redescription, retrodiction, elimination) pattern, in which antecedently validated knowledge is transfactually applied in the systematic reconstruction of the genesis of events, etc., as conjunctures, i.e. as the outcomes of a diversity of determinations, perhaps of radically different sorts. On the assumption, then, that there are structures producing social phenomena analogous to the causal mechanisms of nature, the openness of the systems within which such phenomena occur does not undermine the feasibility of either retroduction from manifest phenomena to generative structures or retrodiction from resolved components to antecedent causes, subject to the same (or similar) constraints of empirical adequacy, consistency, coherence, non-redundancy, relevance, etc. On this account, if social theory consists in the abduction of the abstract from the concrete (C-A), applied work characteristically depends upon the reverse movement (A-C), eventuating in the 'recovery' from the abstract of the concrete, now understood as the resultant of a manifold of abstractly apprehended, discovered, determinants.[8] Knowledge of structures and of their contingent modes of articulation in time would thus appear as distinct moments of scientific activity, in natural and social science alike. Transcendental realism divaricates itself sharply from idealism in comprehending the aim of the first, analogical-retroductive, movement as the apprehension (in thought and, if possible, experimental actuality) of a transfactually efficacious form of determination, co-generating the concrete; so that the 'abstract', though non-empirical, may nevertheless designate what is real.

It has, however, been plausibly claimed that (some) social objects are typically differentiated from natural objects, in that they are *internally complex*, *pre-interpreted* and *transient*, suggesting that we are dealing with sciences which are, at least in some measure, concrete (in the sense of Husserl), hermeneutical (in the sense of Dilthey) and historical (in the sense of Marx).

---

8. See, e.g., K. Marx, *Grundrisse*, Harmondsworth 1973, pp. 100-102 (cf. also D. Sayer, *Marx's Method*, Brighton 1979, Part II).

These characteristics would, if they could be substantiated, at once distance the human sciences from the abstract, objectivistic and nomological sciences of physics and chemistry and, together with the ineluctable openness of their subject matter, explain the total eclipse of the D-N model in the human sphere.[9]

To the extent that social phenomena are internally complex or *holistic*, the explanatory schemata just recapitulated require adjustment. I consider first a strong species of internal complexity. I shall call a combination of structures a '*system*' and a combination of aspects (or facets) of an event, etc. a '*nexus*' when the combination coheres as a whole in that:

(1) the form of the combination causally codetermines the elements; and
(2) the elements causally codetermine (mutually mediate or condition) each other, and so causally codetermine the form.

Diagrams 2.1 and 2.2 overleaf contrast the determination of events within a system and of features within a nexus with the normal open-systemic cases.

In Case II the mechanisms and in Case IV their effects are modified. Clearly both may hold simultaneously. In general the determination of events within a system will result in their constitution as a nexus. But the modulation of effects within a nexus may affect the modus operandi of the mechanisms themselves. In the strong forms specified by conditions (1) and (2), causal interdependency between structures presupposes *internal relations* between them. A relation between the structures or mechanisms $M_1RM_2$ is internal if and only if (which I shall henceforth abbreviate to 'iff') $M_1$ would not act in the way it characteristically does unless $M_2$ was so related to it; it is symmetrically internal if this condition also applies reciprocally in the case of $M_2RM_1$. Where thoroughgoing internal relationality prevails it is natural to think of the structures 'interpenetrating' and as comprising a '*totality*'. But causal structures may interact in a normic or a systematic way, without being internally related or satisfying the strong conditions (1) and (2). Accordingly

---

9.  Cf., e.g., A. Donegan, 'The Popper-Hempel Theory Reconsidered', *Philosophical Analysis and History*, ed. W. Dray, New York 1966.

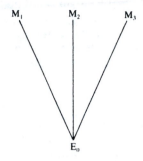

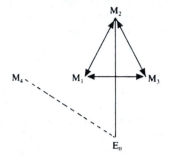

Case I: Determination of Events
in an Open System

Case II: Determination of Events
within a System in an Open System

Diagram 2.1

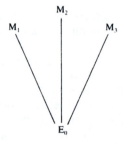

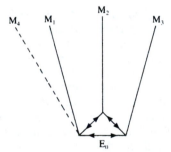

Case III: Multiple Determination
of Events

Case IV: Multiple Determination of
Events as a Nexus in an Open System

Diagram 2.2

systems can be bifurcated into two polar types: 'mechanical'
complexes of externally related interacting structures; and
'organic' totalities of internally related intra-acting ones. But
particular systems may contain both mechanical and organic
connections, and pairs of structures may be related in both
internal and external ways (as so indeed may their relations
too). So that even where structures cohere as a totality, this does

not mean that all causal interaction between them is internal, i.e. identity-affecting.[10] Pervasive internality in a system is compatible with differentiated, and highly specific, causal roles within it; so that existential parity is quite concordant with ontological differentiation and depth. Note, finally, that multilinear determination of events and things at the level of actualities, of $D_a$ in the terms of 1.4, (e.g. joint determination of phenomena by physical, biological, economic and cultural processes or structures) is consistent with a definite ordination in the stratification of being and becoming, including the possibility of unilinear (synchronic or diachronic) explanation of mechanisms and kinds at the level of the non-actual real, of $D_r$-$D_a$ in the terms of 1.4 (e.g. the one-way emergence of biological from physical matter, or, more controversially, determination of cultural by economic forms).

If (some of) the structures generating social phenomena combine in a system, then an abstraction may be found wanting either (i) if it fails to identify or correctly describe a necessary connection; or (ii) if it isolates a necessary connection from others (internally or externally) essential to its existence and functioning. And if (some) social systems are historically developing, then it is easy to appreciate how either kind of illicit abstraction, involving a destratification or detotalisation, may result in the spurious eternalisation of the present, the false universalisation of particular historically conditioned states. If the concrete is a 'condensate' of several necessities, the nature (or, under some descriptions, time) of that condensation is contingent, and can only be descried in particular instances by detailed empirical research.[11] However, in so far as the facts of the concrete episode etc. are qualitatively tempered by the character of the episode as a whole, the 'resolution' accomplished in a practical explanation cannot be a simple mechanical one. And to the extent that redescription of the facets is necessary, practical explanations may unearth new totalities in that sphere of social life. It is this possibility of discovering a

10. In general one can distinguish those tendencies of a tendency T of a kind K to affect or be affected by tendencies of the same or some other kind which are essential to its being the type of tendency it is from those which are not.

11. Cf. A. Sayer, 'Abstraction: A Realist Interpretation', *Radical Philosophy 28*, (1981), and *Method in Social Science*, London 1984, especially chapters 3 & 4.

new totality in a nexus which accounts for the 'configurational' quality of social forms.[12] But totalising 'outwards' from a particular feature is never just a matter of following up further connections; it is always potentially reciprocal, re-illuminating its point of origin. In the social realm, totalising is intrinsically bifocal, operating on two margins of spection: an *extensive* margin, on which ever wider swathes of reality are seen, centrifugally, to be implicated in some specific episode (or structural office); and an *intensive* margin in which the episode (or structural office) is seen, centripetally, to be ever more densely packed. Similarly it is the continuing unravelling of the possibilities of social objects over space and in time which demands the continual rewriting of their geo-histories. If the history of an object is literally 'finished' (as is patently not, at present, the case with Stone Age Man or Ancient Greece or Evans-Pritchard's Azande), then writing it no longer depends upon the mediation of times, but can take the bare form of chronicle.

In the human sciences, ranged between *abstract* sciences and the reconstructed concepts of concrete objects lie *intermediate* and *concrete* sciences. Concrete sciences (like biography) study the ensemble of epistemically significant truths about a given thing, especially as these are formed in the context of what it does and what happens to it. In such sciences the thing is treated as a virtually unique natural kind — as, in a word, an individual — within an empirically identifiable genus;[13] its truths are systematically connected up and synthesised into a structured order; and often presented in the form of a narrative of the story of the becoming and lapsing of that thing, and the waxing and waning of its effects and relations, in time. Intermediate sciences (like ecology) study the confluence or interaction of two or more orders or types of determination in a given kind of thing or system. Economics and linguistics are abstract sciences, social biology (abstract) and economic history (concrete) intermediate sciences, history and biography concrete sciences and revolutions, wars, plagues and people concrete phenomena. It is important to remember that in the social domain, abstract sciences always have a concrete 'mooring' — in history and geography, and in biography (individual and group) — which

---

12. N. Elias, 'The Sciences: Towards a Theory', *Social Processes of Scientific Development*, ed. R. Whitley, London 1971.
13. Cf. E. Husserl, *Logical Investigations Vol. 1*, London 1970, pp. 230-231.

must be understood as a condition for the application of any theoretical constructs. In the human realm, relations of causal priority do not reflect degrees of ontological independence. While there could be magnetic and gravitational fields without tables and chairs, there could not be modes of production or syntactic structures without people.

## The Human Sciences and the Natural Order

Integrative pluralism suggests that the objects of the human sciences are distinct (and perhaps emergent) from, but connected to, and in particular grounded in, nature. More especially, I am going to propose that they are taxonomically and causally *irreducible*, but *dependent*, modes of matter:

(i)     *Dependence* — the objects of the human sciences are unilaterally existentially dependent on those of the natural sciences;[14]

(ii)    *Taxonomic Irreducibility* — the natural sciences are *at present* unable to explain the human world under human descriptions;

(iii)  *Causal Irreducibility* — reference to properties *not* designated by physical theory is (apparently) necessary to explain some *physical* states (viz those resulting from intentional action).

On SEPM, human phenomena are consistent with, and constrained (but not exclusively determined) by, natural laws. SEPM does not require the postulation of any substance other than matter as the bearer of the putatively emergent powers, so that it is not dualist; and it is consistent with a diachronic explanatory reduction, i.e. a natural-historical explanation of the formation in time of the emergent powers, so that it is not preformationist or creationist, i.e. it is metaphysically Darwinian. It is vital to appreciate that only an emergent powers materialism is consistent with a realist interpretation of non-physical

---

14.  It follows from this that any social object presupposes the existence of some material thing, but not vice versa; any social change entails a natural change but not vice versa; and a social phenomenon may be realised in a diversity of modes (Cf H. Putnam, 'The Mental Life of Some Machines', *The Philosophy of Mind*, ed. J. Glover, Oxford 1976) but not necessarily not vice versa — iff emergent causality operates.

(psychological, sociological) explanations of human phenomena; and that a realist interpretation of *sui generis* sociological or psychological explanations of human phenomena is only justified if it can be shown that there are properties instantiated in the human world inexplicable in terms of different sets of conditions of purely natural laws. Ontologically speaking, we are confronted with a stark choice between reductionist physicalism and an emergent powers theory. Of course, explanatory realism might still be justified as a temporary (or indefinite) expedient, pending the prospective physicalistic reduction of the human sciences.[15] But this interpretation of social and psychological theory as 'elliptical' suffers from the embarrassments that ontologically, higher-order phenomena appear highly underdetermined under the appropriate lower-order descriptions, and epistemologically, any choice of higher-order theory seems arbitrary.

If, as Marx and Engels supposed, the unilateral ontological dependence of social upon natural phenomena warrants the assertion of some priority to our interactions with nature in the explanation of our social life, the nature of the grounding must, as will been seen later on, be made more precise than in slogans of the 'as man is only human, he must eat before he can think' genre.[16] All human phenomena have a natural manifestation. But it is clear that just as human beings are more immediately implicated in some segments of space-time than others, viz those that bear their causal mark, so nature is more centrally implicated in some (e.g. medical) than other (e.g. literary) practices; and that the effects of such transcategorial interactions are typically materialised in society as particular technical and cultural products.

---

15. Indeed, this seems to have been the official position of Freud and one phase in the thought of the early Marx. Freud's formal biologism is well-known but Marx's sport with the project of a unified science — 'natural science will in time subsume the science of man just as the science of man will subsume natural science: there will be *one* science' (*Economic and Philosophical Manuscripts* (1844), *Early Writings*, Harmondsworth 1973, p. 355) — is compatible with the notion of a two-way reconciliation or rapprochement between the epistemic orders, rather than a unilinear physicalistic reduction.

16. See A. Collier, 'Materialism and Explanation', *Issues in Marxist Philosophy Vol. 2*, eds. J. Mepham and D-H. Ruben, Brighton 1979, p. 44.

The study of such products, marking the confluence of heterogeneous orders of determination, belongs to linking intermediate sciences of technology, on the one hand, and social biology and social geography (or ecology) on the other.

If technology examines the way in which humanity may appropriate nature, social biology and geography scrutinise the way in which nature, so to speak, reappropriates humanity. Or we could say that whereas in technology nature provides the content for a social form, in social biology and geography, society supplies the content for an essentially natural form. See Table 2.1 below. If the causal intersection of the natural and social defines the practical order, then the relations between these intermediate sciences, concretely enacted in the drama of human history and geography, can be depicted as in Diagram 2.3 below. Note that whereas natural laws fix the boundary (and natural phenomena, the initial) conditions for the social natural sciences, such as social biology, it is economic (political, etc.) laws that set the boundary (and social phenomena, the initial) conditions for the natural social sciences, such as technology.

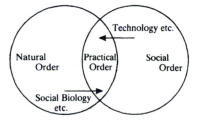

| Content | Form | Science |
|---------|------|---------|
| society | society | social science |
| society | nature | social biology, ecology |
| nature | society | technology |
| nature | nature | natural science |

Table 2.1                          Diagram 2.3

In principle, then, one can distinguish natural from mixed from social determinants of concrete human phenomena, as in Diagram 2.4 below, where the dotted line represents relations of continual constraint and conditioning and where one should imagine feedback loops from the effects $E_a$—$E_c$ back onto the state of the biosphere and so into the specific character of natural determination and conditioning at any moment of time. But it seems likely that the material causes of social phenomena

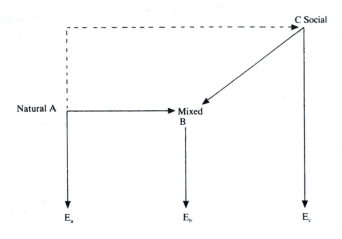

Diagram 2.4

(such as the forms of manifestation of eating, sexuality, ageing, illness or play) can rarely be explained in *wholly* physical or biological terms, so that in general one will be dealing with cases of B-type rather than A-type determination.

Indeed it can be argued that Timpanaro, in his welcome re-emphasis of the role of nature within historical materialism,[17] tends to systematically conflate the socially mediated effects of biological determinants with the determinants themselves, so reducing mixed to purely natural determinations.[18] In effect this drives Timpanaro back onto essentially Feuerbachian terrain, employing an abstract dehistoricised human condition in an unmediated explanatory capacity.[19]

17. S. Timpanaro, *On Materialism*, London 1975.
18. Cf. K. Soper, 'Marxism, Materialism and Biology', *Issues in Marxist Philosophy Vol. 2*, and *On Human Needs*, Brighton 1981.
19. Contrast Marx on the historically developed nature of needs: 'Hunger is hunger, but the hunger gratified with cooked meat eaten with a knife and fork is different from that which bolts down raw meat with the aid of hand and nail and tooth' (*Grundrisse*, p. 42); and of social forms generally: 'A negro is a negro. He only becomes a slave in certain relations. A cotton-spinning jenny is a machine for spinning cotton. It only becomes *capital* in certain relations. Torn from these relations it is no more capital than gold is itself *money* or sugar the price of sugar.' ('Wage Labour and Capital',

On the conception proposed here, social objects are the emergent powers and liabilities of natural ones, subject to continual conditioning and constraint by nature. In specific terms, the emergence of society is shown in the causal irreducibility of social forms in the genesis of human action (or being); and the emergence of mind in the causal irreducibility of beliefs in the explanation of those states of the physical world which are the outcome of intentional agency. The relation between these levels is in principle two-way. But the known effect of natural causes are normally mediated as cultural products (e.g. $E_b$ in Diagram 2.4), and the social effects of human actions in institutions. Whereas metaphysical monism, for example in positivism, has been prone to substitute natural (A-type) for social (C-type) determinations, metaphysical atomism, underlying most idealisms, has been wont to ignore any A-type determining, constraint or conditioning in the social sphere. Scientific realism holds of course that the exact forms of determination cannot be stipulated *a priori*, in advance of substantive natural-historical research. But the integrative pluralism it indicates situates a fuller matrix of possibilities than monism and atomism, accentuating in particular the possibility of mixed or B-type determinations, understood as a resultant of emergent and non-emergent natural structures.

Talk of emergence can easily become vague, if not indeed laced with idealist or romantic overtones. What is mandatory is the specification of precisely those properties of the allegedly emergent domain not explicable in terms of different sets of conditions of purely natural laws. This is the role of what I have termed the 'transformational model of social activity' (TMSA),[20] which I come on to shortly.

---

*Selected Works*, London 1968, p. 81). Could hunger exist for the human species, as naturally endowed, without any social relations? Or is the analogy between hunger and capital exact? Is natural man intrinsically social? Marx claims that 'only within these connections and relations does our action on nature, production, take place ' (*loc. cit.*). Should we add 'and reaction to nature', so affording equal status to our natural liabilities and powers?

20. See *The Possibility of Naturalism*, p. 43.

## 2. Critical Naturalism and the Transformational Model of Social Activity

In the seventeenth century a 'naturalist' was a 'natural philosopher' or 'scientist', i.e. someone who studied and described the causes of phenomena, including human behaviour and morals, without resort to supernatural (or transcendent) agencies. This usage continued into the nineteenth century, with special emphasis, after the Darwinian earthquake, on the explanation of biological, especially human, life as part of the natural order. The implied contrast throughout was with the 'supernatural' and 'supernaturalist'. Nowadays naturalism connotes three related views:

(a) The dependency of social, and more generally human, life upon nature, i.e. materialism (in at least one sense of that term);

(b) The susceptibility of social and natural phenomena to explanation in essentially the same way, i.e. 'scientifically'; and

(c) The cognate character of statements of facts and values, and in particular the absence of an unbridgeable logical gap between them of the kind maintained by Hume, Weber and Moore, i.e. ethical naturalism.

Sense (a) was broached in §1; sense (c) will be discussed in §6. My main concern here is with naturalism in sense (b). This has been the overriding issue of controversy in the philosophy and, to an extent, the practice of the human sciences. Naturalism in this second sense must be straightaway distinguished from two extreme species of it: scientism, which proclaims a complete unity of method, and reductionism, which asserts an actual identity of content (or subject matter) between the natural and the human sciences.

In addressing this issue, transcendental realism does not licence the simple-minded transapplication of results derived from reflection on the conditions of the natural sciences to the social sphere. Rather it is only in virtue of an *independent* analysis, such as will be aired in a moment, that a *paramorphic* relationship between the natural and the human sciences can be set up capable of vindicating the idea that there are (or at least may be) knowable structures at work in the human domain partly analogous but irreducible to (although dependent upon) those discovered in nature, whereupon the material causality of social forms and the efficient causality of beliefs emerge as conditions of intentional agency and discursive thought respectively. Thus any answer to the question 'how is a scientific sociology (etc.), if it is, possible?' will unfurl in at least two stages: (1) an independent derivation of an adequate account of science, based on an accepted and acceptable paradigm; and (2) an independent analysis of the subject matter of the social (psychological, etc.) sciences designed to ascertain the extent to which social (etc.) knowledge can (and if it can, actually does) fall under the generic, or at least paradigm-based, account of science. Such a double-barrelled procedure is essential if we are to avoid the pitfalls of normative methodologism, the external application of a philosophy of natural science, which begs the question (historically posed by anti-naturalists) of the comparability of the two domains; and of meta-sociological empiricism, the naive description of existing social scientific practices, which evades the issue (historically posed by their critics) of their epistemic worth, i.e. their right to the title 'science'. Stage (1) has been conducted in chapter 1 on the basis of analysis of classical physics and chemistry. Why take these sciences as paradigms? Because they form the explicit or implicit contrast which underlies most discussions of the 'scientificity' of the human sciences. But in principle this is only the beginning. For in any fully comprehensive investigation of the epistemic conditions and possibilities of the human sciences, one would undertake comparative exercises with a whole compendium of sciences[21] (and non-sciences such as drama, fiction and art generally), which should then cross-confirm, modify, enrich or amend the results achieved in (1), in a process which would be reciprocal as well as iterative, potentially entraining adjustments in the account (or acceptability) of the initial paradigm. In §3 I shall explore some analogies and disanalogies with evolutionary biology, before proceeding in §4 to a discussion of the specificity of human history.

In the history of the naturalist dispute three broad positions

21. Cf. T. Benton, 'Realism and Social Science', *Radical Philosophy* 27, (1981).

can be delineated: a more or less unqualified naturalism, usually *positivistic* in complexion; an anti-naturalism, erected on a distinctive notion of social reality as pre-interpreted, conceptual or linguistic in character, normally *hermeneutical* in inspiration; and a qualified and *critical naturalism*, grounded in an essentially realist theory of science and a transformational conception of social activity. The positivist tradition is based squarely on the Humean account of causal laws and the deductivist or Popper-Hempel theory of explanation, criticised in Chapter 1.4-1.5, but its roots lie in the neo-Platonism of the late Renaissance. Its maestro is of course Durkheim, but it finds sociological expression generally in behaviourist, functionalist and structuralist thought. The principal harbingers of the hermeneutical tradition are Vico, Herder and Schleiermacher, but its proximate philosophical ancestry is traceable through the work of Weber, Dilthey, Simmel and Rickert to a neo-Fichtean fusion of Kantian dichotomies and Hegelian identities so as to produce a contrasting diptych of the phenomenal world of science and the intelligible world of freedom, grounding distinctions between causal explanation (*Erklären*) and interpretative understanding (*Verstehen*), the nomothetic and the idiographic, the repeatable and the unique, the realms of physics and of history. Its virtuoso is of course Weber, but it infuses phenomenological, ethnomethodological and interpretative sociologies generally. Within this second camp one can discriminate *neo-Kantians*, such as Weber or Habermas, who seek to combine or synthesize positivist and hermeneutical principles, and dualists, such as Gadamer or Winch, who would deny positivism any sway in human affairs. The comet of the third tradition is of course Marx. But Marx is foreshadowed by the realists of the Scottish Enlightenment[22] and, in some measure, as he never ceased to acknowledge, by classical political economy generally. Moreover, the tradition cannot be simply empirically identified with the work of Marxists: it is indeed present there, normally imbued with elements drawn from one or both the other traditions; but it is also present in classical sociology, including the practice of both Durkheim and Weber, and in some recent

---

22. Cf. R. Keat and J. Urry, *Social Theory as Science*, London 1975, p. 97; and A. Swingewood, 'Comte, Marx and Political Economy', *Sociological Review* 18, (1970) p. 335-350.

social thought which seeks to blend the virtues of both structuralist and interpretative traditions in an historically informed and ecologically sensitive way.

Whereas positivists have normally been content to rest their case for their brand of naturalism on relatively *a priori* epistemological grounds, hermeneuticists have steeped their anti-naturalism in ontological considerations, typically the meaningful or rule-governed cut of social life. However, while positivists insist that hypotheses about such features must be subject to the standard operational protocols of any empirical inter-subjective science, hermeneuticists can tellingly score the complete absence of laws and explanations in the human sciences conforming to positivist lore. In defence, positivists are inclined to plead that the social world is much more complex than the natural world (*interactionism*, already anticipated by Mill) and/or that the empirical laws governing it can only be identified at some more basic, e.g. neurophysiological, level (*reductionism*, prefigured by Comte), thus generating familiar regresses in the drive for a more complete and/or atomistic state-description. Of course in as much as the principles — of empirical invariance and undifferentiated instance-confirmation (or -falsification) — underpinning positivism are inapplicable in the natural arena, as urged in Chapter 1, the general epistemological case for positivism collapses, and a special brief has to be mounted explaining why it should, most implausibly, be uniquely tenable in the human estate! On the other hand, the hermeneuticists' concern with intelligibility in explanation applies, properly circumscribed, equally to the natural sciences. At the same time, their ontological point concerning the pre-interpreted, linguistically mediated or conceptualised texture of social life can be accommodated without supposing that these interpretations are incorrigible, insusceptible to scientific explanation or exhaustive of the subject matter of the social sciences.

The aim of critical naturalism, then, is to vindicate naturalism, against hermeneutics, on the basis of a non-positivist, specifically realist, account of science. In as much as it is to be both formally adequate and practically convincing, it will take as its premises in any demonstration, features which are at once highlighted by anti-naturalists and reasonably compelling. A transcendental argument from intentional agency (a sound, yet anti-naturalistically acceptable, premise) implicit in both Marx and Durkheim,[23] establishes the relative autonomy, *sui generis* reality and temporal pre-existence of society, as its necessary means and medium. I turn now to elaborate the heuristic which this argument, which I have presented in some detail elsewhere, implies. In what follows I shall assume that social life is a causally and taxonomically irreducible but dependent mode of matter and that intentional agency pre-supposes the causal efficacy of reasons. These assumptions, again justified elsewhere,[24] are not formally necessary for the refutation of anti-naturalism, but they are indispensable for the development of a plausible realist alternative.

### On the Transformational Model of Social Activity

The T.M.S.A., which may be motivated either by transcendental argument from intentional agency or by immanent critique of the antinomies of social theory, may be regarded as an attempt to articulate the formal conditions for substantive object-constitution in the social sciences via a definition of what must be the case for a *sui generis* science of social objects to be possible. It has already been displayed at work in the shape of the quasi-autopoietic conception of scientific development spelt out in Chapter 1.5. The principal historical forebears of the model, as I understand it, are Aristotle and Marx. Its central features are the definition of human intentional agency as criterial for the social, as distinct from the purely natural sphere; and the characterisation of the onto-logical structure of human activity or praxis as essentially transformative or poietic, as consisting in the transformation of pre-given material (natural and social) causes by efficient (intentional) human agency. The criterion for differentiating the *social* from the purely *natural* material causes is given by their property that, although necessarily pre-given to any particular agent and a condition for every intentional act, they exist and persist only in virtue of human agency. If there are *social* explanations for social phenomena (i.e. if a social science of social forms is to be possible), then what is designated in such explanations, the social mechanisms and structures generating social phenomena, must be social products themselves; and so, like any other social

---

23. See, e.g., E. Durkheim, *Rules of Sociological Method*, New York, 1966.
24. See *The Possibility of Naturalism*, chapter 3.

object, they must be given to and reproduced in human agency. From this cardinal recursive property of the model, expressing the quasi-autopoietic feature that *society is itself a social product* and entailed by the possibility of any non-reductionist naturalism, flow a series of ontological differences from standard conceptions of physics and chemistry, or ontological limits on naturalism. The most important of these, which will be detailed below, are the activity-, concept-, time-space- and social-relation-dependence of social structures. But it is just in virtue, not in spite, of these emergent properties that a *sui generis* social science is indeed possible.[25]

Human activity, then, is dependent upon given materials (means, media, resources, rules), which it transforms. Praxis always involves a physical manifestation as well as an intentional aspect and the presence (or absence) of others, so that it is characteristically articulated both in the dimension of material (and symbolically mediated) transactions with nature and in the dimension of material and symbolically mediated interactions with others. Transformation is always situated in and stretches across space and time; and it is not of course limited to physical production or work on nature, but includes such modalities as the satisfaction of physical needs, communication of meanings, exercise of power, expression of self, etc. If society is the condition of our agency, human agency is equally a condition for society, which, in its continuity, it continually reproduces and transforms. On this model, then, society is at once the ever-present *condition* and the continually reproduced *outcome* of human agency: this is the duality of structure.[26] And human agency is both typically work (generically conceived), i.e. normally conscious production, and reproduction of the conditions of production, including society: this is the duality of praxis. Thus agents reproduce in their substantive motivated productions, the unmotivated conditions governing (and employed in) those productions, and society is both the unconscious medium and the unintended (and generally non-teleological) product of this activity. On the T.M.S.A., society and agents are *existentially interdependent* but *essentially*

25.   *Ibid.*, chapter 2.
26.   Cf. A. Giddens, *New Rules of Sociological Method*, London 1976, p. 121; and J. Lyons, *Chomsky*, London 1970, p. 22, Cf. also P, Bourdieu, *An Outline of a Theory of Practice*, Cambridge 1977.

*distinct.*[27] For while society exists only in virtue of human agency, and human agency (or being) always presupposes (and expresses) some or other definite social form, they cannot be reduced to or reconstructed from one another. Rather they mark the sites of potentially independent sciences, consistent with and conditioned by each other, but referring to different aspects of the same concrete flux of social life. The objects of these distinct (groups of) sciences cannot, of course, be actually isolated, so that there is no question of a predictive testing of the cognitive abstractions required to grasp them. The *social sciences* abstract from human agency to study the structure of reproduced outcomes, the enduring practices and their relations; the *social psychological* sciences abstract from these reproduced outcomes to focus on the rules governing the mobilisation of resources by agents in their interaction with one another and nature. If the sphere of the former is social structure, that of the latter is social (and socio-natural) interaction. They may be linked by the study of society as such, where society is conceived as the system of relations between the positions and practices (or positioned-practices) which agents reproduce or transform, the subject matter of the social science of *sociology.*[28]

Thus whereas the various special social sciences of social objects are concerned with the mechanisms generating particular (theoretically defined) kinds of social practices (whether these practices consist in the conscious following of rules or the unconscious enactment of effects), sociology itself must be conceived, in opposition to the prevalent individualist and collectivist conceptions, as engaged with the social relations within which any human action or social effect must occur. It is thus, understood as an historically specific, regionalised and totalizing science, presupposed in any concrete social or psychological explanation. But just as it would be a mistake to take sociology as the study of the social simpliciter, so it is a mistake to see psy-

---

27. See A. Collier, op. cit. p. 37; P. Manicas 'The Concept of Social Structure', *Journal for the Theory of Social Behaviour* 10(2), 1980; and P. Manicas and P. Secord, 'Implications for Psychology of the New Philosophy of Science', *American Psychologist,* 1983.
28. Cf Marx: 'Society does not consist of individuals, but expresses the sum of interrelations, the relations within which the individuals stand' (*Grundrisse,* p. 265).

chology as the study of the concrete acting self. For, on the one hand, the individual comprises bodily as well as mental processes, and is constituted in part by his or her social relations and the skills and resources available to him or her; and, on the other, there is a need for general theories of psychological phenomena, including the ways in which individuality is experienced and expressed. It follows from this that although the general form of psychological (i.e. mental) phenomena and processes may be universal or species-general, their specific contents (their, as it were, semantics rather than syntax) will be intrinsically social and historically specific, in so far as they are acquired, maintained and transformed in the course of social life. Thus intermediate historically specific sciences of social psychology will always be required to identify the conditions for the applicability of psychological (including psychoanalytical) theories to particular situations.

The T.M.S.A. allows the isolation of a triple set of twinned mistakes: the ontological errors of voluntarism and reification, the constitutive ones of individualism and collectivism and the epistemic ones of methodological individualism and social determinism. Although notionally opposed, the terms of these couples may be formally combined in various pseudo-dialectical hybrids, and in practice they often tacitly presuppose one another. The transformational conception also enables the situation of the closely affiliated weaknesses of the various schools of action-oriented and interpretative sociology, on the one hand, and of structuralist and functionalist thought, on the other. Thus whereas in action-centred sociology (as represented by the diverse utilitarian, Weberian and phenomenological traditions) social objects tend to be seen as a result of or as constituted by intentional or meaningful, essentially individual, human behaviour; in form-centred sociology (as represented by the diverse romantic-organicist, Durkheimian and structuralist traditions) social objects are prone to be seen as possessing a life of their own, as collectives, external to and coercing the individual. On the T.M.S.A., society is not the creation of unconditional human agency, but neither does it exist independently of it; and individual agents neither completely determine, nor are completely determined by, social forms.

The existential interdependence of society and individuals, duality of structure and praxis and dynamic profile of the T.M.S.A. are represented in Diagrams 2.5-2.7 overleaf. On this model, unintended consequences [cf. (1)] and unacknowledged conditions [cf (2)] may limit the actors understanding of their social world, while unacknowledged (unconscious) motivation [cf (3)] and tacit skills [cf (4)] may limit his or her understanding of him or herself. Corresponding to each of these cognitive limits, human scientific knowledge promises a distinct emancipatory benefit — at (2) and (3) via the social and psychological conditions, and at (1) and (4) via the effects and

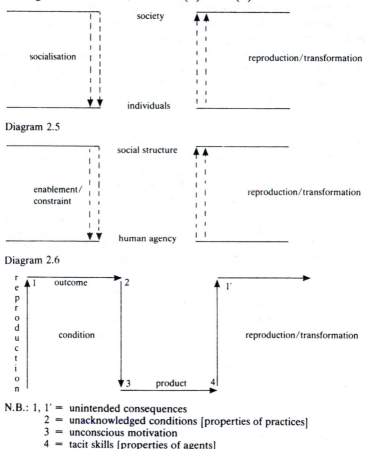

Diagram 2.5

Diagram 2.6

N.B.: 1, 1′ = unintended consequences
     2 = unacknowledged conditions [properties of practices]
     3 = unconscious motivation
     4 = tacit skills [properties of agents]

Diagram 2.7: *The Transformational Model of Social Activity* forms, of praxis, identifying opaque social structures and hidden motivational springs, and disclosing counterfinality and latent or unrecognised powers, etc. (1)-(4) may also be viewed as indicating the foci of the depth social, social praxiological (including phenomenological and ecological), depth psychological and social psychological or poiesiological (including the developmental, ethogenic and technological) group of social sciences respectively.

The continuity, depth and reflexivity of human agency prompt the model of it presented in Diagram 2.8 overleaf.[29] Discursivity presupposes a distinction between real and possible, including ratiocinated, reasons, grounded in the causal efficacy of the former. Where $R_m \neq R_r$ there is the possibility of rationalisation Real reasons are the wants that prompt motivation and, *ceteris paribus*, issue in action.[30] As such they may be regarded as efficacious and effective beliefs, which may be conscious or unconscious, trained on objects of desire, and composing a cognitive-conative-affective vector or perhaps better ensemble (see Diagram 2.9 below). It should be underlined that what is reproduced or transformed in praxis is not just discursive, practical and expressive consciousness, but *sentiment*,[31] comprising, one might say, the form, content, style and *mood* of social being respectively.

In social phenomenology, unintended consequences may take the well-known forms of counterfinality and suboptimality (e.g. in a prisoner's dilemma).[32] The conditions figuring on the left hand side of Diagram 2.8 include the rules and resources agents command in such games. Like all such conditions, they may be unmotivated and unacknowledged. These are properties which a general social phenomenology, whether rational or empirical, cannot itself, without vicious circularity, explain. For such rules and resources are at once historical deposits, and so

---

29. Based on one proposed by A. Giddens, *Central Problems of Social Theory*, London 1979, p. 56.
30. See *The Possibility of Naturalism*, pp. 121-123.
31. Cf. R. Williams' 'structures of feeling' (See R. Williams, *Marxism and Literature*, Oxford 1977, Part 2, chapter 9 and *Politics and Letters*, London 1978, especially pp. 180ff.) Both philosophers and sociologists have been liable to depreciate the significance of the affective domain of 'feelings, meanings and memories' in social life in favour of the (more macho?) cognitive and/or conative realms.
32. See e.g. J. Elster, *Logic and Society*, Chichester 1978, chapter 5 and E. Ullmann-Margalit, *The Emergence of Norms*, Oxford 1977.

always given; and historical reproducts (or transforms), and so always subject to a potentially unrecognised possibility of supercession. The games of the *Lebenswelt* (life-world) are always initiated, conditioned and closed outside the life-world itself.

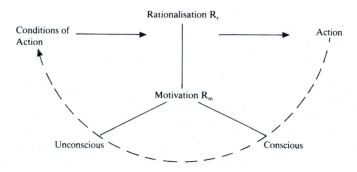

Diagram 2.8: *The Stratification of Action*

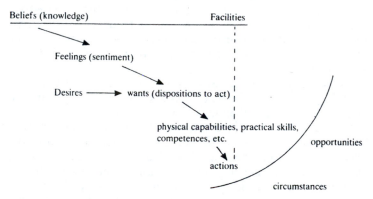

Diagram 2.9: *Beliefs, Wants, Abilities and Action*

The connections between social structures, social relations, human agency or practice and its material content, can be schematically depicted as in Diagram 2.10 on p. 130. This shows praxis, which always occurs at places in time, and its effects, characteristically arrayed in the dimensions of interactions between agents (and groups) and of transactions between agents (and groups) and nature. The second category may be extended to encompass transactions with all non-human things, so including inter alia other sentient animals and socialised physical objects (computers, machines, mines). It is important to remember that the top of the diagram is a (transcendentally and causally) necessary condition of the bottom. Human agency on this conception is an analytically mixed mode, akin to a B-type determination (in the sense of p. 116 above), moored *socially* in a complex of social relations and *physically* at determinate locations in space and time. 'Socialisation', the vital connector between the human being and the agency which reproduces or transforms the social structure, is of course itself a social process in which individuals acquire, mature (grow), develop and mobilise the skills (competences) which they utilise or exercise in their everyday productions (performances). But the continuity of human praxis in an ongoing social activity through a potential plurality of agents must not be confused with the continuity of the praxis of some particular agent through a potential plurality of activities. Both alike depend upon the interaction of individual life-paths and institutional projects, the junction of individual biographies and social histories[33] — intersections and junctions which are the very conditions of the being of the terms they intersect and conjoin.

'Society' itself may be conceived in a number of ways: as (i) the totality of social forms; or, more narrowly, (ii) the totality of social structures or generative mechanisms; or, more narrowly still, (as above) (iii) the totality of human relations within which praxis occurs; as well as in some more theoretically precisely specified manner. A 'practice' cannot be identified either with a 'structure' or with the 'agency' which reproduces or transforms it; it is rather, as it were, the structure at work in praxis — or, to employ a Kantian analogy, the schema· of the structure. Practices are the conveyors of history, but their individuation and articulation raises complex questions which will be considered in §4.

## The Specificity of Social Science

As already mentioned, the activity-, concept-, time-space and social-relation-dependence of social structures can be imme-

---

33. Cf A. Pred, 'Structuration and Place', *Journal for the Theory of Social Behaviour 13(1)*, 1983.

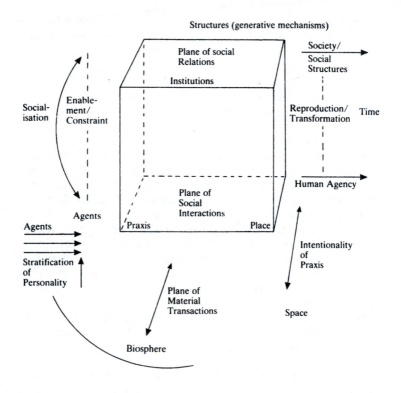

Diagram 2.10: *The Social Cube in a Natural Setting*

diately derived from the T.M.S.A., as four major *ontological* limits on naturalism. As follows:-

(1) *activity-dependence* — Social structures exist only in virtue of the activities they govern, enable and constrain.
(2) *concept-dependence* — Activity is intentional only in so far as it is informed (co-caused) by an agent's beliefs. Hence social activities, and thus structures, are concept-dependent.
(3) *time-space-dependence* — Social activity occurs at a place and takes time, the place and time of the agent; so that it is 'earthed' in the geodesic of the biosphere. Reproduction

of the structures necessary for such activity occurs only in it[34] and so social reproduction stretches over space and time. Social structures, being themselves social products dependent upon social activity, are liable to social transformation (and not merely reproduction) across timespace, that is, in world history. Hence they may (and perhaps normally will) be spacio-temporarily restricted in range, i.e. geo-historically transient.

(4) *social-relation-dependence* — Characteristically, social activity occurs when agents occupy positions and engage in practices effectively given to them, which they reproduce or transform. The network of relations between such positioned-practices is itself a social structure reproduced or transformed in agency. But defining the point of articulation of structure and praxis (the dual point), it is a condition for every other practice dependent upon its specific articulation. And since all social reproduction and transformation is dependent upon some such articulation (or its absence), a structure of social relations is both necessary for every other social structure and a condition for the identity of any social form.

Besides these cardinal limits, three other ontological differentiae are important: the relational, internally complex and interdependent inscape of social structures.

(5) *relationality* — social structures are materially present only in persons and the results of their actions. The *identity* of social effects (the ultimate explananda of social science) depends upon their constitution in and by systems of (conceptualised or conceptualisable) *difference*, their 'meaning', so that social effects are intrinsically relational or relation-dependent in form. This must not be confused

---

34. More precisely, it occurs only in virtue of the reproduction of the social possibility or power, in social activity, of the physical bearer of, or some physical basis for, the social structure or quality. Cf., e.g., information storage systems. Remember that the continuity of the physical basis of social properties takes in the commonplace 'discontinuous continuities' of contemporary theoretical physics and everyday technology — the continuities of fields, waves, pulses and jumps, as well as of lines, flows, solids and surfaces.

with the sense in which all phenomena, whether natural or social, depend for their *identification* upon semiosis; or the more specific sense in which social structures, and a fortiori social phenomena, are *social-relation-dependent* (just defined above). Are social structures, like their effects, intrinsically relational in physiognomy? There are two paradigms for the non-actual real, viz the powers of a particular or kind, and the relations between the elements of a system. But the consideration, implied by the T.M.S.A., that social structures are themselves social effects (reproducts/transforms) entails that they must be aligned under the second paradigm, save in respect of those properties where the system may be treated as a particular or which are essential to sociality as such.

(6) and (7)

   *internal complexity and interdependency* — Their importance stems from the relative 'richness' or 'modularity'[35] of structures and skills (competences) in comparison with events and acts (performances). But this excess of real possibilities over historical actualities is consequent upon any ontological stratification, is not special to the social domain, and does not *per se* carry holistic implications. What motivates the latter is rather the fact that social structures typically display far greater coherence than the processes which reproduce or transform them, suggesting internal complexity; and that they often disclose far less variance than one would expect *a priori*, suggesting inter-dependency or their binding as totalities. Of course the extent of such inter-dependency and the nature of any organising or binding principle or structure (such as 'man', 'mode of production', 'relations of production', 'social formation', 'state', *Volksgeist*, etc.), like the degree of internal complexity, are only determinable in the context of specific empirical inquiry.

It should be noted that ontological features (5)-(7) are not peculiar to the social field; nor is (3) unless taken as 'historicity' in conjunction with (1) and (2) (and (4)). (3) immediately situ-

---

35. See, e.g., N. Chomsky, *Rules and Representations*, Oxford 1980, pp. 40ff and *passim*.

ates a quasi-endogenous modality of change. It is the condition that social structures are social *products* that makes a *social* science possible; the condition that they are *structures* (non-actual but real; stratified) that makes a social *science* possible. The essential insight of the T.M.S.A. is that the social structure is neither foreign to nor something chosen by agents; rather it is what they reproduce or transform in the course of the more or less routine conduct of their everyday lives, as historically specific and axiologically necessary means and media. On the T.M.S.A., social life, in virtue of its recursive quality, possesses a fundamentally non-teleological dynamic, in as much as agents reproduce or transform, for the most part (but not necessarily[36]) in an unconscious and unmotivated way, the very structures which they must draw upon and utilise, and which they are constrained and frustrated by, in their substantive practical productive activities. And it enables us to accept both the 'objective' and 'subjective' aspects of social existence without illicitly conflating them.

In addition to the ontological limits of naturalism, there are three other major sorts of limit: epistemological, relational and critical. The most important *epistemological* limit, the ineradicably open calibre of social systems, accounts for the absence of (ontologically) crucial or decisive test situations, the breakdown of any significant explanatory/predictive symmetry and the need to rely on exclusively explanatory, non-predictive criteria for the rational assessment and development of theories in the social sciences. Because social structures are necessarily unperceivable ('present only in their effects'), empirical confirmation will always be indirect, i.e. via the detection of the effects of the structures. At the same time the recognition that the identification of social practices (activities and acts) depends upon the mediation of meanings requires an extended notion of the empirical.[37] A further extension of this (woefully under-

---

36. Rational political action becomes possible when agents become aware of the conditions of their routine practices and motivated actions.

37. In some respects it would be preferable to employ the notion of the '*a posteriori*' — for this takes in the essential point that the outcome of our inquiries in hermeneutic mediation and sense-perception alike are not already implied (though they will normally be limited) by hypotheses (theories, conceptual frames, etc.), while allowing us to forego the implication that understanding a sentence or an act is the same as or can be reduced to what it depends upon: viz sense-perception or observation. Contra J. Bennet (*Kant's Analytic*, Cambridge 1966, p. 213) 'what people

theorised) concept is called for to the extent that confirmation of theoretical constructs turns on such considerations as 'well-being' (health, or even the satisfaction of human needs).

The principal *relational* limit stems from the circumstance that social science, consisting of social beliefs, comprises part of its own field of inquiry. Metaphysically, this necessitates paying heed to the distinction between the *existential intransitivity* of the object (or ontic$_2$) of some particular transitive inquiry (or epistemic$_2$) and the potential *causal interdependency* between the processes of, and governing, the production and reproduction/transformation of social cognitions and their objects. The relational limit leads on, as we shall see in detail in §6, to the *critical* limits, presaging the collapse of the fact/value and theory/practice dichotomies. For the consideration that the subject matter of the social sciences includes not just social objects, including both beliefs and their social causes, but beliefs about those objects permits an explanatory critique of false (and other modes of inadequate) consciousness, and being, entailing judgements of value and action without parallel in the field of the natural sciences. The inference schemes indicated here vindicate a modified form of ethical naturalism — sense (c) on p. 118 above. But if social science is conceived in this way as essentially explanatory critique, it is imperative to understand such critique reflexively, non-voluntaristically and materialistically, i.e, as conditioned by human dependency on the natural order, i.e. naturalism in sense (a) on p. 118 above.

It is just because of these differences, constituting the cognitively significant features of the, so to speak, emergent or non-natural but causally efficacious 'surplus' (embedded within nature in socialised regions of space-time), which we nominate 'society', that a non-reductionist naturalism is feasible. Hence it is not despite, but on account of, them that the two characteristic modalities of scientific explanation which I adumbrated in 1.5 (and recapitulated in 2.1) still apply here, albeit in modified form. Thus the empirically-controlled retroduction of explanatory structures from (here, conceptualised) phenomena, and

---

say' is *not* 'just a special case of what objects do'. In Kantian terms, one could say that the 'forms of intuition' in observation and understanding are *qualitatively* different, although complementary and practically interdependent.

the synthetic reconstruction of networks of (here, internally related) transfactually efficacious causal structures at work in the production of events, etc. in conjunctures, are possible here in the social, as in the natural, world; but the social sciences will be historic, reflexive, critical and totalising in a way in which classicial physics and chemistry were not. On the critical naturalist approach, then, the social sciences can be sciences in exactly the same *sense* as the natural ones, but on the strict condition that they are science in *ways* as specific and different as their objects.

There are two further steps to take. As society is only manifest in (and exists only in virtue of) intentional agency, and intentional agency depends upon (or even just consists in) acting on beliefs, the argument must be completed by showing the causal irreducibility of beliefs (and of mental states generally) in the genesis of physical behaviour. And for this both (a) the causal efficacy (and so reality) of beliefs and (b) their irreducibility to purely physiological states must be established. Elsewhere I have argued apropos (a) that reasons must be causes if they are to discharge their explanatory burden and if the concept of agency is to be saved and for theoretical and practical discourse to be possible, which depend alike on a distinction between real, *qua* causally efficacious, and possible reasons; and that indeed intentional behaviour just is behaviour in so far as it is caused by reasons. Apropos (b), the synchronic emergent powers materialism (S.E.P.M.) I have advocated is in support of a conception of mind as a biologically emergent ensemble of powers of matter with irreducible explanatory principles of its own. S.E.P.M. is counterposed to reductionist physicalism (e.g. central state materialism) and behaviourism, which collapse those powers to their physical basis and exercise respectively, and to immaterialist dualism (or idealism) which hypostatise (or transcendentise) them.

For critical naturalism, then, social science takes the form of *conditioned critique*, incorporating a historically situated hermeneutics as premises for the empirically-controlled retroduction of the internally related causal structures (totalities) producing the manifest phenomena of social life. In contradistinction from the hermeneutical point of view, actors' accounts are both *corrigible* and *limited* by the existence of unacknowledged conditions, unintended consequences, tacit skills and unconscious motivation; but in opposition to the positivist position, these accounts form the logically indispensable *starting points* (constituting the ultimate explananda) of social scientific inquiry. From the perspective of immanent critique it can be shown that just as positivism fails to sustain the intelligibility of experimental and applied natural scientific inquiry, hermeneutics falters over the very features of social life such as *Verstehen*, dialogue and conceptual change, which it trumpets. Moreover these features presuppose for their intelligibility crucial aspects of the categorial framework employed in natural science (existential intransitivity, causality, etc.), just as the positivists' sponsored features presuppose communicative understanding and the mediation of meanings (e.g. in the 'teamwork' normally required for the experimental testing or technical application of a theory). At the metacritical level, on to which we step in chapter 3, further and more striking parallels and analogies between these will become apparent. For the moment, we can leave their internecine feud behind us.

### 3. Socio-Evolutionary Concepts, Functional Explanation and Human History

*Men make their own history, but not of their own free will; not under circumstances they themselves have chosen but under the given and inherited circumstances with which they are directly confronted.* [38]

As I noted in §1, a non-reductionist realism or natrualism in the human sciences presupposes some kind of emergence, with the most plausible position being perhaps that social objects just are the emergent powers of natural (material) ones, subject to continual conditioning and constraint by nature; so that the sociosphere appears, on S.E.P.M., as a taxonomically (and therefore epistemically) necessary and causally (and so ontologically) real, but dependent mode of matter. The T.M.S.A. was then introduced and justified in §2 as an attempt to specify the social content of this emergent surplus. But I also recorded in §1 another kind of natural-social link, in which natural processes

---

38. K. Marx, 'The Eighteenth Brumaire of Louis Bonaparte', *Surveys from Exile*, Harmondsworth 1973, p. 146.

separately or jointly generated effects in the social arena (as A- and B-type determinations respectively, and in such intermediate sciences as social biology) and conversely *sui generis* social processes produced, e.g. in technology, deliberate and various feedback effects on the biosphere. The T.M.S.A. was accordingly seen not just as embedded in nature, but as in continuous causal exchange with it. This second kind of link specifies, then, a causal rather than an existential connection. I now turn to a third kind of link, in which the social surplus is modelled on specifically biological concepts or theories (either directly or indirectly, via the modelling of social or psychological processes on physical theories informed or inspired by biological analogies).[39] We thus have three orders of social-biological (or, more generally, natural) connections:

(α)   the biological as an *existential basis* for social phenomena and processes (cf S.E.P.M.);
(β)   the biological in *causal interaction* with social phenomena and processes (cf B-type determinations);
(γ)   the biological as a *model* for the understanding of *sui generis* social phenomena and processes.

In respect of (γ), I propose to argue that a modified evolutionary schema furnishes one useful, if limited, framework for situating social change, on the condition that it is understood as presupposing the T.M.S.A. and provided that basic ambiguities in key terms such as 'adaptation', 'function', etc., are resolved. (In as much as other explanatory frameworks are required, social things will need to be located in a multiply connected paramorph in the sense of 1.5.) In §2 I addressed the question 'How is a social science possible?' against the background of classical physics and chemistry. An investigation of the negative analogy in evolutionary biology, which is already historical and relational[40] (although not of course social-relational) in calibre, should then confirm the practical and conceptual character of the sociosphere.

Rejecting the projection onto the human estate of concepts

---

39.   See, e.g., D. Bohm, *Wholeness and the Implicate Order*, London 1980.
40.   That is, its mechanisms are only actualised relationally, i.e. across sets of relations between the members of a species or different species.

more or less immediately derived from the *Weltanschauung* of classical mechanics, with its intimate affiliation with positivism and behaviouristics, it is tempting to look to new developments in the physical and biological sciences in pursuit of models, paradigms and insights.[41] In §5 I will consider whether, if we are not old-style Newtonian machines and also not only animals, we could nevertheless perhaps after all just be machines, but new-fangled Turing-based, 'functional' ones. Here I am concerned with the issues prompted by the requisitioning of evolutionary, populational, ecological or generally 'green' concepts, theories and approaches for redeployment in the human meridian. In this context it is of course imperative to distinguish (i) the *literal*, i.e. non-analogical, use of green concepts and theories to describe natural modes and aspects of determination in concrete social life, which is uncontroversially proper; from (ii) their *analogical* use to model non-natural modes and aspects of determination; and from (iii) their illicit literal, i.e. *reductionisι*, use to describe these modes and aspects, which is from a realist standpoint, quite illegitimate. Note that to the extent that evolutionary biology is conceived merely as a source of *analogy*, two forms of reductionism — of content, in biologism, and of form in 'social Darwinism' — are straightaway pre-empted. Unfortunately, it is not always clear from the work of human ecologists whether or not they are asseverating an actual identity of content in an ontologically reductionist monism, especially as they frequently fail to elaborate the disanalogy (discontinuity or emergence) involved. It is thus perhaps worth remarking that while the mechanist world-view could never satisfactorily handle the ideas of qualitative difference, complexity and change, any epistemological continuism, whether Engels', Bergson's or Bohm's, is going to sit uneasily with ontological discontinuism or pluralism and leave itself exposed to reductionist pressure.

The context in which socio-evolutionary concepts are mooted today differs markedly from that pervading the social Darwinism of the closing trine of the nineteenth century.[42] It is

---

41.  For discussion of this approach, see my 'The Consequences of Socio-Evolutionary Concepts for Naturalism in Sociology', *The Philosophy of Evolution*, ed. U. Jensen and R. Harrë, Brighton 1981 and 'Beef, Structure and Place', *Journal for the Theory of Social Behaviour* 13.1, 1983.
42.  Cf., e.g., D.R. Oldroyd, *Darwinian Impacts*, Milton Keynes 1980.

informed, on the one hand, by a fuller understanding of the basis and import of the Darwinian revolution; and, on the other, by a turning away from positivist and historicist philosophies of science and history. Thus while the internal coherence and explanatory power of evolutionary theory have been enhanced by gene-theoretic elaborations of it,[43] it is now clear that Darwinism is not, in any simple sense, a doctrine of progress and even less, for any particular species, of survival. Rather, in retrospect, Darwin's immense historical significance can be seen to lie in the way in which, in proposing a plausible explanation of natural functionality or adaptiveness without invoking the notion of a purposive or all-encompassing being or implying either consciousnes or design,[44] he radically undermined the idea of teleology in nature. The reason for the apparent 'original complicity' or pre-established harmony between species and environment (or subject and object, or part and whole) — that primal mystery which is such a pervasive feature of our experience of nature (and which has dug such an inexhaustible well for philosophical rumination) — is simply that, if and when the pair are ill-suited or mismatched, the species (or subject or part), but, note, not in general the environment (or object or whole), dies away; so that, as Collier has aptly remarked, 'nature will always produce the appearance of design *if* it produces the appearance of anything'.[45] In this way, then, as Marx wrote to Lasalle, Darwin not only dealt 'the death blow to "teleology" in the natural sciences ... but also set forth [its] rational meaning in an empirical way.'[46] (That is to say, he empirically explained its apparently rational ground — or, perhaps better, rationally explained its apparently empirical ground.)

---

43. See, e.g., R. Dawkins, *The Selfish Gene*, Oxford 1976 and D. Howe, 'Units of Evolution', ed. U. Jensen and R. Harré, *op cit.*

44. Although its affinity with Kant's 'purposeless purposiveness' and 'unsocial sociability of man', Adam Smith's 'invisible hand' and Hegel's 'cunning of reason', all teleologically-imbued, left a penumbra of ambiguity, exploited to the quick by the social Darwinists. This affinty derived in part from the social, specifically Malthusian, analogy Darwin self-consciously employed.

45. A. Collier, 'In Defence of Epistemology', *Issues in Marxist Philosophy Volume III*, eds. J. Mepham and D.H. Ruben, Brighton 1979, p. 85 (my italics).

46. 'K. Marx to F. Lasalle', January 16, 1861, *Selected Correspondence*, London 1975, p. 117.

At the same time, it should, I hope, be abundantly clear from the argument of Chapter 1 that the actualist (deductivist and determinist) ontologies underpinning positivism and historicism are fatally flawed; that, indeed, they are inconsistent with the very possibility of experimental and applied science. Moreover, scientific realism implies the untenability of any ontological reductionism or epistemological monism (such as exemplified by Wilson's biologism[47]), and more generally of any unilinear or monocausal approach to history (at any level). Despite the difference in context between contemporary social ecology and late nineteenth century social Darwinism, there are a pair of fallacies common to both of them which it is worth isolating at the outset: the fallacies of supposing that because A survived or flourished at time $t_i$ it must therefore (being 'fitted') survive or flourish at $t_n$; and/or that because x occurred at $t_i$ it was bound (being 'apt') to have done so. Both are patent paralogisms: logically they involve the crude mistake of *post hoc ergo propter hoc*; ontologically they presuppose actualism (as introduced in Chapter 1.4); while epistemologically they amount to variants of the explanatory genetic and transhistorical justificationist fallacies discussed in 1.4. Nevertheless they are widespread, being endemic to any unhistorical application of evolutionary concepts in the social world, constituting a quasi-Darwinist illusion or ecomyopia, overlooking certain fundamental realist and materialist theorems essential to any authentically Darwinian or ecological approach. The point of these remarks may be summed up by saying that *social life is not a success story* and *things could have been* (just as they might be) *different.*

### Human Ecology and Social Adaptation

Social life is no success story; and ecological failure is epistemologically just as, if not more, significant than success. Intrinsic to any truly ecological perspective is a real asymmetry between animal (organism, species, population, agent, act, etc.) and environment. When species and environment (or subject and object, or part and whole, or individual and society), mismatch, it is the species, subject or part, not the environment,

---

47. See E.O. Wilson, *Sociobiology*, Cambridge 1978; and for critical commentary on it, M. Midgley, *Beast and Man*, London 1979

object or whole which 'gives', goes under. This is the *ecological asymmetry*. From the perspective of any given animal or act (perceptual, or cognitive or otherwise), the environment supplies 'affordances'[48] — more generally, possibilities (opportunities, dangers, etc.) of various kinds, just as society does for the individual agent, institution, etc., although the environment would not be what it is independently of the totality of animals, acts, etc., just as society wold not be at all without human agency. Without the last sentence, the world would no doubt be slightly different, but without the rest of the world the last sentence would have been infinitely more so! While focusing on completed, successful actions, surviving species, etc., may encourage the eductive paralogism, looking at failed, incompleted, bungled actions (unsuccessful species, fractured individuals, conflictural relations, contradictory systems, etc.), may set us on the steep path to science. For in bringing out just those features of a successful action or adaptation which the very success of the action tends to elide or obscure, it silhouettes what needs to be explained and guards against any reversion to a pre-Darwinian view of the world as either obvious (cf. empiricism) or numinous (cf. idealism), concepts equally antithetical to science. Indeed a rich vein in the human sciences from Marx, Durkheim and Freud through to Garfinkel has confirmed the usefulness of the postulate of the methodological primacy of the pathological.

The ecological asymmetry is connected, via the finitude of acts and of the life-cycles or organisms, to two other major asymmetries, viz. the *temporal asymmetry* between past and present, marking the real irreversibility of time; and the *axiological asymmetry* between constraints and enablements, marking the condition that the class of acts we cannot perform is always infinitely greater than the class of those we can. These in turn are related to the binding of the present by the massive presence of the past, and the pervasiveness of social quasi-entropic processes in time, i.e. the conversion of free (open) possibilities into bound products. However, while an emancipatory practice cannot do anything about the temporal asymmetry, it can aspire to divert the axiological one, by

---

48. See e.g. J. Gibson, *The Ecological Approach to Visual Perception*, Boston 1979.

uncoupling the present from the causality of the past and by replacing depotentialising (disempowering, oppressive) by potentialising (empowering, enhancing) structures.

Standing in for the genuine temporal asymmetry, which is between the real determinacy of the past and the real indeterminacy of the future, one often finds a spurious one, that between the fatality of the past (conceived as the realm of structure, explanation and the descriptive direction of fit) and the freedom of the future (conceived as the dominion of norm, justification and the prescriptive direction of fit). Underlying this bogus asymmetry is frequently the failure to differentiate *epistemic* and *real* possibilities (and underlying that, normally, the conflation of the transitive and intransitive dimensions in the epistemic and ontic fallacies). For the past may be over and totally determinate, but this does not mean that it was determined, i.e. governed by laws such that nothing else could have happened. If 'I could have climbed the Eiffel Tower yesterday' correctly describes a real power or possibility I had (yesterday), then it is still true today, even though I did not in fact climb the Eiffel Tower yesterday (and even if I have since lost the ability or opportunity to do so). 'I could have climbed the Eiffel Tower yesterday' describes a real possibility open to me then, whether it was realised or not. Reducing real to epistemic possibilities conduces to *historical justificationism* (e.g. 'given conditions in the Soviet Union in the 1920's ... Stalinism had to occur'). And the obverse of historical justificationism is the denial, or what amounts to the same thing, the Kantian noumenalisation or the existentialist oceanic hyperinflation of the circumscribed reality of free agency now. Freedom is irrespective of the arrow's flight, no regarder of the river's flow.

### Natural Functions and Human Adaptation

The following five analytically distinct steps are involved in the scientific explanation of some phenomenon or feature, A, in terms of its function, F:

(α) *dispositional power claim*, P (e.g. a cow's tail (A) has the propensity to swish away flies (B); or increasing size up to a point in the steel industry (A) yields economies of scale (B));

(β) *functional gloss* on P (this property is useful, functional, adaptive or good for some end, e.g. species survival or profit; that is B is the (or a) function of A);

(γ)     *consequence claim*[49] (it is because of this property, P. that cows possess — or rather *came to possess* — long tails (A));

(δ)     *theoretical elaboration of the mode of connection,* between dispositional property, P, and consequent, A, presupposed in (γ), or of adaptation or functionality of a specified type (e.g. Darwin's theory of chance variation and natural selection);

(ε)     detailed *natural history* of the particular case, presupposing (δ) (e.g. short-tailed cows perished).

Note that, on this exegesis, functionality is a mere gloss on the effects or consequences of the exercise of a disposition, either synchronically within the structure of an ongoing thing or system and/or diachronically on its formation, maintenance or demise. (β) as such plays no further part in the schema — either in any consequence law or in its structural explanation or in its applied explanatory use. Conversely the other components of the schema may be invoked without (β), i.e. the implication that P is functional for some end, or with a quite contrary import, as when our explanatory attention is fixed on the demise of the dinosaur, or the short-tailed cow. It is the theoretical elaboration, (δ), of the mode of connection presupposed at (γ) which *ipso facto* rationally explains the appearance of teleology, here in the guise of the functional gloss (β).

What is sometimes dignified as a functional fact, F, must therefore be unpacked into:-

(α) the dispositional power, P, normically understod, i.e. as A tends to do (suffer, produce, etc.) B, under conditions $C_1 \ldots C_n$ in virtue of its nature N; and

(β) the gloss, F, on which P is conceived as functional (useful etc.) for some end, where B is a function of A, given the context or environment D (including $C_1 \ldots C_n$) and an end or end-function E, and where, given E, A may be said to be 'adapted' to D and D contains or is characterised by whatever makes B useful.

---

49.   This term is adapted from G.A. Cohen, *Karl Marx's Theory of History,* Oxford 1978, chapter 8.

But what precisely is meant by 'functional' and 'adapted' here? It is clear enough that the root notion is the idea of 'aptness', 'match' or 'fit' between an object and its situation — e.g. species/environment, agent/activity (cf. 'aptitude'), action/context (cf. 'aptness') — with 'adapting' signifying changing so as to become more apt. Obviously from a naturalistic perspective, the drive or mechanism of adaptive change, including any ends identified or imputed, must be sought immanently within the context of (mis)fit itself. But is there a more general criterion of fit — such as the Darwinian measure of adaptation as the differential reproductive rates of alternative or coexisting populations within a given habitat? Assuming that the end of existence (survival), a condition for any other end (save extinction), is satisfied, then it is clear that in the human realm provision must be made for a multiplicity of criteria of adaptiveness, and that in social life such 'surplus criteria' are chronically, and of course fatally, contested. Moreover in social life such contests are not only (or even typically) about how to become (more) apt, but rather about what to become apt for, as parts (but not all) of the human habitat are comprehended as social products, as historical transmits and so possible historical transforms.

A consequence statement may be analysed straightforwardly as A exists, occurs, develops, etc. because of P (or P glossed as F), i.e. as P tends to produce A; that is, if A tends to do (suffer, produce) B, then A tends to exist, occur, survive, flourish etc., in some more or less specified context D. This does not involve any mysterious 'backwards causation'. In a consequence statement it is the prior or concurrent existence of a dispositional property which explains the existence or persistence mentioned in the antecedent of the tendency statement specifying the disposition. In Darwinian theory it is the past, not the current, adaptive value of a feature which causally explains its occurrence. (Thus we may note in parenthesis the possibilty that a social trait or feature may persist and be effective long after the conditions apposite to it have disappeared).[50] It should be noticed that a consequence claim is (1) contingent, (2) regulatively useful and (3) justifiable. (1) It is defeasible on the grounds either that the disposition does not hold or that it does

---

50. Cf. the comments on the regressive binding of the present by the past on p. 101 above.

not account for the consequent. (2) Although it does not explain the mode of connection between the dispositional property and consequent, in indicating the need for an elaboration of this, it points science towards (δ). (3) Even in the absence of the knowledge of the consequence-producing or adaptive mechanism, M, in virtue of which P tends to produce A, we may have grounds for supposing that such a mechanism exists (i.e. we may know *that* P caused A without knowing *how*[51]). In each of these respects a dispositional consequence claim is exactly on a par with, indeed just is a particular kind of, causal power one. Note that we are only justified in asserting the consequence statement in the explanation of some particular phenomena if we have grounds for supposing its antecedent is instantiated, that is, that the tendency specified in the dispositional claim (α) is, or has been, exercised or operative. Thus the 'double causality' of a consequence claim, whether glossed or unglossed, just consists in the property that the existence of some feature (of a kind, species, individual, system etc.) is explained by the (prior or contemporaneous) exercise of a prior or contemporaneous causal power of this feature. But it is important to keep the two causal power claims, and accordingly the dispositional and consequential mechanisms — the mechanisms implied in (α), Mα and (γ), Mγ respectively — distinct. Thus the (technical) mechanisms by which cows swish away flies, or scale produces economies are not the same as the (natural-historical) mechanisms by which short tailed cows

---

51. This corresponds to the Humean or protolegal level of natural necessity (see 1.5 above). G. McLennan (*Marxism and the Methodologies of History*, London 1981) correctly points out that the functional dependencies Cohen invokes presuppose causal elaborations of realist ilk. However, as Cohen's argument is that at any particular time such elaborations may be unavailable, it is vital to explicitly conceptualise historical materialism as an ongoing research programme (in the TD) — a lacuna in McLennan's book — committed to a scientific realist ontology (in the ID) — a dimension Cohen lacks. Thus as Elster underlines ('Belief, Bias and Ideology', *Rationalism and Relativism*, ed. M. Hollis and S. Lukes, Oxford 1982, p. 147n) there just are no examples of consequence explanations conforming to Cohenesque desiderata. But the moral of this is not, as Elster supposes, methodological individualism and rational action theory; but that theoretical explanations in human history require *explicit* commitment to a transcendental realist ontology of transfactually efficacious structures rather than one of Humean, Hempelean or Davidsonian sequences of events.

perished or rationalisation in the steel industry occurred. Note, finally, that on Darwinian, and more generally populational, elaborations of consequence laws, the environment or context D is integral to the operation of the mechanism; so that whereas the form of an ordinary causal law can be adequately glossed as 'if X then Y' or here 'if P then A', a Darwinian consequence law must be parsed as 'if D and P then A'; or, more fully, as 'if D and if A then B, then A' or as D. $(A \rightarrow B) \rightarrow A$. Remembering that D contains or is characterised by B, the form B. $(A \rightarrow B) \rightarrow A$ represents our jejune experience of that pervasive complicity whose mechanism Darwin set out to explain.

The error of functionalism can now be quickly isolated: it consists in the supposition that the mere fact that if a feature existed it would play some useful role suffices to explain it. On the contrary what one requires to be justified in making a consequence claim are grounds for supposing that the dispositional property and consequent are normically connected. Darwin's theory of chance variation and natural selection comprise one way in which a consequence claim of the 'cow's tail' type can be elaborated and so defended (amended etc.). Alternative, e.g. Lamarckian, providential and quasi-purposive explanatory sketches can easily be constructed. The gene-complex selection theory constitutes a further, second-order, elaboration on the mechanism of natural selection. (See Diagram 2.11 below.) The mutation/selection (M/S) and replicator/interactor (R/I) conceptual frameworks are 'explanatory formats' which must be applied to concrete natural-historical circumstances for the explanation of particular cases at stage ($\varepsilon$) above.

Refining a classification originally proposed by Toulmin,[52] four basic modes of elaboration can be specified: (1) intentional; (2) homoeostatic; (3) developmental and (4) populational. The intentional mode includes not just the purposive, calculative paradigm central to utilitarian theory, but the non-calculative, non-deliberative modes of acting and adapting tacitly, practically, expressively and unconsciously. The second mode covers the cases of homoeostatic causal loops, self-regulation through feedback and reflexive self-regulation. The third mode, lately in vogue with the work of Piaget, Chomsky

52. S. Toulmin, 'Human Adaptation' ed. U. Jensen and R. Harré, *op cit.*, discussed in my 'The Consequences of Socio-Evolutionary Concepts', see p. 138 n. 41.

and Habermas, encompasses in principle both nativist and non-nativist theories. Finally, the populational mode must be extended to incorporate the possibility of quasi-Lamarckian and other non-strictly Darwinian mechanisms, i.e. mechanisms which do not presuppose the causal independence of chance variation and selective perpetuation. This taxonomy has several advantages. It enables us to pinpoint the weaknesses of social thought of utilitarian, organicist-functionalist, historicist and biologistic cast in the one-sided accentuation of one of these modes to the virtual exclusion of the others. It situates the possibility of a quasi-teleonomic array of goal-realisation through purpose, feedback, programme and selection. It leaves the relation between the modes open (e.g. is a deliberately initiated, reflexively self-regulated, developing, maladapted practice possible?) Finally it clarifies two senses in which the populational mode must take epistemic precedence —

(i) in as much as it is biologically well-grounded, the other forms of adaptation natural-historically presuppose it;

(ii) it alone locates a central place for disfunctionality and afunctionality (logically including eufunctionality), maladaptation alongside fit.

There are however four major disanalogies of the populational paramorph, at least in its Darwinian paradigm, for understanding social reproduction and change. First, social reproduction is neither automatic nor blind. On the contrary it depends upon the accomplishments of skilled agents, about their tasks, drawing on and so reproducing the social structure, accounting for themselves and the social orders in which they exist in very definite ways. The intentional mode is much more centrally implicated in social than in other orders of biological life. Biological models in the social sciences have been prone to emphasise unintended consequences at the expense of human agency; so that it is salutary to remember that human history — the place, time and meaning of selection pressure on practices — consists, as Marx put it, in '*nothing* but the *activity* of men in pursuit of their ends'.[53] The form of social replication is not a parameter external to the historical process. It just *is* that process, considered under its structural aspect, as it unfolds in the way, whatever it happens to be, socialised individuals collect-

---

53. K. Marx, *The Holy Family, Selected Writings*, ed. T. Bottomore and M. Rubel, Harmondsworth 1963, p. 75.

ively begin, live, share, transmit and end their lives. Moreover the activity- and concept-dependent nature of social reproduction renders it liable to critique and conscious change. Secondly, whereas Darwinian theory upholds a rigid separation between mutation and selection conditions, and the modes of replication and interaction, in the social zone these poles are causally interdependent and mutually interpenetrating. In Lamarckian theory mutation conditions are 'coupled on'[54] selection conditions, i.e. $S \rightarrow M$, as e.g. in market research; and in the social world selection conditions may also be coupled on mutation conditions, i.e. $M \rightarrow S$, as in advertising, propaganda, etc. More generally a typical pattern is provided by $S...M'...S''...M'''$, etc., i.e. mutant practices are intelligible in context, which they actively transform, generating reinforcement and resistance. Completely Darwinian socio-evolution implies a voluntarism of social practices; complete Lamarckism, a determinism of social processes. Moreover, from a transcendental standpoint this side of infinity — that is, on the one hand, this side of utopia and on the other, of extinction, i.e. within human history — social adaptation can be neither total nor nil. So we need a theory of the interinfluence of relatively independent M- and S-conditions, and of the dialectic of adjustment and tension, accommodation and subversion between form of life and setting. Both requisites call for a theory of agency — or more precisely of *agents* (their classes, relations, interests, etc.) — as the mediating link between selecting environments and mutating practices.

A third disanalogy, the possibility of multiple and conflicting criteria, has already been noted. But this only carries ontological force inasmuch as the differential criteria are or might be *acted upon*. i.e. in virtue of the activity- and concept-dependence of 'memetic',[55] in contrast to genetic, codes. Together these differentiae restore the practical, conceptual, totalising and critical tasks of the socio-evolutionary, in contrast to the bio-evolutionary, sciences. But this leads on to a fourth disanalogy: that in the social world alone functionality, insofar as it becomes a project of social-political action for human agents, need not be just a gloss. That is to say ($\beta$), the functional gloss on the dispositional power (see p. 142 above), can be reflexively incorporated into any mechanism of social change. For fit, or the

---

54. Cf. S. Toulmin, *Human Understanding Vol. 1*, Oxford 1973, p. 338
55. R. Dawkins, *The Selfish Gene*, pp. 206 ff.

lack of it, *matters to people* — whether in the cognitive medium of incoherent narratives; in the communicative medium of thwarted intentionality; or in the great practical media of unfulfilled possibilities, frustrated needs, unwanted determinations and oppressive relations. Each of these can become, in specific circumstances, the object of a transformative praxis. Only in the human sphere does historicity enter, as a material force with an efficacy of its own, into history. Only here is history written (or told); and made as well as done. For only here is experienced the hope that history, conceived as the understanding of the past, can be reflexively incorporated into our experience of history as the enactment of the present and so inform history as the process of the production of our future, already shaped and conditioned, ramified and constrained, but still unselected, open, yet to be made.

### The Limits of the Evolutionary Analogue

Pursuing the implications of the gene-theoretic elaboration of the M/S framework, Harré has suggested that the social analogues of genes (replicators) and organisms (interactors) are rules and practices respectively.[56] Without offering any detailed justification here, I want to propose the following alternative interpretation of the model:

lineage = history = temporal sequence of replicators
replicator = social structure
$interactor_1$ = practice/institution
$interactor_2$ = agent
environment = ensemble of $interactors_1$, embedded in biosphere.

I prefer the category of social structure to that of rule, both because only causally efficacious rules are replicators and because social replication always involves resources as well as rules (memetic matter as well as form). I distinguish two types of social interactor (and *a fortiori*, collectives): practices are generated by social structures, but it is through the medium of human agency that selection pressure operates. Accordingly, I distinguish two types of individuating narrative, corresponding to the *longue durée* of institutions and the biographies of indi-

---

56. See R. Harré, 'The Evolutionary Analogy in Social Evolution', eds. U. Jensen and R. Harré, *op. cit.*

viduals. (See Diagram 2.13 and compare with Diagram 2.10 on p. 130 above).

In the social case the mode of replication is activity (and so interactor$_1$ and $_2$-dependent); but the mode of reproduction of the population (of practices) is the very process of copying, the mode of replication of the social structure (memetic order) itself. A species is a naturally self-producing system. But society is neither naturally produced nor self-reproducing. So if the R/I format is not to lapse into reductionism (memes as genes) or reification (memes as self-reproducing), it must presuppose the T.M.S.A., i.e. human agency as the medium and vehicle of reproduction, without of course seeing replication as its consciously intended outcome. As Harré has pointed out 'all populational theories conceive of change as defined in terms of the replacement of a population of one type by a collection of individuals of another, under the condition that there exists a *real relation* between the members of the successive populations'.[57] It is the role of the T.M.S.A. to specify this real relation of replication, on which human agents reproduce the codes governing their activities in the course of, and as the necessary means of, those very same activities they govern. The argument here thus converges on the argument in §2: the T.M.S.A. defines at one and the same time the emergent surplus from nature and its mode of reproduction (replication). That this is so is because this social surplus has no material existence other than in the course of its continual re- and transformation in the durée of human praxis.

However, although the M/S framework presupposes the T.M.S.A., it cannot just be replaced by it. For the great merit of that framework is that it delineates the way in which the environment, the ensemble of causally interdependent and more or less internally related interactors$_1$, in their physical setting, mediated by the practical activity and consciousness of interactors$_2$, may exert selection pressure on particular interactors$_1$, whether pre-existing or new: so as to either inhibit them

---

57. Cf. R. Harré, *Social Being*, Oxford 1979, p. 368. The disanalogies between socio- and bio-evolution which Harré notes throws the transformational character of the social process into heightened relief. For such phenomena as non-simple lineage ordering, replicative innovation, selection on replicators, causal interaction between replicators, direct causal relations between interactors$_1$, Lamarckism and reinforcement all turn on the activity- or concept-dependence of social evolution.

(Darwinian mechanism) or encourage them (Lamarckian mechanism). As such it situates one of the kinds of ways in which endogenously generated 'adaptive' transformations in the social structure can occur. But it should be stressed that transposition of the framework to the social domain leaves the nature of the adaptive mechanism open: it is a framework for situating change, not — in the social world — an explanation of it. To illustrate, understood as a scheme for situating changes in populations (or transformations in the numbers) of practices of a specified type, the simplified form of the Darwinian case can be represented in the following 'survival matrix':

[I]  (i)  $K_A t_1 \ldots K_A t_n$
(ii)  $K_{-A} t_1 \ldots -K_{-A} t_n$

This tells us that of two populations only the one possessing the attribute A survived over $t_1 \ldots t_n$, but it does not explain why or how. For comparison, consider a needs explanatory format. Roughly, an individual or population N may be said to have a need for X at $t_1$ iff it lacks it at $t_1$ and it cannot continue to survive, or survive as a good or flourishing specimen of its type or species, unless it comes to possess X within some further time period, say $t_i \ldots t_n$.[58] This can be represented in the matrix:

[II]  (i)  $N_{-X} t_1 \ldots N_X t_n$
(ii)  $N_{-X} t_1 \ldots -N_{-X} t_n$

Here again this tells us merely that of two individuals only the one which came to acquire the attribute X over $t_1$ to $t_n$ survived at or by $t_n$, but leaves the nature of this need and the manner and means of its satisfaction unexplained. In short, such formats are not substitutes for, but logically presuppose, substantive social theories (of a realist and transformationalist hue). It is also clear that a M/S framework for situating social changes requires at the very least supplementation by other schemata allowing for change consequent upon sheer teleology, counterfinality, imposed exogeny (e.g. conquest), auto-subversion (internal to a structure), conflict-resolution, contradiction-

---

58. Cf. A. Kenny, *Freedom, Will and Power*, Oxford 1975, pp. 48 ff. This definition of needs will be broadened in § 5.

resolution, territorial spread, material resource exhaustion and discovery etc.

Some consequences of the transformational timbre of social evolution should be briefly summarised. The duality and interdependence of replicators and interactors$_2$ (implied by the duality and interdependence of structure and praxis), means that there is only a virtual, but nevertheless real, distinction between them. They are not distinct things, but different (as generative and generated) aspects of the same process, seldom in one-to-one relation. While the relational texture of the subject-matter of social science casts doubt on standard formulations of the micro/macro contrast, its pre-existing and holistically changing configuration implies that no transformation is total and all reproduction is transformation. This means that theoretical sociology must be historical in character and necessitates reformulation of the synchronic/diachronic contrast. The T.M.S.A. implies that there is neither logical nor epistemic asymmetry between the explanation of (relative) stasis, i.e. continuity, and (relative) change. Specifically, to the extent that either are seen under the figure of a consequence explanatory scheme, an elaboration is required of the mode of connection between the presence or absence of the dispositional property and the consequent continuity or change. It is equally a mistake to suppose an ontological asymmetry by hypostatising the social system as something which would (somehow) reproduce itself *unless* prevented. Tradition, invention, routine, habit, etc., whether considered as general phenomena or in particular cases, in principle all require social explanation (even if the explanation should turn out to be obvious or trivial or take the form of a principle of least action). Change and lack of change in the social world are on a par.

Let me conclude by reiterating the most important elements of disanalogy between biological evolution and social transformation. In the biological case, while adaptation, in whatever mode it is elaborated, presupposes a causal connection between the changing features and historical outcomes, on the Darwinian paradigm this does not involve either teleology or causal influence from the environment on the genesis (as distinct from selection and perpetuation) of those changes. By contrast, in the social case, teleology, in the special form of intentional agency, is involved as an indispensable condition and a part-cause of adaptive changes; mutations, i.e. transformations in practices, must normally be seen as at least weakly coupled on their environment and so cannot be treated as random (as on the Darwinian prototype); and the selective perpetuation of selected variants can never be regarded as self-explanatory. Finally, as we shall shortly see, inasmuch as social science may reveal a discrepancy between social objects and beliefs about those objects and may come to socially explain such a social discrepancy, then we may and must pass to a critical assessment of the social causes responsible for it. Such a critique, inasmuch as it casts light on unsuspected or recondite sources of determination, facilitates the development of emancipatory practices oriented to emancipated (free) action. And in this process implicit selection criteria — criteria of adaptiveness — are brought to consciousness, subject to critical scrutiny and themselves more or less transformed. When unreflected processes are rendered amenable to conscious control, we are free to fulfil our natures.

Human history is faster, more interconnected and complex, praxis- and concept-dependent and value-impregnated than biological history (some of these differences are relative, some appear absolute). Biological time is itself a fleeting now in the longer curve of natural history, in turn a flash of light in the hollow sound of eternity. Some, but not all, human history can be modelled on a populational schema which (i) respects the interdependence of social replication and interaction and social selection and mutation and (ii) presupposes, in its elaboration of the mode of connection between adaptive (and non-adaptive) features and their historical consequences, a transformational and relational view of social activity. If this is done, social 'evolution' will take on a new meaning, just as 'mass' has done in twentieth century physics, as the model gradually severs its connection with its parent-source and comes to acquire an autonomous life of its own. That said, it is important to remember that much human history just *is* (and will always be) natural history, both in the sense that the human species is evolving biologically, and in the sense that the natural and social life of the species is continually subject to the determinations of our ecological environment, in which we have been lately so dramatically intervening.

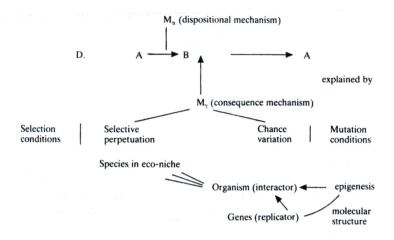

Diagram 2.11: *The Stratification of Evolutionary Theory*

## 4. The Problems of Topology, Conceptuality and Critique

*Anyone who sets out in this field to hunt down final and ultimate truths ... will bring home little, apart from platitudes and commonplaces of the sorriest kind: for example, that generally speaking men cannot live except by labour; that up to the present they have been divided into rulers and ruled; that Napoleon died on May 5th 1821, and so on.*[59]

The T.M.S.A. immediately generates two interconnected problems, which bear on the themes of structural, integrative pluralism (IP) and of multiple, holistic and mixed determinations discussed in §1, viz.: (1) how are the social practices to be identified, and especially individuated?; and (2) how are the individuated practices to be interlaced or intricated (e.g. should one attempt to incorporate them within a unified explanatory scheme such as historical materialism purports to provide?) The problem of individuation may be broached, as we shall see, by reference to agents' own accounting procedures,

---

59. F. Engels, *Anti-Dühring*, Moscow 1969, p. 109.

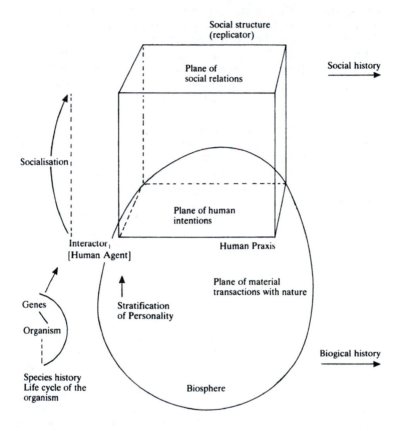

Diagram 2.12

| existential ↑ | R _____ social structure | |
|---|---|---|
| interdependence | I₂ _____ social practice | duality of structure<br>longue durée |
| of society and | [I₀] _____ human praxis | duality of praxis<br>flow of day-to-day<br>existence |
| human agent ↓ | I₁ _____ human agent | individual life<br>histories<br>(biographies) |

Diagram 2.13: N.B. The levels R, $I_2$ [$I_0$], I are not in one-to-one correspondence

but agents may lack (especially in the contingent historical context of a systematically atomising society) any clear conception of the interrelations between their activities.

Integrative Pluralism indicates that here again we need to be able to think the simultaneity of distinctions and connections, so that the various practices are conceived as non-identical but causally, and possibly internally, related to one another. And once more it becomes mandatory to insist in principle against both monism, whether in essentialist or reductionist guise, which would scout the differentiation of the practices, and eclecticism or pluralism, whether or an empiricist, rationalist (e.g. structuralist) or idealist sort, which would efface their interconnections. In its most general form, this issue is a problem for any human historiography at three main levels: (1) within human ecology; (2) within social science; and (3) within some particular social scientific explanatory scheme such as historical materialism, where it is of course familiar as the problem of reconciling the notion of the relative autonomy of the superstructures (repudiating monism) with that of their ultimate determination by the economic base (rejecting eclecticism).

At level (2) the tangram is that of the interdigitation of the preferred explanatory scheme with supplementary and/or alternative and/or incompatible schemes. These possibilities stem from the ($\alpha$) multiplicity and ($\beta$) plurality of causes characteristic of open systems (in the ID) and ($\gamma$) the plurality of possible hypotheses (in the TD) respectively. Thus it might be maintained[60] that while history has a definite shape or structure which dialectical materialism articulates (*contra* eclecticism at this level), historical outcomes are co-determined by individual actions, natural causes, accidental circumstances etc. too.[61] The question now arises as to whether these additional elements should be understood as independent determinations on historical outcomes, on analogy with A in Diagram 2.4 above, or perhaps more plausibly (but less heretically) as subject to mediation by the historical process, as described by historical materialism, by analogy with B, or by some mix or both; or whether, alternatively, these extraneous factors are not strictly

60. See e.g., G. McLennan, *op. cit.*
61. Cf. G.V. Plekhanov, 'The Role of the Individual in History', *Fundamental Problems of Marxism*, London 1969.

(methodologically or substantively) incompatible with historical materialism — that is to say, refute it or at least severely restrict its range. Setting this last possibility on one side for the moment, Diagram 2.14 is a partial analogue of Diagram 2.4, where C′ represents the intra-theoretically described determinations, B′ the mixed or extra-theoretically mediated determinations and A′ the extra-theoretically described determinations. If a similar integrative pluralist orientation were feasible at level (3), i.e. for the theoretical elaboration of historical materialism itself, the result for human historiography would be a nesting of integrative pluralisms (or IPs) as depicted in Diagram 2.15 below.

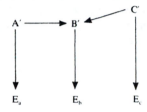

Diagram 2.14

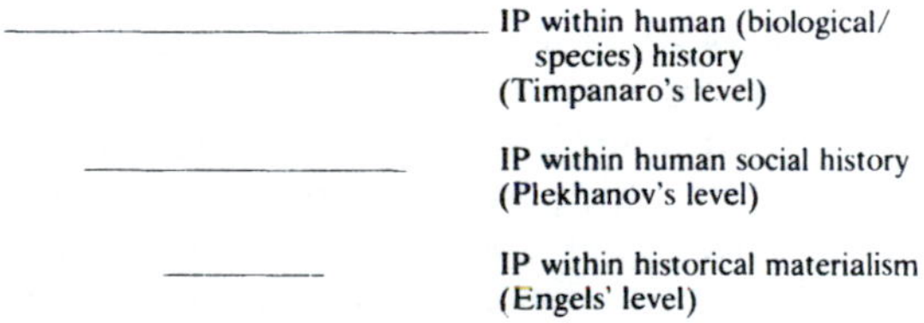

---------------------------------- IP within human (biological/
                                     species) history
                                   (Timpanaro's level)

--------------------------- IP within human social history
                           (Plekhanov's level)

-------------- IP within historical materialism
              (Engels' level)

Diagram 2.15

The relations between the nests may be conceived as ordinated by non-reductionist, non-actualist principles of the explanation of higher-order by lower-order mechanisms or processes, while the phenomena identified under the descriptions of each level would remain subject to the principle of multi-level as well as multiple determination spelt out on p. 106 above. It should be unnecessary to underline that such a hierarchy provides only a framework (and heuristic orientation) for the empirically-controlled *investigation* of the patterns of coherence which emerge within human history.

I turn now specifically to level (3), the problem of the elaboration of an integrative pluralism within historical materialism. Crude forms of the latter layer the social cake into economic basis and political and ideological superstructures, and one can still find residues of this in Althusser. Attempts to slice it in terms of interest and orientation have fared little better, as can be seen by the problems besetting Habermas's cognitive-interest theory.[62] The general difficulty with both objectivist and subjectivist taxonomies is that any concrete practice will normally reveal a plurality of different aspects; so that progress on this problem requires clarity about precisely what one is trying to individuate and articulate. On the transcendental realist ontology, these are the non-actual but real structures at work generating different aspects of the concrete flux of social life and their systematic and developing interrelations; that is to say, the problem of identifying and connecting practices is subsumed under, or rather theoretically replaced by, that of classifying and explaining the structures at work in them.

Althusser's influential work on the topology of historical materialism in fact consists in an uneasy synthesis of two kinds of resolution to Engels' problem: (i) the quasi-mechanistic formula that the economy determines the 'weightings' of the levels of the social structure, and in particular which level is dominant;[63] and (ii) the quasi-holistic formula that the elements of the social structure are determined by the configuration of the structure itself (which may of course be asymmetrically weighted).[64] Neither supply adequate resolutions of the problem either within the topography of historical materialism or in its more general aspect, and clearly both formulae need to be fully elaborated in models of causal determination explicitly applicable to particular research fields.[65] But this leads on to a more general difficulty with any such scheme. For it is an implication of the T.M.S.A. that there can be no general a-historical theory

---

62. See, e.g., T. McCarthy, *The Critical Theory of Jürgen Habermas*, London 1978; and *Habermas: Critical Debates*, ed. J.B. Thompson and D. Held, London 1982.
63. L. Althusser, *For Marx*, London 1969.
64. L. Althusser and E. Balibar, *Reading Capital*, London 1970.
65. See, e.g., E.O. Wright, *Class, Crisis and the State*, London 1978, especially chapter 1.

of articulation,[66] that the relations between the elements of the social totality (including the operative forms of causal determination, and even perhaps the feasibility of an orientation such as that of IP) may change along with the elements themselves. Consequences of this are that regional theories — in Poulantzas's sense[67] — must always take the shape of historically specific intermediate sciences; and that if social/historical theory develops by constructing nets which, when thrown over reality, continually augment our understanding, the best net at any moment of time will be both sensitive to and liable to change,[68] as the distinct ontic modalities of 'becoming true' and 'making true', join that of 'being [is] true', in our epistemic armoury. (In 'becoming true' there is no time-independent distinction between ($\gamma$) and ($\beta$), the plurality of hypotheses and causes; in 'making true' there is no belief-time-independent distinction between them.)

Social practices, unlike their interconnections in a social totality, must be already conceptualised in experience. So we can reason analogically-retroductively from these conceptualisations — reflecting 'self-understood forms of social life'[69] — to the conditions and structures explaining them. Such an analysis may of course, once completed, disclose a systematic discrepancy between the individuation (and identification) of the practices entailed by the theory and that implicit in the experience or explicit in the understanding of the agents of that practice. There cannot therefore be a final resolution of the problem of individuation outside that of the problem of articulation; and the practical resolution of both problems depends upon the construction of substantive theories which maximise total explanatory power. This is the only 'organon'[70] available to the human sciences.

---

66. Cf. K. Marx to N. Mikhailovsky, November 1877, *Selected Correspondence*, London 1975, p. 294.

67. N. Poulantzas, *Political Power and Social Classes*, London 1973.

68. Cf. C. Wright Mills: 'we do not know any universal principles of historical change [because] the mechanisms of change ... vary with the social structures we are examining'. If the point in open systems, with their countless conjunctures and compounds, is seldom to find a single key, but rather to crack a combination lock, in social life the numbers on the combination are continually changing.

69. K. Marx, *Capital Vol. I*, Harmondsworth 1976, p. 75,

70. I. Kant, *Critique of Pure Reason*, London 1970, p. 26. (cf. K.R. Popper, *Conjectures and Refutations*, London 1963, p. 64.)

### On the critique of interpretative fundamentalism and the corrigibility of agents' accounts

The T.M.S.A shows what may escape (and so be misconstrued by) consciousness in our conscious activity. But are there perhaps elements in our experience or aspects of our consciousness of which we must be — cannot help but be — certain? And which, because of this, are perhaps exempt from the possibility of historical supersession?

The history of post-Cartesian philosophy is largely the attempt to establish just such an Archimedean point for knowledge, free from the possibility of error and impervious to every form of doubt. Thus in its classical empiricist avatar, knowledge was conceived as incorrigibly grounded in (or even exhausted by) sense-data or operations. Of course we now know that there are no foundations of knowledge, that there is no uniquely privileged level, moment or operation, that there are no *brute data*, that the facts already contain a certain 'sedimented' reading of the world (that natural facts are social institutions), and that the relationship between theories and facts is not that between a human idiom and a given world, but between two interdependent conceptualised spheres, one of which is paradigmatically taken as referring to objects apprehended in experience.

In short, we now know that the facts are interdependent and changeable; and science itself appears, as one might anticipate on the T.M.S.A., as a historical process of levels and connections, a weighted network, without foundations, developing in time. This view does not dispute the epistemic value of experience; on the contrary, transcendental realism claims, against irrealism, to uniquely sustain it. But it interprets this not as the absolute privilege of a *content*, but as dependent upon the ontological and social *contexts* within which the significant experience occurs.

Now insofar as there has been a real advance in recent analytical philosophy of the human sciences, it lies in recognition of the significance of the condition that (wo)man is a self-interpreting and self-motivating animal, a member of a story-telling species, whose language, beliefs and stories are in some manner necessary for and productive of his or her life; so that social reality faces the scientific neophyte as already *pre-interpreted*, as linguistically and cognitively 'done', prior to any scientific enquiry into it. These pre-interpretations are *not* externally related and contingently conjoined to what happens in the human sphere, but internally related to and constitutive of it.[71] It was natural then, in the slipstream of this insight, to suppose that these interpretations (or beliefs) would constitute the base or foundation of social knowledge; to regard them, as consisting, so to speak, in *brute interpretations* (or beliefs), whether such data-analogues were conceived positivistically (monologically) as immediately available to the investigator or dialogically (in a sort of hermeneuticised Kantianism) as dependent upon work within his or her own culture. Thus there came about a transposition of the familiar thematics of classical philosophy in a hermeneutical key — more plausible than the original, perhaps, because nature is not self-interpreting, but little different in logical form or epistemological effect. For both the reductionist thesis that social knowledge is *exhausted* by, and the milder position that it is *rooted* in (and so must be *consistent* with) self-interpretations inexorably induce a displaced hermeneuticised scientism and a consequent 'disavowal of reflection'.[72] In both variants the doctrine of the incorrigible — because ontologically constitutive — foundations of social knowledge secretes, like its positivist prototype, as an inevitable corollary, the thesis of the *neutrality* of social science. This doctrine and its corollary imbue, in one way or another, the various schools of interpretive sociology; they possess parallels in both historicist and structuralist interpretations of historical materialism (where the privileged level is defined by the revolutionary praxis of the proletariat or the self-validating practice of theory respectively); and exert an extensive influence in contemporary culture quite generally.

Of course Hegel demonstrated long ago that the fundamentalist programme is both radically incomplete and viciously circular,[73] in that it not only cannot establish its own legitimacy,[74] but must (implicitly or explicitly) presuppose some unvalidated 'knowledge'. And it is clear that, in these respects, any Vichian *facimus* must share the same failings as the

---

71. Cf. C. Taylor, 'Interpretation and the Sciences of Man', *Review of Metaphysics 25*, (3), 1971; and A. McIntyre, *After Virtue*, 1981.
72. J. Habermas, *Knowledge and Human Interests*, London 1972, p. VI.
73. G.W.F. Hegel, *Phenomenology of Spirit* (1807), Oxford 1977, Introduction.
74. Cf. K. Gödel, *On Formally Undecideable Propositions*, New York 1962.

Cartesian *cogito* (or a Bachelardian *cogitamus*). For just as Descartes must have assumed some content to initiate his axiomatic play, so for Vico, God or man must already have some matter to make their worlds, and what an agent does not make (what it must take to make) it can have no privileged understanding of, just as what an ego cannot prove it must remain uncertain about. On the transformational model, of course, we do not make the conditions or consequences, skills or motives of our intentional making (cf. Diagram 2.7 on p. 126 above); so that our beliefs about, or interpretations of, our actions cannot be constitutive in the requisite sense. Moreover the T.M.S.A. recognises that we never start, cognitively or more generally socially, any more than we can begin biologically, from scratch: that we are always in the predicament of the tinker, having to mend our cognitive tools on the job; that we learn to swim in the water, not on the beach. Fundamentalism, whether in Cartesian (objectivist), Pascalian (conventionalist) or Vichian (interpretative) guise, and whether decked out in Kantian (transcendentalist) trappings or not, always obscures the historically situated, epistemically interested and transformative — practical, social, contingently critical and historical — contours of cognitive, normal-ising and interpretative work.

In scrutinising the social-incorrigibilist position in more detail, two main types of argument for it can be discerned: one more strictly Vichian, the other more Herderian in conception. The Vichian argument claims that one and the same knowledge is used to generate as to explain (account for, justify) behaviour; that the stock of knowledge we use to act is just the stock we use to think (and explain) that action — a condition that may be grounded in some notion of the identity (or affinity) of our powers to initiate and to monitor behaviour,[75] so, as it were, superimposing a transcendental unity of agency on that of consciousness. The more hermeneutically slanted argument contends that it is actors' interpretations which uniquely and exhaustively constitute the social world, extracting it from a mere assemblage of physical happenings, so that it is only and sufficiently by reference to these interpretations, that is, the actors' own understandings, that the *sui generis* reality of their social world can be saved.

---

75. See e.g. R. Harré and P. Secord, *The Explanation of Social Behaviour*, Oxford 1972.

(a) In considering the Vichian argument the beliefs (motives) that prompt or rationalise action must be distinguished from the practical knowledge employed in it. Both are important. For we are only in the intentional domain, and so on the site of the human sciences, insofar as organisms — agents — possess beliefs that their actions manifest a certain property. The belief may be unconcious, unformulated or tacit, and it may be wrong; but it must be there or we are indeed dealing with purely natural phenomena. Second, all actions, even so-called basic ones, utilise or consist in the exercise of skills, whether learned or innate. The motivating belief or reason prompting the action may be regarded as an initial condition for the exercise of the ability displayed in the action. But the ability or skill itself may be *tacit*.[76] That is, we need not be able to *say* — as distinct from do (and normally, but not always show) — how to do what we know very well how to *do* (or vice versa, as in the case of the hamfisted theoretical engineer) — even when, as Chomsky has made abundantly clear, the first-order skills are themselves verbal, discursive ones. Indeed we are bound to presuppose more than we can prove (Gödel), know more than we can tell (Polanyi), notice more than we can see (Whitehead), if such acts are to be possible at all. Thus generally, the consciousness at work, the knowledge exploited, in action may be — and at some level must always be — practical rather than discursive, tacit and inexplicit, spontaneous not reflective, a matter of know-how rather than know-that,[77] the performance of a competence. So such knowledge cannot immediately ground, even if it is held to furnish the ultimate empirical touchstone of, a discursive theoretical science (cf. the social poiesiological group — see p. 126 above).

Of course the agent plays a special rôle in the verification of accounts, both of the mechanisms utilised in practical abilities and of motives. But practical knowledge or competence is never epistemically self-certifying. For any particular act will normally display much else besides the ability in question or it may not in fact display it at all (the behaviour may be accidental, or over-determined by other unrelated causal processes); and its identification as an ability of a specified type (under a sufficiently specific description) will normally depend upon a

---

76. M. Polanyi, *Personal Knowledge*, London 1958, esp. chapter 4.
77. G. Ryle, *The Concept of Mind*, Harmondsworth 1963, esp. chapter 2.

thorough hermeneutic and historical permeation of the culture in which the skill is exercised (cf. ($\alpha$)-($\gamma$) on p. 156 above). Turning now from skills to motives, notice that the assumption of relative privilege for an agent's account of her reasons depends upon the notion of the causal efficacy of her beliefs — for otherwise there would be no reason to prefer her's to an outsider's account — but that such a notion at the same time establishes an ontic distance between the agent's belief and any particular expression or statement of it, grounded in the existential intransitivity of the belief at the moment (or for the duration) of its efficacy, entailing the corrigibility of any description of it. On the other hand, once it is accepted that an action is distinguished from a mere movement by the condition that it has a belief for its cause, then it is easy to see that some of the agents' beliefs *must* be efficacious, and that unless most of our everyday beliefs were in fact efficacious, and we were in general able to identify *which* of them were, communication and interaction generally would be impossible.

However it does not follow from this (i) that the beliefs are generally true (as distinct from efficacious and statements of them generally veracious);[78] (ii) that any *particular* belief about whether or not a belief is causally efficacious or generative is true, since there will always remain a gap between any causally efficacious belief and a description of it, which may sometimes (for a variety of well-rehearsed reasons) be easier for an outsider to bridge; (iii) that our beliefs about the causes of (which may include reasons or grounds for) the causally efficacious beliefs are true. It is one thing to know that a person is polishing an icon, quite another to know *why* s/he is doing so. Of course this distinction between the immediate and underlying causes of actions (between causes, and causes of causes, of actions) is relative to our normal ways of identifying and describing actions. But these are in turn relative to our normal ways of

---

78. Although it is not a necessary condition of an intentional action, and for the correct identification of the intention of an action, that the action does in fact possess the property for the sake of which it is performed (so that veracity and truth are distinct), a parallel argument to that employed in the text would show that while there may be particular, systematic and underlying discrepancies between intention and property, general mismatch at the ordinary level would render the identification of the problematic cases impossible.

acting, i.e. to the types of acts which we do in fact intentionally (and successfully) perform. Thus in a psychoanalytic community, for instance, the distinction would be shifted only to the extent that its members successfully acted on analytic theories! To summarise, then, although practical life would be impossible unless we possessed certain skills, it is not a condition of practical life that we know the mechanism of these skills; and although communication and interaction in particular would be impossible unless we were normally able to identify agents' immediate reasons for acting, this does not mean either ($\alpha$) that we must be always able to do so or, more fundamentally, ($\beta$) that we must be able to identify the underlying reasons for (or causes of) those reasons — nor of course does this argument establish that communication and interaction will always be possible (cf. 1.6 above). ($\beta$) of course situates the possibility of the systematic misdescription of underlying or structural causes in ideological mystification or psychological rationalisation, i.e. of 'self-misunderstood' forms of social life or agency.

(b) In considering the hermeneutical motivation for the doctrine of social foundations, the meaning of an act (or utterance) must be distinguished from the agent's intention in performing it. Again both are important. Although the immediate intentions of agents or meanings of actions cannot normally be misdescribed for mutual understanding or functioning, well-oiled language-games to be possible, both intentions and meanings may be opaque to agents occasionally, at the level of everyday interaction and systematically, at the level of the underlying reasons for any meanings of their behaviour. The meaning of an action is a social fact which, to the extent that the action is intentional under that description, is utilised by the actor in the production of her performance. But the reason why the agent performs the act is a fact about the person which cannot be read off or deduced from its social meaning. The question 'why is X exchanging rings with Y?' is not exclusively or exhaustively answered by reference to the fact that this is part of the ceremony (act) of getting married. I want to argue that an agent's beliefs as to the reasons for her actions may be both explicably false (and in particular both false and necessary), and that both agents' statements or assessments of the meanings of their actions, and the meanings themselves, may be, in interesting ways, corrigible.

It is clear that for any action $\psi$, the agent N may be unaware

of, or misdescribe (before, during or after $\psi$), her real, i.e. the causally efficacious (whether underlying or immediate), reason, say s, for $\psi$. Such a misdescription, say p, of the motivating stimulus, s, for $\psi$ — which we may write as p[-s] — may of course itself be a necessary releasing condition for $\psi$. In this case, then, p is *false* inasmuch as it misdescribes s, so rationalising $\psi$, but *necessary for* $\psi$, insofar as $\psi$ would not occur without it (or perhaps some other suitable releasing condition, in which event p would only be contingently necessary for $\psi$). And in a simple depth-psychological model, p might be *necessitated* (generated) *by* s, s.p jointly codetermining as stimulus and releasing conditions $\psi$, i.e. s → p[-s]. sp[-s] →$\psi$ (or more simply s → p → $\psi$. This paradigm may be readily extended to include 'outer' as well as 'inner' causes, where outer causes encompass all causes other than the agent's reasons — e.g. social and natural conditions (with natural conditions covering those internal as well as those external to the agent's biological frame). Thus it might be true that sp would not have occurred but for some somatic condition, P, and the misdescription of some social structure S, in an ideology I, where the social structure itself generates I — i.e. when
(S → I[-S]). P → (s → p[-s]. sp[-s]) → $\psi$.
Obviously various combinations of inner and outer causes are conceivable.

What of meanings? If acts are what are done in or by actions, then it is uncontentious: (i) that an agent may be unaware of some of the acts s/he performs, i.e. that s/he may be unaware of some of the meanings of what s/he does; and (ii) that acts, as well as actions, may come to be redescribed in the course of history. By a development of the argument in the preceding paragraph, it is easy to appreciate how lack of awareness may be a causally necessary condition for action. But in what ways can the attribution of meanings by an agent be wrong? And in what ways can meanings be positively misidentified? Meanings at the ordinary level of day-to-day interaction and transaction with nature cannot be generally misattributed within a culture, but they can certainly be misattributed: (a) by a particular agent and in any particular case; (b) for some systematic class of acts; and (c), most importantly, at the level of the underlying, structural causes of (or grounds for) behaviour. What agents do in praxis is never simply motivated, intentional production, but is always also (normally unmotivated) reproduction and transformation of the conditions of production, including especially social structures. Agents may be simply unaware of this dimension of their praxis (these acts that they perform); or they may describe them in quite inadequate ways. Moreover they may not be able, in their language, to describe them in anything but inadequate ways, or even at all. Particularly significant here is the possibility (already noted in 1.3) of a contingent generalisation of Gödel's theorem in the direction of a *critical depth semantics* or meta-critique. This aims to pinpoint what cannot be said, articulated or expressed *in* a particular language or conceptual system about what is said or done, presupposed or shown *by means of* it; or, generally, what cannot be said in a language about what is done in the society which the language articulates — a critique which leads quickly into the critique of the society itself, inasmuch as causal relations can be established between this linguistic-conceptual constitution and the structure of the society concerned. Agents may thus be unaware, or positively misdescribe, or be unable adequately to describe some of the most significant meanings of actions which they intentionally perform. Only if we have been tacitly destratifying semantic space to the level of some foundational 'given' should we feel any surprise or unease at this.

In general, then, the generative rôle of agents' skills, wants and beliefs and of social beliefs and meanings must be recognised, and their authenticity and epistemic significance respected, without lapsing into an interpretative fundamentalism by conferring (discursive status and) incorrigibility upon them. But how do we isolate agents' beliefs and social meanings in particular in the face of the corrigibility or absence of statements of them? Agents' accounts (or the lack of them) are more than just evidence: they are internally related aspects of what they are about. Hence any resolution of the problem of identifying agents' beliefs must be two-way, it being incumbent upon the social student to avoid both the pitfalls of arrogant dismissal of and fawning assent to first-person accounts.[79] But agreement between agent and student, if and when it can be reached, hardly seems either sufficient or necessary for an adequate identification at the level of the deep, underlying or strange. Interpretations (including self-interpretations) here can

---

79. Cf. R. Bernstein, *The Reconstruction of Social and Political Theory*, Oxford 1976, p. 203.

only be checked out in that always more or less contingently circumscribed field of the agents' developing biography or, at the societal level, history — that is, total development (not just discourse). If judgements about beliefs cannot be separated from judgements about activity, judgements about meaning — again presupposing a two-way resolution (in the shape of a dialogical fusion of horizons)[80] — are inseparable from judgements about explanatory adequacy. Thus the so-called 'problem of the indeterminacy of translation' (which is only a special case of the general problem of the underdetermination or theory by evidence) can only be resolved in practice by selecting that translation which is *explanatorily most adequate* (whether or not it is most charitable) in the context of what is already known about the organisation of the particular society in question (and of societies in general) — a context which may well of course be modified by the explanatory choice. The most adequate explanation will save the maximum of significant phenomena in the subject-matter at issue, showing in that subject-matter precisely the degree and the type of rationality that makes this possible. *Mutatis mutandis* similar considerations apply to the problems of how 'thick',[81] 'fuzzy', 'quantifiable', 'vague' etc. social descriptions should be. Some social practices are vague, others are ambiguous and they should be described accordingly.[82] Some epistemically significant phenomena are countable, others are not; some activities, such as smalltalk, are intrinsically fuzzy, others, such as many ceremonies and routines, may be precisely defined; some social episodes are densely packed, others, like a desert trek or a slow train journey in the early hours of the morning, may have no interior. The only general rules to follow are: (i) engage dialogically with one's subject; (ii) maximise total explanatory power; and (iii) make one's analysis as precise, but only as precise, as 'the nature of the subject permits'.[83]

---

80. Cf. H.G. Gadamer, *Truth and Method*, London 1975.
81. Cf. H. Geertz, *The Interpretation of Cultures*, New York 1973.
82. Vagueness and ambiguity are sometimes confused. Vagueness inhabits the shading, soft-edged, open textured conceptual universe of Wittgenstein and Waismann, the world of rule and context. Ambiguity, on the other hand, points towards the conceptual spheres of ambivalence and contradiction, plumbed by Marx and Freud, the world of structure and code. Needless to say both are indispensable categories of social analysis.
83. Aristotle, *Nicomachian Ethics*, Book I. 1094 b 25.

## 5. Facts and Values: Theory and Practice

*Science is meaningless because it gives no answer to our question, the only question important to us, "what shall we do and how shall we live?"*[84]

I now intend to show that the human sciences are necessarily non-neutral; that they are intrinsically critical (both of beliefs and their objects) and self-critical; that accounts of social reality are not only value-impregnated but value-impregnating, not only practically-imbued but practically-imbuing; and that in particular they both causally motivate and logically entail evaluative and practical judgements *ceteris paribus*. I will not be so concerned with the way in which factual and theoretical judgements are predisposed by value and practical commitments. This is partly because these connections have been better recognised,[85] but more because I want to address myself to an historic aspiration: the hope that the human sciences might yet come to be in a position to cast some light on the question 'which really interests us', of what to do and say, feel and think.

On the thesis advocated here, social science is non-neutral in a double respect: it always consists in a *practical intervention* in social life and it sometimes *logically entails* value and practical judgements. In particular the possibility of a scientific *critique* of lay (and proto-scientific) ideas, grounded in explanatory practices based on recognition of the epistemic significance of these ideas, affords to the human sciences an essential emancipatory impulse. Such a *conatus* does not license an unmediated transition from factual appraisals to practical imperatives in particular situations. But mediated by the explanatory power of theory and subject to the operation of various *ceteris paribus* clauses, we do nevertheless pass securely from statements of fact to practice. Appreciation of the emancipatory dynamic of explanatory theory dissolves the rigid dichotomies — between fact and value, theory and practice, explanation and emancipation, science and critique — structuring traditional normative discourse.

---

84. L. Tolstoy, quoted in M. Weber, 'Science as a Vocation', *From Max Weber: Essays in Sociology*, New York 1946, p. 143.
85. See e.g. C. Taylor, 'Neutrality in Political Science', *The Philosophy of Social Explanation*, ed. A. Ryan, Oxford 1973.

Besides the positivist and irrationalist creeds of the neutrality and impotence of social science, together with their sundry (e.g. hermeneutical; historicist) displacements, I will also be objecting to a rationalistic intellectualism or *theoreticism* which conceives social science as immediately efficacious in practice. This view, which comes in traditional-authoritarian, utilitarian-technocratic (including reformist socialist, e.g. Fabian) and Stalinist variants, is often coupled with, or indeed founded on, a barely disguised contempt for the cognitive worth of the actors' point of view.[86] In opposition to it, I want to insist that social science always only happens in a context which is at once always understood, preconceptualised, and codetermined by non-cognitive factors too. So that, on this stance, social theory appears, at its best, in the form of *conditioned critique*. As critique, it presupposes and engages with those preconceptual-isations; as conditioned, it is subject in its genesis, reception and effect, to extra-scientific, extra-cognitive and non-ideational, as well as scientific, cognitive and ideational, determinations (whose critical understanding is itself part of the business of theory). This is of course an implication of historical *materialism*. To understand critique as conditioned by agencies outside itself is not to impugn its explanatory power (or normative force), merely to be realistic — that is, self-reflexively scientific (descriptively and explanatorily adequate) — about its practical impact.

On the position advanced here, knowledge, although necessary, is insufficient for freedom. For to be free is: (1) to know one's real interests; (2) to possess both (a) the ability and the resources, i.e. generically the power, and (b) the opportunity to act in (or towards) them; and (3) to be disposed to do so. An interest is anything conducive to the achievement of agents' wants, needs and/or purposes; and a need is anything (contingently or absolutely) necessary to the survival or well-being of an agent, whether the agent currently possesses it or not. Satisfaction of a need, in contrast to the fulfilment of a want or purpose, cannot ever *per se* make an individual or group worse off. Notice that freedom can be no more the simple recognition,

---

86. See e.g. from the Fabian camp, 'we have little faith in the "average sensual man", we do not believe he can do much more than describe his grievances, we do not think he can prescribe his remedies', B. Webb, *Our Partnership*, entry for 24th December 1894, London 1948.

than escape from, necessity. Engels and Sartre must be adjudged equally wrong insofar as circumstances, capacities, wants (and/or needs) etc. contain non-cognitive components. It is salutary to remember that there is a logical gap between 'knowing' and 'doing' which can only be bridged by 'being able and wanting to do in suitable circumstances'. It is my contention that that special qualitative kind of becoming free or liberation which is *emancipation,* and which consists in the *trans-formation,* in self-emancipation by the agents concerned, *from an unwanted and unneeded to a wanted and needed source of determination,* is both causally presaged and logically entailed by explanatory theory, but that it can only be effected in *practice.* Emancipation, as so defined, depends upon the trans-formation of structures, not the alteration or amelioration of states of affairs. In this special sense an emancipatory politics or practice is necessarily both grounded in scientific theory and revolutionary in objective or intent.

Although I argue that social science sometimes entails, often informs and always affects values and actions, I am far from holding that either can be wholly determined by or analytically reduced to social science. Social science cannot determine or uniquely ground values, because there are other good things in life besides explanatory knowledge; and it cannot determine, or on its own rationally inform, action, because this is always a matter of will, desire, sentiment, capacities, facilities and opportunities as well as beliefs.

Moreover, to resolve the jaded dichotomies by elucidating the rational connections between the terms customarily dichotomously opposed, in no way gainsays the categorial differenti-ation of the poles. Here again, as before, on an integrative pluralistic approach, we must think the unity of distinctions within (and as) connections.

I am taking it for granted that human beings are character-ised by a biological basis, the capacity for intentional agency and for the reflexive awareness and organisation of such agency and by a thoroughly social existence. What is normally meant by 'consciousness' refers to those aspects of our praxis in which we are (progressively) (i) sentient, (ii) aware, (iii) attentive, (iv) reflexively self-aware, attentive and articulate and (v) occupied in planned (controlled, deliberate, integrated), reasonable (intelligent, well-grounded, responsible) collective, coordinated or mutual activity. Although Turing-based and more generally computational models can capture some features of human intelligence, they cannot do justice to either the biological or the social dimensions of our praxis, in which all the other features of our conscious (and unconscious) life and agency are marinated.[87] For insofar as we are machines, we are *sentient* ones, related by homologies to other animals (and not merely analogies with man-made machines). Moreover, our characteristically human powers (such as speech) are both ontogenetically rooted in the maturation of an organism and phylogenetically steeped in the (biological) history of an evolving species. Our sense of self and agency are pervaded with affect, and when we attach significance and meaning to the world of objects, others and ourselves we do so, from our ontic standpoint, as feeling organisms. Second, if we are sentient machines, we are also *mobilising* ones, situated *ab initio* in a pre-formed, potentially public social world. And in our transformative causal agency, mobilising pre-existing structures, we endow the world with consequences, realising (or not) our purposes in it, and conferring meaning upon it, including the physical and cultural products of our agency (such as Turing machines), reproducing or transforming those structures in the course of our agency.[88] Human consciousness, understood as an aspect of human praxis, is an irreducibly bio-social product in a psychological mode.

Science informs values and actions which in turn motivate science, so one is in effect dealing with fact-value and theory-practice helices here. These helices can be rationally developing precisely to the extent that there is a sense in which facts and theories non-trivially entail values and practices but not vice-versa. To simplify matters I will consider in the first place only relations involving practical judgements rather than actions (the connections between the two will be considered shortly).

---

87. Cf. ed. P. Secord, *Explaining Social Behaviour*, London 1982.
88. Cf. Marx: 'A spider conducts operations which resemble those of a beaver, and a bee would put many a human architect to shame by the construction of its honeycomb cells. But what distinguishes the worst architect from the best of bees is that the architect wills a cell in his mind before he constructs it in wax. At the end of every labour process, a result emerges which had already been conceived by the worker at the beginning, hence already existed ideally. Man not only affects a change of form in the materials of nature; he also realises [ *verwirklicht*] his own purpose in those materials', *Capital Vol. I*, Harmondsworth 1976, p. 284.

The asymmetry between the F → V and T → P relationships, on the one hand, and the V → F and P → T relationships, on the other, stems from the consideration that whereas factual and theoretical considerations not only predispose and motivate, but, in favourable epistemic circumstances (to be spelt out in a moment) and subject to the operation of various *ceteris paribus* clauses, logically entail value and practical judgements; value and practical commitments, while they may (and in general will) predispose and sometimes motivate, do not (non-trivially) entail factual and theoretical judgements.[89] It is just these asymmetries which make the helices potentially rational ones: that is progressively developing spirals, rather than merely self-confirming, and so self-destroying, more or less rapidly vanishing circles. The helices can be set out as in Diagrams 2.16 and 2.17 below, where the double lines indicate relations of

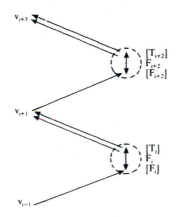

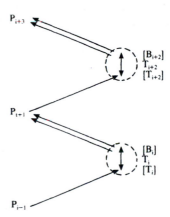

Diagram 2.16: *Fact/Value Helix*

N.B. F,V stand for fact-theory complexes and values respectively; [F], [T] stand for factual and theoretical components within fact-theory complexes.

Diagram 2.17: *Theory/Practice Helix*

N.B. T,P stand for theory-belief complexes and practices (and actions) respectively.
[T] [B] stand for theoretical and other (e.g. evaluative) components within theory-belief complexes.

89. If 'ought' implies 'can', the non-trivial implication of a power is a pre-supposition, not an entailment, of the ought-statement — an implication which depends on a theory (i.e. factual knowledge) of the agent and his or her circumstances. (Cf. N. Cooper, *The Diversity of Moral Thinking*, Oxford 1981, p. 181.)

entailment and causal influence (inclination, etc.) and the single lines causal influence only.

The scientistic denial of the value-impregnation of factual discourse, involving the reification of propositional contents, shares with the positivistic denial of its converse, viz. the value-impregnating character of factual discourse, a naive extentionalist theory of meaning (whether in physicalist, sensationalist or Platonist guise). Moreover, it shares with the theoreticist conception of the unmediated efficacy of theoretical discourse a neglect of the non-cognitive bases of action, spawning a voluntarism of theoretical praxis; while the converse 'practicist' error (of anti-intellectualist irrationalism) ignores the cognitive bases of action. There are hyper-naturalist and hyper-rationalist analogues of theoreticism and scientism respectively. Theoreticism, as defined above, leads naturally to the denial that practice (to the extent that it is not merely a redescription of theory) plays any rôle in the generation or development of theory. Similarly ethical hyper-naturalism tends to the denial of any causal impact of values on the process of theory. These errors can be tabulated as below, where the treble arrows indicate unmediated efficacy or direct expression.

| | | | |
|---|---|---|---|
| F | $\nrightarrow$ | V | positivism (and displacements) |
| V | $\nrightarrow$ | F | scientism |
| F | $\Rrightarrow$ | V | ethical hyper-naturalism ($\rightarrow$ V $\nrightarrow$ P) |
| V | $\Rrightarrow$ | F | ethically based epistemological idealism[90] |
| T | $\nrightarrow$ | P | irrationalism |
| P | $\nrightarrow$ | T | hyper-rationalism |
| T | $\Rrightarrow$ | P | theoreticism ($\rightarrow$ P $\nrightarrow$ T) |
| P | $\Rrightarrow$ | T | ultrapositivism (or ultra-pragmatism) |

Table 2.2

Once the value-implications of theory, and the rational assessability of wants (in virtue of their grounding in beliefs) is established, then Diagram 2.9 on p. 128 can be modified as in Diagram 2.18 below. The bases of action may be classified into five broad types: cognitive, conative, affective, dynamic and cir-

---

90. E.g. of a subjectivist, pragmatist, emotivist, existentialist — or a quasi-objectivist (e.g. Platonist or intuitionist) — sort.

cumstantial.[91] The *dynamic* bases of action[92] comprise the *powers* necessary to perform an action in appropriate (normal or specified) circumstances. These powers may be subdivided into two general kinds: the *competences*, including practical capacities, skills and abilities of various sorts; and the *facilities*, including political, economic, normative (moral, legal, etc.) resources and more generally possibilities. Competences constitute the *intrinsic*, facilities the *extrinsic* dynamic bases of action. It is plain that an agent may possess a competence without the corresponding facility and vice-versa. The five bases of actions are only analytically separable. Thus there are cognitive competences, facilities to acquire competences, etc.; and in general for any category of agent and act the bases will be causally connected and often internally related. All the bases of action have structural conditions and effects, and each basis is in general necessary for any action, so that in particular the intrinsic/ extrinsic contrast cannot be identified with the praxis/structure distinction. The circumstantial basis of action is a holdall, which includes structures not directly implicated in the action and the whole welter of material and social conditions and contingencies that comprise an agent's 'context'. It is the dynamic basis of action, and the coincidence of competences and facilities in human transformative agency, that lies at the heart of the transformational conception of social activity espoused here.

As already intimated in §2, inasmuch as theoretical and practical explanations (of the patterns recapitulated in §1) succeed in identifying real, but hitherto unrecognised conditions and patterns of determination, they immediately augment our knowledge — of the objective and subjective conditions and the effects and forms of praxis. And hence, *ceteris paribus*, they augment both the rationality of our actions and the degree, or possibility, of our freedom (on the definition enlisted above). But there is a significant asymmetry between the extrinsic dynamic and circumstantial bases of action and the others. Any

91. I here include the volitional under the conative basis of action. But it is arguable that the will, comprising the unity of a well-functioning ego, should be accorded a distinct place.

92. Cf. G.H. Wright, *An Essay on Modal Logic*, Amsterdam 1951. Neglect of the dynamic bases of action amounts to forgetting the historicity of the agent and her *Umwelt*; and by assuming the existence of competences and facilities, it obscures the politics of their development, acquisition and distribution.

beneficial effect of knowledge on action, e.g. in the direction of enhanced rationality or greater freedom, at these levels presupposes mutual or collective effort; and as in general each base is necessary for any action, such effort is a condition for the realisation or implementation of *any* scientifically inspired change. In short, the benefit of any scientific enlightenment depends upon a *politics*. Politics may itself be conceived most abstractly as any practice oriented to the transformation of the conditions of human action; more concretely, as practices oriented to or conducted in the context of struggles and conflicts over the development, nature and distribution of the facilities (and circumstances) of human action; more starkly, as practices oriented to the transformation of the structured sets of social relations within which particular social structures operate and particular social activities occur. Insofar as emancipation depends upon the transformation of structures, and such structures are general (extensive), a *self*-emancipatory politics, oriented to that transformation of unwanted and unnecessary source of determination, will of course need to be a *mass* (extensive) one. But such a politics *need* not be necessary for the transformation of particular or local constraints or for constraints stemming from the subjective (psychological) conditions, or (poiesological) forms or (praxiological) effects as distinct from the objective (social-structural) conditions of action.[93]

My core argument is simple. It turns on the condition that the subject-matter of the human sciences comprehends both social objects (including beliefs) and beliefs about those objects. Philosophers have been prone to ignore the internal relations connecting them: empiricists by obectivising beliefs (naturalising them or otherwise undermining their epistemic significance, scouting the IA of consciousness, in the terms introduced in 1.3); idealists by bracketing objects (in one way or another extracting the belief from the historical context of its

---

93. It is of course plausible to conjecture systematic relations between the zones analytically differentiated in Diagram 2.7 on p. 126 above, especially in view of the intrinsically social content of the objects of the psychological groups of sciences. In which event it is plausible to suppose that while an emancipatory practice in the other dimensions will not take the form of a mass politics (but that of an individual one — say speech-therapy) they may presuppose such a politics as a historically facilitating (or enabling) condition.

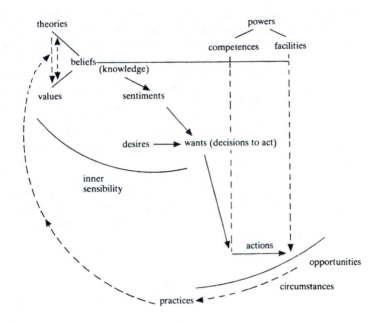

Diagram 2.18: *The Five Bases of Action and Practices, Values and Theories*

formation, denying the EA of consciousness). These relations, which may or may not be intra-cognitive — depending upon whether the first-order object is itself a belief — are *both* causal and epistemic. In the ontological or intransitive dimension of some particular belief (or epistemic$_2$) we are concerned with relations of causal *generation*; in the epistemological or transitive dimension with relations of representative adequacy (truth) and *critique*. But it is the causal relation of generation which grounds the epistemological programme of critique.

Let a belief P, which has some object O, have a source (causal explanation) S. I am going to contend that if we possess:

(i) adequate grounds for supposing P is false; and
(ii) adequate grounds for supposing that S co-explains P,
then we may, and must, pass immediately to
(iii) a negative evaluation of S (CP); and
(iv) a positive evaluation of action rationally directed at the removal of S (CP).

That is, inasmuch as we can explain, i.e. show the (perhaps contingent) necessity for some determinate false consciousness, or perhaps just some determinate consciousness under the determinable 'false', then the inferences to a negative evaluation of its sources and a positive evaluation of action oriented towards their dissolution are, *ceteris paribus*, mandatory. Of course such action can only be rationally justified to the extent that there are grounds for supposing the source dissoluble (or sufficiently transformable). The notion of false consciousness employed here simply involves in the first instance that of disjuncture, mismatch or lack of correspondence (representative adequacy) between belief and object. But, as I shall presently show, this general pattern of argument may be readily extended to accommodate more interestingly specific forms of false consciousness, and indeed more generally of defective or unfulfilling being. However it should be made plain that the T.M.S.A. does not *per se* licence the supposition of a society without some false consciousness or, more generally, socially remediable ills.

In principle this pattern of inference applies equally to beliefs about *natural*, as well as social, objects, on the condition (and to the extent) that the relevant *source* of false consciousness, S, is itself a social, or at least socialisable, object, i.e. an object amenable to social control (or influence). But then S cannot be the same as O and will not, at least insofar as it is praxis-independent (e.g. the speed of light, the specific gravity of mercury), be internally related to O; and neither S nor P can, at least in the praxis-independent case, be causal conditions for the genesis or persistence of O (or some causal condition or effect of O), as in the cases of psychological rationalisation and ideological mystification, where S, P and O are typically causally interrelated.[94] Only in the cases of beliefs about social objects can the illusory (or more generally defective) character of con-

---

94. Weak quasi-natural analogues of these explanatory-critical modes, where the proximate source of mystification S′ is an artefact or naturalised social object or alternatively a socialised natural object, as in some forms of primitive fetishism, are usually subject both to B-type mediation, i.e. they are mixed modes in the sense of § 1, and deeper forms of explanation on which S′ is socio-theoretically redescribed. It is not the physical properties of shoes which explains the shoe fetishist's fetishism, but the meaning shoes have in his or her life, which once understood, shows the shoe as a (condensed) code for something else, some specific socio-somatic configuration.

sciousness be a condition of what it is about. However, given that beliefs about nature are social objects, *all* the modalities of false consciousness may apply to our understanding *of*, as distinct from *in*, science.

I shall call (i) the *critical* and (ii) the *explanatory* condition. Of course even if the critical condition alone is satisfied, then we also pass immediately to a negative evaluation of P (CP), and of actions based on or informed by P (CP). But I want to distinguish this kind of '*criticism*' which, although it formally violates and so refutes 'Hume's law',[95] remains silent on the causes of error, from an '*explanatory critique*'. Criticism, in Marx's words, 'knows how to judge and condemn the present, but not how to comprehend it'.[96] The essence of Marx's objection to criticism may, I think, be stated thus: it employs value (and especially, although not necessarily, moral) terms in the absence of any kind of causal grounding. At its best, i.e. if elaborated in naturalistic (i.e. non-intuitionist or -emotivist) form, it can furnish objective grounds for belief and action which, if true, extend our freedom. But criticism says nothing *about*, although it may of course (intentionally or unwittingly) causally affect, the (causal) conditions of action, the springs of belief and behaviour, the sources of determination. And so it cannot illuminate the topic of the transformation of the sources of determination from unnecessary to rationally wanted ones. Only a discourse in which the explanatory as well as the critical condition is satisfied, can be intrinsically emancipatory.

'Depth-explanations' may be undertaken at each of the levels corresponding to the four kinds of limits on actors' knowledge identified earlier (see Diagram 2.7 on p. 126 above), corresponding to the subjective and objective conditions of action, and its effects and forms in both the dimensions of interactions between agents and transactions with nature. Templates of these types are provided by the Freudian theory of rationalisation; the Marxian theory of ideology; phenomenological and ecological studies of the mechanisms of interactional and natural-

---

95. See R. Hare, *Freedom and Reason*, Oxford 1963, p. 109. This attribution has been (in my opinion unconvincingly) disputed – see e.g. A. MacIntyre, 'Hume on "ought" and "is"', *Against the Self-Images of the Age*, London 1971. The vexed passage in Hume is at *A Treatise of Human Nature*, ed. L.A. Selby-Bigge, Oxford 1965, III. 6.1, p. 468-70.
96. *Capital Vol. I*, p. 639 n.

transactional counterfinality; and developmental and structural studies of the mechanisms of operational-instrumental-technical and communicative-presentational-moral competences (e.g. in the work of Piaget, Chomsky, Habermas and Goffman).

The fine structure of most of these explanatory species is considerably more complicated than that depicted in the bare form of an explanatory critique. Moreover many, perhaps most, of the significant depth-theorists at the praxiological and poiesiological levels have both disclaimed any critical intentions and formulated universalistic theories — with questions of facilities, blockages and structural change marginalised. Despite this, I think it can be shown that, shifting the marginalia into more central loci, transitions from facts to value and theory to practice can be effected in essentially the same way as in the Marxian and Freudian paradigms. I cannot attempt to demonstrate this here. Instead I want to focus on the logical structure of an explanatory critique. The possibilty of such a critique constitutes the kernel of the emancipatory potential of the human sciences; and the possibility of the effectivity of such a critique in human history comprises perhaps the only chance of non-barbaric, i.e. civilised, survival for the human species. But to illustrate the possibilities here fully, I want to develop the argument on a series of levels, which may be regarded as so many ratchets of historical reason.

## 6. Reason and the Dialectic of Human Emancipation

*The world has long since dreamed of something of which it needs only to become conscious for it to possess in reality ... To obtain forgiveness for its sins mankind need only declare them for what they are.*[97]

Seven levels of rationality may be identified as follows:

| Level I: | Technical rationality | |
|----------|----------------------|---|
| Level II: | Contextually-situated instrumental rationality | Instrumental reason |

---

97. 'Marx to Ruge', September 1843, *Early Writings*, Harmondsworth 1975, p. 209.

| | | |
|---|---|---|
| Level III: | Practical rationality | |
| Level IV: | Explanatory critical rationality | |

Critical reason

practical = criticism

explanatory = critique

| | |
|---|---|
| Level V: | Depth-Explanatory-Critical rationality |
| Level VI: | Depth-rationality |

Emancipatory reason

| | |
|---|---|
| Level VII: | Historical rationality |

Historical reason

## *Instrumental v. Critical Reason*

At the first two levels, no attempt is made to question the logical heterogeneity (and impenetrability) of facts and values. Despite this, the human sciences may still have (so to speak, contingently) emancipatory implications in virtue of (i) their use as sheer technique and (ii) their effects, in the context of the existence of relations of domination, exploitation and oppression.

### *Level I: Technical Rationality*

Patently, the human sciences may be used, like any other sciences, to achieve more or less consciously formulated and justified ends, which may of course be adjudged either (and more or less) good or bad. In particular, explanatory theories may be used, in conjunction with statements of particular initial conditions, to generate technical imperatives akin to 'put antifreeze in the radiator (if you want to avoid it bursting in winter) CP'. If such imperatives ever appear to depart from the ends-means schema, this is only because they implicitly presuppose a context of human purposes in the domain of their intended applications. This is the only kind of rationality positivism knows.

### *Level II: Contextually-Situated Instrumental Rationality*

The human sciences, even at the rung of instrumental reason, are not symmetrically beneficial to the parties involved in relations of domination, etc. For, in the first place, explanatory knowledge increases the range of real (non-utopian) human possibilities, which may of course also mean decreasing the range of imagined ones, by showing certain of these to be purely imaginary.

But CP this will tilt the balance of (in a broad sense) political argument, discussion, vision and choice against the status quo. This is quite consistent with the existence of only a simple external connection between knowledge and politics.

Secondly, even on an instrumental interpretation, explanatory knowledge appears as a necessary condition for rational self-emancipation — whether what the agent seeks emancipation from be the oppression of individuals, groups, classes; of practices, institutions, organisations; of relations, structures and systems; of material situations, ideational complexes, interactive networks; or of remediable lacks, incapacities and unfulfilments — acting as unnecessary, positively or negatively, by their presence or absence (or by their commissions or omissions), compulsions or constraints on action. Hence the oppressed, dominated, exploited, repressed, denied have an *interest* in knowledge which their oppressors lack, in the straightforward sense that it facilitates the achievement of their wants and the satisfaction of their needs. And their oppressors, or more generally the oppressing agency, inasmuch as their (or its) interests are antagonistic to the oppressed[98], possess an interest in the ignorance of the oppressed (and perhaps even in their own ignorance of the nature, or the fact of their oppressing). Thus the human sciences, and at a remove philosophy, cannot be regarded as *equally* 'a potential instrument of domination' or of 'the expansion of the rational autonomy of action'.[99] The human sciences are not neutral in their consequences in a non-neutral (unjust, asymmetrical) world. And it is just this which explains their liability to periodic or sustained attack by established and oppressive powers.

### Level III: Intra-Discursive (Non-Explanatory) Critical or Practical Rationality

The point has been well made[100] that any science depends upon

---

98. This depends on the balance of what they stand to lose and to gain if they forego their oppressing.

99. A. Giddens, *New Rules of Sociological Method*, London 1976, p. 159.

100. R. Edgley, 'Marx's Revolutionary Science', *Issues in Marxist Philosophy*, *Vol. III*, eds. J. Mepham and D.H. Ruben, Brighton 1979,

intra-discursive criticism, i.e. criticism of other actually or possi-bly believed (and therefore potentially efficacious) theories, hypotheses etc. Acceptance of some theory T entails CP a series of negative evaluations: on theories incompatible with it, on beliefs such theories underpin, on actions sustained or informed by them. Although 'X is false' does not just *mean* 'don't believe (act on) X', it certainly CP entails it. Conversely 'X is true' entails 'act on X (in appropriate circumstances) CP'. It is just this that makes applied science, and indeed any rational or even intentional (speech or other) action possible. (*That* there is a link between beliefs and actions is transcendentally necessary; what this link is, is a topic for the various sciences). It is only if one were to deny any ontological connection between beliefs and actions, or theory and practice that one could plausibly sup-pose that a change in theoretical judgements does not entail a change in practical judgements CP. But denying such a con-nection makes practical discourse practically otiose. Again this point is consistent with a contingent relationship between a science and its subject-matter; and it applies, quite indifferently, at the level of intra-discursive critical rationality, in all sciences alike. All the sciences, then, irrespective of their subject-matter, are intrinsically critical, and so evaluative.

*Mutatis mutandis* this point applies to all discourse at what might be called the level of practical rationality. A truth claim typically involves both a prescriptive or imperative ('act on X') and a descriptive or evidential ('X is grounded, warranted, justi-fied') component or dimension. What distinguishes truth claims in science from those in ordinary life is not their logical structure, but the nature of their evidential requirements, which incorporate various logical, empirical, inter- and intra-theoretical controls; the object or referent of the truth claim, which is characteristically a causal structure or explanatory mechanism; the persons (and communuties) to which the claim is made and presented for redemption and ratification; and the sorts of uses to which the claim, if it is both validated and true, can be put.

## Level IV: Explanatory Critical Rationality

All the sciences make judgements of truth or falsity on beliefs about their object domains. But the human sciences, in virtue of the distinctive feature of their domain, that it includes, *inter alia*, beliefs about social objects, also make (or at least entail) judgements of truth or falsity on (aspects of) that domain. And such belief/object correspondence, or lack of it, appears immediately as a legitimate object of social scientific explanation. To recapitulate the central argument: if we have a consistent set of theories T that (i) shows some belief P about an object O to be false, and (ii) explains why that, or perhaps some such false (illusory, inadequate, misleading), belief is believed (or held), then the inferences to (iii) a negative evaluation of the object (e.g. system of social relations) accounting for the falsity of the belief (i.e. mismatch in reality between the belief P and what it is about O) and (iv) a positive evaluation of action rationally directed at removing (disconnecting or transforming) that object, i.e. the source(s) of false consciousness, appears mandatory CP. This could be represented, informally, in the inference scheme below as:

*I.S.1.* (i) $T > P$. (ii) $T \exp 1(P) \rightarrow$ (iii) $-V(S \rightarrow I(P) \rightarrow$(iv) $V\phi_{-s}$ and we certainly seem to have derived value conclusions (CP) from purely factual premises.

Now for some possible objections.

1. It might be objected that 'P is false' is not value-neutral. But if it is not value-neutral, as is indicated by the prescriptive component involved in truth claims, then the value-judgement 'P is false' can be derived from premises concerning the lack of correspondence or mismatch of object and belief (in the object domain). Moreover, as assuming that such judgements are intrinsic to any factual discourse, we are nevertheless able to infer from them, together with explanatory premises, conclusions of a type which are *not* intrinsic to *every* factual discourse (viz. those specified in (iii) and (iv)), we do have a transition here that goes against the grain of Hume's law, however it is supposed to be interpreted or applied. On the other hand, if 'P is false' is value-neutral, then the inferences to 'P ought not to be believed (CP)' and 'Don't believe (act upon) (CP)' certainly seems inescapable.

2. The suggestion that science itself presupposes or embodies commitment to certain values such as objectivity, openness, integrity, honesty, veracity, responsibility, consistency, coherence, comprehensibility, explanatory power, etc.

should certainly be welcomed — suggesting as it does that the class of the 'value-neutral' is as empty as that of Austin's original 'constatives'.[101] But it does nothing either to salvage Hume's law or to invalidate inference types (iii) and (iv). These turn on the special feature of the sciences of belief that commitment to truth and explanatory power entail the search for theories which will often possess value-implications that cannot be regarded as conditions of, or as already implicit as anticipations in the organisation of, scientific activity in general.

3. It might be maintained that, although inference type (iii) is valid, (iv) is faulty, so that no commitment to any sort of action is entailed by the critical explanatory theory. But this is not so. For one can reason straight away to action directed at removing the sources of false consciousness, provided of course that one has good grounds for supposing that it would do so, that no ill (or sufficiently overriding ill) effects would be forthcoming, and that there is no better course of action which would achieve the same end. Naturally the inference scheme, as a philosophical reconstruction, does not determine what such practical-critical-revolutionary action is: that is the task of substantive theory. Of course the injunction 'remove (annul, defuse, disconnect, dissolve, transform) sources of false consciousness (CP)' does not specify *what* the sources are, any more than 'lying is wrong' tells us which statements are lies.

Behind this objection, however, lie two considerations of some moment. First, the kind of theory underpinning (iv) may be different from the explanatory theory at (ii) informing (iii). Diagnosis is not therapy. We may know that something is causing a problem without knowing how to get rid of or change it. Secondly, an explanatory critique of this type does not in general specify how we are to act after the source of mystification (false consciousness) is removed. It focuses on action which 'frees' us to act, by eliminating or disconnecting a source of mystification acting as an unwanted source of (co-) determination, replacing that source with another wanted (or perhaps just less unwanted) one, so permitting (absolute or relative) liberation from one stream of constraints or compulsions inherited from, as the causalities (and casualties) of, the past.

---

101. See J. Austin, 'Performative-Constative', *Philosophy and Ordinary Language*, ed. C, Caton, Urbana 1963.

But it does not tell us what to do, if and when (and to the extent that) we are free. Thus emancipated action may (and perhaps must) have a different logical form from emancipatory action.

4. Granting this, it is clear that there is still a gap, or rather two gaps, between the positive evaluation of a course of action at step (iv), in what I shall now discriminate as a practical (evaluative) judgement, and that course of action. The first gap is that punctuated by the *ceteris paribus* clause. Spanning this gap takes us to what I shall call a concrete axiological judgement (CAJ), prescribing what is to be done in the particular circumstances which actually prevail. The second gap is that which holds between such a judgement and the prescribed action. This gap has endeared itself to generations of philosophers under the rubric of the problem of *akrasia* or 'weakness of the will'. Crossing it transports us into the realm of practice proper. Can these gaps be bridged? It should be remembered that some, perhaps implicit, CAJ is always present (and so formed) and some action or other is always performed; so that, unless we are to ascribe a mysterious spontaneity at these levels, the question is never *whether* but *how* the gaps are bridged, and in particular whether they can be rationally crossed from the side of theory — i.e. whether general judgements can be applied to particular situations and particular judgements translated or enacted into practice.

There is nothing special to evaluate or practical discourse about the need for a CP clause: all statements which possess or presuppose an ontic or assertoric content of any generality require it in the context of their actual or possible applications in open systems. The multiplicity and plurality of causes and the transfactuality of laws all disclose evaluative counterparts. For just as what happens in open systems is determined by a multiplicity of causes, what is to be done in them will be determined by a multiplicity of evaluative, theoretical, dynamic and conjunctural (circumstantial) considerations. Further, just as the same mechanism may be exercised in the generation of a plurality of events and the same (kind of) event may in general be codetermined by a plurality of mechanisms, so the same value or goal may be manifest in a plurality of acts and the same act may satisfy (*inter alia*) a plurality of possible values. Moreover the virtue or rationale of an end or possibility is no more undermined by the applicability in some particular situation of countervailing, modifying or reinforcing values and rights than gravity is undermined by the existence of double-decker buses or multi-storey houses. The fact that exactly and only what is to be done can rarely, if ever, be uniquely deduced from general maxims, which accounts for the barrenness of universalisability even as a purely formal criterion (or test) or morality or conduct, stems from these features of action-situations:

1. their ineradicable *openness*, which vitiates deducibility in particular instances or actualities in the sphere of practical (as of theoretical) reason;
2. their *diversity*, under the dense (thick) and highly specified (and differentiated) descriptions under which we must and do normally act;
3. their *historicity*, which vitiates the universality of norms, placing them under the sign of an actual or possible scope restriction.

The kinds of action situations of normative concern to us rarely, if ever, repeat themselves;[102] but it does not follow from this that the same underlying or generative causes are not present at work in them. What follows from the collapse of any *normative actualism*, such as Kantian prescriptivism, utilitarianism or natural law theory, is not the subjective e.g. expressive, pragmatic, spontaneous or intuitive, character of normative discourse (as e.g. in emotivist, existentialist or intuitionist ethics), but the historically specific *or* mediated character of norms, understood tendentially as transfactually applicable (within the restrictions imposed upon their range or realisation by their historically transient or mediated nature). A transcendental realist ontology requires, it will be seen, as much readjustment in ethics as in epistemology. In the particular case at hand the warrant for the transfactual applicability of the con-

---

102. When they do it is usually either under conditions of historical stasis or neurotic (or quasi-neurotic) compulsion, both profoundly historical configurations; so that the repetition itself becomes the particular action situation requiring explanation and change. But if the surface structure of the moral world has more of the aspect of Bergsonian continuous novelty than Nietzschean eternal recurrence, it is important to remember that this surface has a historical, relatively enduring, depth to it — precisely the object of explanatory social science and emancipatory political action.

tent of the practical judgement, (iv), in some particular concrete axiological judgement, (v), is given by our grounds: (a) for the existence, in the domain of the CAJ's application, of the trans-factually efficacious, mystifying structural source of determination, S, specified in the explanatory theory at (ii); and (b) for the feasibility of the emancipatory strategy commended in (iv). This at once justifies the CP clause at (iv) and sanctions the CAJ at (v).

But how do we pass from (v), the CAJ, to (vi), action? The CAJ, as so far specified, is grounded in purely factual considerations, including the agent's assessment of her or his own powers (capacities and facilities). The agent is to be conceived as always already acting, but for any transformation in her praxis, all the bases of action must be satisfied (or allayed); so that even if we suppose that the CAJ is sincerely held (cognitively instantiated), there can still be no guarantee, or even strong presumption (at least at this stage of the argument), that the agent will in fact act in the self-prescribed way. All that can be said is that: if the CAJ is sincerely held and can attach itself to any necessary additional affect and/or desire, so as to find expression in a want; and if the agent can muster the appropriate powers and the circumstances are as described or presupposed in the CAJ; then the action *must* occur. If this does not happen we will naturally look for conflicting wants, changed circumstances etc. The CAJ licenses only the supposition of a predisposition (if a want is a disposition), or (metaphorically) an inclination, orientation, charge, pressure, force or bent in the direction of the action. Theory cannot affect the transition from theory to practice. Only practice itself can do that. It is in this sense that the explanatory critique is always *conditioned* critique.

Our schema thus allows for the following notionally distinct stages: (i) theoretical critique (satisfaction of the critical condition); (ii) explanatory critique (satisfaction of the explanatory condition); (iii) value judgement; (iv) practical judgement; (v) concrete axiological judgement; (vi) transformation in agent's praxis; (vii) emancipatory action, i.e. praxis oriented to emancipation; (viii) transformative praxis, consisting or culminating in the dissolution or progressive transformation of structural sources of determination (emancipating action); (ix) emancipated (free) action.

An inference scheme analogous to ISI applies in the case of the natural sciences. For inasmuch as they are concerned in their own substantive critical discussions not just to isolate and criticise, but to comprehend and causally explain, illusory or inadequate beliefs about the natural world, then they too — assuming the second-order standpoint of the intermediate sciences (in the terminology of § 1) of the natural sociology (or social psychology) of belief — may come to explain false consciousness of nature at least partially in terms of human causes (e.g. faulty instruments, inadequate funds, superstition, the power of the church, state, party or corporations, etc.). This could be represented by

$$I.SI'\ \text{(i) } T > P.\text{(ii) } T\ \exp\ I(P_n) \to \text{(iii) } -V\ (S_s \to I(P_n)) \to \text{(iv) } V\psi_{-s_s}{}^{103}$$

It is of some interest to dwell on this standpoint. Natural science is here conceived as a resultant, product or vector of both natural and cultural (or more generally social) determinants, so that beliefs about nature appear as akin to a mixed or B-type determination (on human actions, etc.) in the sense introduced in § 1. This can be represented in a simple parallelogram of forces, as in Diagram 2.19. In Diagram 2.20 such a parallelogram is used, more specifically, to depict the effect of experience in a theoretically pre-formed context,[104] and more especially to illustrate the way in which experimentation may select within a theoretically defined range (as argued in 1.4). In Diagram 2.21 the parallelogram is used, more broadly in a topological transform of Diagram 2.4 on p. 116 above, to represent the formation of mind or B-type modes generally, and to represent the historical mediation of trans-human-historical or species-general determinants. (These two interpretations of

---

103. The case referred to in § 5 (p. 179 above) where a praxis-dependent natural object acts as a source of false consciousness can be represented as:

$$ISI^*\ \text{(i) } T \to P.\ \text{(ii) } T\ \exp\ I(P_n) \to \text{(iii) } -V(S_{n\psi} \to I(P_n) \to \text{(iv) } V\phi_{-sn\psi}$$

Where a socially irremediable natural object causes systematic false consciousness it is possible to imagine a *deploring* stage (iii) without a stage (iv). Whether this is or would be a rational, as distinct from a likely, attitude is another matter.

104. Cf. D. Bloor, *Knowledge and Social Imagery*, London 1976, chapter 2.

2.21 are distinct: many natural determinations are in their determining form not trans-human-historical.)

In virtue of their explanatory charter, the human sciences must make judgements of truth and falsity and these, in the context of explanatory theories, entail value judgements of type (iii) and (iv), so that inasmuch as they are in a position to give well-grounded explanations of false consciousness, then, the human sciences *must* and the natural sciences *may* (mediately, via the natural sociology of belief) come to form judgements on the causes, as well as the contents, of consciousness. *Mutatis mutandis*, similar considerations apply to judgements of rationality, coherence, consistency etc. Thus I.S.I. can be generalised in the cognitive direction represented in I.S.2 below, where X (P) stands for the contradictory character of some determinate set of beliefs viz.

*I.S.2*    $T > P. T \exp X(P) \rightarrow -V(S \rightarrow X(P)) \rightarrow V\phi_{-S}$

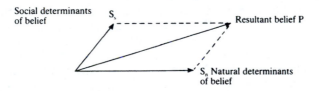

Diagram 2.19

Diagram 2.20

Mind, B-type or historically
mediated determinants

Social, C-type or
historical
determinants

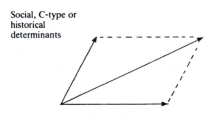

Natural, A-type or trans-human-
historical (species-universal)
determinants

Diagram 2.21
[N.B. These interpretations are distinct]

But the human sciences are not only concerned to explain *'cognitive* ills': their *explananda* are not exhausted by beliefs. Their manifest takes in the explanation of such *'practical* ills' as ill-health, misery, repression, including the socio-economic ills of oppression, brutality, war, exploitation, poverty, waste, etc. and the psycho-social ills of pathological violence, neurotic compulsion, boredom, hysteria, etc.; and, in between such ills and the cognitive ones, the *'communicative* ills' of deception (including self-deception), distortion, etc. Together they comprise such generic ills as frustrated needs, ('unwanted') subjection, unused resources, or underdeveloped powers (competences and facilities), unfulfilled possibilities and thwarted (intra-subjective, inter-subjective and collective intentionality (amounting to *'irrationalities')*, plus gross inequalities in the distribution of powers and liabilities between agents (classes, groups, etc.) (constituting *'injustices')*.

This immediately indicates two further lines of development. First, I.S.1. can be straightaway generalised to deal with the explanation of non-cognitive ills, with a corresponding deduction of evaluative and practical judgements, as in I.S.3

and I.S.3′ below, where I-H stands for ill-health and S-D. for systematic self-deception:

*I.S.3*   T exp. I-H. -V (I-H) → -V(S → I-H) → V$\phi_{-s}$

*I.S.3.′*   T exp. S-D. -V(S-D) → -V(S → S-D) → V$\phi_{-s}$

Clearly ill-health and systematic self-deception may constitute unwanted sources of determination, and insofar as they can be dissolved or replaced by a less unwanted source, so that they are *ipso facto* unnecessary, such a pattern of argument may directly inform emancipatory strategies. However, it will be immediately obvious that these deductions, despite their evident epistemic and practical weight, are no longer from purely factual premises or from what is immediately or self-evidently constitutive of purely factual discourse; and so they do not formally refute Hume's law. It is precisely on this rock that most previous attempts at its refutation, including Searle's attempted derivation of an 'ought' from the notoriously tenuous institution of 'promising',[105] have foundered.

But further reflection shows another possibility here: namely that there are *non-cognitive* conditions, such as a degree of good health and the absence of marked asymmetries in political, economic and the other modalities of power, for discourse (including factual discourse) in general to be possible. If this is correct, then a formal derivation of an 'ought' can proceed as in

*I.S.4*   T > P. T exp.I-H. T exp. (I-H → I(P)) → -V(S →I-H) → V$\phi_{-s}$; and

*I.S.4′*   T > P.T exp.S-D. T exp. (S-D → I(P)) → -V(S → S-D) → V$\phi_{-s}$.

What this highlights is that *practical* or effective (including here communicative) *freedom*, and in particular freedom sufficient to enable the agent to activate or summon all five orders of consciousness specified on p. 171, may well be a condition for engagement in any explanatory-emancipatory discourse. But

---

105. See J.R. Searle, *Speech Acts*, Cambridge 1969, chapter 9.

emancipation from specific constraints (whether psycho-social or social in form or origin) may be a prior condition for such practical freedom. Clearly this situates the possibility of various kinds of vicious circle (leading to historical and biographical or compound stasis or regression), in which the entrapped lack the means to understand the means of their entrapment and so cannot find or consciously employ the means for escape or release from it. Equally it grounds the possibility of various virtuous historical circles, on which emancipation from a specific constraint or compulsion and enhanced practical freedom conduces to an explanatory-emancipatory discourse. Here the historical limits and transformational tendencies of structural sources of determination checking the satisfaction of needs or the realisation of possibilities are identified, informing strategies and practices, in turn empirically and practically facilitating the development of theory, in the helical way indicated in Diagram 2.17.

Is there a sense in which IS1 and IS2 are *epistemically* prior to their non-cognitive generalisations? Yes, inasmuch as empirically controlled retroduction to explanatory structures always occurs in the context of, and typically (in science) assumes the form of, criticism of beliefs (consciousness) — scientific, proto-scientific, ideological, lay and practical. But this does not mean that such beliefs and/or the structures which explain them are necessarily causally prior or most important in the subject-matter under study; or that their study must take precedence in the organisation of scientific work, once that subject-matter has been thoroughly hermeneutically permeated and, if and when necessary, its consciousness of itself critically explained; or that an explanatory critique of consciousness is not itself historically conditioned and limited by factors external to the society from which it arises, such as the existence of practical (and communicative) freedoms from various orders of constraint and compulsion, as exemplified in IS4 and IS4'.

Let me summarise the argument to this stage. On the view advanced here the critical rôle of the human sciences in human history is not an optional extra: it is *intrinsic* to their explanatory function — for this depends indispensably on the identification and description, and proceeds naturally to the explanation, of ideas. If the critical condition in an explanatory critique of consciousness expresses the intrinsic aspect (IA) of any science of consciousness, the explanatory condition expresses the extrinsic aspect (EA) of such a science. To reject the former, objectivistically, is characteristic of empiricism: it ignores the relation between beliefs and their objects (P and O). To reject the latter, subjectivistically, is typical of idealism: it ignores the relation between beliefs and their causes (P and S). An explanatory critique unites both aspects. If what lies behind the failure to sustain practical rationality at Level III is the (implicit or explicit) denial of an ontological connection between beliefs and actions, theory and practice; the basis of the failure to sustain explanatory critical rationality at Level IV is the failure to recognise the possibility of an explanatory link between the truth value of a belief and its causal genesis, reception and effect. If criticism without explanation is impotent, explanation without criticism will often just be simply false. Although the explanatory critique of consciousness has a certain epistemic priority, the paradigm may be readily extended to other facets of social being, including inter alia those which are effective conditions for explanatory-critical science. The human sciences appear then as necessarily subversive and auto-subversive, in a stratified and changing social world.

## Emancipatory Reason

### Level V: Depth-Explanatory Critical Rationality

The most thoroughly explored applications of IS1 and IS2 involve the phenomena of psychologial *rationalisation* and *ideological mystification*. These phenomena are characterised by two distinctive features:

(1) a doubling of necessity between misrepresentation P and source S so that the, or some such, misrepresentation is not only causally necessitated by, but causally necessary for, the persistence or modulation, reproduction or limited (non-essential) transformation of its source; and

(2) an internal relationship between source S and object O, so that the misrepresented object O is either the same as, or at least causally (and essentially) dependent on, the source of the misrepresentation S.

Thus in the simple depth-psychological model considered in § 4 we had

(5)     $s \rightarrow p[-s].sp[-s] \rightarrow \psi$; or more simply

(5)'    $s \rightarrow p \rightarrow \psi$

where the agent N misdescribed the real (i.e the causally efficacious) reason, s, for $\psi$ by p; where p was itself a contingently necessary releasing condition for $\psi$; and where p was itself generated, in context, by s. To explain ths, we now posit a structure S such that $\psi$ is (perhaps contingently) necessary for its persistence or modulation as in

(6)     $S \rightarrow (s \rightarrow p[-s].sp[-s] \rightarrow \psi) \rightarrow S'$; or, more simply

(6)'    $S \rightarrow (s \rightarrow p \rightarrow \psi) \rightarrow S'$

Given $s \neq p$, i.e. p [-s], the evaluative and practical deductions proceed as in IS1.

This paradigm may be extended to include the self-mystification of forms of social life or systems of social relations in ideologies. Thus, the contradictions which mystify Colletti[106] turn simply on the necessary coexistence in social reality of an object and a (categorially) false presentation of it, where it is the inner (or essential) structure of the object which generates the categorially false presentation (or appearance). (7) is isomorphic with (5):

(7)     $E \rightarrow A[-E]. EA[-E] \rightarrow P$, or more simply

(7)'    $E \rightarrow A \rightarrow P$; and (8) is isomorphic with (6):

(8)     $R \rightarrow (E \rightarrow A[-E]. EA[-E] \rightarrow P) \rightarrow R'$ or, more simply

(8)'    $R \rightarrow (E \rightarrow A \rightarrow P) \rightarrow R'$

where E = essence, A = appearances, P = practices and R, R' = the modulated reproduction of some system of social relations (such as the capitalist mode of production).

The sense in which the misrepresentation A is not only necessitated by, but necessary for E, invites comparison with the populational and consequence explanatory frameworks discussed in § 3. The basic form of a consequence explanatory

---

106. L. Colletti, Marxism and Dialectic, *New Left Review 93*, 1975.

framework was, it will be remembered, given by d.(a → b) → a.[107] Can this capture the sense in which A is necessary for E? Provided that we understand this quasi-adaptive necessity, in terms of the T.M.S.A., as the necessity of appearances for practices which reproduce (or modulate) a mode of production essentially characterised by certain relations, the A → E link can be represented by the following survival matrix, illustrating the case of *eliminative generation*:

(9)  (i)  $K_e A_{tl}, \ldots\ldots K_e A_{tn}$
     (ii) $K_{e\text{-}Atl}, \ldots\ldots \text{-}K_e A_{tn}$

This quasi-adaptive or 'functional' relation can then be represented as $(K_e A_{tl} \rightarrow P_{etl}) \rightarrow K_e A_{tn}$

But to capture the E → A link, the *productive generation* (or preventive selection) of the quasi-adaptive (reproductive) property, we need a matrix of, in populational terms, a more Lamarckian kind:

(10)  (i)  $K_e \text{-}A_{tl} \ldots K_e A_{tn}$
      (ii) $K_e \text{-}A_{tl} \ldots \text{-}K_e \text{-}A_{tn}$

The appearance-generative relation can then be represented by $K_{etl} \rightarrow (P_{atn} \rightarrow K_{atn})$, yielding a population characterised at $t_n$ by $K_e A_{tn}$, i.e. by the presence of the 'functional' property (appearance). If we rationalise times, and combine the quasi-Lamarckian and quasi-Darwinian moments, we obtain the following pattern:

(11)    $K_{etl} \rightarrow (K_e A_{ti} \rightarrow P_{eti}) \rightarrow K_e A_{tn};$

or, more fully,

(11)′   $K_e A_{tl} \rightarrow K_{eti} \rightarrow (K_e A_{tj} \rightarrow P_{etj}) \rightarrow K_e A_{tn},$

which render the substance of (E → A → P) → R′ and R → (E → A → P) → R′ respectively in (8).

Can anything be said here about whether there are any general conditions on the internal structure, E, of a quasi-self-reproducing system, T, which generates and contains within

---

107. I have altered the notation from that used in § 3, p. 146, viz. D.(A → B) → A, to avoid confusion with the examples under substantive discussion here.

itself (i.e. T) a functionally necessary misrepresentation (A) of itself? It seems plausible to suppose that E must possess at least sufficient internal differentiation to justify attributing to it a '*Spaltung*' or *split*; and that if T is to be capable of endogenous (essential) transformation, rather than merely modulated reproduction, the split must constitute, or be constituted by, *antagonistic* (opposed) *tendencies*. But apart from the Colletti style contradiction built into the notion of the system's misrepresentation of itself, it seems *a priori* unlikely that what the human sciences may empirically discover about the various structural sources of its consciousness will justify the application of a single unified category of 'contradiction' to those structures. Instead, one might conjecture a galaxy of concepts of contradiction clustered around the core notion of the axiological indeterminacy generated by the logical archetype (together with the evaluative connotations this secretes). The specific concepts of contradiction would then achieve their individuation in the constraints they impose upon such indeterminacy, and in their theorisation of its form. Note however that in the relationship between a feature of social life and its systematic misrepresentation (most generally, in ideologies) there does seem to be a species of contradiction which has analogies with, but is non-identical to, that between a notion and its dialectical supersession in Hegel. And it can be plausibly maintained that the possibility of such an essence/appearance contradiction which, once it both exists and has been discovered, is susceptible to a purely analytic description, is a condition of any human science (or mode of self-reflection).

Perhaps the most justly famous depth-explanation, that in Marx's *Capital*, has the logical structure of a triple critique: of theories, of the practical consciousness such theories reflect or rationalise and of the conditions explaining such consciousness, viz.

I.S.12: $T > P_d . T \exp (S \rightarrow (A \rightarrow P_d)) \rightarrow -V(S \rightarrow (A \rightarrow P_d))$
$\rightarrow V\phi_{-s}$,

where $P_d$ stands for theoretical and discursive consciousness and A is proxy for practical consciousness, in a reproductive scheme which would look something like

(13)     $R \rightarrow ((E \rightarrow A[-E]).(E.A[-E] \rightarrow P_d[-A[-E]])).$
$E.A[-E]. P_d[-A[-E]] \rightarrow P) \rightarrow R'$

at least as an initial simplification. (Characteristically, the relations between theoretical and practical consciousness will be much more complex, and there is a sense in which any adequate symbolic representation needs a way of tying practical consciousness more closely to practice, which in turn requires more modulated differentiation.) But in Marx and the Marxian tradition generally, the criticised (discursive and practical) consciousness is regarded not just as false but as ideological — where ideology is counterposed to science. In addition to the *critical* and *explanatory* conditions one thus finds a further set of *categorial* conditions. Here beliefs are typically criticised for their *unscientificity simpliciter* (as in the critique of vulgar economy) and/or for their incapacity to sustain the irreducible *specificity*, the *sui generis* reality, of the subject-matter of the domain (as in the critique of classical political economy). Thus in reification, fetishism, hypostatisation, voluntaristic conventionalism, organicism etc. social life is presented, in one way or another, in an a-social (and so de-historicised) mode — a condition rooted, for Marx, in the alienation and atomisation characteristic of capitalism as a specific form of class society. For example, on Marx's analysis, the wage form collapses a power (labour power) to its exercise (labour), the domain of the real to the actual, while the value form fetishistically represents social relations in the guise of natural qualities. The critique of these gross categorial errors can be represented as

I.S.14   $T > P. \ T \exp -S_c (I(P)) \rightarrow -V(S \rightarrow -S_c(I(P))) \rightarrow V\phi_{-s}$

I.S.15   $T > P. \ T \exp -S_o (I(P)) \rightarrow -V(S \rightarrow -S_o(I(P))) \rightarrow V\phi_{-s}$

P once more stands for consciousness generally; $-S_c$ and $-S_o$ stand for the unscientific and desocialising character of the forms in question; and the double bracketing reminds us that we are dealing with categorially illusory forms, not merely illusory beliefs.

*Marxian* critique of consciousness differs from *Baconian* critique of illusion in that it does not merely pinpoint obstacles in the way of cognitive experience, but isolates forms which structure and inebriate experience. But it differs from *Kantian*

critique in that it understands these forms as objective systems of constraints, historically produced, reproduced and potentially transformable, which explanatory theory may show to be either (1) quite simply false, in not being properly or validly applicable to experience at all — in a first-order critique of consciousness, as e.g. in the case of the wage form; or (2) true but systematically self-misunderstod or -misrepresenting, in being validly applicable to experience but only *within* certain historical limits, contrary to the form's own self-presentation — in a second-order critique of consciousness, as in the case of the value form. It is analogous to *Hegelian* critique in that it sees reflection on the conditions of possible knowledge as at once reflection on a system of humanly produced constraints, but it differs from it, in that the medium of this reflection is explanatory theory, the form of the constraints are transcendentally real and historically defined, and the agency of their dissolution is transformative (e.g. class) praxis rather than speculative experience. It anticipates too the great insight of *Nietzschean* 'critique' that 'among the conditions of life might be error'[108] but locates the source of error in structural causes, neither fated nor fixed.

The characteristic mistake indicated in a second-order critique, the self-dishistoricisation, especially detemporalisation or eternalisation, of a social form can be regarded as a cognitive error analogous to that pinpointed in IS2, as in

I.S.2′   $T > P.T \exp -t(P) \rightarrow -V(S \rightarrow -t(P)) \rightarrow V\phi_{-s}$

where -t stands for detemporalisation, with the categorial nature of the error brought out in

I.S.16:  $T > P. T \exp -t(P) \rightarrow -V(S \rightarrow -S_o(-t(P))) \rightarrow V\phi_{-s}$; or as in

I.S.17:  $T > P. T \exp -S_o((F(t_1 \ldots t_i)T(t_i \ldots t_j)F(t_j \ldots t_n))(P)) \rightarrow -V(S \rightarrow -S_o((F(t_1 \ldots t_i)T(t_i \ldots tj)F(tj \ldots tn))(P))) \rightarrow V\phi_{-s}$

What, finally, are we to make of Engels's celebrated rebuke to

108. F. Nietzsche, *The Gay Science*, New York 1974, p. 121.

Lafargue: 'Marx rejected the political, social and economic ideal you attribute to him. A man of science has no ideals, he elaborates scientific results and if he is also politically committed he struggles for them to be put into practice. But if he has ideals, he cannot be a man of science, since he would then be biased from the start'.[109] While interests both predispose and motivate analyses and their acceptance/rejection in the human sciences, so that Engels's scientistic repudiation of the V → F connection is disingenuous, it remains the case that no value judgements other than those already bound up in the assessment of the cognitive power of Marx's theory are necessary for the derivation of a negative evaluation of the capitalist mode of production (CP) and a positive evaluation of action rationally oriented towards its transformation (CP). Thus the political commitment that Engels attributed to Marx as, so to speak, a contingent extra, can (on the assumption that Marx's depth explanation is correct) be logically grounded in his scientific practice alone. Of course the theories now required to confirm, extend, develop or refute Marx's own analyses can only be consequent upon engagement in investigations of comparable scope and penetration.

## 7. Depth, Rationality and Change

*From the beginning we are unlogical and therefore unjust beings and we can know this: this is one of the greatest and most insoluble disharmonies of existence.*[110]

Clear paradigms exist in the human sciences of IS1-4, most notably in the traditions inaugurated by Marx and Freud, but also in some of the work of the theorists of the day-to-day lived world of social interactions with one another and material transactions with nature (e.g. in the understanding of such phenomena as counterfinality). But is there a sense in which the *application* of these inference schemes, and hence of the type of explanatory critique they presuppose, is transcendentally necessary? That is, is there a respect in which these schemes are

---

109. F. Engels to P. Lafargue, 11 August 1884, *Correspondence Engels-Lafargue*, Paris, p. 235.
110. F. Nietzsche, *Werke in drei Bönden*, Munich 1954, Vol. I, p. 471.

not only, as I have shown, necessary for the explanatory projects of the human sciences, but necessary for the unbounded projects and conduct of everyday life? And if there is, how are these types of project interconnected?

## Level VI: Depth-Rationality

To set the scene, imagine two interlocutors X and Y. Let us suppose that one of them, Y, experiences some frustration in her life. The other, X, can be thought of, if one likes, as a proxy for 'social science'. Y's frustration may be associated with a belief Q which she cannot get rid of (e.g. an obsession) or some circumstance C (e.g. of unemployment) which seriously constrains her. Let us suppose X surmises the existence of a structural source of determination S inducing Q or C. What is to be done? Consider three possibilities here: (i) Y continues to suffer under Q or C; (ii) some non-discursive and/or external procedure or event (e.g. force, medication; or a coup d'état) removes Q or C so that, under heavy sedation, she no longer believes Q or she now works, under conditions of forced labour, in the arms industry, as the new regime prepares for an expansionist war; or (iii) X and Y jointly institute an enquiry into the conditions producing or inducing Q or C with a view to identifying the responsible causes and taking, or helping to take, appropriate remedial action.

Which of these possibilities is to be preferred? Adoption of solution (i), i.e. stoic acceptance of irrationality, is a counsel of despair. Moreover it cannot be generalised to the first person case of doubt (or more generally choice) without vicious axiological regress. Solution (ii) can be ruled out on the grounds that it is not emancipatory, in that it does not replace an unwanted with a wanted source of determination but merely counteracts or replaces the effects of one unwanted source of determination with another [or in the second case, perhaps, one unwanted form of expression of the same source of determination with another unwanted expression of it]. This has the corollary that inasmuch as the original source of determination is not defused, even if it is successfully counteracted, it may continue to exert a latent power. Moreover it can also be argued that the externally imposed end-state does not constitute, but merely simulates, the originally desired end state (Y wanted not merely to be free not to think Q but to be free to think -Q (not Q), R, S and T etc.).

The alternative (iii) of a depth enquiry (D-I) is possible where reason fails but has not yet exhausted its resources; and it is practicable, where Y's beliefs and actions are generated or underpinned (positively compelled or negatively constrained) by un- or incompletely-known (or unacknowledged) processes, and where Y seeks to understand them in order to undermine, abrogate or transform them. A D-I may be defined generally as any co-operative enquiry, which includes the frustrated agent(s) concerned, into the structure of some presumed set of mechanisms, constituting for that agent an unwanted source of determination, with a view to initiating, preserving or restoring the agent's wellbeing, including her capacity to think, speak, feel and act rationally.

Four points must be immediately noted about this definition. What constitutes an agent's wellbeing cannot be stipulated *a priori*, but must itself be discovered, in relation to the agent's antecedent notion of her wellbeing in the course of the explanatory critique and emancipatory practice such a D-I pre-supposes. And what is rational cannot be laid down in advance but must likewise be determined, in relation to our pre-existing ideas of rationality (comprising its nominal essences, so to speak), in the context of the D-I itself. That said, it is important to avoid the presumption that rationality is (i) a universal or monolithic concept, (ii) exclusively epistemic or cognitive in character,[111] (iii) primarily applicable to statements rather than actions, projects (practices) etc., (iv) equivalent or analogous to consistency in argument. The rationality of a (line of) historical action is not the rationality of a pattern of formal argument. But while the latter always depends upon the former, logical consistency is never sufficient and frequently violated in rational transformative praxis (e.g. in the diachronic development of science). Secondly, although the concept of a DI has been intro-

---

111. Remember that the epistemic priority of critiques of inadequate consciousness does not carry over into their sociological priority over critiques of defective or unhappy being generally. If we tacitly work with a cognitive conception of rationality, then we must accept the paradox that it is not rational to be fully rational because there are non-cognitive bases and aspects of and determinants upon [optimally-rational, as indeed all] action. Cf. H. Meynell who remarks: "It is not intelligent or reasonable, after all, to treat men as though they were beings wholly determined by intelligence and reason, and not at all affected by emotion or physical desire [as well]', *Marx, Freud and Morals*, London 1981, p. 182.

duced as an ideographic, practically-oriented *application* of some or other determinate explanatory critique, the *theory* at the heart of the critique itself depends crucially for its own development and empirical confirmation on such investigations (whether on living or historically reconstructed materials). Accordingly the links between theory and practice, and pure and applied research, though not eliding their distinctions, are bound to be much tighter than in the natural sciences (as is indicated by the internal limits on naturalism discussed in § 2 and exemplified in the helix of Diagram 2.17). Thirdly, corresponding to the different types of inference scheme outlined in § 6 above, there will be different forms of DI. These must not, however, be hypostatised. For the explanation of cognitive ills will in general make reference to practical and communicative ills, and vice versa; poor facilities may induce competential ills and affective malaises, etc. We are here in the world of interdependence and internal relations, as well as of depth, diversity and historical change. Finally, consider the desire for emancipation which motivates the DI. If and when historically transformable and unnecessary sources of the determination of ills are identified, an emancipatory drive can neither be posited *a priori* nor predicted in historicist fashion. It cannot be posited *a priori* for, although it is a necessary truth that people act on their wants, it is not a necessary truth — but on the contrary plainly false — that they always act on their interests and needs. And it cannot be predicted in historicist manner, not because of some special cussedness on the part of people's desires, but because historicism is, as a species of actualism, false in the social and natural world alike. However the desire for emancipation from specific, and more or less systematically interrelated, sets of compulsions and constraints, understood as a socially produced social object, will be a critical topic for metainvestigations, which must then be reflexively incorporated into the substantive theory of the practice from or for which emancipation is sought. Thus once such a meta-DI, investigating the emancipatory drive, has been iteratively incorporated into the explanatory diagnostic theory of the malevolent structure, it may then inform the strategic emancipatory theory of the transformative practice. At the same time, these theories may reciprocally modify and enhance the emancipatory drive.

The structure of a simplified D-I may be elucidated as follows:

(1) Y wants to, but is unable to perform an act, or a systematic class of acts, ψ, where a relatively general and grounded view of human nature, shared by X, suggests that ψ should be possible. The status of this presupposition will be discussed shortly. This inability is experienced by Y as the frustration of a need or the unfulfilment of an objective possibility.

(2) Scientific realism suggests that there is, or may be, a mechanism M preventing ψ, either by constraining, blocking or by compelling not ψ.

(3) General explanatory theory T investigates the structure of blocking/compelling mechanisms in the domain in question under the control of empirical data and researches.

(4) The application of T to Y depends upon the agent Y, as well as the scientific investigator X. For it is Y's interpretations, actions and determinations that are at issue. Subjectivity in the human sciences is not an obstacle: it is an essential part of the data. But ontological authorship does not automatically transmute to epistemological authority. The Y-dependence of the D-I means that Y must have a really efficacious interest in disengaging M or at least in a class of acts, which may now be expanding, of the ψ type which M prevents. And that co-investigator X must not have an interest in the distortion of M-descriptions or their application with respect to ψ or to Y. Concretely this raises the question of the costs of emancipation for Y, and of the conditions under which it may be a second-best solution for Y; and it presupposes, on the part of X, the willingness to learn (in the general spirit of Marx's Third Thesis on Feuerbach) and the continual development both of T and of X's own self-understanding.

(5) At a deeper level the success of the detailed investigation of the way in which M works so as to prevent Y's ψ'ing depends upon an internal differentiation within the experience of Y, at least insofar as Y's own practices are interwoven into its effectivity (implying rejection of the empiricist/utilitarian notion of emancipation as the alteration of the external circumstances of effectively autonomised individuals).

Moreover it should be reiterated that cognitive emancipation depends in general upon non-cognitive conditions; and that cognitive emancipation is necessary but insufficient for full, human emancipation (as shown by the example of the slave who knows only too well that he is a slave but still remains one). In fact *dissonance*, not liberation (or the rational elaboration of an emancipatory strategy), may be the immediate result of enlightenment. And such dissonance may lead either towards practical-critical-transformative-revolutionary action or alternatively to despair. Moreover, constraints upon cognitive emancipation itself are imposed by the imbrication of ideologies into the practical contours fixed by the material imperatives in social life (in historical materialism), by the preformation of ideational contents (in psychoanalysis) and by the projects of others (in social phenomenology). Hence emancipation can no more be conceived as an internal relationship within thought (the idealist error) than as an external relationship of 'educators', 'therapists' or 'intellectuals' to the 'ignorant', 'sick' or 'oppressed' (the typical empiricist mistake).

(6) The object of the D-I is emancipation, but we must allow the possibility that the D-I will reveal the $\psi$-preventing mechanism to be unchangeable (under the current and/or foreseeable, including all co-produceable, sets of circumstances under which Y lives) and/or that the view of human nature which grounded the presumption in favour of its changeability to be radically flawed. And we must allow the possibility that the initial want for $\psi$ is not a 'happy' one, in that though Y wants it, it may not 'suit' her, i.e. be in accord with what the D-I shows to be or consist in (or to be fulfilling of, or to move towards) her nature; so that, though she wants it, she not only does not need it, but has a positive need not to $\psi$. In the D-I, or rather in the theory-practice helix it initiates, wants and prescriptions are themselves transformed. Note further that although it is not possible for Y to continue to want something that is knowingly not in her nature,[112] her socialised nature is in itself in continuous transformation (so that nothing of empirical import follows from this analytic truth); and, more importantly, that there can be no *a priori* guarantee that it is only in human nature or a particular agent's nature to do what is conducive to her survival, flourishing, happiness, wellbeing *even* if she knows what this is: only an historical experience, incorporating the D-I, can disclose Thanatos or Kali or manicheanism to be myths. It is the possibility of needs/wants conflicts that I had in mind in defining emancipation in § 5 as the transformation from an unwanted and unneeded source of determination to a wanted and needed

---

112. If this appears to happen, we will expect that the agent's nature has been incompletely or wrongly specified; or alternatively that it has changed.

one. Certain forms of labour may be (either always or at least under all conceivable historical circumstances) both unwanted and constraining, but nevertheless needed. Conversely, unless a source of determination is unwanted, the emancipation is not self-emancipation and is unaccompanied by any experience of enhanced well-being or possibility by the agents concerned.

Emancipation itself may be conceived either (i) as the process of the changing of one source or order or mode of determination $S_1$ into another $S_2$; or (ii) as the act of switching from $S_1$ to $S_2$, both $S_1$ and $S_2$ perduring, but $S_1$ in a de-activated state.

Now, I want to propose that the possibility of a D-I is a transcendental condition of any human science, and hence at a remove of any science or philosophy and of every rational practice or act of self-understanding at all. If the fundamental norm of theoretical discourse is descriptive or representative adequacy or truth, that of practical discourse is the fulfillment, realisation or satisfaction of human wants, needs and purposes. If there are real grounds (causes) for belief and action, then it is possible we are mistaken about them, and if we fail in truth we may also fail in satisfaction. There are three possible responses to this: we can deny it, and revert to a form of *fundamentalism* — this is the path of classical philosophy; we can shrug our shoulders with a '*tant pis*' and carry on with the ordinary business of living — this is the homely way of *commonsense*; or we can seek to identify the causes of our truth — and satisfaction — failures — this is the royal road to *science*. On this road, the question which interests us is no longer merely the simple one of the causes of belief and action, it is the question of the causes of these causes: it thus presupposes an ontological *stratification* within the constitution of our theoretical and practical agency which classical philosophy and commonsense join hands in denying. To enquire into the causes of error is the same thing as to enquire into the possibility of rationalisation, self-deception, deception of others, counterfinality and systemic (ideological) mystification; and to enquire into the conditions of these cognitive-communicative malaises immediately raises the question of the conditions of practical ones — from ill-health to brutal oppression. And to enquire into the causes of practical failures — from the frustrated projects of individuals to the missing, misidentifying or misunderstanding of historical opportunities of eliminating ills or realising goods — is at the same time to enquire into the conditions of possibility of impossible relations and the conditions of impossibility of possible ones; and to enquire into the conditions of the dehiscence of needs and possibilities, of the conditions of frustrated needs and unfulfilled possibilities of satisfying them, immediately raises the question of the mechanisms of cognitive — communicative smokescreening at work. To stress, the explanatory critical discourse is not about whether we may be said to act or choose or believe or know, it is about the structural sources of the options from which we, in our everyday practices, more or less freely, choose. This is a question which can only be taken up by the depth human sciences (at their various — e.g. historical, phenomenological, psychodynamical — levels). In the human sciences the problem of error, oppression, etc. must thus be fused — in the explanatory-critical D-I — with the problem of the causes of error, oppression, etc. as part of the programme, paramorphic (but non-identical) to that of Kepler, Galileo and Newton, of the investigation of the shifting deep structures, moving like continental plates, producing, in myriad forms, the turbulences and routines of our historical experience, the manifest phenomenology of everyday social life.

I stated above that the D-I is prompted or informed, at the initial stage, by a view about human nature, which will be refined, revised or refuted (or perhaps confirmed and consolidated) in the D-I itself. It is this view which forms the characteristically ethical ingredient associated with the D-I, or more generally explanatory critique (cf. Diagram 2.16 on p. 173 above). Such an anthropology need not, and, on the transformational view, should not, be an a-historical one. But some anthropology is the condition of any moral discourse at all. As ontology stands to epistemology, so anthropology stands to ethics; indeed one could say that anthropology just is the ontology of ethics. Just as a theory about the nature of the world is implicit in any cognitive claim, a theory about the nature of (wo)men is implicit in any moral one. (And it is easy to identify analogues of the epistemic and ontic fallacies here. Extreme examples are provided by Kantian formalist prescriptivism and Benthamite naturalistic utilitarianism respectively.) To say that 'X is good for an agent (or agents) N', or that 'N ought to $\phi$' is to say that the nature of N is such that A or $\phi$'ing promotes or realises or fulfils N's (species, class, group, individual) nature — conduces, in some more or less vital way, to N's survival or flourishing — as that nature essentially is and/or has been biologically and historically (psycho-socially) formed. Notice that this is not to say that N necessarily wants 'A' or 'φ' — it is just this which gives moral dialogue its characteristic normative bite. Moreover this leaves open the question of the universality of the nature that is presupposed in moral discourse. Now it seems grossly implausible to suppose that human beings do not, qua human beings, share characteristics (such as purely physical ones!) which differentiate them as members of the same species from members of different species: there is a scientifically impeccable ground for this assumption, viz. in their common genetic constitution. At the same time, this 'common nature' is never expressed in anything but thoroughly socialised, more or less historically specific and very highly differentiated forms. We cannot identify a common nature under psycho-socially meaningful descriptions. There is the further consideration that the transformational view espoused here suggests that essential forms of a psycho-social kind, considered as real because causally efficacious, are the products of prior transformations and/or in the process of contemporary transformation and/or subject to the possibility of future transformation, although it should be noted that the T.M.S.A. does not assert the non-existence of summative social universals. I suggest that the most plausible resolution of these three desiderata lies in the supposition that any particular agent N* possesses a 'nature'[113] which can be componentialised into at least: (i) a common human nature, grounded in genetic structure and manifested in certain species-wide capacities (e.g. language-use); (ii) an historically specific nature, of a quite highly differentiated kind, whose development was initiated at the time and place of birth, deriving from class, gender, occupational positions, experience, etc., shared in common with other agents subject to the same general determinations; (iii) a more or less unique individuality. (i) never manifests itself in anything but a historically mediated form, although it is *not* itself human-historical in constitution (cf. the analogue of B-type determinations depicted in Diagram 2.21 on p. 191 above; just as a person's individuality ((iii) above) is only ever expressed in some or other socially *classifiable*

---

113. It should be unnecessary, but is nevertheless perhaps advisable, to make it explicit that the concept of a nature here, and human nature in general, is not to be hypostatised. It functions purely syncategorematically, acting as a placeholder for, and awaiting filling by, substantive scientific descriptions.

ways. What (i) licenses is the supposition of the existence of universal powers (and liabilities), certainly needs and very probably wants (and so interests). Now it is of the first importance to appreciate that it is not an argument against the universal existence of a power or need (or basic ground in nature) that it can only be exercised or realised where certain historically specific circumstances are present (any more than it is an argument against the existence of a magnet's power to attract iron filings when there are none about). Neither is it an argument against the existence of a power or need that its existence can only become articulated and recognised under definite historical conditions. If moral discourse is, as I have suggested, grounded in historical anthropology and this is componentialised in the manner just proposed, then we can allow that it makes sense to ascribe the *existence* of rights (and goods) for all human beings *qua* human beings, in virtue of their possession of a common (although always historically mediated) nature, ultimately grounded in their biological unity as a species, composed in particular of common powers and needs [albeit manifest in a myriad variety of historically different ways], even though these rights (and goods) can only come to be formulated as demands, recognised as legitimate and exercised as rights under very definite historical conditions. To collapse a right to the historical conditions of its recognition, realisation or exercise is to commit some ethical form (as distinct from analogy) of the epistemic fallacy, grounded in the actualist collapse of anthropology.[114]

Now if the emancipation is to be *of* the human species, or some proper subset of it, the powers of the emancipated community must already exist (although perhaps only as powers to acquire or develop powers) in an unactualised form. (It should never be forgotten that the world is not just the totality of what is actually the case, but includes what might or could be, grounded in the structural properties of things, as well.) The key questions for substantive theory then become: what are the historical conditions for the actualisation of these powers (competences and facilities)?; what are the transformative

---

114. A good example of this error is provided by MacIntyre's criticism of A. Gewirth's *Reason and Morality*, (Chicago 1977) in *Against Virtue*, London 1981, pp. 64-65, when MacIntyre equates the existence of a right with the intelligibility of the making of a claim to it, which is patently always highly specific and local in character.

tendencies at work?; whence come the historical agencies for change? etc. Such questions, which transport us to Level VII of historical rationality as such, cannot be answered outside the context of some specific theory.

But can anything be said about the conditions of possibility of emancipatory practices in general? For emancipation to be possible, the following conditions must be satisfied. First, *reasons must be causes*, or discourse is ontologically redundant (and scientifically inexplicable). But the potentially emancipatory discourse, given the T.M.S.A. and the general conception of an open world, can only codetermine action in an already pre-structured, practical and collective context. Second, *values must be immanent* (as latent or partially manifested tendencies) in the practices in which we engage, or normative discourse is utopian and idle. I think that Marx, in conceiving socialism as anticipated in the revolutionary practice of the proletariat, grasped this. And it is on this feature that Habermas's deduction of speech-constitutive universals also turns.[115] But if there is a sense in which the ideal community, founded on principles of truth, freedom and justice, is already present as a prefiguration in every speech-interaction, might one not be tempted to suppose that equality, liberty and fraternity are present in every transaction or material exchange; or that respect and mutual recognition are contained in the most casual reciprocated glance? It is an error to suppose that ethics must have a linguistic foundation; just as it is an error to suppose that it is autonomous from science or history. Third, *critique must be internal to* (and conditioned by) *its objects*, or else it will lack both epistemic grounding and causal force. But it follows from this that it is part of the very process it describes, and so subject to the same possibilities of unreflected determination and historical supercession it situates. Hence continuing self-reflexive auto-critique is the *sine qua non* of any critical explanatory theory.

Fourth, at the emancipatory moment, there must be a *coincidence of subjective needs*, experienced as affective and effective drives, informed by vision, imagination, daring and explanatory theory, on the one hand, *and of objective possi-*

115. J. Habermas, 'Towards a Theory of Communicative Competence', *Enquiry 13*, (1970).

*bilities*, already at or close to their historical conditions of realisation, as the articulated and achievable goals of groups, rather than merely the abstract properties of structures: a dynamic coincidence of competences and facilities in a conjunctural combination of cognitive, conatative, affective conditions and circumstantial context. Finally, for emancipation to be possible, *knowable emergent laws must operate*. Such laws, which will of course be consistent with physical laws, will be set in the framework of explanatory theories elucidating the structures of cognitive and non-cognitive oppression and the possibility of their transformation by men and women. Emancipation depends upon the untruth of reductionist materialism and spiritualistic idealism alike. On reductionism — if the physical process level is $L_p$, and the level at which emancipation is sought is $L_e$, then either $L_p$ completely determines $L_e$, and no qualitative change is possible; or qualitative change is possible, and the laws of $L_p$ are violated. On idealism — either emancipation is entirely intrinsic to thought, in which case it is unconditioned and bondage and irrationality become inexplicable; or, if it is conditioned, it cannot be intrinsic to thought. Emergence is a condition of explanation, which in turn is a condition of emancipation. The possibility of emergence is not of course the reason why an emergent powers theory, if it is, is true. It is rather that if human beings, and social forms in general, are emergent from but conditioned by nature, then there is at least the possibility that, provided 'we do not anticipate the world with our dogmas but instead attempt to observe the new world through the critique of the old',[16] the human sciences could still be of some benefit to the greater majority of humankind.

## 8. A Note on History

'*Even the most accurate of histories, if they do not exactly misrepresent or exaggerate the value of things in order to render them more worthy of being read, at least omit in them all the circumstances which are basest and least notable; and from this fact it follows that what is retained is not portrayed as it really is, and that those who regulate their conduct by*

---

16. 'Marx to Ruge', September 1843, *Early Writings*, p. 207.

*examples which they derive from such a source are liable to fall into the*
*extravagances of the knight-errants of Romance, and form projects*
*beyond the power of performance.*[117]
'*The only thought which philosophy brings with it [to history] is the*
*simple idea of reason, the idea that reason governs the world; and that*
*world history too is a rational process.*[118]

The essential ground of the distinction between social science
and history is that between the domain of the real and the
actual, between structures (and possibilities) and events (and
concrete things). History and social science are not differentiated by time, but by task or focus of explanatory interest.
For, on the one hand, everything, once it has happened, is (in
the) past, which begins with the pulsating-passing of the
present. And, on the other, social theory treats of structures
which are spatio-temporally earthed, reproduced (extended or
distanciated[119]) and transformed, and so must be understood as
materially spatio-temporalised (geo-historically restricted),
dynamic (and open, i.e. unbounded, unfinished and ongoing)
and subject to (praxis-dependent) change. In the concluding
section of this chapter I want to explore some of the implications of the transformational character of social activity (and
*a fortiori* of social structures), which necessitate a greater overlap of professional and research interest (or shared interface of
explanatory concerns) between the historian and the social
scientist, than the bare event/structure distinction *per se* would
indicate and greater than that which is normally feasible in the
field of non-human nature.

Let us look first at the social theorist. Space and time enter
immediately into the T.M.S.A. in the three respects just mentioned (and elaborated more fully in § 2). Giddens has aptly
referred to the 'repression' of time in social theory.[120] Its consequence — the naturalisation, and hence eternalisation of the
status quo — is evident enough.

---

117. R. Descartes, *Discourse on Method, Philosophical Works of Descartes,*
    *Vol. I*, ed. E. Haldane and G. Ross, Cambridge 1970.
118. G.W.F. Hegel, *Lectures on the Philosophy of World History*, translated H.
    Nisbet, Cambridge 1978, p. 27.
119. A. Giddens, *A Contemporary Critique of Historical Materialism*, London
    1981, p. 4.
120. A. Giddens, *Central Problems of Social Theory*, London 1979, p. 3.

But this repression was always thinly disguised. Consider, for instance, the ease with which spatio-temporal concepts are employed in the metaphorical characterisation of ordinary life. Thus we say of a remark that it was 'untimely' or 'out of place'. One way of putting the central insight of contemporary time-geography[121] is that such metaphors are to be taken, at least partially, literally: that social being is to be conceived, whatever else it is, as bodily being; so that social structures are to be earthed in space and situated in time, and their reproduction (or transformation) to be seen as a space-time flow. The geo-historicisation of social theory does not, however, warrant an ontological conflation of (relatively enduring, transfactually efficacious) structures with the continuous flux of surface show. Nor does it vitiate a modified synchronic-diachronic contrast, reformulated in terms of the structure-event differentiation and manifest in the distinction between theoretical ['vertical'] and practical ['horizontal'] explanations, where theory need not to static but can depict, in abstract fashion, flows, cycles and movements in a multiplicity of topological modes (e.g. as in Marx's reproduction schemata), tendentially applicable to concrete historical situations.[122]

Within theory itself, as so (dynamically) understood, a non-exhaustive discrimination can be made between: (α) *structural* principles (properties, operations, tendencies, contradictions), i.e. attributes which essentially characterise, under some more or less theoretical redescription, and so define it as a structure of a particular kind; and (β) *historical* principles etc., i.e. those which only hold or apply for a certain period of the structure's duration (which may be contingently co-extensive with the

---

121. See e.g. N. Thrift and A. Pred, 'Time Geography: A New Beginning', *Progress in Human Geography 5*, (1981) pp. 273-286.
122. In this respect my T.M.S.A. differs from Giddens' structuration model. I think this difference is connected with the fact that I am inclined to give structures a firmer ontological grounding and to place more emphasis on the pre-existence of social forms. (It is because social structure is always a given that I prefer to talk of reproduction and transformation, rather than structuration, which, I think, still retains voluntaristic connotations. For me, structuration is always, so to speak, restructuration.) There are other differences, some of which I have noted elsewhere ('Beef, Structure and Place', *Journal for the Theory of Social Behaviour*, Vol. 13 no. 1, 1983), but the basic thrust of the models are, at least at an abstract level, highly convergent. Cf., e.g., A. Giddens, *Profiles and Critiques in Social Theory*, London 1982 and *The Constitution of Society*, Cambridge 1984.

duration of the structure itself). The genesis, span and demise of these historical principles may be determined by a (more or less interrelated) combination of endogenous and exogenous processes and factors. The principles themselves may be entirely unique or novel in the history of the structure; or they may consist in the unfolding or development of properties essentially constitutive of it. They may, as it were, supervene upon the normal operations of the structure; or they may be integrated out of and/or into its essential modus operandi — for instance, securing the satisfaction of the intrinsic enabling conditions for the exercise of an original power or liability of the structure, converting it into a 'tendency$_2$'[123], that is, into a power in readiness, predisposed to be articulated. It is such historical tendencies$_2$, derived at ($\beta$), especially when they comprise auto-subversive or structure-replacing ones, i.e. tendencies to structural transformation, which ground the emancipatory strategies motivated, fixed and informed by the explanatory-critical empirically controlled retroduction of possibilities situated or opened up by structural theory proper at ($\alpha$). Note that the onset and/or realisation of historical tendencies may be necessary, without their space-time location or geo-date being so. That Socrates, being a man, must die is necessary; but neither the time nor place of his death is determined by biological theory. The limits of the reproduction of a structure may be fixed by the properties of the structure itself, but if, when, where and how these limits are reached can only be explained (or their possibilities assessed) at some more concrete level of investigation.

The ground of the distinction between 'pure' and 'applied' work in natural and social science alike lies in the enduring and transfactual efficacy of structures, in virtue of which they possess tendencies which are applicable to particular situations not deducible from the theory of the structure itself. Here the theorist has the task of elaborating the implications of the structure, empirically identifying and confirming its nature and properties, developing the explanatory-taxonomic niche into which the structure fits, etc. The applied scientist can use that knowledge (e.g. in concrete explanatory work), but its use always depends upon discovering whether the initial conditions

---

123. See *A Realist Theory of Science*, p. 231.

for the operation of the structural tendency were (are or may be) satisfied, what other tendencies etc. were at work in the production of the explanandum-event or episode etc., how their effects were modified, etc., none of which can be read off from 'pure' theory alone. This gives the applied scientist quite distinct explanatory tasks.[124] In social science theoretical knowledge can be transfactually applied and used in any concrete explanatory work subject to the same, plus some further complicating, controls as in natural science (discussed in §§ 1-4 above). But the structures which applied social scientists invoke in the explanation of phenomena occurring within the concrete open flux of social life, only exist in virtue of that flux, which continually reproduces, restructures, reconstitutes afresh and re-forms (or transforms) those structures which apply; and such structures may be themselves only relatively enduring. Thus if the pure scientist is typically concerned with structure and the applied scientist with events, their concerns fuse in the social sphere in the study of *process* where structure meets events; that is, in the study of the mode of becoming, bestaying and begoing of a structure or thing, i.e. of its genesis in, distantiation over and transformation across space-time. Process is not an ontological category apart from structure and event; it just is structure (or thing), considered under the aspect of its story — of formation, reformation and transformation — in time. Insofar as s/he is, and must be, concerned with this story, the social scientist ceases to be a purely abstract and becomes a concrete theorist; and insofar as the historian is — and must be — concerned with that story, s/he ceases to be a merely applied and becomes a concrete scientist.

Recognition of the concrete character of social life and of its constitution and reconstitution in space-time, makes it important to distinguish different orders of temporality in social life, different levels at which a temporalised story can be told: (1) individual biography (the life-history of the individual; (2) the life-cycle of the human being, including of course the chronic fact of finitude; (3) the flow of day-to-day existence at the level of intentional agency; (4) the *longue durée* of institutions, defined structurally; (5) the development of specifically

---

124. Needless to say, the applied scientist may have other, e.g. practical (say engineering), interests. *Mutatis mutandis* similar considerations hold here.

human history in world history; (6) the biological history of the human species, inserted into the global history of species and genera, itself inserted into the geo-physical history of the solar system (and ultimately the universe). These levels are all already identified in Diagram 2.12 and 2.13 (on pp. 154-5 above). But there are other significant orders of temporality — most importantly, at the levels of group biography and class (more generally, theoretically defined, i.e. explanatorily significant, group) history; regional history, defined in terms of geo-administrative or political or ethnic or national coordinates; and the socio-psycho-somatic history of the individual. If social structures are always geo-historically earthed (that is, if they are 'space-time travellers'), complex, interconnected and changing, then it makes sense to suggest that ultimately social theory means and depends upon doing 'world-history'. But even a description of the process of world history would not actualistically exhaust the content of social theory or collapse abstract structures to concrete universals. For a complete world history would not only show why whatever occurred, occurred, just as it did; it would also reveal how, if agents had acted differently, employing the structures to hand and under the same determinate circumstances, different outcomes would have ensued. That is to say, a comprehensive natural history of the human species would not cease to be metaphysically transcendental *realist* and practically explanatorily *critical.*

If the social sciences' primary focus of explanatory interest is in structures and their interdigitation in different (historical) forms of society, it should never be forgotten that neither exist save as constituted in and by human practice, and that the data for the empirical assessment and development of theories about them can only be drawn from concrete historical (including of course contemporary) research. Although social theories can be refuted, they cannot be confirmed or creatively elaborated, independently of the fruits of the historian's skill — for human history is the only testing ground for social science, the open lab. into which almost anything may wander and from which the most vital piece of evidence may seem free to leave at ease.

Let us, then, now turn explicitly to the historian. His or her rôles include: (1) the applied scientific explanation of conjunctures, compounds and concrete universals; (2) definition of the (space-time) boundary conditions for the existence and transfactual efficacy of particular social structures and for their articulation into determinate (theoretically defined) forms of society (and sociality); (3) the elaboration of intermediate and concrete theory (including theory of world-history); (4) critical assessment of *all* social theory. In principle, the historian may chose to explain any social event (or conjuncture) or to trace the trajectory of any social thing (or compound) in a structured reconstruction of the formation of the event or narrative of the development of the thing.

But naturally, the historian will be most anxious to explain, at least in the first place, explanatorily (and/or evaluatively and so, by the argument of §§ 5-7, normally also explanatorily) significant events and things. The social scientist, by contrast, may be more interested in typical or scenic events (and things), and may look to the historian for taxonomic assistance in the classification of social objects, rather than (or at least in addition to) explanatory help in the explanation of their generation. What are the appropriate criteria of significance? From the vantage point of the T.M.S.A., significant events are transformative events, and significant things are (actually or possibly) transforming ones. Insofar as significant things are defined by the historian by reference to their transformative power and effects, and the object of transformation is itself a social structure, the historian patently presupposes social theory for the identification of historical episodes, as well as for their explanation, viz. via the transfactual employment of theoretically-elaborated (and -grounded) structural principles, tendencies etc. The historian, *qua* applied scientist, then, is concerned with the *nodal points* and the *motive agencies* in the past and present (and the likely and possible futures) of human history. Such nodal points include: (1) connector points, which interpose one into another type of process; (2) branch points, foreclosing certain possible lines of development; (3) jump points, creating a new horizon of possibilities; (4) saddle points, inducing stasis or even regression; (5) break points, actually consisting in or substantively contributing to a rupture of social structures and/or their constellation in a totality; (6) trigger points, initiating or powerfully augmenting such a transformative process; (7) predisposing points, securing the satisfaction of the enabling conditions for such a process, e.g. the inception of a (tendentially) auto-subversive tendency$_2$. In addition, the historian may be empirically interested in events, episodes or processes which, in one way or another pre-select, limit, inhibit, disconnect, shape, mediate or (technically) over-determine the actual course of the temporal development of some explanatorily significant social thing. Any entity counts as a 'thing' if it possesses sufficient internal complexity, organ-isation, structure or coherence to count as a unit (or system) or a class (or part) of such units or a complex of relations between or within such units or classes or parts, or if it consists in any earthed function of any of the foregoing. Any entity counts as a 'social thing' provided that it satisfies the prerequisites of sociality elaborated in § 2 — in particular the criteria of activity-, concept-, space-time- and social-relation-dependence. Any such social thing can be accorded the dignity of a narrative, in which we may possess more or less interest. But whether or not a social thing is explanatorily significant cannot be settled outside the elaboration and historical sifting of social theory.

The transformational theory of social activity presupposes a view of causally active agents and structures, always already more or less complex and pre-formed (out of prior transforms), endowed with and endowing themselves with powers, liabilities and tendencies to change, moving, in interaction with one another, irreversibly through time in a radically open world in the direction of a future *still to be made.* That is to say, the T.M.S.A. presupposes (1) the real irreversibility of time; (2) the irreducibility of structures to events and, *a fortiori*, of possibility to actuality, as dual aspects of the historical process; and (3) a categorial asymmetry between explanation and prediction. These three transcendental conditions of the possibility of any science of history are intimately connected. The determination of events by causes does not entail that events either exist or are predetermined prior to their being caused by the agents etc. which cause them. Causal agents are integrated things which, at least in the social world, can never be reduced to simple atomistic conditions (or effects) of their past formation, present composition or future behaviour. And the systems in which such agents act can never, from the standpoint of their action (or indeed any other), be closed. This means *inter alia* that although *retrospectively* we can give well-grounded explan-ations of their behaviour, namely in terms of their structural powers, liabilities and dispositions; *prospectively* we are never (or very rarely) in a position to do this, just because we do not know which out of the myriad of possible sets of circumstances (in principle intrinsic as well as extrinsic to the agent) will actually materialise.

It is the irreducibility of things to their formation and the non-determination of events prior to their causation ('their time') which accounts for both the temporal asymmetry of causes and effects and the irreversibility of causal processes in time. Those of a transcendental idealist cast of mind sometimes object to Russell's 'spatialisation of time', viz. his attempted elimination (following McTaggart himself) of McTaggart's A-statement series, i.e. '$E_i$ is future/past/now' in favour of the B-statements series, i.e. '$E_1$ is before, after or simultaneous with $E_2$,'[125] by pointing to such phenomena as our non-indifference to equivalent events in different temporal directions from us. Only a fool (or perhaps an inmate?) would feel, one supposes, the same one week after the start of a ten-year jail sentence as one week from its end.[126] However, to account for this, and other phenomena attesting to our supreme non-indifference to temporal location, we do not need to suppose that time is moving through us. We account for such phenomena much better by supposing that we are moving through time, as in effect time-travellers on our historical world-lines (embedded in world-history), producing not the future (which as a notion is always either formal or [present-] relative), but its content. If time is moving through us, the future is already, as it were, laid out and fully formed, as on the Parmenidian/Laplacian/Russellian/Quinian view, save that it is now awaiting the privilege of being experienced by us — in exactly the same way as the end of a movie is already completed half-way through its showing. But we are not spectators in a completed scenario; we are actors, actresses, camera crew and stage-hands, making the film on location. Time indeed is indifferent to us, but we are not indifferent to it; and we are not indifferent to it because we move, for a duration, through it, making and being made in it. In this process our explanatory consciousness of the past can inform our understanding of the present and illuminate projects and strategies for a future, shaped but unmade.

The notion of differential historical temporalities associated with twentieth-century French structuralist historiography,

---

125. See J. McTaggart 'The Unreality of Time', *Mind 18* (1908), and, for a discussion, D.H. Mellor, *Real Time*, Cambridge 1981, Chap. 1 et passim.
126. See, e.g., N. Schlesinger, 'How Time Flies', *Mind 1982*, pp. 50 ff.

especially the work of Braudel, Bloch and the *Annales* School, is a fruitful one. But it raises the problem of how the differential temporal planes are to be related to one another. We need, it would seem, an IP type way of non-reductively integrating the different temporalities. There are two plausible responses to this. One is to suppose that time itself must be deconstructed and analysed as a mixed mode subject to the codetermination or mediation of higher order times by lower order, more basic, ones. The other, which I prefer, is to retain the notion of a unified temporal order and replace the problem of relating different times by the problem of relating different rhythms (patterns of flow, cycles, ratchets, spirals, novelties and finitude etc.) and modes of becoming of different orders, kinds and levels of structure, including our subjective awareness and experience of these rhythms, phases etc. The spatio-temporal unity and commensurating measure of these different transformative processes would be the simple one imposed by the geophysical location of Earth.

I have criticised actualism sufficiently above. It is however worth stressing that the duality of structure and praxis in historical process implies the symbiotic, but non-reductive, complementarity of social science and history; and that the irreducibility, but interdependence, of historical possibility and actuality implies the distinctiveness, but mutuality, of what I earlier characterised as the intrinsic and extrinsic aspects of consciousness. Scientific critique will never make our decisions, or perform our actions for us. These require judgement, choice and deliberation as well as effort. But criticism uninformed by scientific critique, wherever that is both necessary and possible, may quite properly be assessed 'ill-judged' (under-grounded). I have also discussed the explanatory/predictive symmetry thesis sufficiently elsewhere. That thesis follows of course as an immediate consequence of actualism. But it is just worth making two connected points here. First, it is quite extraordinary how many philosophers have found it possible to construct a methodology or speculative ideal for history upon the dogmatic formula 'whenever this, then that'. For the single most obvious feature of history is that it never in fact (exactly) repeats itself (and only exactness will do for the Humean's purposes here). Hence if we are to have a science of history, upon which truly general (transfactually efficacious) and informative (i.e. non-trivial), though not necessarily spatio-temporal universal, knowledge can be brought to bear, generality cannot possibly be sited at the level of events, but must instead be pitched at the level of what *is* general in the human-historical world. These are not events, but the generative structures co-producing them — although always complexely and mediated through intentional agency, such structures are causally efficacious and (relatively) enduring, as any (surviving) agent in the world must tacitly know. Second, transcendental realism implies a total rejection of all prediction-based (positivist and historicist) accounts of science, whether in the natural or social domains. It entails repudiating the positivist, Comtean-Baconian view of science as *savoir pour prévoir*, the instrumentalist Berkeleyan-Machian conception of science as a mnemonic or heuristic device; the deductivist Humean-Millian view of science as subsumption under empirical regularities; and the idea common to both inductivists, such as Carnap, and deductivists, such as Popper, that predictive power (success or failure, respectively) is the acid test of theory. All these theories presuppose, of course, spontaneously occurring closed systems, which are not in general — and never in the social world — available. In open systems, criteria for theory assessment cannot be predictive and so must be exclusively explanatory; deducibility can at best serve as a criterion for our knowledge of tendential necessities; theories cannot licence the prediction of events, although they can be used in the explanatory retrodiction of structures; and the aim of science once more becomes, as it was initially with the Greeks and then again in the seventeenth century, that of understanding rather than manipulating nature.

This leads into a final topic, which is related to the spatial dimensions of our social practices about which I have so far said little. This is the question, described by Kant in 1784 as 'the problem which is both the most difficult and the last to be solved by the human race'[127] — which I will paraphrase in contemporary terms as follows: Is not the development of a truly universal or cosmopolitan sensibility, rooted in a shared sense of our common humanity, and of our shared place, Earth, a condition, in present circumstances, for the very survival of the human species? Posing this question in Kantian terms does not entail

---

127. I. Kant, 'Idea of a Universal History with a Cosmopolitan Purpose', *Political Writings*, Cambridge 1970.

endorsing a Kantian solution of it. Kant supposed that the 'unsocial sociability' of man, guided by Providence or Nature, would eventually issue in the establishment of an international confederation of nations. As is well-known, Hegel rejected this idea. Implicit in the notion of a state was that of a boundary, and hence that of a contradictory plurality of states, in which war played an inevitable part, and for which the only compensation lay in the philosophical comprehension of world history, understood as the progressive development of the idea of freedom. If we reject this scenario and the speculative sleight of hand by which Hegel transports us from the sphere of objective to that of absolute spirit (populated by the constellations of art, religion and philosophy), then it is natural to turn to the possibility of explanatory critique and putatively emancipatory practice in the tradition of Marx and historical materialism. There is the relatively minor difficulty here that Marxism, not least in its classical mould, fully shared the manipulative, instrumentalist orientation to nature and place integral to the development of nineteenth-century capitalism. The more major difficulty is one of time. In the long run the answer may be socialism, but in the immediate-short run the question is survival, non-extinction. There is no way of bypassing historical mediations in any resolution of this profound and pressing ecopolitical problem. But could it be that its very difficulty and urgency provide rudiments for a possible solution? Could it be that affect, in the form of a heightened sense of time, and the possibility it conveys of literally global displacement, could so concentrate sensibility on our common planetary locale and our species' interest in its survival as to avoid an early terminus for it? What we need in order to feel at home in the world is not the infantile fantasy that it was made for us; but the mature post-Darwinian recognition of the ecological asymmetry: that it is more true to say that we were made for it,[128] and that we survive as a species only insofar as second nature respects the overriding constraints imposed upon it by first nature. From this nature, although it is always historically mediated, we can never, nor will ever, escape. If Kant is not to have been proved awesomely right, the emergence of a cosmopolitan sensibility, necessarily interested and no doubt organised and motivated by

---

128. Cf. M. Midgley, *Beast and Man*, London 1979, p. 145.

gender, class, generational, party, occupational, and a host of conjuncturally determined socio-economic, political, aesthetic, scientific and religious interests and experiences, may be an indispensable ratchet in the self-transformative process of the human species in the direction of a more fully human, and at least longer, and perhaps more emancipated, being.

# 3

# The Positivist Illusion: Sketch of a Philosophical Ideology at Work

*'"Facts?" he repeated. Take a drop more grog, Mr. Franklin, and you'll get over the weakness of believing in facts! Foul play, Sir"'[1]*

It is my aim in this chapter to describe the way in which a philosophical system, such as positivism, can function as an ideology for science and other social practices. I want to focus on positivism because of its intrinsic historical importance; because the impasse in contemporary philosophy of science diagnosed in chapter 1 takes the form of an incomplete critique of it; because it continues to inform the philosophy, and to an extent the practice, of the human sciences (as noted in chapter 2.2); because it describes an analytical limit or pole with respect to which many other philosophies can be defined and their *modus operandi* delineated and because many other philosophies tacitly presuppose it, even when nominally and perhaps virulently opposed to it.

Bachelard remarked on the striking *décalage* or discrepancy between the *diurnal* philosophy of scientists, that is the philosophy implicit in their spontaneous practice, and the *nocturnal* philosophy of philosophers. But what is more striking

---

1.   Wilkie Collins, *Moonstone* (quoted in P.K. Feyerabend, 'How to be a Good Empiricist', *The Philosophy of Science*, ed. P. Nidditch, Oxford 1968, p. 12).

is that it is to the nocturnal philosophy of the philosophers that scientists tend to return when they self-consciously reflect upon their conscious practice. Newton, Engels, Freud, Einstein in different ways attest this phenomena. What explains the discrepancy? How are we to account for the fact that even, and sometimes especially, the greatest scientists seem systematically deluded about the nature of their work? More generally, how are we to account for systematic misconceptions about science, among scientists and non-scientists alike? What is the source of 'false consciousness' about science?

This chapter attempts to sketch the elements of a partial answer by considering the implication of the hypothesis that the efficacy of philosophical ideas about science, including their efficacy in science, turns on the way in which they rationalise social practices, including non-scientific ones. (Thus, for example, their intra-scientific mystifying function may depend partly on the way in which they mystify extra-scientific practices.) Specifically, I want to illustrate some ways in which philosophies can act as ideologies for science and other forms of social activity, by employing a Marxian concept of ideology in the analysis of the mode of generation, reproduction and transformation of ideological effects by a particular cognitive system, namely positivism, inasmuch as it takes science for its topic. Because for the bulk of this chapter I will be working with a rather abstract conception of positivism, I commence my argument with a brief overview of positivism as a historical tendency of thought.

## 1. Positivism in context

Although positivist themes are already identifiable in antiquity, in the Middle Ages (especially in the writings of William of Ockham) and in the work of Francis Bacon and the British empiricists generally, the term 'positivism' was first used systematically by Saint-Simon. It was adopted by his erstwhile secretary Auguste Comte, to express the ideas that the world consists of phenomena which are real, useful, certain, precise, organic and relative and that knowledge consists in and only in the description of the coexistence and succession of such phenomena. As is well known, it became an extremely influential intellectual and cultural trend from the mid-nineteenth century onwards, forming the backbone of the generally accepted view of science. If positivism has now become, as Raymond Williams has remarked, a 'swear-word by which no one is swearing',[2] this is because unlike, say, the terms 'empirical' and 'scientific', it is no longer used 'positively' to describe or prescribe a criterion of authentic knowledge, but merely 'negatively' to critically assess or situate one or more of its constituent themes. Thus contemporary disputes about the extent to which, say, Poincaré's conventionalism or Popper's fallibilism are 'positivist' are, in part, disputes over which features of positivism were of greatest historical moment or cognitive interest — that is, in part, attempts at a real definition of positivism as a causally efficacious movement of thought.

At its most general, positivism is a theory of the nature, omnicompetence and unity of science. In its most radical shape it stipulates that the only valid kind of (non-analytic) knowledge is scientific, that such knowledge consists in the description of the invariant patterns, the co-existence in space and succession over time, of observable phenomena; and that the role of philosophy is analysis and perhaps summary of and/or propaganda for scientific knowledge, as so conceived. As a species of empiricism it is characterised by a reductionist view of scientific theory, a deductivist notion of scientific laws and a phenomenalist interpretation of scientific experience. Its naturalist insistence on the unity of science and scientistic disavowal of any knowledge apart from science induce its aversion to metaphysics, insistence upon a strict value/fact dichotomy and tendency to historicist confidence in the inevitability of scientifically mediated progress. Most of positivism is already contained elegantly expounded in the writings of Hume. But the strident anti-dogmatism of late nineteenth (and twentieth century) positivism — sure of itself and of its understanding of science as the 'representation of

---

2.  R. Williams, 'Postivism', *Keywords*, Glasgow 1976, p. 201. Positivists are of course notorious for disclaiming the accolade. But it is seldom appreciated that they are, in their own terms, perfectly justified in so doing. For the Humean theory of causal laws presupposes the complete independence of all predicates, and hence the arbitrariness of all definitions, so that there is no cognitive significance to the 'label'. At the same time the emotivist theory of values entitles them to repulse the pejorative load (quite properly) accruing to the term 'positivism' by resisting its application to themselves.

facts without the admixture of any theory or mythology'[3] — was never tempered by the wistful scepticism of the Enlightenment.

Comte envisaged the sciences as a hierarchy, resting on mathematics and developing progressively through astronomy, physics, chemistry and biology to sociology. On the Comtean eschatology, all thought evolves through three stages: the theological, when man represents natural phenomena as a product of supernatural agencies; the metaphysical, in which supernatural forces are replaced by abstract depersonalised ones; and the positive, when man finally relinquishes the search for inner or hidden causes and essential natures and sets the powers of reason and observation to describe the (presumed) invariant show of phenomena, thereby achieving technical mastery over them: '*savoir pour prévoir, prévoir pour pouvoir*'.

A similar, though more radically empiricist and libertarian, approach was elaborated in Britain by J.S. Mill, while Spencer pursued Comte's evolutionary theme, treating evolution, agnostically, as susceptible to interpretation in either materialist or spiritualist terms. Spencer's agnosticism found epistemological counterparts in Haeckel's 'neutral monism', Avenarius's 'empiriocriticism' and Mach's 'sensationalism'. On Mach's theory, sensations were neither physical nor psychical, but neutral elements which figured in the simultaneous constitution of both subject and object; facts were relatively stable clusters of sensations connected to, and dependent upon, one another; and knowledge was motivated by economic rather than explanatory interests, its end being the progressive adaptation of the human organism to its environment.

Mach's sensationalism chimed in well with the logical atomism developed by Russell and Wittgenstein, whereby the propositions of a language could be reconstructed as truth-functional complexes of atomistic components: atomic propositions in correspondence with atomic facts. Together these theories were the decisive influences on the logical positivism of the Vienna Circle of the 1920s and 30s, whose leading members were Carnap, Neurath and Schlick. The Vienna circle is best remembered for its aggressive employment of Hume's rigid and purportedly exhaustive dichotomy between analytical and

---

3.   Or in Bacon's original, 'The very contemplation of things as they are, without superstition or imposture, error or confusion, F. Bacon, *Novum Organum*, Book I, CXXIX Oxford 1889.

empirical truths in the guise of a criterion of meaningfulness, which also served as a principle for demarcating scientific and non-scientific discourse: the famous *verifiability principle*, initially formulated by Schlick as 'the meaning of a proposition is the method of its verification'. A number of difficulties soon appeared. First, the principle itself was evidently neither analytic nor empirical and so ought to be meaningless; on the other hand, treating it as a linguistic recommendation merely displaced the conundrum onto our grounds for accepting the recommendation. Secondly, on the principle, both historical propositions and scientific laws (which, being universal, could never be conclusively verified) turned out meaningless. To meet this difficulty, Carnap weakened the criterion to allow a proposition as meaningful just in case some empirical evidence would count for or against it, i.e. if it was confirmable or more generally *testable*. Popper's response to the problem was to admit non-scientific propositions as meaningful, but to substitute *falsifiability* as a demarcation criterion, adducing historical and moral as well as logical grounds for this. Finally, the principle seemed to entrain solipsism; or if specifically fortified with an intersubjective or 'public object' interpretation, e.g. by being couched in a physicalist (Neurath) or operationist (Bridgman) rather than sensationalist idiom, it lost incorrigibility and thence algorithmic determinacy and uniqueness (one and only one decision for each proposition).

In the period since the Second World War the elements of the positivistic view of science have gradually fallen apart whilst leaving, as we saw in chapter 1, its underlying ontology intact. The idea of theory-independent facts, constituting the incorrigible foundations of knowledge, was rendered suspect by the later Wittgenstein's critique of the possibility of a private language (and hence of the solipsistic individualism which positivism seemed to entail) and by an increasing awareness of the magnitude and pervasiveness of actual scientific changes — that is, by a growing appreciation of the sociality and historicity of science. The other lynchpin of the positivist view, the idea that laws can be represented as truth-functional complexes of atomistic facts, arrested in sense-perception, has been undermined by acknowledgement of the irreducibility of intensional relations between predicates and of models and analogies in scientific explanation and development — that is, by comprehension of the irreducibility, uneven and stratified character of scientific theory. At the same time there has been growing acceptance of the view that positivism, in its obsession with the observable and manipulable, reflects a form of technical-scientific practice embodying only a limited, partial and/or historically restricted human interest. A direct line of descent links Comte, via Durkheim to functionalist sociology, and the conceptual resonances between philosophical positivism and behaviourist psychology are plain. Both the theory and practice of a positivistically unified science have been attacked by anti-naturalist and non-positivist naturalist writers concerned to identify and save the specificity of the human sciences, as we saw in chapter 2. In this chapter I intend to move on from the transcendental realist and critical naturalist development of these critical shifts in an attempt to explain, in what I earlier called the metacritical dimension (MD) of the philosophy of science (1.3 above), the perennial appeal of positivism (and *a fortiori* the incompleteness of much contemporary anti-positivism). For if positivism is philosophically 'dead', it survives and kicks in the sciences — as a current of thought in the natural sciences, and as considerably more than that in many of the human ones.

In this chapter I shall be treating positivism as an abstract but transfactually efficacious (and so real) cognitive structure, mechanism or apparatus — a real tendency of thought which, when I consider it abstractly, I will simply designate as 'P'. My theoretical definition of positivism, of P, is of a philosophical system whose essential tenets are already to be found in Hume. It may be provisionally justified by two considerations. First, however precisely positivism is defined, the historical significance of Humean empiricism on its development, and its importance for both 'positivist' (Comte, Mill, Mach, Carnap, Hempel) and 'anti-positivist' (Kant, Whewell, Poincaré, Campbell, Popper(?)) alike is undeniable.[4]

Secondly, the system P reconstructed here describes a pole not merely in relation to which other philosophical positions may be defined, but a pole in relation to which they have had typically to defend and justify themselves — to such an extent that P has come to exercise a kind of shaping hegemony in the

---

4.    Cf. L. Kolakowski, *Positivist Philosophy*, London 1972, p. 43.

philosophy of science:[5] to constitute, one might say, its underlying determinant, if not always locally dominant, mode of production.

P is, in the first instance, a theory of the nature, limits and unity of knowledge. Particular knowledge is of events sensed in perception; general knowledge is of the patterns such events trace in space and over time which, if it is to be possible, must be constant (the Humean theory of causal laws). Sense-perception exhausts the possible objects of knowledge. Conversely any object of sense-perception constitutes a possible object of knowledge. Thus the cognitive claims of theory, metaphysics, morality, ethics, politics, religion and hermeneutics alike are rejected; and man is located squarely as an object within the system of objects in which he acts. P is a limit form of empiricism.

P is a theory of knowledge. But any theory of knowledge presupposes an ontology. For it must be assumed, implicitly if not explicitly, that the knowable world is such that it is or consists in objects of the specified type. Thus the Humean theory, on

---

5.  Thus in major respects the Humean critique of ontology has shaped, at least until very recently, almost all subsequent philosophy of science — either directly, in the empiricist and Kantian traditions; or indirectly (and in inversive reaction), in the romantic (e.g. Bergsonian) and dialectical-materialist (Engelsian) traditions, mediated in the latter case by the transitions Kant-Fichte-Schelling-Hegel-left Hegelianism. Moreover, it is significant that even when it is 'positivism' itself that is in contestation, as in the '*Positivismusstreit*' of the 1960s (see especially T. Adorno *et al.*, *The Positivist Dispute in German Sociology*, London 1976), the disputants typically accept an essentially Humean account of natural laws and of natural scientific theories. Thus, for Habermas, for example: 'In the empirical-analytical sciences ... theories comprise hypothetico-deductive connections of propositions, which permit the deduction of law-hypotheses with empirical content. The latter can be interpreted as statements about the covariance of observable events; given a set of initial conditions, they make predictions possible. Empirical-analytical knowledge is thus possible predictive knowledge', J. Habermas, *Knowledge and Human Interests*, London 1972, p. 308. This is a succinct statement of the D-N model of explanation of Hume, Mill, Popper and Hempel, together with its attendant corollary, the thesis of the symmetry of explanations and (potential) predictions. The fact that this model is restricted to closed systems means that Habermas's 'knowledge-constitutive interest in prediction and control', allegedly structuring the natural sciences, can no longer be seen as a *universal* condition rooted in an *undifferentiated* relation between human beings and nature. Instead a distinction between experimental and technical action, and a foriori the interests 'guiding' them, becomes mandatory; and the question of the conditions (intrinsic and extrinsic to both science

which P pivots, presupposes an ontology of closed systems and atomistic events, comprising the objects of actual or possible experiences. Moreover any theory of knowledge presupposes a sociology, in the sense that it must be assumed, implicitly if not explicitly, that the nature of persons and the institutions they reproduce or transform is such that knowledge could be produced in the specified manner. In this way the Humean theory presupposes a view of people as passive sensors of given facts and recipient recorders of their given constant conjunctions, which has the corollary that knowledge can always be analysed as a purely individual attribute or possession.

A theory of knowledge, such as P, thus *automatically* constitutes two dimensions in the philosophy of science: an intransitive dimension (ID) or philosophical ontology; and a transitive dimension (TD) or philosophical sociology. But in parallel fashion it presupposes some philosophical method by which its results are produced, and hence, explicitly or implicitly, a theory of philosophy, so constituting a metacritical dimension (MD) or philosophy and historical sociology of philosophy, just as its results constitute a metaphysics. Positivist philosophy, notoriously, in what I characterised in 1.3 as the 'positivistic illusion', denies this. P presupposes, then, as necessary conditions of its results: an ontology of empirical realism, a

---

and technology) for the assumption that knowledge in the natural sciences is pursued subject to an interest in possible technical control must itself be posed. (Cf. N. Stockman, 'Habermas, Marcuse and the *Aufhebung* of science and technology', *Philosophy of Social Sciences, Volume I*, 1978, pp. 15-35). This is not a minor matter, but points to a fundamental flaw in Habermas's Kantian project of attempting to render ontological mediations as epistemological divisions. *Mutatis mutandis*, similar considerations apply to all those theories that picture scientific knowledge as grounded in, or growing under, an interest in prediction, manipulation and/or control — e.g. M.B. Hesse, *The Structure of Scientific Inference*, London 1974, (see e.g. p. 284), and S.B. Barnes, *Interests and the Growth of Knowledge*, London 1977. Such theories, despite their power and sophistication, amount to so many critical-theoretical, philsophical or sociological isotopes of an *actualising instrumentalism*. This reflects only a phase of the natural scientific process, a particular historically circumscribed form of technology and a restricted class (not a universal human) interest. The distinction between laws and their empirical grounds, and between open and closed systems (see 1.4 above) means that: (i) science must be viewed as essentially explanatory and only subsidiarily predictive; and (ii) theory must be differentiated from its applications. It is of course characteristic of positivism to conflate these. (Cf. also R. Keat and J. Urry, *Social Theory as Science*, London 1975, p. 191.)

sociology defined by a mechanistic or behaviouristic model of man, and a reductionist, self-abnegating (and so self-refuting) conception of philosophy — that is, a philosophy lacking a concept of itself, and of these three transcendental necessities to which any theory of knowledge is subject.

P is a theory of the nature, limits and unity of knowledge. But it is not a theory of its *possibility*. Knowledge is for P quite unproblematic. A given fact, it never enquires for a moment into its conditions or seriously contemplates the possibilities that it might not have been or of its demise. (In this it is irredeemably pre-critical, objectivistic and historicist.) But knowledge is a transient historical phenomenon, whose conditions are subject to both philosophical analysis and scientific investigation. Foremost among the conditions that can be established by *a priori* argument are, I argued in chapter 1:

(1)   the independent existence and transfactual efficacy of causal structures and things (the intransitive objects of knowledge) (in the ID);

(2)   the social production of knowledge by means of antecedent knowledge (the transitive objects of knowledge) (in the TD);

(3)   the irreducibility and science-susceptivity of the discourse (philosophy) in which such propositions and their contraries are expressed (the metacritical conditions of knowledge) (in the MD).

Any system such as P which fails to satisfy (1)-(3) is immediately vulnerable to transcendental refutation. But if (1)-(3) are indeed necessary conditions of scientific activity then any system not satisfying them will have in *practice* to contain them or their consequences, or at least a gesture in their direction, in the shape of some compromise formation, as a proper subset. And it will transpire that some of the most interesting ideological effects of P are generated by the requirement that that system satisfies what, if it is to be any use at all, it formally denies. In such cases the mechanism of effect-generation, of ideology-application and reproduction is necessarily *covert* or disguised. And it is in the inconsistent system, 5, which results that the tremendous versatility or flexibility of positivism as an ideology lies. S is produced by the transformation of the core system P by what I shall call the 'axiological operator', A, viz.

(4)   P $\triangleq$ S ... theory application.

As contradictory conclusions can be derived from an inconsistent system, the particular conclusions actually derived from S, on particular occasions of its use, can only be explained by factors external to it, e.g. by the conscious or unconscious uses to which it is put and/or the causal roles it characteristically performs in the wider social sphere (which may be relatively enduring or ephemeral, and internal or external to science). However there are other ideological effects of P which are *overt*, in the sense that they are generated as straightforward consequences of it, whether they are recognised as such or not (and hence whether the effect is manifest or latent). These consequences need not, at least in as much as the core system P is not itself formally inconsistent or overdetermined, give rise to permutable results, and hence can be explained as immanent necessities of P itself, however the latter is explained.

If S is to be applied and used, P must itself have already been constituted and produced. But P is not just false, but categorially false and grossly implausible to boot. And its mode of production as a system, susceptible to overt and covert uses, depends upon the tacit presupposition of theses, which only transcendental realism, represented by (1)-(3) and their implications and elaborations, can coherently or adequately sustain.

In this operation, a determinate outcome P is derived from an internally inconsistent ensemble, viz.

(5)   C $\triangleq$ P ... theory production.

(5) presents in a certain respect the mirror image of (4), but here the mechanism of ideology production, i.e. the generation of the core system P, deployed in the generation of covert and overt effects, is necessarily covert or disguised. So P, although liable to overt or covert *uses*, is necessarily covertly *produced*. The T.M.S.A. suggests that it is plausible to look to the characteristic effects or uses of S in the production of social objects, and in the reproduction or transformation of the social structures governing and employed in these productions, for explanation of the production and reproduction and transformation of P; that (5) is to the explained, at least in part, in terms of the typical results and consequences of (4), i.e. in terms of the overt and covert effects flowing from P's misrecognition

of the nature of the world, society, science and itself. P accumulates an ideological value in contemporary society in both ways. But if overt results are perhaps more important in the misrepresentation of being, in the ID, covert ones hold sway in the TD, in the mystification of the process of science itself. However I shall insist that we need to understand a complex philosophical ideology, such as P, at at least four levels:

[1] *theory-production*, or deep-structure; here C $\subseteq$ P

[2] *theory-constitution*, or surface-structure; here P

[3] *theory-application*, or use; here P $\triangle$ S;

[4] *concrete historical mediation* of [1]-[3], leading to detailed case histories, say of Hume or the Vienna Circle.

There is no question of collapsing P to the conditions or mechanisms of its production or those of its use. Only [1]-[3] are attended to here, so what is essayed is not a full explanatory critique, merely a proto-explanatory sketch, limning possible frameworks for more specific natural-historical investigations.

P is, or purports to be, a theory, even if only by default, of much else besides science. But in this chapter I can deal with it only insofar as it is a theory of science. However, even in this limited respect, P, as just intimated, acts as an ideology for social practices other than science. It does this partly by generating an ideology *of science*, for society as it were, to complement the one it generates *for science*; and partly by encouraging, either by injunction or resonance, certain substantive conceptions of the nature of nature, society, people and their interconnections. In resonance, it reflects and in general tends to reinforce interests, preconceptions and images at work sanctioning the wider social order, including those in substantive social science.[6] In resonance, social theory assumes a metaphorical or metonymic existence in the transfigured form of epistemologies. I had better make it clear at the outset that in speaking of an effect of an ideology I mean nothing other or apart from its conscious or unconscious uses, or more or less systematic kinds of use, by agents in determinate historical contexts; similarly in

---

6. In this respect it acts as the obverse of what Buchdahl has styled a philosophy of science's 'analogical grammar'. See G. Buchdahl, *Metaphysics and the Philosophy of Science*, Oxford 1969, p. 37.

talking, when I do, of its 'function', I merely refer to its causal impact, mediated via use, on the reproduction (or transformation) of some social structure (cf. 2.3 above).

If P is an ideology, we must attempt to ascertain its necessity. That is to say, we must ask: to what extent does science necessarily appear to agents in positivist guise, i.e. as something other than it really is. P is a wholly inadequate philosophical position. But this does not mean that it possesses no measure of necessity as a scientific one, whence it may derive some of its *prima facie* compelling power. The significance of this is that positivism has always coexisted in symbiosis with anti-scientific romantic reaction (a reaction which, now that science has come to be glossed as merely one social activity among others, has ineluctably penetrated its citadel in the philosophy of science itself).[7] A critique of this debris of the Enlightenment, which must throw its satellite into relief, is essential if, in developing a social science of human history, we are to resist the seductive doctrinairianisms of the apostles of dogma and spontaneity, method and anti-method alike. At the same time this should help us steer our way to a fairer assessment of the role of science in history and its significance in contemporary culture and politics. My aim, then, is to examine the degree to which P as a theory of science is explicable by the ways in which it mystifies or otherwise rationalises scientific and other social practices. Before seeking refuge in the heaven of Marxism, it will be instructive to glance at the sociology of knowledge to see to what extent the clouds of empiricism here are lined with truth.

## 2. Metacritical Preliminaries: Sociology, Science, Ideology

### I. The Contribution of the Sociology of Knowledge

In seeking to scientifically explain scientific beliefs and practices, the sociology of knowledge usurps philosophy's self-anointed crown. For traditionally, insofar as philosophy regarded science as susceptible to explanation, it was assumed to be explained by 'scientific method', about which philosophers disagreed but which was, at any rate, adumbrated by them as indeed the signal object of their discourse. Broadly speaking,

---

7. See, e.g., P.K. Feyerabend, *Against Method*, London 1975.

philosophers divided into two main camps: (α) the classical *rationalist* position, whereby science is, or should be, the realization of philosophy (cf. the speculative illusion, identified in 1.3 above); and (ß) the opposed, typically *empiricist* position, whereupon philosophy is, or should only be, the self-description of (and/or self-propaganda for) science (cf. the positivistic illusion)[8].

A corollary of (α) is that science should have no effect on philosophy (cf. Popper; Lakatos); of (ß) that philosophy should have no effect on science (cf. Feyerabend; and, in a very different way, Bachelard). Positivism is of course logically based on the second position.[9]

But this may take the form of either (i) a scientistic *sociologism* (repudiation of the intrinsic or normative aspect (IA) of science, and more generally consciousness) or (ii) a normative *me-*

---

8.   On both conceptions, the field of legitimate historical or sociological concern was characteristically restricted to the origins of scientific method, or of the conditions for its supremacy or of deviance from it — the cause, in the most naive inductivist accounts, of error. (Cf. J. Agassi, *Towards an Historiography of Science*, The Hague 1963). In any event it was rigidly bounded by the limits of the applicability of the concept 'science', so that no scientific explanation of science was deemed necessary, or indeed possible. Thus, for instance, for Lakatos it is still philosophy which decrees what science or sociology (in the shape of external history) could and could not explain, the best philosophy being the one which minimised sociology's role. (See I. Lakatos, 'The History of Science and its Rational Reconstructions', *Philosophical Papers Volume 2*, Cambridge 1978.) What I characterise immediately below as scientistic sociologism, manifested by the work of Kuhn and his disciples, remains within this problematic, merely reversing its terms, i.e. opting for (ß) and then — their twentieth-century innovation — adopting a first-order, rather than a second-order, stance, being postivistic in science (sociology) rather than merely *about* science. The reader may like to be reminded how transcendental realism differentiates itself from the traditional positions. It rigorously discriminates scientific and philosophical ontologies. The former consists in what is established in some scientific activity or other. The latter comprises what is presupposed by it. Thus a science/philosophy distinction, rooted in the relative primacy of the former, is preserved against the possibility of both speculative and positivistic reductions (dissolutions). Moreover both the forms taken by science (generally, the movement from manifest phenomena to generative structures) and its realisability in a particular domain remain contingent questions. Hence transcendental realism is not a monism and it is only weakly or conditionally (but nevertheless is) prescriptive. Nor is it 'objectivist' in either method or results. For it is predicated on the immanent critique of existing conceptualisations of historical practice, and it situates itself, these conceptualisations and those practices, within the framework of the very same historical process which social science describes and in which philosophy intervenes.

*thodologism* (renunciation of the extrinsic or historical aspect (EA) of science). (i) and (ii) are equally faulty — for to conceive science merely as object means to be unselfconscious about one's own science and acritical about actually existing scientific practices; while to consider it purely as subject undermines the possibility of a historical ground for one's own methodological commendations and historical judgements.

On its traditional self-decreed prerogative, then, philosophy took for its prime subject-matter knowledge, of which science constituted the paradigm or the whole. And philosophy and science were linked as subject and object, norm and action or *explanans* and *explanandum*. Either science was the realisation

9.  But support for it has also emerged in more surprising quarters — in the work of the British post-Althusserians, especially Hindess and Hirst. For example, Hindess argues that the invocation of philosophical theories in the explanation or criticism of scientific or pseudo-scientific practices is always illegitimate in that it involves the supposition that there is a real empiricist (of whatever) process of knowledge. (See B. Hindess, *Philosophy and Methodology in the Social Sciences*, Hassocks 1977, p. 189). This presupposes a rationalist conception of the production of discourse (*ibid*, p. 216), which is a special case of the rationalist conception of action according to which 'the act or its product is conceived as the realisation of a conceptual totality' (*loc cit.*) or more generally an 'idea'. This argument presupposes the old Kantian dichotomy of noumenal and phenomenal worlds, or in modern garb of reasons and causes, whereupon human action can have only a physical explanation (determination). Besides undermining the status of Hindess's own 'critique', which must depend for its efficacy upon the detection (see *ibid*, pp. 224-8), and correction (and therefore upon the operation in theoretical practice) of just such a 'rationalist' mechanism of action (that is, of a mechanism for the realisation of ideas in the material world — for a defence of which see my *The Possibility of Naturalism*, especially chapter 3), it vitiates the possibility of any Marxist politics, or, as is notoriously conceded, historiography or concept of ideology. Thus 'ideological analysis' is reduced to an utilitarian 'calculation of political consequences' (see P. Hirst, 'Althusser and the Theory of Ideology', *Economy and Society* 5: 4, 1976, p. 396). And we have the doctrine that: '"reality" does not conceal its essence from us any more than it reveals it to us ... [so that] the terms illusion, misrecognition, etc. only have a meaning in ideology, they have no place in the real object under investigation', B. Brewster, 'Fetishism in *Capital* and *Reading Capital*', *Economy and Society* 5: 3, 1976, p. 347. These sentiments may be perfectly proper to natural science, but they are irrelevant to social science which, together with ideology, is internal to its subject-matter. An account that cannot think the necessity for both, and the irreducibility of, the concepts of thought and being (see B. Hindess, *op. cit.*, p. 198; P. Hirst, *op. cit.*, pp. 407-9) must lapse into idealism where concepts are part of being. The origin of these errors is clear. It lies in Althusser's initial inadequate

of a self-evident philosophy and philosophy was science self-conscious of itself; or philosophy was the expression of science and science was self-evidently itself. The sociology of knowledge in principle dissolves the circular paralogism. For both philosophy and science, and hence their real, imagined and possible connections, now become topics for substantive scientific research — research which, however, *contra* scientistic sociologism always presupposes some (reflexively, and iteratively modifiable) methodological orientation, that is, the virtuous methodological circle of 1.3 above.

The sociology of knowledge has amply demonstrated that neither rationalist nor empiricist approaches to the philosophy-science relation can be historically sustained. Thus while extra-scientific (or generally a-rational) factors of both cognitive and non-cognitive kinds may exercise a keen influence on the formation of scientific products, it is equally clear that changing philosophical theories do at least sometimes act as a major (independent and non-neutral) determinant on scientific outcomes. For instance, in the first respect, the impact of developments in water and steam technology on thermodynamics[10] or of Galton's political and eugenic concerns on the development

---

theorisation of the concepts of the 'real object' and the 'thought object'. His failure to provide an apodeictic status for, or indeed given any real function to, the former rendered it as disposable as a Kantian ding-an-sich — a service duly performed, against the continuing materialist letter of Althusser's texts (see, e.g., L. Althusser, 'Is it Simple to be a Marxist in Philosophy?', *Essays in Self-Criticism*, London 1976, especially pp. 191-4), by his erstwhile British disciples. The result of the collapse of the intransitive dimension is a reduction of Marxism to a semiotics in which, just because the concept of reference has no place — in contrast to what in reality is a semiotic *triangle* of sign (word, etc.) concept and object (or referent) (see, e.g., G.D. Martin, *Language Truth and Poetry*, Edinburgh 1975) — no *materialist* explanation of signifying processes, that is, in terms other than of other signfying processes, is possible. But signifying is not a practice, it is an aspect of practice; and the signifier not only shifts and slides, it connotes and denotes and must itself be susceptible of an act of reference for any signifying (and *a fortiori* critique of signifying) to be possible. Signification is inscribed within and partly constitutive of practices, which are contained within and partially constitutive of the social world, itself contained and efficacious in the natural world in which we breathe. Incidentally, what follows from the inadequacy of empiricism as an account of the cognitive process is that it cannot be consistently realised and so will tend to generate in practice what I have called covert effects.

10. See, e.g., D. Cardwell, *From Watt to Clausius*, London 1971.

of his statistical techniques, have been fully documented.[11] I am here concerned in part with the way such extra-scientific influences may be mediated by philosophical ideas. For example, Duhem's ontological reductionism, and in particular his hostility to all attempts to conceptualise in science a reality not given to the senses was partly motivated by his profound religious convictions;[12] its philosophical expression was eased by the fact that he was following a hallowed ('denying reason to make room for faith') groove, already sanctioned, indeed sanctified, by Kant. But it led him to deprecate Maxwell's electromagnetism in favour of Helmholz's and to ignore Lorentz's work in atomic physics.

Turning explicitly to the influence of philosophical ideas on scientific practices, the sociology of knowledge has clearly shown that such a link does at least sometimes exist, just as the converse connection must surely hold — thus it would be difficult to exaggerate the importance of Newtonian mechanics for the subsequent trajectory of philosophical thought. But the link is not of the simple triumph of reason over dogma (superstition, etc.) kind postulated in rationalist hagiography. Koyré, for example, has argued very forcibly that the Galilean project is unintelligible unless seen as an attempted revindication or posthumous revenge of Platonism, 'as a return to Plato, a victory of Plato over Aristotle'.[13] Forman has argued persuasively that there is a connection between the development of quantum mechanics and the philosophical hostility to determinism and commitment to *Lebensphilosophie* characteristic of Weimar culture.[14] Young has attempted to demonstrate a link between Darwin's scientific work and his commitment to 'unif-

---

11. See R. Cowans, 'Francis Galton's statistical ideas: the influence of eugenics', *Isis Vol. 63*, pp. 509-28; cf. also B. Barnes and D. MacKenzie, 'Biometrician v Mendelian: a controversy and its explanation', *Kölner Zeitschrift für Soziologie*, 1975; and S. Rose, 'Scientific racism and ideology: the IQ racket', *The Political Economy of Science*, eds. H. Rose and S. Rose, London 1976.

12. See, e.g., P. Duhem, 'The Physics of a Believer', *The Aim and Structure of Physical Theory*, New York 1962, pp. 273-311.

13. A. Koyré, *Metaphysics and Measurement*, London 1965, p. 15. See also A. Koyré, *Galilean Studies*, Hassocks 1978.

14. P. Forman, 'Weimar culture, causality and quantum theory, 1918-27', *Historical Studies in the Physical Sciences Vol. 3*, Philadelphia 1971, pp. 1-115.

ormitarianism'.[15] More broadly, work has begun on the question
'what must society and social relations be like in a system which
generates and reproduces the forms and relations characteristic
of specific scientific products'[16] by tracing the characteristic
forms of social relations implied by 'arithmomorphic'[17] (rather
than 'dialectical'), 'restricted' (rather than 'unrestricted' or 'configurational')[18] and closed (rather than open) systemic sciences.
At a more general level it is clear that fictionalist (and instrumentalist) interpretations of scientific theory have been consciously employed to obstruct and subvert the development of
realistic scientific theories, e.g. by Brodie in chemistry in the
1870's and by Friedman in economics in the 1950s.[19] And the
interpolation of philosophical reflection in the practice of a science, proto-science or pseudo-science needs no emphasis in
such fields as contemporary micro-physics, evolutionary theory,
paranormal psychology and above all the human sciences generally.

---

15. R. Young, 'Darwin's metaphor: Does nature select?', *De Moniste, Vol. 55*,
    pp. 442-503. See also generally B. Barnes and S. Shapin, *Natural Order:
    Historical Studies of Scientific Culture*, London 1979.
16. P. Colvin 'Ontological and Epistemological Commitment and Social
    Relationships in the Sciences', *Sociology and the Sciences Yearbook 1977:
    The Social Production of Scientific Knowledge*, eds. P. Mendelsohn, P.
    Weingart and R. Whitley, Dordrecht 1977.
17. N. Georgescu-Roegen, *The Entropy Law and the Economic Process*,
    Cambridge, Mass., 1971, especially chapter 2. Entropy — the conversion of
    'free' into 'bound' energy — entails a radical 'irreversibility' in nature, and
    hence introduces the necessity for concepts of qualitative, rather than
    merely quantitative change.
18. R. Whitley, 'Changes in the Social and Intellectual Organisation of the
    Sciences', ed. P. Mendelsohn *et al.*, *op. cit.*
19. See B. Brodie, *The Calculus of Chemical Operations*, London 1876, and
    M. Friedman, 'The Methodology of Positivist Economics', *Essays in
    Positive Economics*, Chicago 1953, pp. 3-43. Friedman's main aim was to
    undermine the validity of criticisms of neoclassical economics directed at
    the unrealism of its assumptions. Brodie's project was to construct a
    chemistry without atoms. So successful was Brodie's system, which was
    intellectually entirely parasitic upon (in the sense that it was merely a
    Boolean transform of) Daltonian chemistry, in the positivist and anti-
    theoretical climate of the 1870s that at a meeting of the Chemical Society
    in London only one out of the sixty members present was prepared to
    countenance the existence of atoms! (For an account of this bizarre episode
    in the history of chemistry, see R. Harré, 'Philisophy of Science, History
    of', *Encyclopaedia of Philosophy Vol. 6*, ed. P. Edwards, London 1967,
    pp. 200-201.) Friedman's success can be counted, in part, by the numbers
    currently unemployed.

It would seem, then, from the sociology of knowledge that philosophical ideas play a part in explaining scientific beliefs and practices (and vice versa); and that both, together with their connections, must be explained by reference to a matrix which allows for the effectivity of external as well as internal factors, and numbers among the former non-cognitive as well as cognitive influences. However, the sociology of knowledge has tended to a systematic objectivism about its own field of enquiry, resolutely renouncing any normative or critical assessment of its subject-matter, whilst at the same time abstaining from reflexive causal investigations into its own context of determination, tending to a complementary subjectivism about itself, repudiating at once the IA of the object under study and the EA of the sociological enquiry studying it. The former presupposes that the truth or falsity of a belief (or the rationality or otherwise of a practice) is irrelevant to its explanation; the latter that the explanation of a belief or practice is irrelevant to its truth or rationality, etc. The former implies the absence or externality of causal relations between a belief and its object, the latter the effective extrusion of the enquiry from its social sources, leading to a practical destratification or detotalisation of both investigated and investigating social forms. 'Hypostatisation of subject, deintentionalisation of object; idealism of content, empiricism of form' would seem to be a fair description of at least leading tendencies within this sociological current's practice.

If Marxism is to mark any advance on its progeny, it must therefore presumably be because it is capable of restratifying and retotalising social forms, reconnecting the subject and object of social enquiry and more generally both to their objects and their sources (in the terminology of 2.5), furnishing principles of articulation and plausible explanatory hypotheses, in a distinctive research tradition, for the structures and relations established, while being methodologically self-conscious about what it is doing. The effectivity of some particular cognitive product, such as P, would then be explained in terms of the way it is and has been drawn upon and used by historically situated agents in the reproduction and transformation of a structured totality of causally (and internally) related and developing moments, encompassing both the explanandum object, P, and its explanatory theory, which must therefore be able to historically comprehend itself.

## II. Ideology in the Marxist Tradition

As is well known, the term 'ideology' was initially coined by Destutt de Tracy to denote the scientific study of ideas, but was then used pejoratively by Napoleon Bonaparte to refer to the fanciful and impractical schemes of Enlightenment theorists like de Tracy. This connotation was stretched and then transformed by Marx and Engels in the mid-1840s to characterise the mystified and mystifying abstraction of the thought of their contemporaries from the real processes of history. In the schematic topography of historical materialism, such ideas were designated as part of, or at least alongside the superstructure, ultimately explicable in terms of the economic base; while in Marx's critique of political economy, the characteristic pattern of explanatory critique, first cut on German philosophy and utopian socialism, was refined to definitively overarch the earlier Baconian, Kantian and Hegelian critiques of illusion, although not without unresolved difficulties of its own. Subsequently there has been a tendency in both radical historicist, e.g. Gramscian, and structuralist, e.g. Althusserian, Marxism, paralleling developments in non-Marxian thought (e.g. Mannheim and Lévi-Strauss or Lacan respectively) to emphasise the 'positive' notion of ideology as expressing the values or world view of a particular social class (group or sometimes milieu);[20] or to effectively extend the concept to embrace the entire cultural sphere, understood as more or less mystificatory. It should be clear from the argument of chapter 2 why I regard both developments as mistaken. In particular if emancipation is to be possible, well-grounded explanations of false consciousness and more generally ill-being must be capable of informing self-conscious transformative practice, unfettering human productive, developmental, life-enhancing and consumptive powers and possibilities. I shall therefore adopt a classical Marxian orientation to the concept of ideology here.

Within this conceptual line, ideologies are ($\alpha$) explicable systems of false, especially categorially false (or otherwise inadequate) systems of effective ideas, ($\beta$) explained (or at least situated) in terms of the particular historically restricted and/or sectional, especially class, interests they, normally unwittingly,

---

20. Cf. J. Larrain, *The Concept of Ideology*, London 1975.

serve in the process of the production, reproduction and transformation of human material being. ($\alpha$) registers formal, ($\beta$) material or substantive criteria. I tackle the formal criteriology first, borrowing from an earlier discussion[21] and formalising considerations broached in 2.6 above.

To designate a system of ideas I as '*ideological*' we must possess a theory (or coherent set of theories) T such that:

(1)    T can explain most, or most of the significant, phenomena, under its own descriptions, which are explained by I under I's descriptions, where these are incommensurable with those of T (see 1.6 above).

(2)    T can explain in addition a significant set of phenomena not explained by I.

(3)    I cannot satisfy either (i) a criterion of scientificity, specifying the minimum necessary conditions for a practice or production to qualify as 'scientific', and/or (ii) a criterion of domain adequacy, specifying the minimum necessary conditions for a theory to sustain the specificity (e.g. the historical or social character) of its subject-matter.

(4)    T can sustain both (i) and (ii).

(5)    T can explain the reproduction, indicate the limits and delineate any auto-subversive or more generally transformative tendencies of and upon I, specifically

(5')   in terms of a level of structure or network of connections described in T but absent from or obscured in I, so that T possesses a depth or totality that I lacks.

(6)    T can account for its historical genesis and conceptualise its present situation.

(1) and (2) comprise the *critical*, (3) and (4) the *categorial* and (5) and (6) the *explanatory* conditions for the characterisation of a belief system or practice by or in terms of another as 'ideological'. (3) and (4) presuppose that T, or some metatheory T* consistent with it, elaborates the appropriate criteria. The argument of 2.2 implies that in the final analysis there can only be a relative, heuristic distinction between (i) and (ii), as what constitutes scientificity in the study of X depends upon the *sui generis* characteristics, the X-reality or X'ishness, of X. Employing the

---

21.   *The Possibility of Naturalism*, Brighton 1979, Appendix to chapter 2.

notation introduced in 2.6 the conditions can be chalked as

$$T > I; T \text{ dem } (-S_c(I) \text{ v } -S_o(I)); \text{ and } T \exp (-S_c(I) \text{ v } -S_o(I))$$

where 'dem' stands for 'demonstrate' (here the unscientific and/ or desocialising nature of I), licensing the evaluative and practical judgements of the kinds spelled out above, so that ideology-critique is intrinsically evaluative in virtue of its explanatory power and practically as well as theoretically subversive or enhancing. It should be remembered that if the term ideology is necessarily correlative to science, the T theory which permits us to situate a belief as ideological will always consist in or include a social scientific one, even where the belief is one about nature. And it bears re-emphasis that while we are only warranted in characterising a system of beliefs as 'ideological' if we can explain, or are on the road to explaining, it, we cannot in general adequately explain beliefs about the social world without establishing their truth or falsity, etc. ('critiquing them', in the vernacular). Explanation and criticism are irreducible and complementary aspects fused in the explanatory critique. A sociologistic rejection of the criterion of false consciousness, by those who wish to define ideology solely in terms of its serving concealed, historically restricted, particular or sectional (non-universal) interests or its embodying 'unnecessary' forms of domination, in fact does a subtle *disservice* to the actor's point of view. It suggests that one might be able to detect those interests or forms without a theory capable of showing how these beliefs and practices arise as more or less adequate, intelligible and rational responses to the systemic irrationalities, mystifications and oppressions in which those interests and forms of domination are expressed. *Mutatis mutandis* similar considerations apply to the converse theoreticist mistake — the indiscriminate over-extension of the notion of false consciousness — save that here the disservice is obvious and blatant, and theory itself is left without a point of view, a point of view *from* which to be true.

pass now to the substantive or material criteriology, concerned with the elaboration of the explanatory and metaphysical (in the sense of metaphysics $\beta$, as explicated in 1.3) principles to be engaged in the construction of particular research hypotheses. The general desideratum is of course to avoid both idealism and reductionism (whether of an expressivist or economistic) kind, while retaining some clear, non-trivial and historiographically plausible content to the theory of the primacy of the mode of production of human material being in the organisation of human social life. This presupposes commitment to (perhaps historically specific) principles of hierarchy, totality and relative autonomy. I have considered the problem under its more general — integrative pluralistic — rubric in Chapter 2 § 4. Here I touch on it only insofar as it is necessary for the development of a proto-explanatory framework for a philosophical ideology of and for, in, about and against science — such as P.

All three terms — science, philosophy, ideology — pose problems for standard historical materialist topographies. If anything belongs to the material forces of production, then the embodied *applications* of natural science in augmenting human material productive powers must surely do so. But it would be quite wrong to infer from this that the *production* of natural scientific knowledge and the reproduction or transformation of natural scientific practices can be treated as independent variables of the historical process. In chapter 1 I argued that science must be conceived as a process of the production of thought by thought, in which the transformation of nature in experimental activity, plays a key role. Here I want to regard science, as distinct from its technological applications, as a specific mode of production in its own right, itself constituted by a unity of forces and relations of production, but located firmly within the 'superstructure': that is, as relatively autonomous from but intricated into (and configurationally determined by) the seeded structures and social relations of other sectors of social life, set in a totality conditioned and ordinated by the mode of production of material life itself. The degree and kind of autonomy and of extra-scientific determination will depend crucially upon the particular science concerned, its conjunctural significance and the role it plays in the longer time across which socio-economic relations of production are reproduced and transformed.

If anything belongs in the superstructure, presumably philosophy must do. But again matters are not quite so simple. For, on the one hand, possessed of its own distinctive discursive tradition and characterised by a peculiarly ruminating, regurgitating, tenor of production, philosophy appears only weakly coupled on the changes in the relations of treadmill and market place, as the paucity of plausible Marxist explanations of philosophies attest. Yet, on the other hand, as a line of questioning anywhere presupposed and answering almost everywhere pregiven (i.e. prior to the question), there is a sense in which philosophy underpins all currency of mind, in whichever particular practices minted. One might perhaps distinguish between philosophy as rarefied *professional discipline* and philosophy as ubiquitous *practical presupposition.* I am here concerned with the kind of way in which a rarefied product, such as P, can become a commonplace or colloquial idiom.

Finally, it should be clear that ideology cannot be treated as a homogeneous Parmenidian block and just assigned to the superstructure. For all practices, including those of commodity production, reveal an ideational aspect, which may or may not categorially mystify them (i.e. rate as ideology in terms of the criteria (1)-(6)) and through which they are at least partly constituted (as Marx's analysis of commodity fetishism amply illustrates). Accordingly it is important to severalise different ideational complexes entwined and/or associated with different practices, including both scientific practices and the ones identified in any particular formation as basic. These systems may be more or less internally differentiated, and they may be causally and internally related to one another as well as to the practices which carry them. They may fuse into an organic whole or they may prove more or less cognitively or practically separable or neutral. Their mystifying (or emancipatory) role may or may not be an aspect of the practice. Finally any particular ideology, properly so-called, may be classified with respect to practice, object, target, source and medium or vehicle of expression.

In this chapter, then, I want to outline the rudiments of an account of the real conditions for the efficacy of the misrepresentation of reality in P. In so doing I shall be primarily concerned with the isolation of the (relative) invariants that explain its reproduction, rather than with the ontologically coequal (but logically secondary) question of its genesis and changing historical fortunes. To explain the latter one would need to look into changes in scientific and social theories and to social structures generally. Thus it would be surprising indeed if the relative backwardness of chemistry in comparison with physics (and the dominance of atomistic and contact rather than singularity and field theoretic interpretations of the latter), or the rise of the individualistic mode of thought associated with the growth and consolidation of capitalism (and reflected in Enlightenment culture broadly), were not important features in the establishment of modern positivism. Moreover I intend to focus, for purely heuristic reasons, on the cognitive rather than the non-cognitive conditions for the reproduction of P; and within the former, on those which depend on the categorially false misrepresentation of reality, as distinct from those which do not (of which Newtonian mechanics provides a prime example). But it has been convincingly argued that a low level of the development of the productive forces in science — of the material forces of enquiry — together with a system of general economic production in which the dominant form of human relation to nature is manufacture or factory production (depending upon the organisation of effectively quasi-closed systems in the interests of capital) were major material prerequisites for the development of modern positivism.[22]

## III. Science Versus Ideology in the Critique of Positivism

Does P satisfy the formal criteria for the characterisation of cognitive structures as 'ideological'? In chapter 1 I ventured an immanent critique of, *inter alia*, positivism, adduced grounds for preferring transcendental realism and furnished reasons for asserting it to be true; so that the critical conditions (1) and (2) are satisfied, viz.

(α)   TR $>$ P ... critical conditions.

Notice that for the elucidation of what I characterised in section 1 as a covert mode of generation or production, we must be warranted in asserting not just the falsity of an idea or system, but the truth of a further incompatible one. That is, we need to be able to say how the world really is. For how the world really is, is here a condition for the way in which the refuted idea really, but covertly, operates. I shall refer to this as an *assertoric*, rather than a merely conditional, *critique*. In the next two

---

22.   Cf. N. Stockman *op. cit.*, pp. 15-35.

sections I will review the way in which fundamental categorial confusions in P, situated by transcendental realism, entail its incapacity to sustain appropriately levelled analogues of (3) (i) and (ii), namely the reality of being and the sociality of science, satisfactorily sustained by realism (4); so that the categorial conditions (3) and (4) are satisfied, to wit

(β)　TR dem $(-S_c^* (P) . -S_o^* (P))$ ... categorial conditions.

I will then embark on a limited proto-explanatory sketch of P, and reflexive self-situation of transcendental realism, so going some way to fulfilling the explanatory conditions (5) and (6) whence

(γ)　TR exp $(-S_c^* (P) . -S_o^* (P))$ ... explanatory conditions.

where TR includes transcendental realism plus substantive historio-sociological theories consistent with it.

　　Satisfaction of (α) − (γ) entitles us to score an explanatory critique of P. This is not the same as a Hegelian supercession or *Aufhebung*, because in a critique of this kidney nothing internal to thought need be preserved. Thus when, for example, in the identification of its covert effects, the contrary of an idea or system is affirmed, it will not in general be the contrary of the initial, self-understood idea, but the idea as redescribed by the refuting theory, the *redescribed contrary*, that is affirmed. Such redescription does not make a false proposition true, but shows the falsity of the proposition as, and for, what it really is.

　　Satisfaction of (α) − (γ) can be expressed as

[a]:　TR $\overset{\text{crit}}{\rightarrow}$ P ... explanatory critique ... (theoretical pre-supposition)

I earlier (p. 233, above) represented the mode of application and production of P by

[b]:　P $\triangle$ S ... theory-application ... (practical presupposition);

and

[c]:   C $\overset{\text{G}}{\to}$ P ... theory-production ... (poietical presupposition)

respectively. I left the generative complex C and the operator G undefined, but noted that P presupposed, for its production as a philosophical theory, the satisfaction of what it formally denied, just as it presupposed this for the generation of some of its most potent practical or applied consequences. This is to say that P possesses a covert mode of production, and a range of covertly generated effects. Both C and G constitute internally inconsistent ensembles composed of realist and irrealist elements.

Clearly insofar as they issue in determinate outcomes, viz. P and the particular uses of S, these outcomes must be explained by factors external to the complexes. [b] and [c] comprise of course moments in the explanatory critique P, i.e. in [a]. Inasmuch as S and G contain or imply realist components, i.e. components which only transcendental realism can fully, adequately or consistently sustain, and inasmuch as [a] is approached via immanent critique, realism may be said to constitute, contain or imply at [a]-[c] respectively a *theoretical, practical* and *poietical* presupposition of P. It should be stressed, however, that immanent critique alone does not licence the transition to assertoric critique, and that C, P and S are all theoretically here — transcendental realistically — redescribed; so that the three presuppositions of P are not Hegelian sublations of it, and their isolation depends upon ineradicably heteronomous processes of critical transformation.

I am going to contend that the mode of reproduction of P depends largely, although not exclusively, on its ideological efficacy in generating ideologies rationalising and so mystifying the bourgeois social order, normal science and common sense and/or technocratic expertise. But if P depends for its efficacy on the normally unconscious and unmotivated applications to which it lends itself, this should not obscure the fact that it has first (logically, not chronologically) to be produced. This is the special work of the deep structures of philosophical thought — what I shall call the 'grid-work' of philosophical consciousness, and G is the grid operator or 'gridator' of philosophical ideology, pulling the strings and weaving the strands of philosophical false consciousness. [c] and [b] correspond to the moments of theory production and application respectively. They are directly connected via the internality of the relationship between the theoretical production of a philosophical ideology and its applied uses, including simple defence by injunction or subtle support by resonance with lower-level theoretical, practical and lay ideologies. This is one reason why it is misleading to think of [c] and [b] as corresponding to the internal or philosophical and the external or extra-philosophical conditions for the reproduction (or transformation) of P. Diagram 3.1 schematizes the mode of production and reproduction of P, from the general standpoint of the T.M.S.A. developed in chapter 2; and Diagram 3.2 illustrates the internality of the relations between the generation of theory and its effects. Note that here it is the role of theory to reproduce or transform the efficacious structure; and the reproductive momentum and transformative pull is provided by P's social role or effect. Philosophy even seems to disappear at an intervening variable, viz.

$$ C \unlhd P \rightarrow P \unrhd S \simeq C \rightarrow S $$

But this appearance of a disappearance is an illusion, *the* positivistic illusion, half-real here. For before positivism can be re-produced, it must not only be produced, it must exist. *This* is the site of professional philosophy, the more or less conscious constitution and reconstitution of ideas and theories carried in a high discursive tradition. Three orders, of theory-production (deep-structure), of theory-constitution (surface-structure), and theory-application or use, are the minimum necessary for any critical explanation of the reproduction of an ideology such as P.

(Thus we have $C \unlhd P$; P; $P \unrhd S$).

### 3. Coordinates of the positivist account of science

I have said that P presupposes an ontology of closed systems and atomistic events constituting the objects of actual or possible experiences and a sociology of atomistic individuals consisting in passive sensors of given facts and registers of their given constant conjunctions.[23] In 1.4 and 1.5 I showed that constant conjunctions are not generally spontaneously available in

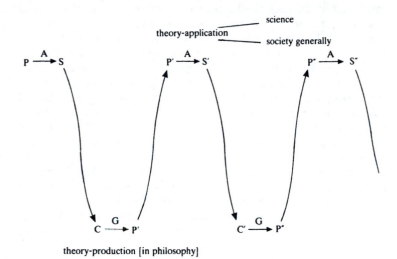

theory-production [in philosophy]

Diagram 3.1: *Mode of Production, Reproduction and Transformation of P*

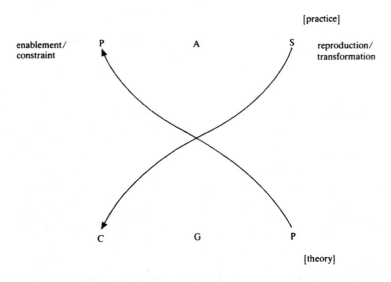

Diagram 3.2: *Duality of Production and Use of P*

nature, but rather must normally be artificially and assiduously produced in the socialised laboratories of science, so that causal laws and the other objects of experimental work must, if that work is to be intelligible, be ontologically independent of the patterns of events (the domain of the actual) and the praxes of agents (the domain of human subjectivity) alike; but that, conversely, if scientific discovery and development is to be possible, the concepts and descriptions under which we apprehend and comprehend them must be located within the indelibly social process of science. Accordingly, experiences, together with the facts they ground, plus the constant conjunctions comprising the empirical (actual) grounds for causal laws, are social products; but the objects to which they grant us access, such as causal laws, exist and act quite independently of science. Now, as I noted in 1.7, P cannot sustain either the idea of an independent reality or that of a socially produced science. Instead, these ideas, which constitute preconditions for an adequate account of science, the philosophical analogues of (3) (i) and (ii) in § 2.II above, become crossed, resulting in a *derealized reality* and a *desocialised science*. For, as in the interests of its fundamentalist conception of the tasks of philosophy, it allows the desired account of our knowledge to inform and implicitly define the presupposed account of the reality known by science, so as to better ensure a correspondence between them, a naturalised science is purchased at the expense of a humanised nature. And it is in this transaction, or rather in the philosophical crucible in which it occurs, that the most fateful ideological consequences of P are forged.

Let us scrutinise the mechanism of this peculiar chemistry in more detail. For P, our knowledge of the world consists only of atomistic events of states of affairs sensed in perception. If the world consists only of such events, then of course any connection must be the product or contribution of mind, so that no concept of natural necessity can be sustained. Moreover, if particular knowledge consists only of knowledge of atomistic events, then general knowledge can consist only in the knowledge of their relationships, more particularly of co-existence in space and succession over time, which must be assumed con-

---

23. For full demonstration and documentation, see my *A Realist Theory of Science*, 2nd edition, Brighton 1978, especially chapter 2.

stant. And so the Humean theory depends upon a view of conjunctions existing independently of the human activity normally necessary for them, and hence upon a *fetishism* of the systems within which the conjoined events occur. But in similar fashion it depends upon a view of what is given in immediate sense-experience as a fact constituting an atomistic event or state of affairs existing independently of the human activity necessary for it, and hence upon a *reification* of facts. When the conjunction of such facts are reified and identified with causal laws, science becomes a mere epiphenomenon or *Doppelgänger* of nature. The condition of the reduction of causal laws to experience in P is a denial of the social character of science, and more especially of its nature as work, involving the transformation of antecedent objects, both material and ideational. Thus at one stroke the ground is removed from the possibility of a sociology, history or scientific understanding of science; and the concept of the empirical world, expressing the epistemologisation of being, finds its ideal complement, meaning and ground in the *a priori* naturalisation, and so ontologisation, of knowledge in a reified account of science. In this respect, subjective super-idealism appears as the honest face of classical Humean and positivistic empiricism, because it shamelessly proclaims what the latter only slyly insinuates: the anthropomorphic constitution of being in the essential epistemological attribute of cognising subjects or knowledge-producers.

Positivist philosophy is thus founded on two category mistakes: the *derealisation of reality*, i.e. the collapse of the ID, entraining the epistemologisation of being, covered and cloaked by the epistemic fallacy; and the *desocialisation of science*, i.e. the collapse of the TD, resulting in the ontologisation of knowledge, the point of the exercise, manifesting and realising the ontic fallacy. In P, facts usurp the place of things and constant conjunctions those of causal laws. But the price of the reification of facts and the fetishism of the systems within which the events they describe occur is P's incapacity to sustain (or, as in practice, it *must*, to sustain in anything other than an ambivalent or equivocal way) the ideas of the existence of things independently of our perceiving them and of the transfactual (universal) applicability of laws and efficacy of things in open systems, i.e. where no constant conjunctions obtain.

The structure of the positivist account of science is represented in Diagrams 3.3 and 3.4 opposite.

There are two critical moments in the theory of the production of particular knowledge. In the first, the real content of science is reduced to or reconstructed from atomistic events apprehended — or stated — in sense-experience (Axis I) and in the second, these facts are treated as either identical to ('phenomenalism') or in one to one correspondence with ('material object empiricism'), the objects to which the referring expression, in the sentence with which they are stated, refers (Axis II). Such things may be physical objects, sensations or operations. Now whether the facts are identified with the statements or the features, the vital correspondence or identity between them is secured by the apprehension of the features in autonomised sense-experience — that is, in a moment of pristine subjectivity, free from the effects of all preformed or extraneous, including theoretical, content, so that in it man becomes a pure sense-object of the world. For any such extraneous matter would affect the completeness, and were it to be variable, the uniqueness of the correspondence (or identity), which must thus be secured by a theory of ostensive or operational definition. In this way the ontology of our world consists not (or not simply) of things to which we refer, but of facts of which we are aware, which are also (in sense-consciousness) meanings we cannot help but intend.

In the theory of the production of particular knowledge, then, the *autonomised sense-experience* constitutes the *form* in which knowledge is acquired and the *reified fact* the *content* that is expressed. This determines a theory of the production of general knowledge isomorphic with it. For the atomicity of the events generated by the autonomised character of sense-experience necessitates, as a condition of the possibility of general knowledge, the constancy of their conjunctions. And this in turn entails the fetishism of the systems within which the conjoined events occur and results in parallel equivocations, viz. over the transfactual efficacy of structures and things of a kind and the transfactual applicability of natural laws. The fetishism of systems at Axis II′ presupposes of course a fetishism of conjunctions of events, and thus through the reification of facts already established at Axis II, the fetishism of their conjunctions. It should be underlined that empirical realism is at once a condition for and a consequence of the denegation of ontology in operations, to be examined more closely in the next section, which traverse the dotted line in Diagrams 3.3 and 3.4

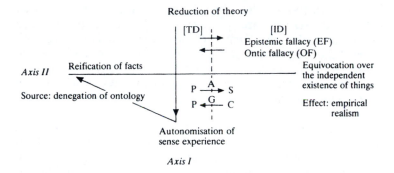

Diagram 3.3: *The Core Structure of Positivism: the Production of Particular Knowledge*

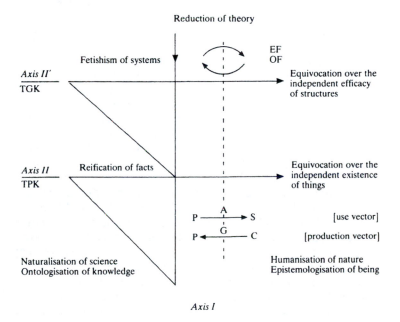

Diagram 3.4: *Generalisation of the Core Structure: the Production of General Knowledge*

N.B. TPK = Theory of (production of) particular knowledge; TGK = Theory of (production of) general knowledge.

in both directions, The central coordinates of the positivist account of science are given then by the *reification* and *atomisation* of facts. Such facts and their conjunctions both exhaust the real content of science and determine the knowable nature of the world, i.e. fix science in its ontology and ontology as only a matter for science. Together they establish the development of knowledge as *monistic* and its structure as *deductive*.

In reconstructing a system of thought such as P it is important to distinguish the philosophical reasons or motives for consciously performed moves, their underlying structures, which need not be at all obvious, and their manifest and latent, covert and overt results and consequences, which need be neither intended nor noticed and may obtain in quite remote practices. I turn to underlying structure in § 4. P results *inter alia* in the impossibility of scientific change, a point on which its anti-monistic critics have fastened (cf. 1.5), and in the impossibility of explanation in open systems or more generally of knowable natural necessity, onto which its anti-deductivist critics have latched (cf. 1.4). And P generates as consequences of these results, amidst much else, ideologies of science and society. At the level of the philosophical constitution and reconstitution of P, such results can only be explained in terms of the need felt for an epistemically certain base. For it is this that necessitates the atomicity of the events perceived (or perceptions), requiring *seriatim* the constancy of their conjunctions. But what explains the need? To refer to the existence of a tradition which has historically perceived incorrigible foundations for knowledge as a need is an insufficient explanation — for it begs the question of why this tradition has perdured. I think that the need can only be explained in relation to the solutions it engenders; and that these must be explained, at least in part, in terms of the results and consequences they justify and/or prohibit or otherwise produce or prevent. If correct, this has the corollary that if the relations between a philosophy, the problems it sets itself and the solutions it yields are internal ones, the solutions may also be to problems posed by equations, interests and practices other than, and sequestered from, its own.

P's problem, which determines the formal constitution of its results, is that of the 'problem of knowledge'. As Lukács presented it, 'acknowledging as given and necessary the results and achievements of the special sciences, philosophy's task is to exhibit and justify the grounds for regarding the concepts they construct as valid'.[24] That is, philosophy's task is the certification or indemnification of our knowledge to the title of 'knowledge' in response to the possibility of sceptical doubt. This means that two desiderata in particular must be met: (α) scepticism must be allayed, tamed or otherwise domesticated — this is the *epistemic function*; and (β) it must be shown how this allaying 'carries over' or transmutes to our actual knowledge — this is philosophy's *cognitive* — or 'carrying-over' — *function*. Now empirical realism is *made* for this problem-field. For it perfectly satisfies its requirements. It attaches our knowledge, analytically, to the world, so demonstrating that it is knowledge of what it claims to be; and, in so doing, it renders it insusceptible, whether by nature or convention, of further justification, so showing that it is naturally or practically certain — thus guaranteeing (α) and (and as) (β).

The problem-field's epistemic function itself presupposes philosophy and normalising functions, and its cognitive function realist and social functions. In P's case these functions are respectively self-abnegating, objectivistic, empirical and individualist. We shall watch them at work anon. Empirical realism, it will be recalled, is susceptible to both empiricist (including conventionalist as well as positivist) and transcendental idealist interpretations. Moreover it is consistent with non-reductionist forms of empiricism and historicised forms of transcendental idealism in which the unilinearity and uniqueness of the fact-theory relation is snapped. It presupposes an individualistic sociology but not an irredeemably reifying one. A caveat is necessary concerning my use of the term 'reification'. In saying that an account of facts is reified, I am not saying simply that on it facts are regarded as things. For indeed facts *are* things; but they are social, not natural things, belonging to the transitive world of science, not the intransitive world of nature. Moreover, merely to possess a non-reified view of facts, to see them as dependent upon human activity, is insufficient for an adequate concept of them as social. For in voluntaristic superidealism they are presented as created, rather than merely sustained and transformed, in human activity, so that in this way their inde-

---

24. G. Lukács, *History and Class Consciousness*, London 1971, p. 110.

pendent social reality, and characteristic *sui generis* coercive power, is scouted. Conventionalism is a hybrid of voluntarism and reification. On it, what is to count as a fact, or the empirical world generally, is decided voluntaristically, being constituted in and by human agreement. But, once established, the convention is treated as binding and constitutive of a universe of facts, conceived positivistically, as reified. In conventionalist mythology, agents decide that or which of their transmits are to be reified for them; but the primary equation of empirical realism — empirical ontology $\rightleftharpoons$ individualist sociology — remains intact, not least because such decisions never occur and are only implausibly and (explicably) mystifyingly imputed. In chapter 1 we saw that even where, as in neo-Kantianism, theory is accorded a role in the production of facts, the philosophy of science has typically not called into question the ontology of empirical realism (thus *inter alia* jeopardizing or irrationalising theory's newly-won status). In particular it continues to view constant conjunctions as necessary, if no longer sufficient, for laws. It thus continues to presuppose the fetishism of the systems within which such events occur at Axis II', so that pure positivism continues to exercise an open hegemony at the level of conceptions of general knowledge and agency. But a moment's reflection suffices to show that no actualist closure is tenable without actualist elements, identified and known under the descriptions in terms of which they can be shown to be constantly conjoined; that is, there can be no Humean generalisations (plus) without (at least) Humean particulars, and no Humean-parsed agency without (at least) Humean things. There is no midway station between empirical and transcendental realism.

Three operations then determine the surface structure of P: a *fusion* of the world and experience, crystallised in the doctrine of empirical realism; a *reduction* of knowledge to the level of experience which is, as constitutive of the nature of reality itself (thanks to the fusion achieved), held to be certain; and a *denegation* of philosophical ontology — of philosophy *per se* in the positivisic illusion and of ontology specifically in the epistemic fallacy — expressing in that surface structure the very content that it opposes. I descend now from the surface structure of P, the currency of its circulation with other social practices, to its deep structure, located in the 'hidden abode of production' where we shall discover, in the murky depths of philosophical false consciousness, not only how positivism produces, but how positivism is produced. Space precludes investigation of more than one moment of this production. But it is a crucial one: the generation, in the 'grid of phenomenalism', of a reified account of science, through the transactions effected by and necessary for empirical realism, in the theory of the production of particular knowledge: the isolated, naturalised fact.

## 4. The Grid of Phenomenalism

P, we have seen, depends upon the idea of a statement/feature conformity. Two general forms of such conformity may be defined: identity, as in phenomenalism; or correspondence, as in 'material object empiricism'. According to phenomenalism, things just are, or at least must be analysed as, clusters of actual or possible experiences; whereas material object empiricism attempts to preserve the idea that (at least some of) the objects apprehended in sense-experience exist independently of it. As it is clear that the language of science is, or encompasses, a material object language, only a material object empiricism can satisfy the cognitive or carrying over function (cf) or desideratum ($\beta$) (on p. 257 above), intrinsic to the problem field within which P is constituted. This desideratum may be explicated in terms of the *realist* and *social* functions (rf and sf). These may be expressed as the imperatives to satisfy, however minimally, the ideas of an independent reality and an irreducibly social science. Insofar as these ideas are transcendentally necessary, the realist and social functions must be satisfied *in practice* for the theoretical generation, as in C ⊊ P, and for the practical application or use, as in P ⊿ S, of even the most idealist and solipsist philosophies of science.

Now P's problem is to show how our actual knowledge, which is or depends upon a knowledge of material things, is justified. But merely to assert a correspondence between knowledge and the world leaves the former still vulnerable to sceptical attack. For we have not as yet furnished any guarantee that our statements, which would be true if they were in perfect or exact correspondence with the given facts, are indeed true. Only with such a guarantee can we be sure that we have indeed come right up against the world, i.e. found the base of our knowledge — or made this base of knowledge ours. And it is the task of phenomenalism, at what I will call 'Level II' of analysis, to arm material object empiricism at Level I with this missing guarantee, so incorrigibly grounding our present claims to knowledge. Specifically this means that the phenomenalist must resolve the problem of scepticism to satisfy the epistemic function (ef) or desideratum ($\alpha$) (on p. 257 above), generated by the philosophical problem-field within which P is formed. The objective of the phenomenalist exercise is thus:

(i)    the generation of a class of incorrigible sense-datum propositions, so as to satisfy ef;
(ii)   the transference, through programmes of normative reconstruction and/or descriptive analysis, of the incorrigibility of the sense-datum propositions to material object ones, so satisfying cf (rf and sf).

Most criticism of phenomenalism has centred on (i). And important though it is, I am not going to rehearse or expand upon it here. For it is (ii) that is the crucial step in the production of P as an indemnified account of science. Now it is clear that if sense-datum propositions are to be capable of doing the job for which they are designed, they must stand in a relationship of entailment or equivalence to the propositions they are held to ground or analyse. But such a relation cannot hold in *all* cases as is shown by consideration of the very examples — illusions, hallucinations, etc. — that phenomenalists invoke in motivation of their programme. Hence either the inference is never legitimate or it is only acceptable if a prior decision has already been made in favour of the corresponding material object opposition. So that it is now our material object knowledge that is required to justify or analyse its alleged sense-foundations! That is to say, if an inference beyond a subjective state of mind is possible, there is no need for the introduction of sense-datum propositions; conversely, if it is not possible, sense-datum propositions cannot ground or explicate our existing public knowledge. Either way, phenomenalism is devoid of cognitive point. Phenomenologically, this is reflected in the fact that it is my consciousness of a material object that is required to identify sense-data as the objects of my consciousness. Hence although phenomenalism claims a direction of analysis,

$$r_{sd} \rightarrow m_{sd} \rightarrow m_{mo} \rightarrow r_{mo}$$

(where r = reference; m = meaning; sd = sense-datum proposition, mo = material object proposition), it actually depends in epistemological reality upon a precise reversal-viz.

$$r_{mo} \rightarrow m_{mo} \rightarrow m_{sd} \rightarrow r_{sd}.$$

In saying this I am concerned only with the direction, and no more underwrite the validity of the links than denying that N believes himself to be a unicorn commits me to a belief in their existence. The completely extensionalist character of the links can only be explained by reference to the assumption of an isomorphism between knowledge and the world, already implicit in the surface structure of P and for which phenomenalism purports to furnish proof and guarantee. Analogously at TGK within the (equally false) perspective of an isomorphism, it is only if we already have grounds for supposing a law that we are entitled to infer a natural invariance. It is (grounded) laws that licence induction and eduction, not the other way round.

The result of the phenomenalist exercise is thus a redefinition of the world in which the genuine incorrigibility of spurious propositions is transubstantiated into the spurious incorrigibility of genuine propositions. But the supposition of the incorrigibility of the latter is the effective precondition, as well as the real meaning, of the transition. The subjective certainty expressed in a state of intuitive awareness finds its objective counterpart in the fact that the material object proposition states. Thus underlying the solipsism of level II is a theory of the absence of inconsistency; and underpinning scepticism, certainty.

The structure of the grid of phenomenalism is presented in Diagrams 3.5-3.7 below. For the generation of TPK, P needs to assume both of two incompatible positions as conditions for each other. It needs a material object empiricism to satisfy its *empirical* realist function; it needs a phenomenalism to satisfy its *fundamentalist* epistemic function. The empirical realist function (rf) acts, as it were, as a proxy within empiricism for the realist imperatives of science; the fundamentalist epistemic function (ef) expresses, so to speak, the demands of the philosophical (problem-of-knowledge) problem-field. Material object empiricism is the (real) condition of phenomenalism and phenomenalism is the (formal) condition of material object empiricism. But they are mutually inconsistent, in that the former avers what the latter denies: namely that real objects exist independently of consciousness. Hence the transformational complex necessary for the production of TPK is internally inconsistent. It follows that the particular results actually derived must be explained by factors *external* to the complex. Such a constraint is clearly necessary to prevent the derivation of any well-formed result from the complex G. This can be formulated as a general theorem to the effect that the determinant outcomes of internally inconsistent (and so formally indeterminate) systems can only be explained by reference to factors, uses or principles not contained within the system. This theorem represents an inverse of Gödel's. The resolution of contradictions is never just a matter of immanent or internal necessity, but always presupposes external constraints upon or selection of outcomes.[25] Thus, to put it another way round, given the external functions, viz. rf and ef, which the generative complex of material object and phenomenalistic empiricism is required to satisfy for the production of TPK, the latter is uniquely determined, subject to qualifications to be discussed below, and so explained. These functions, rf and ef, must then of course be related to and partially explained in terms of their characteristic effects in the social totality, including in the latter both the practices P characteristically justifies, discredits, insulates, etc. and the relatively autonomous organisation of the discursive traditions of philosophy.

It is worth stressing that the isomorphic character of the relationship between knowledge and the world (whether this takes the form of correspondence or of identity) can only be explained by reference to the surface structure of P (as illustrated in Diagram 3.5). Hence there is no question of explaining deep structure in isolation from surface structure; or, to change the analogy, philosophical production from the principles of exchange (of non-equivalents) which govern the circulation and distribution of its products. They are internally related. It also follows from this that the transformational complex C cannot be reduced to a simple combinatory of transcendental realist and positivist components. All that can be

---

25. No amount of soul-searching will ever cause Buridan's ass to move left or right. Yet if and when it actually moves, we will naturally look to something not contained within the Buridanite description of its situation (including of course a (causal) change in that situation) to explain why it does so.

claimed is that the production C $\unlhd$ P itself requires or presupposes components, such as commitment to a material object
language, which only transcendental realism can consistently or
coherently sustain. For instance, any empirical realist satisfaction of the realist function must face problems when confronted with the phenomena of scientific change and open
systems. P will thus need to find a way of handling them in
theory and/or in practice — presumably by the incorporation of
further realist elements, i.e. elements which only transcendental
realism can adequately sustain, into its generative (C) or applied
(S) matrices — at the price of further inconsistencies (but also
ideological opportunities). In this respect C can be regarded as
an inconsistent ensemble, not of positivist and transcendental
realist principles, but of irrealist and realist ones (in the sense
explicated in 1.2).

Diagram 3.6 depicts the interdependence of phenomenalism
and material object empiricism. Step (ii) (on p. 260 above) of
the phenomenalist exercise, or rather its reversal or inversion,
now appears as a condition of step (i). Level II (material object
empiricism) is seen to be a condition of Level I (phenomenalism) and surface structure, in the shape of the tacit presupposition of isomorphism, to be a condition of deep structure, the
sphere of its supposed proof. Inversion marks the general form
of inconsistency in the poietic production of P, in C $\unlhd$ P, just as
ambiguation marks the general form of inconsistency in its
practical applied use, in P $\triangle$ S. The conditions of the transition
from Level II of analysis establish a series of equivalences
between the material and the sensuous, public and private, contingent (or doubtful) and necessary (or certain) etc. The combination of the equivalences established by the transition with
the results of the fetishism already presupposed at Level I, i.e.

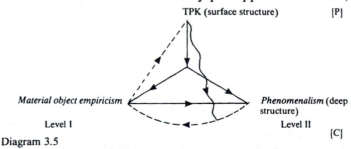

TPK (surface structure)      [P]

*Material object empiricism*      *Phenomenalism* (deep
                                   structure)

Level I                          Level II
                                                [C]
Diagram 3.5

N.B. Continuous lines represent directions of actual presupposition, dotted lines direction of formal proof, and the wavy line the direction of informal philosophical motivation.

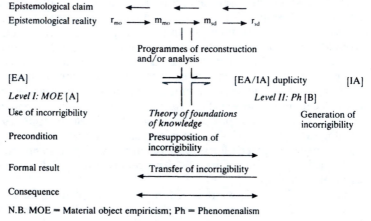

N.B. MOE = Material object empiricism; Ph = Phenomenalism

Diagram 3.6: *The Grid of Phenomenalism*

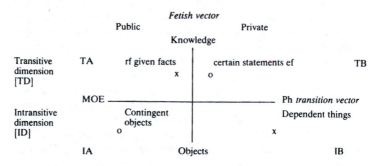

Diagram 3.7

N.B. 1. *Empirical realist function* (rf): Given things + dependent facts → given facts + dependent things; cf. transcendentally real world + social knowledge → individual knowledge + empirical world.

*Fundamentalist epistemic function* (ef): contingent statements + certain objects → certain statements + contingent objects.

2. *Fetish vector* — material principle: isomorphism; formal results: equivocation — ambivalence — duplicity.

mode of critique: establishment of non-isomorphism; hence P presupposes contraries for the applications in practice (cf. [b] on p. 249 above).

*Transition vector* — material result: exchange; formal principle: inversion (e.g. reversal of directionality).

mode of critique: establishment of non-equivalence of terms of exchange; hence P presupposes contraries for its generation in theory (cf. [c] on p. 249 above).

the knowledge/world isomorphism assumed in the surface structure of P, results in the constitution of *certain statements* in the TD, satisfying the fundamentalist epistemic function at the price of contingent (or doubtful) objects in the ID; and of *given facts* in the TD, satisfying the empirical realist function, at the price of dependent things in the ID. Let us examine the micrologic of this grid-work, this algebra of false consciousness, in more detail. Any position in A (at Level I) necessitates as its condition a position in B (at Level II) and vice versa. But any position in the TD (T) characteristically constitutes a position in the ID (I). Hence TA has a unique image IB and TB a unique image IA in the opposite quadrant of Diagram 3.7. The condition of the possibility of reified facts (erf) is dependent things. That is, given facts are only possible in practice because we have dependent things in theory. Conversely, the condition of certain statements in science (fef) is contingent or doubtful objects in being. But both realist and epistemic functions must be satisfied. Given the character of these functions, subject to certain provisos, the structure P is uniquely determined in theory, viz. $C \xrightarrow{G} P = C \xrightarrow{\text{erf;fef}} P$, where the grid operator G can now be defined in terms of the empirical realist and fundamentalist epistemic functions (abbreviated to erf and fef respectively).

These vectors specify only the *dominant* tendencies of the system, explicable, I shall suggest, in terms of the results and consequences they justify, permit or otherwise co-produce. They are subject to the following provisos. First, the cognitive and epistemic functions may be further unpacked, producing correspondingly richer systems upon the same basic structure. Second, additional terms and functions may be introduced, resulting in more complicated structures. Third, one *could* argue, using the same structure, with equal facility to, for instance, the doubtfulness of our public knowledge as a condition of the possibility of the phenomenalist programme. For if certainty is distributive, doubt — which is its condition — is too. That is to say, just as things can be viewed alternatively as given or dependent according to whether the epistemic or realist operator is applied, so alternative operations can be performed on statements. I shall call this general type of move, which establishes the malleability and commutability of intra-theoretical (or -discursive) results, a κ transform. Fourth, standard results are additionally subject to non-systematic abrogation in any particular case, via an epistemological *ceteris paribus* clause, in what I shall call a λ transform.

Subject to these provisos, P is in principle determined: that is to say, the grid-work accomplishes the entropic transformation of a 'free grammar' into determinate and relatively fixed 'sentences'. But any constraint upon its possible uses as an ideological system is immediately removed in practice by a converse operation, viz. P $\triangle$ S, resulting in the characteristic equivocations or ambivalences, depicted in Diagrams 3.3 and 3.4 (on p. 255 above), encapsulated in 'empirical realism' and its correlate, 'naturalised knowledge' (facts, conjunctions, systems etc.). These are of course already anticipated in the transitions necessary for the production of P. For *in practice*, we must have a realist function (which I shall write as 'rf*') which applies to the ID and not just to the TD of science: that is, which presupposes, even if it cannot think (let alone apodeictically prove) the reality, the givenness of things, as opposed to and distinct from, facts: discursivity rather than reification. This is shown by reflection on the Hume-Hegel line of anti-sceptical argument elaborated in chapter 1.4, the considerations developed more generally in that chapter and the very conditions necessary for the establishment of P in theory (the tacit presupposition of a realist contrary of phenomenalism and of the direction of transference posited in it (step (ii) on p. 260 above)). The axiological operator A thus inverts and so undoes the work of the grid, but now on the basis fashioned by it (so that this is a determinate negation, in Hegelian jargon). Thus we have a 'free' grammar once more — free, that is, for the generation of whatever ideological effects are deemed fitting or required. But it is a free grammar constructed upon, freed from and packaged into certain exemplary sentences. The result, a sharp determinate figure blending and dissolving indeterminately into a contrasting contradictory ground, is a most convenient property for P, as for any idological system of similar hue. For the core, P, fixing standard interpretations, secures economy; the contrast, affording it a duplicity and, more generally, plasticity of structure and use, enables it to respond in some measure — in what I shall call a μ transform — to most conceivable contingencies, while the penumbra in between successfully camouflages the transition between them.

A general theorem follows from this: whenever we have TR > X, where X is susceptible of transcendental refutation, then either we have a philosophy which is consistent with its episte-

mology, but of no use to science; or one which is relevant to science, but more or less radically inconsistent with its epistemology. Formally, this duplicity is manifest in certain antinomies or internally destructive dilemmas, some of which were reviewed in 1.4. (Remember the two other faces of the Humean theory of causal laws: the Humean problem of induction and Poincaré's problem of transduction). Proximately it is in the contradictory ensemble yielded by the necessity to hold both of two incompatible positions that the most fertile ground of ideology, and the prerequisite for the generation of covert effects, lies. The transformational possibilities of such a system are limited only by the number of terms that can be introduced and, in practice, by the number of non-equivalent (non-vacuous) functions that must be uniquely satisfied.

By viewing the inconsistent system S as the immediate field for the generation of ideological effects, are we not in danger of explaining too much? No. For (i) practical imperatives (injunctions, prohibitions, commendations, etc), overt and general resonance effects flow directly from P. Further (ii) P forms the standard, normal or typical interpretation of S. And (iii) P's existing terms and relations delimit the possible range of covert effects and constrains, via considerations of coherence, relevance and plausibility imposed by P, the introduction of new terms and relations. The grammar is free but possible discourses are constrained. So within the ensemble described by S, P remains dominant, as illustrated in Diagram 3.8 below. A general schema for the production and reproduction of P is presented in Diagrams 3.9-3.12.

What remains to be explained, however, is the function of the functions erf and fef that fix the surface structure of P. I shall consider this fully shortly. But the principal ideological consequences of the grid should already be clear. Given facts, generated by the empirical realist function, produce an ideology *for* science, while certain statements, generated by the fundamentalist epistemic function, produce an ideology *of* it. Thus the transference of certainty to scientific knowledge, accomplished in the grid-laboratory of philosophical ideology, establishes its development as monistic, dehistoricising it and rationalising the scientific status quo; while the identification of what is immediately apprehended in sense-perception as certain encourages a set of beliefs generally comforting to the common sense of humankind. So knowledge is *certain*, its development

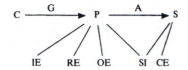

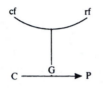

N.B. IE = Injunctive effects
(practical imperatives, etc.)
RE = General resonance effects
(e.g. replication or
concordance of underlying
figures, interpretations,
relations, etc.)
OE = Overt effects[26]
SI = Standard interpretations and
uses of S fixed by P
CE = Covert effects

Diagram 3.8; *Primacy of P within S*

is monistic. At the same time it is *safe*, it does not threaten the spontaneous consciousness of ordinary life, for it is constructed out of units available to the latter. In consequence of the grid-operations, then, science becomes as certain as what exists and as commonplace as the activity — perception — that establishes it. The condition of the satisfaction of the empirical realist function (erf) in the ID, viz. that of dependent things, is equally flattering to human vanity, while that of the satisfaction of the funda-mentalist epistemic function (fef), the contingency of objects, plays a key role in the generation of a general social ideology. The question — of scepticism — which initiates the philo-sophical play must be posed, if only so that philosophy can give the answers to the question its functions demand.

There is a parallel to the grid of phenomenalism in the *grid of actualism,* at the level of TGK. Here analogously deductive-nomological and inductive-probabilistic concepts of law prove necessary for each other (the former to meet the realist, the latter to satisfy the epistemic, function); universal general-isations are bought at the cost of restricted laws; and the

---

26. These need not be explicitly formulated as descriptions, nor need they even be conceptualised (as distinct from concept-dependent). But in general all the ideological consequences of a system such as P will be mediated by some of the discursive consequences of S.

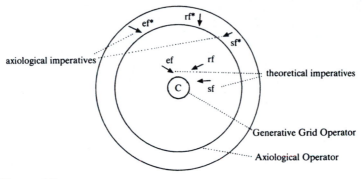

Diagram 3.9:

N.B. Operators G and A are determining bounds (circumferences) of C and P respectively.

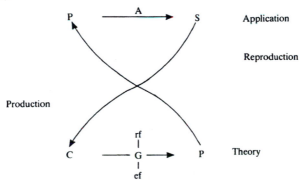

Diagram 3.10: *Production and Reproduction of P*

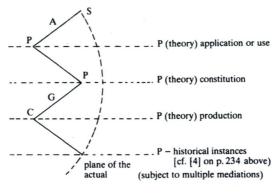

Diagram 3.11: *Production, Constitution and Application of P*

270

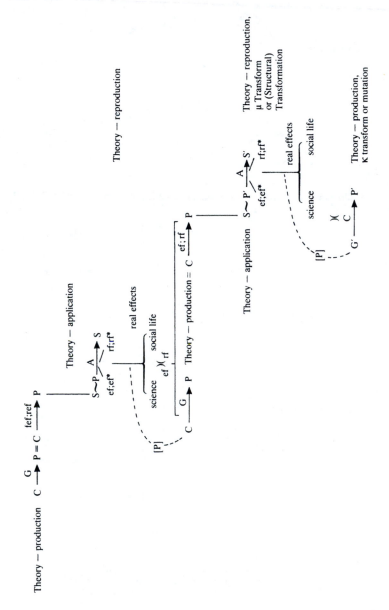

Diagram 3.12: *Production, Reproduction, Application and Transformation of P*

explanation of phenomena in open systems becomes impossible, a consequence which *inter alia* vitiates the possibility of any social science or science of history. Hence positivism, in the very move with which it seeks to vest scientific products with certainty, comes to radically undermine the potential scope of application and critical significance of science, betraying itself in unmistakeable terms as an *anti-scientific scientism*. But before coming on to these effects, I want to look first at the versatility of its structure. Later we shall have to probe more deeply into the production of its problem-field and the constitution of its results.

## 5. Synchronic transformations of the grid

Mutability is a feature of all social forms, endemic malleability a feature of a historically significant class of ideological ones. Synchronic transformations, transformations *within* an unchanged structure, must be analytically distinguished from diachronic transformations or transformations *of* a structure. Of course particular historical instances of ideological lability will often combine aspects of both. In the concluding sections of this chapter I will briefly indicate some historical transformations of P. Here I want to examine three modalities of synchronic transform to which P is pliable, viz.

[μ] or applied extra-theoretical or practical use transforms;

[κ] or intra-theoretical intra-discursive or generative transforms; and

[λ] or *ceteris paribus* type transforms of both μ and κ kinds.

To illustrate these transforms I will consider only the empirical realist and fundamentalist epistemic functions as specified in § 4, using only the simple grid introduced there, as defined by the following eight points:

dependent facts; given facts; certain statements; doubtful statements — abbreviated as DF; GF; CS; DS
contingent objects; determinate objects; given things; dependent things — abbreviated as CO; DO; GT; DT

I shall wield this grid in exemplification of both theoretical and applied operations, but the interpretation of the grid differs importantly in the two cases. For in the poietic or productive moment, being is subjectivised so as to generate incorrigibility; while in the practical, applied and reproductive moments being is objectified so as to enable reference to a common public world. In § 4 I glided over this distinction, which is not of course made within the phenomenalist programme and indeed cannot be consistently sustained within any empirical realist frame, but it will now assume some importance for us. The facts remain the same, but the interpretation of the things to which they refer differ as, or rather more radically than, shapes and colours differ from bodies and waves.

P is the kernel of the system S, whose structural pliability and, as we shall see, historical elasticity, is quite remarkable. Thus it can generate an ideology of technocratic expertise and managerial authority as well as, and perhaps to go with, its quasi-egalitarian mystique of commonsense and everyman; and it can incubate an ideology of theoretical and practical doubt, of anti-scientific scepticism and neo-Luddite nihilism as easily as either. In the intransitive dimension it can indue an ideology of despair and fatalism, of stoic or sceptical temper, as readily as it hatches an ideology of caprice and contingency of inductivist or indeterminist stamp. S is the ideal answer to every apologist's prayer, an Alice-in-Wonderland Elysian paradise where words can mean anything we say (we choose to mean by them).

Taking the empirical realist function, rf, mapping given facts onto dependent things, two basic $\mu$ transforms are sanctioned within S:

$\mu 1$, the *fetish dual* or (duplicate), $\overline{rf}$, licenses movement across the TD/ID divide, viz. from given facts to given things (epistemic mapping) or from dependent things to dependent facts (ontic mapping). The source of this fetish dual lies in the equivocation between knowledge and being in the isomorphism or fusion involved in any anthroporealism, or more generally epistemological definition of being. This generates a duplicity or ambivalence which endorses free movement from (epistemically relevant and defined) predicates of knowledge to being and vice versa. The predicates thus span the TD/ID divide represented by the horizontal line in the grid, and the philosophical ideologue can commute freely from knowledge to being and back again.

μ2, the *covert complement,* rf′, licenses movement from an irrealist to a realist position, viz. from given to dependent facts (epistemic transition) or from dependent to given things (ontic transition). The source of the covert complement lies in the practical (axiological-transcendental) necessity for realist positions, i.e. for positions which only transcendental realism can adequately sustain.

μ1 and μ2 permit the definition of two other transforms: μ3 the *realist dual,* rf\*, a realist transform of the empirical realist function with given things mapped onto dependent facts, transmuting rf to the notional initial function for the production of P, noted under Diagram 3.7 (see p. 264 above). It should be unnecessary to reiterate that the dual here is not realism but what the practical necessity for transcendental in empirical realism implies. It is, if one likes, a compromise formation, resultant or residue of incompatible frames. These frames are equally irreducible to the compromise outcome, which only transcendental but not empirical realism can consistently describe.

μ4 the *irrealist complement,* ′rf, licenses movement from a realist to an irrealist position, viz. from dependent to given facts (epistemic transition), or from given to dependent things (ontic transition), retracing the illictly presupposed direction of transference in the production of P.

The same types of transform may be defined in respect of the fundamentalist epistemic function. Note that armed with μ1 and μ2 the applied philosophical ideologue can travel *anywhere* s/he likes on the grid, armed with μ3 and μ4 as well *anyway* s/he pleases. Introducing additional terms and functions increases the transformational possibilities of the system up to an exponential upper bound. The duals are relations expressing *categorial* or functional *duplicity* and *practical ambivalence,* the complements are positions expressing *predicative commutability* or contingently *practical inversions* in use. The four types of transform of rf are represented in Diagram 3.13 below.

Let us look at some of the ways S can exploit these transformational possibilities in the generation of an ideology of expertise. Thus, making covert use of the real gap between scientific and lay knowledge — a gap which is artificially augmented by the present division of labour, system and forms of education as well as by the distribution of educational opport- unities — it can straightaway employ the covert complement rf′$_e$, moving directly from given to dependent facts, i.e. facts conceived as dependent upon the expertise, know-how or more generally work of science. Alternatively, the ideological reasoner could argue from the dependency of things, sup- posedly established in philosophical argument (the rf), to the dependency of facts, applying an ontic fetish dual transform rf$_o$. Or again, s/he could take the epistemic fetish dual ($\overline{\text{rf}}_e$) to given things, and parologize thence, operating the realist dual (rf*) to dependent facts in science. These possibilities are illustrated in Diagram 3.14.

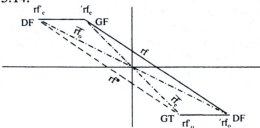

Diagram 3.13: *Type of μ Transform*

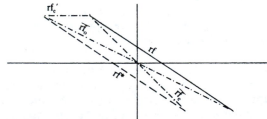

Diagram 3.14: *Ways of Generating an Ideology of Expertise*

Diagram 3.15 shows some of the ways in which S can pro- create a science-sceptical ideology. It can either directly oper- ate the covert complement in the transitive dimension from certain to corrigible or doubtful statements (ef′$_e$); or it can move from the established contingency of objects (by the ef), along the ontic fetish dual transform ef$_o$, to the contingency of state- ments; or, it can apply the epistemic fetish dual $\overline{\text{ef}}_e$ to yield determinate objects and thence proceed, via the realist (non- fundamentalist) dual form of the (fundamentalist) epistemic function, viz. ef*, to the corrigibility or uncertainty of science.

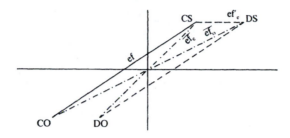

Diagram 3.15: *Routes to Nihilism*

The possibility of voluntarism is already built into the constitutive structure of P in the shape of the man-dependency of things and the absence of human-independent (natural) necessity. But a contrary outcome, fatalism, can as easily be assimilated. Thus, operating the transitive covert complement of the realist function ($rf'_e$), the apologist can wean contingent from given facts and then, operating the realist dual ($rf^*$), surmise the givenness of things, the naturalness of the status quo, insinuating human impotence in the face of it and the advisability of accepting it, at least grudgingly if not gracefully. Or, relying on the transitive covert complement of the epistemic function ($ef'_e$), the move can be made, via its realist dual ($ef^*$), from the contingency of statements to the necessity of objects, glossed actualistically as a Laplacean determinism. These two ideological pathways are depicted in Diagram 3.16. The reader will be able to produce the same ideological results in other more or less plausible ways.

I turn now to the intra-theoretical or κ transforms. These are discursive possibilities opened up by the matrix within which P is formed. It will be recalled that whereas phenomenalism *claims* a sequence of transition from the subject-dependency of given things to certain statements to given facts to the determinacy of contingent objects, it tacitly *presupposes*, in epistemic reality, precisely the reverse movement, namely from the contingency of determinate objects to given facts to certain statements to the givenness of subject-dependent things. This is re-illustrated in Diagram 3.17, where the dotted arrows mark the direction of claims and the solid ones that of presuppositions.

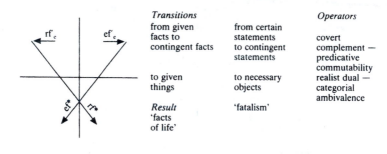

<table>
<tr><td>Transitions</td><td></td><td>Operators</td></tr>
<tr><td>from given<br>facts to<br>contingent facts</td><td>from certain<br>statements<br>to contingent<br>statements</td><td>covert<br>complement —<br>predicative<br>commutability</td></tr>
<tr><td>to given<br>things</td><td>to necessary<br>objects</td><td>realist dual —<br>categorial<br>ambivalence</td></tr>
<tr><td>Result<br>'facts<br>of life'</td><td>'fatalism'</td><td></td></tr>
</table>

Diagram 3.16: *Pathways of Despair and Resignation*

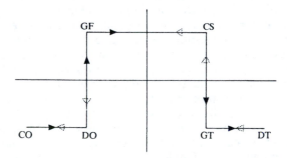

N.B. DF = dependent facts; GF = given facts; CS = certain statements; DS = doubtful statements; CO = contingent objects; DO = determinate objects; GT = given things, DT = dependent things

Diagram 3.17: *Claims and Reality in the Protean Grid of Phenomenalism*

For the sake of analysing the discursive possibilities of this structure it may be divided into four quadrants composed of facts, statements, objects and things respectively, characterised by the following pairs of predicates: dependent/given, certain/corrigible (doubtful), contingent/determinate (necessary) and given/dependent respectively.

Three major types of transition are implicated here:

(1) from knowledge to being, and vice versa;
(2) from subjective or private to objective or public, and vice versa;
(3) from doubt or contingency to certainty or determinacy, and vice versa.

(1) is represented by the horizontal line through Diagram 3.18 splitting the grid from above to below into knowledge and being or into the transitive and intransitive dimensions. This I shall call the *fusion* frontier. (2) is represented by the vertical line splitting the grid from right to left into subjective and objective or private and public — the *transition frontier*. (3) is represented by the boundary of the line dividing the space of the grid into outer and inner, the sphere of contingency and doubt from the sphere of determinacy and certainty — the *fundamentalist frontier*.

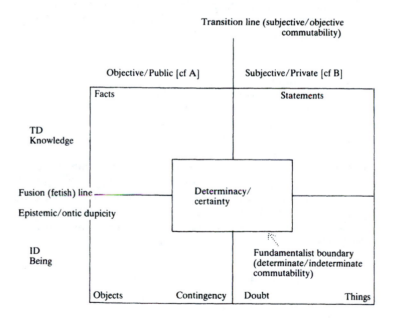

Diagram 3.18

Analysis of the internal structure of the production of P has revealed that we must move from left (cf. public) to right (cf. private) in order to pass from right to left, and that we must come out of the box, into the realm of contingency and doubt, before we can jump back in. (Cf Diagram 3.17 above). So an inversion of P's theory is not only necessary for its use in practice at S; but in these two respects, that is, across the transition and fundamentalist frontiers, for the very production of the theory itself at C. At the same time, at the fusion frontier, a categorial duplicity and theoretical ambivalence in P spans the TD/ID divide. So we have two-way movement across the fusion (fetish), transition (subjective-objective) and fundamentalist (determinacy-indeterminacy) frontiers, generating ontic/epistemic duplicity, subjective/objective commutability and determinate/indeterminate commutability respectively, in each case of both formal and presupposed types. A tacit κ transform can be defined corresponding to each of the presupposed moves in P's generative grid. Thus, following the direction of presuppositions indicated by the solid arrows in Diagram 3.17), we can define:

$\kappa t_1$, determinating transform (CO to DO)
$\kappa t_2$, ontic fusion transform (DO to GF)
$\kappa t_3$, subjectivising transform (GF to CS)
$\kappa t_4$, epistemic fusion transform (CS to GT)
$\kappa t_5$, indeterminating transform (GT to DT).

Combining these with (a) the formally sanctioned transitions (as indicated by the dotted arrows in Diagram 3.17); and generalising through with (b) the epistemic/ontic fusion already implicit in the surface structure of P (allowing DF→CO, CO→DF; DS→DT, DT→DS), results in the following matrix of possibilities:

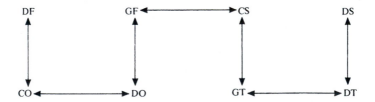

If we now recursively apply the epistemic and ontic fusion transforms to the subjectivising, objectivising, determinating and indeterminating operations the circle of discursive possibilities is overdetermined and closed.

There are two other significant types of intra-theoretical transform besides those that result from combination of the tacit, formal and fusion operations:

κλ, stemming from the need for preformal or informal motivation of the phenomenalist, or more generally formal or official, philosophical programme; and

κμ, stemming from the close links between theoretical and practial discourse here as elsewhere in the social domain.

Thus, referring to the skeletal grid structure immediately above, it is easy to see how the 'gaps' can be filled in by invoking κλ or κμ type moves. For the dependency of facts and the corrigibility of statements are precisely the circumstances adduced in motivation of, and which are deemed to require, the phenomenalist programme (κλ) and so can always be called upon when the ideological going gets sticky.[27] In respect of the κμ type of move, it should be remembered that the distinction between theoretical and applied discourse is a realist one: for the phenomenalist, even outside the study, things just are clusters of actual or possible experiences, licensing an ever-ready subjectivising discursive transform — here, e.g., from DO to GT with a corresponding objectivising complement.

This leads on to the third type of transform, λ transforms, which in effect operate as generic CP escape clauses for theoretical, λκ, or applied, λμ, discourse. λκ has no systematic basis within P. But it is philosophically very important in allowing the philosophical motivation of a system or theory to drop out of the theory it motivates. Such phenomena as illusions, hallucinations, etc. cannot be incorporated into the formal structure of the phenomenalist programme without vitiating it, any more than experimental activity can be incorporated into the Humean theory of causal laws without undermining it. Yet both are indispensable to the motivation of the philosophical

---

27. Analogous discursive interposition is common in the metatheoretical reflections of scientists. They may, for instance, cite philosophical considerations developed on the basis of analysis of their theoretical framework in support of the framework, or alternatively — Mach's is a good case in point — in criticism of them.

theories concerned. The λκ transform achieves metaphysical closure by dropping the motivator from the motivated; it is the saving grace of all metaphysical systems, including Hegel's explicitly phenomenological one, as hitherto known. More generally, it is necessary for any philosophical theory which is either internally inconsistent or inconsistent with its pre-formal, informal or meta-formal grounds or inconsistent with transcendentally, empirically or practically indisputable features of reality and/or which cannot situate such inconsistencies adequately within itself.

The λμ transform is an applied CP clause designed to safeguard P from pseudo-falsification in an open world. In principle some such clause will always be necessary for any theory at any level. But P can provide no consistent defence of its use. This can only be done from a non-actualist metaphilosophical standpoint, which understands cognitive structures as transfactually efficacious. P's λμ transform is thus a covert complement of its practice. With the partial exception of the λμ transform, all the transforms we have been looking at are so many illicit strategems of ideological thought, necessary for an irrealist system in a realist world.

## 6. Ideology in the transitive dimension: the concept of a fact

The transference of certainty to scientific knowledge and the identification of its objects as given, achieved in the grid of phenomenalism, constitutes, in the TD, ideologies of and for science respectively. In the establishment and employment of such ideologies, the concept of a fact assumes a pivotal role. Charged in the very moment of its constitution with certain very specific ideological duties, it fulfils them effortlessly in our discourse. What, then, is its proper analysis?

Rejecting reification, one might take a fact as a 'true assertion' or alternatively, as in Strawson's formula, as what a true statement states.[28] Neither will do, for we discover facts in the sense that we don't true assertions; and we make statements in a way that we don't facts.[29] Rather it is as if they were made

---

28. See P.F. Strawson, 'Facts', *Truth*, ed. G. Pitcher, New Jersey 1964, p. 38.
29. Moreover, what is stated should be a statement; and statements but not facts can be true or false. Furthermore it is unclear how statements, as distinct from the persons who state them, can do (or state) things.

for us. Why don't we make facts? Because, as the etymology of the word indicates, they are *already made*. In stating facts we are acknowledging results already achieved, the results being achieved (in the domain of empirical enquiry) by *readings*, of which the varieties of sense-experience, and its epistemic analogues, constitute special kinds of skill. But of course we discover, as well as state, results; the facts pre-exist their discovery as results to be achieved (just as they pre-exist their statements as achievements). They are *potentialities* of the conceptual schemes or paradigms governing our enquiries which, when actualised, comprise discoveries. For example, Cavendish's determination of the universal gravitational constant was only possible in virtue of Newtonian mechanics. But within the field opened up by the *Principia* it was a discovery. A fact, then, is a potentiality which is actualised in discovery, sustained in (discursive and non-discursive) practice and objectified in sense-experience. If a fact is a potentiality of a conceptual scheme, a truth — in the sense of 1.8 — is a potentiality of the possibility of a conceptual scheme.

Facts then are possibilities inherent in the cognitive structures agents reproduce and transform but never create, with voluntarism, committed in conventionalism (and more radically, in super-idealism), and reification in positivism, forming contrasting and complementary mistakes. Facts are indeed paradigmatic social institutions. They are *real*, in as much as but for them certain determinate states of the physical world, for which our intellectual agency is a necessary condition, could not occur. They are *social*, in as much as, though dependent upon human agency, they are irreducible to a purely individual production. But although all facts are social results, not every social result is a fact: facts are the results of specific cognitive, and more especially empirically grounded, processes of social production.

Is the positivist concept of a fact to be dismissed, then, as a simple delusion? Not quite. There is no doubt that the concept of a fact as what is more or less immediately apprehended in sense-perception accords well with our *spontaneous* consciousness in science. For we have learnt from Wittgenstein, Hanson and others,[30] as well as from gestalt psychology, that, at least in

---

30. L. Wittgenstein, *Philosophical Investigations*, 2nd edition, Oxford 1968, pp. 193 ff. and N.R. Hanson, *Patterns of Discovery*, Cambridge 1965, chapter 1.

the case of so-called 'epistemic perception'[31] we tend to perceive objects under concepts and descriptions such that, as Harré has put it, we 'read propositions off the world'.[32] That is, we tend to read the world like the time from the clock, *as if* it were constituted by facts. Moreover, this stance governs our moments of perplexity, when we imagine the world as a coy, secretive or dissimulating partner in a possible dialogue, and our planned empirical investigations, when we think of the world as writing a script we want to read, in a code that we must first decipher, if we are to read it aright. It is this *factualising* consciousness which positivism simplifies, misrepresents but reflects. What is involved in the categories in which philosophical false consciousness thinks the concept of a fact is not therefore so much a crass error, as a superficiality, reflecting the way in which, in epistemic perception, social reality, in the form of our own prior cognitive reproducts and transforms, naturally presents itself. In this sense the fact form is an objective mystification, partly analogous to the value form, generated by the very nature of the activities in which we engage. Thus we represent facts as hard, stubborn, brute, recalcitrant.[33] A considerable mystique accrues spontaneously to the concept. This is alright if the source of the mystique and of the resistance of facts to voluntaristic (or decisionistic) change is located firmly in the social structure, where it belongs, and not in the natural world, where positivism, following commonsense, places it.

Diagram 3.19 attempts to represent the relationships at work in the constitution and reconstitution of the fact form. Theory generates the phenomenal forms and schemata in and through which we read the world; which, when the reading is practical or spontaneous, are reflected in the ideological categories of positivism; which in turn undergird the normal practice of science, so reproducing theory. BD signifies, so to speak, the cut of everyday life (or normal science). Repudiating the positivist concept of fact, i.e. reification at C, would not destroy our spontaneous concept of a fact, i.e. objectivication at B. But, by situating the historicity of our readings of the world, and hence the possibility of changes in them, it would allow greater ration-

31. F. Dretske, *Seeing and Knowing*, London 1969, chapter 1.
32. R. Harré, *Principles of Scientific Thinking*, London 1970, p. 195.
33. Cf. P. Herbst, 'The Nature of Facts', *Essays in Conceptual Analysis*, ed. A. Flew, London 1956, pp. 134-136.

ality in the development of theory and so enhance our scientific literacy.

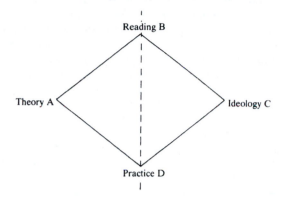

Diagram 3.19: *Reconstruction of the Fact Form*[34]

Facts then are real, but they are historically specific social realities. The mystification attached to them derives from the condition that, in our spontaneous way of thinking and in the philosophy — positivism — which reflects this, the properties possessed by facts *qua social objects* are transformed into qualities belonging to them as *natural things*. Fetishism, by naturalising facts, at once collapses and so destratifies their generative or sustaining social context and the mode of their production, reproduction and transformation in time, *ipso facto* dehistoricising and enternalising them. The fact form then acts so as to obscure, from scientists and non-scientists alike, the historically specific (cognitive and non-cognitive) structures and relations generating sense-experience in science. And so we could say of positivism, as Marx said of 'vulgar economy', that it is content to 'stick to appearances in opposition to the law which regulates, and explains, them'.[35] A degree of necessity

---

34. Diagram 3.14 is based on an analogy with the more general schema in *Possibility of Naturalism*, p. 89. Cf. also N. Geras, 'Marx and the Critique of Political Economy', *Ideology in Social Science*, ed. R. Blackburn, Glasgow 1972; M. Godelier, 'Structure and Contradiction in *Capital*', *ibid*; and J. Mepham, 'The Theory of Ideology is *Capital*', *Radical Philosophy* 2 (1972).
35. K. Marx, *Capital Vol. 1*, London 1961, p. 307.

attaches then to positivism in the TD. Its concept of a fact reflects our *spontaneous* consciousness in science. Nevertheless it is a concept which must be transcended in our *reflective* consciousness. For the facts are, as Marx said of the process of circulation, merely 'the phenomena of a process [production] taking place behind it'.[36] To stop at this spontaneous consciousness is not only mistaken in philosophy but damaging for science. For the facts are not what are apprehended in sense-experience (things, events, etc.), but the products of the conceptual and cognitive structures in terms of which our apprehension of things is organised.

It is only if, through a capacity to become conscious of the role of theory and prior thought generally in the production of that spontaneous consciousness, scientists can achieve sufficient distance from it to understand it as a social product, that they can come to conceive the possibility of a rational criticism, justification, elaboration or development of such factualising consciousness, and situate its content as comprising only one (and not necessarily the best) of a plurality of possible readings of the world. Such reflective distancing, which presupposes of course the necessary (pluralistic) institutional forms, becomes the more important once it is appreciated that theories are liable to only or predominantly produce results which harmonise with their own basic conceptualisation of the world. Incapacity to 'defactualise' in such a situation can lead the scientist all too easily into a dozy bask in the retrojected glories of earlier objectifications of thoughts, misconstrued as natural givens.

The fact form dishistoricises and destratifies science. In both respects there is a partial analogy with Marx's analysis of the value form. But in contrast to the value form, it is difficult to see the fact form itself (as distinct from its specific contents), and so (one might surmise) the objective mystification in which it is enveloped, as historically transient: i.e. as anything other than necessary for any conceivable mode of discursive social life. Furthermore it is difficult to fix an immediate sense to the concept of alienation, or to the possibility of a non-alienated form of existence, here. One might, however, relativise the concept of alienation in this domain to refer not to the domination of agents by social products, but to their domination by a false

---

36. K. Marx, *Gundrisse*, Harmondsworth 1973, p. 285.

consciousness of their relationship to those products. Such second order alienation is of course equally a social product, but unlike the first order spontaneous mystification seemingly implicit in any epistemic discourse, it is palpably not necessary and so is potentially historically transformable.

Parelleling the destratification and dehistoricisation of science is a destratification and dehistoricisation of being. The condition of reified facts in the TD is dependent things in the ID. This entails the denegation of ontology, screened by the epistemic fallacy, and the destratification of reality. Such a destratification is necessitated metaphysically, by the anthroporealist definition of being; meta-epistemologically, by the postulate of knowledge-world isomorphism in P's cognitive function; and epistemologically, by the assumption of a naturalised moment of fact-constituting or factualising consciousness. The latter is implicit at TPK in phenomenalism and at TGK in the actualist presumption of the spontaneity of constant conjunctions (of events perceived or perceptions) constituting causal laws. The dire consequences of ontological destratification will clearly be greatest when science has yet to set foot or secure itself on the royal road; when the first great, empirically controlled, retroductive leap from manifest phenomena to generative structure has still to occur and where only pseudo-science, or at best proto-science, and mythology (whether of a magico-religious or rationalist-humanist kind), reign.

## 7. Ideology in the Intransitive Dimension: Constant Conjunctions and Social Atoms

P's implicit ontology pivots on the Humean theory of causal laws. And it is this theory, is consort with its sundry tropes and corollaries, which is most pregnant with ideological potential in the ID. Now it should be obvious from the discussion in Chapter 1 that the mystification in the constant conjunction, in contrast to the fact, form is not an objective mystification pertaining to the nature of reality itself, but is quite simply false, an illusion properly so-called — or more akin to a philosophical hallucination than a mirage. If we want a Marxian analogue for it we must turn from the value to the wage form. For just as, according to Marx, wages are not what they appear to be —

they are not the value of labour, but of labour power — so causal laws are not the constant conjunctions of events that, when generated under artifically produced and deliberately controlled conditions, comprise their empirical grounds, but the tendencies of mechanisms ontologically irreducible to them. The analogy may be pressed further. For just as, according to Marx, the category mistake in political economy consists in the confusion of powers and their exercise, so the category mistake in philosophy consists in the confusion of powers (tendencies) and their realisation. Distinguishing between the domains of the real and the actual and between open and closed systems forges a way, in the teeth of the flat and uniform ontology of Humean empiricism, to a stratified and differentiated ontology of transfactually active causal structures and things. For Marx the social function of the wage form — not how it is intended, but how it acts — is to conceal the reality of exploitation, unpaid labour, the source of surplus value. What is the act of the constant conjunction form? It acts, I am going to propose, so as to conceal the reality of structures irreducible to events, and more particularly of social structures to human actions and of societies to individuals. In this way it defuses the possibility of science in the field of human affairs, especially of a science (or sciences) of the conditions and possibilities of change in the unwilled structures at work in social life, the only possible ground of human emancipation. The constant conjunction form is, like the wage form, 'as irrational as a yellow logarithm'.[37] But equally 'if history took a long time to get to the bottom of the mystery of wages, nothing on the other hand, is easier than to understand the necessity, the raison d'être, of this phenomenon'.[38]

It is of course the case that the constant conjunction form has a domain of plausibility in describing the Humean moment of a dialectic in the experimental (and some other) natural sciences (see 1.4 above). But it cannot describe its own conditions: it must, of metacritical necessity, apply a $\lambda K$ transform to, or pass over in silence, the human agency normally necessary for such conjunctions. Moreover the consciousness it depicts is nowhere that of science, which everywhere marks a distinction between necessary and accidental sequences, and treats its knowledge as applicable in closed and open systems alike. Thus no-one (I

37. K. Marx, *Capital Vol. III*, London 1961, p. 798.
38. K. Marx, *Capital Vol. I*, London 1961, p. 540.

hope) supposes that if a nuclear war were to destroy our planet this would violate Newton's laws. No chemist imagines that chemical bonding ceases to occur, and no physicist holds that electronic currents might desist from flowing outside the laboratory, so that the relationships described by say Prout's hypothesis or Ohm's law no longer or no further apply. And yet modern philosophy, in contradistinction to the spontaneous practice of science, has seldom doubted that the Humean analysis specifies at least necessary conditions for the attribution of causal laws. Hence. it would seem that the explanation for the constant conjunction form must lie *outside* science, in the ensemble of practices (including philosophy) constituting the rest of society.

In the Humean sieve, reality filters out as unstructured, undifferentiated and unchanging. The knowable world contains neither hidden, but discernible, mechanisms, nor powers (or real possibilities) of which we are not at present, but may presently come to be, aware. Being is dissipated in and exhausted by the fleeting, yet relentlessly uniform, qualia of experience, comprehended in or constructed out of the categories of untutored commonsense.[39] Such reductionism transposed to the human zone has especially deleterious consequences. In perfect resonance with the positivist concept of science as a behavioural response to the stimulus of given facts and their conjunctions, society is conceived as composed of individuals, motivated by given desires and conjoined (if at all) by contract.[40] When it becomes necessary, as it inevitably does, to view the constituents of such a society, viz. atomised individuals, as agents, as acting subjects rather than merely reacting objects, a measure of consistency is preserved by the simple expedient of endowing man with an additional faculty called

---

39. The space denied to science can then of course be used to make room for human freedom from causal determination. Kant, for instance, cleared the ground for belief in the existence of God and the immortality of the soul (the Romulus and Remus of religious faith) and thus prepared the way for both anti-naturalist hermeneutics and countless modern science/religion compromises.

40. Against this model of man see N. Chomsky, 'Review of B.R. Skinner's *Verbal Behaviour' The Structure of Language*, eds J. Fodor and J. Katz, New Jersey 1965. For the roots of it in seventeenth century political thought, see C.B. MacPherson, *The Political Theory of Possessive Individualism*, Oxford 1962.

reason to service his desires. An individual's freedom then consists in his ability to calculate his own best (or sufficient) interests in relation to his given desires, i.e. to perform an optimising or satisficing calculation. Utilitarianism (in the IA) is the natural handmaiden to positivism (in the EA).[41]

An atomistic individualism is both consequence and condition of P. But it cannot be overstressed that, while the powers and properties of social structures and human beings are existentially interdependent and conjuncturally co-determining, they are ontologically irreducible. The reason why wars are fought is not the same as the soldiers' reasons for fighting them. I am going to suggest that the most general ideological result of P in the ID is the rationalisation of individualistic theories of social practices, of which collectivist theories are merely the reified or organicist complement. P's result is obtained partly by resonance, inasmuch as it encapsulates and constructs its theory of knowledge, and implicitly being, around an elementary behaviourist/utilitarian model of man, as empirically determined but essentially inductively or deductively rational; and partly by specific injunctions and prohibitions, in which doctrines of methodological, economic, political atomism/ individualism are propagated and alternatives blocked. A mystique of elemental man in the ID chimes well with the mystique of ordinary commonsense in the TD. Both are equally vacuous. For as the content of commonsense is always given by

---

41. A completely objectivist social science is as much a cipher or surd as a solipsist science. Its pursuit merely results in the unconscious functioning of an implicit subject in ontology. Thus it is significant how Skinner reverts to a mentalistic terminology in the description of his own project as the 'intentional design of a culture' (B.F. Skinner, *Beyond Freedom and Dignity*, London 1972, p. 175), necessary to solve 'the terrifying problems that face us' (*op. cit.*, p. 4) and 'if the human species is to continue to develop' (*op. cit.*, p. 175). Just as the behaviourist must see himself or the species as a self-conscious subject, so the utilitarian must conceive others or society as manipulable objects. Thus Bentham writes in justification of the 'necessasry evil' of punishment, 'the immediate principal end of punishment is to *control* action. The action is either that of the offender or of others: that of the offender it controls by its influence, either on his will ... in the way of *reformation*; or on his physical power ... by *disablement*; that of others it can influence no otherwise than by its influence over their wills ... in the way of *example*.' (J. Bentham, *Introduction to the Principles of Morals and Legislation*, ed. W. Harrison, London 1948, chapter XIII, Section 1.2, p. 281, n. 1.)

some specific (albeit, possibly very general) theory; so the content of behaviour or goals is always dependent upon some specific structured social (albeit, possibly frequently recurring) context.

Hume articulated the corollary of this model well when he declared that 'mankind are so much the same in all times and places, that history informs us of nothing new or strange'.[42] Of course, when and where implicit assumptions of the model transparently break down, when the gap between Hume's 'Hindu' and his Englishman seems too wide, then history (or its spatial counterpart, anthropology) of a type is invoked. But it is history understood as the entelechy of the present (and of the here as distinct from the there) — history as the progressive realisation of a present which appears as its end, at once telos and finis. So we could say of this conception, with Marx, that history exists for it only in the past (as diversity always takes place elsewhere), that because it 'does not know that human history is nothing but the continous transformation of human nature',[43] for it although 'there has been history ... there is no longer any'.[44] In this way, historicism, understood as a prevalent present-centred doctrine of progress, which may be epistemically displaced (projected onto a moment in the future or retrojected onto a time, e.g. a golden age, in the past), is not just a historical concomitant of positivism. Rather it is an essential epistemological complement to positivism, generating an indispensable $\lambda\mu$ transform for it. Historicism, in the sense of an event-eductive or predictive/prophetic view of history, is already explicit in P's commitment to an actualist and deductivist conception of laws, explanation and theory within the framework of a positivistically unified science. So P acts in the ID as an anti-historical historicism, just as it operates generally in the TD as an anti-scientific scientism. Analogously, if there are, as I argued in Chapter 2, internal connections between social theory, social objects and social values, then P's repudiation of any intrusion of a normative discourse in

---

42. 'Would you know the sentiments, inclinations and the course of life of the Greeks or Romans? Study well the temper of the French and the English.' D. Hume, *An Enquiry Concerning Human Understanding*, Oxford 1963, p. 8.
43. K. Marx, *Poverty of Philosophy, Collected Works* Vol. 6, London 1975, p. 192.
44. K. Marx, *ibid*, p. 174.

social science identifies it, in the IA, as a descriptivist pre-scriptivism or a de-evaluating evaluator. In the same way it appears in the MD as the most outrageously speculative meta-physics[45] — an anti-philosophical pure (non-heteronomous) philosophy.

Hume's dictum betrays the *a-priori* and ahistorical limits of P. Its *a priori* basis lies in its ontological commitment to a general social praxiology of utilitarian cast, with only the initial conditions but not the essential content of theory empirically decided. Its ahistorical bias lies in its epistemological and methodological commitment to the dogmas and directives of actualist philosophy of science. The circumstance that social systems are not spontaneously, and cannot be experimentally, closed renders actualist methodologies irrelevant for the human sciences. But the *attempt* can still be made to appy them, gen-erating in its wake a range of covert effects. Thus, P cannot think through the feature that the human sciences must begin their long haul to scientificity without the facility of being able to observe or trace the effects of the undisturbed play of the latent structures of the world in the way sometimes available to the experimental natural sciences. But it is this very same in-ability which enables it to afford to a system all the benefits and dignities, such as resistance to actualist pseudo-falsification, properly conceded to scientific theories, when such systems may have no lease on that title at all: i.e. rate as substantive ideology. P thus comes to provide vital defensive cover for established social theories and doctrines, theories interwoven into the established order, *das Bestehende,* whatever and wherever that is — especially when coupled with the cult of the naturalised social product or fact. P's incapacity to think the distinction between structures and events, and especially social structures and human actions, exacerbates a continuing con-ceptual confusion and methodological obfuscation in the human sciences of the sort about which Wittgenstein complained in the psychology of the 1940s.[46] The chief methodological problem confronting the social sciences remains that received philosophy of science is at one and the same time *ontologically too*

---

45. Who knows a Humean causal law; who has experienced or suffered a sense-datum?
46. L. Wittgenstein, *Philosophical Investigations,* 2nd edition, Oxford 1958, p. 232.

*restrictive* (inhibiting creative theory, blocking the path to science, the move from manifest phenomena to generative structures) and *epistemologically too permissive* in that, in the absence of relevant explanatory *a posteriori* criteria of theory appraisal and development, it is all too easy for any general approach (and easier still for a conceptually confused or barren one, once it has become institutionally entrenched) to effectively immunise itself from criticism, making illicit or covert use of *ceteris paribus* or *mutatis mutandis* or *etc.* (holdall) clauses. Their chief *conceptual bottleneck* remains the lack of a coherent way of articulating human agency, the sole possible mode of material existence of social forms, with the evident reality and causal power of those forms as integrated structures which are in no sense human creations. (It is these blocks which the realist account of science and the transformational model of social activity are designed to clear.) This situation is aggravated by the epistemic arbitrariness of current disciplinary boundaries in the ambit of the human sciences. And in the institutional circumstances that actually prevail, social science still all too readily degenerates into some form of technical expertise, oriented to the pious *a priori* elaboration of empirically uncontrolled and unexplanatory verities, on the one hand, and to the incessant count or (attempted) measurement of the unquantifiable or the insignificant, on the other. Here positivism's incapacity to think the condition that makes it plausible in the experimental natural sciences continues to exert a heavy toll. The effect of the causally efficacious presence of necessary absences in its way of thinking being, science, society, philosophy and (wo)man is that, to recall the Wittgensteinian image, problem and method continue to pass one another uncomprehendingly by.[47]

P is a stratified conceptual totality. Thus if closed systems are a condition of the possibility of P, the condition of the condition is a particular conception of (tacitly gendered) man — necessary for the presumption of the ubiquitous spontaneity of closed systems, which is uniquely consonant with a fully (and so even partially) Humean world. On this model, man is pictured as a passive, essentially isolated spectator, a 'glassy essence' reflecting, a waxen impress, computer printout or recipient

---

47. *Loc cit.*

recorder of the given world; rather than as an always already formed and forming agent practically and co-operatively engaged in making or attempting to make sense (among other social products) in, out and of a complex structured and changing world, awake and attentive, listening and watchful, learning. On P's model, man is 'blank paper', the unused blotter, unwritten reader, absorbing the writing of the world which is simultaneously the reading of its facts. But the meaning of the writing is the reading it disguises and justifies. The result of the representation of our readings in the form of a writing is not only to conceal the possibility of different scripts, but of readings unavailable to unpracticed or jaded eyes, of unsighted structures visible only in the glow of their effects and of mechanisms which must first be heard before they can be visually transposed. So if the meaning of the writing is the reading it disguises, the meaning of this meaning is the immediate and universal legibility of being (in empiricist ontology) and a particular behaviourist-utalitarian model of man, as the absent reader, empirically determined but calculative, turns the pages of his world to his maximum advantage.

## 8. Ideology in the Metacritical Dimension: Presence of an Absence

## 9. Equivocations, Problem-field, Generalisations, Displacements and Results

As the epistemic fallacy collapses the ID and the ontic fallacy the TD, so the positivistic illusion, the self-abnegation of philosophy in favour of science, effaces the MD. P in this way attempts the perfect crime, eliminating all trace of crime, crimed against and criminal, decomposing and vapourising as it constitutes the three dimensions of the philosophy of science. And the positivistic illusion is the special trick by which the mechanism and medium (philosophy) of production and the producer, P, vanish, depositing in their stead only the bare image of the relentless play of actual invariants on empty atoms, of the uniformly given on the identically blank. P then applies an erasing $\lambda\kappa$ transform to the performance in which it produces this still-born scene, disavowing not only its own role but the very possibility of such a performance. 'Me? No, not me. But science' is its alibi, and when questioned as to its self-identity replies 'Who, me? You don't wish to know that, surely'; and when still further pressed, at last relents, confiding 'Just call me by my second name, "science"'.

P's problem field can now be more precisely defined as an anthroporealist (cognitive function) and fundamentalist (epistemic function) one. It presupposes the satisfaction of realist and social functions, specifying knowledge-being and society-individual connections, on the one hand, and philosophy and normalising functions, specifying philosophy-science and object-norm connections, on the other. In each respect P's position is overtly reductionist, but covertly dualist. It is therefore structurally ambivalent and internally (axiologically) inconsistent, with *both* of the opposed terms in each case reductively (exhaustively, exclusively) engulfing the other, so implicitly and bivalently consuming the terms and hence the structure of its constitutive functions. Thus the effect of the epistemic fallacy in empirical realism is the ontologisation of knowledge in the ontic fallacy. The outcome of the atomistic individualist sociology is reification and an exhaustively socialised (because intrinsically empty) concept of man. The upshot of the repudiation of philosophy in the positivistic illusion is a totally *a priori* and deductivist account of science as omnicompetent. And the consequence of P's hypernaturalist objectivism is a subjectivist (and prescriptivist) redefinition of being. But paradox is only the surface form of categorical error. These functions must be examined more closely.

P's cognitive function, considered as a species of anthroporealism, can be defined by the formula, empiricist ontology $\rightleftharpoons$ individualist sociology. It seeks to fuse being and knowing in a reciprocal atomisation and collocating closure of both. The reified fact presupposes the autonomised mind of the subject absorbing it, just as the fetishised system presupposes the behaviourist-utilitarian skeletal model of man as the subject recording it. As the price of the reified fact is the dependent thing, so the autonomous, unformed, pure sense-object is secured only at the cost of absent others, that is, a solipsism with the individual cut off from predecessors and contemporaries and ultimately his own prior and contemporaneous states. The positivist social function is then given by the equation: present others + constructed (formed) self → autonomous (unconstrained, unformed) self + absent others. In the deep structure of P it is this model of man which imposes its imprint on the model of being, at least as much as the corpuscularian action-by-contact cosmology. Moreover it perhaps also goes some way to accounting for the dominance of that cosmology as a specific interpretation of Newtonian physics which, although heuristically invaluable, was never theoretically unchallenged and never empirically validated.

To illustrate the interdependence of epistemic and ontic fallacies in P, let me re-present the way in which being is subjectivised by it so as to impart incorrigibility to knowledge and objectivise facts. I have argued (in the terms introduced in § 1 (see p. 234 above)) that P must be understood at the level of [1] theory-production, C $\overset{G}{-}$ P; [2] theory-constitution, P; and [3] theory-application, P $\overset{A}{-}$ S. To obtain certainty, being must be subjectivised, to apply it objectivised, in a reversible transition which can be illustrated by rotating our familiar basic grid through 180° as in Diagrams 3.21 and 3.22 below. This transform, allowing the philosophical ideologist to commute freely between [1] and [3], and *a fortiori* between the κ and μ pliabilities, may be dubbed the ϱ transform.

The analogue of the ϱ transform at TGK allows the transition to and from actualism in theory to an equivocal transfactualism in practice. Diagram 3.23 depicts the immediate source of the equivocations referred to in Diagram 3.22 and in generalised form in Diagram 3.3 and 3.4 on p. 187 above. Reified facts are at one and the same time determined by given things in theory, expressing the ontic fallacy, and presuppose as their overt conditions the unknowability of such things in practice, in accord with the anti-ontologism expressed in the epistemic fallacy.

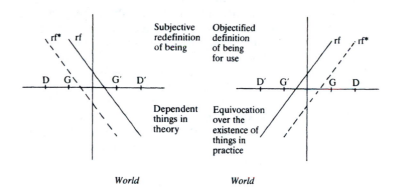

Diagram 3.21: *Theoretical Form of rf*          Diagram 3.22: *Applied Form of rf*

N.B. rf = Empirical realist function; rf* = realist dual of empirical realist function.

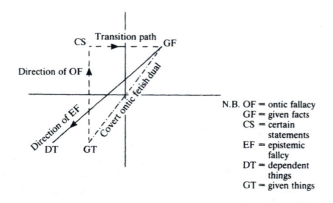

Diagram 3.23: *Proximate Source of Equivocation over Existence of Things*

Diagram 3.23 itself embodies an equivocation, as P does, between the subjective sense-world of consciousness and the objective world of things (supposedly resolved by the phenomenalist rending of the latter into the former, so as it were continually reconstituting afresh in daily practice the foundational poietic moment of P). To disequivocate we need to differentiate and then recombine theoretical subjective and applied objective forms as in Diagram 3.24. Theoretically, it is in the transference of the certainty imparted by given things to sense-statements to objectivised facts that the ground of the ontic fallacy lies. But in practice the naturalised fact is viewed as an effect of an objectified, public thing. Note that in Diagram 3.24 the dependency/doubt axis is eliminated from objectified knowledge, squeezed out by the double determination of knowledge by being.

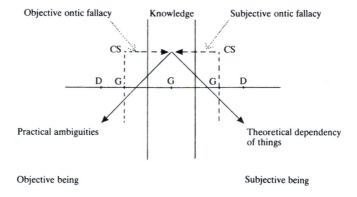

Diagram 3.24

Finally Diagram 3.25 indicates by the device of spacing them the three moments necessary for the understanding of P, and Diagram 3.26 presents a transcendental realist metacritical representation of what is going on. In Diagram 3.26 experience, and the facts it grounds, appear, as in Diagram 2.19 in Chapter 2.6 (p. 190 above), as a resultant of both natural and social determinations. But the epistemic fallacy, as represented by the mixed line, screens the role of theory, on the one hand, and of knowable things, on the other, in the constitution of facts and experience. The way is now clear for the projection of facts onto

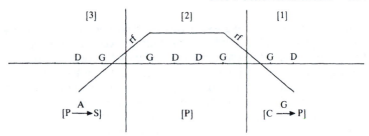

Diagram 3.25

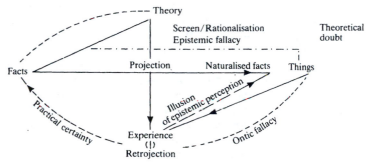

Diagram 3.26

things, thus their naturalisation, and the retrojective determination of facts, via an epistemically autonomised experience, in an epistemological boomerang, by themselves; so consolidating and reconfirming established theory — which appears as the real beneficiary of the whole exercise here. The diagram makes it clear that the reified fact form has an objective basis in the spontaneous illusion of epistemic perception discussed in § 6 above. It is in this way, then, that the reified fact comes to rationalise the theoretical status quo in the practice of normal science.

Before passing on to the fundamentalist side of P's problemfield, some brief general comments. First the basis of the protoexplanatory critique lies in the isolation of *contradictions* between P's theory or self-conception at [2] and its practice, either in the practice of its production at [1] or in the practice of its application at [3]. In this broad sense the critique remains fundamentally immanently-based. These theory-practice contradictions appear immanently in the form of *denegations*, in the sense that the critiqued theory is shown to unwittingly express and unconsciously presuppose the very content it would deny. But the ground of the denegation and the contradiction lies in the *transcendental-axiological necessity* of the denied position, appropriately redescribed. Denegation and axiological inconsistency are just two forms in which these transcendental necessities are historically played out. Second, the form in which the necessity is contained by the critiqued system is that of a *compromise* or vector, e.g. here between realist and irrealist themes — the effect, to speak metaphorically, of the *attempt* to realise the unrealisable. These compromises may be crystallised in the shape of a realist dual of or covert complement to its theory, to and from which the system may freely swing in practice; or it may take some other form, such as that of an internal division or split, or a displacement of the attempt elsewhere in a historically new or condensed form. Third, insofar as the necessity is contained within a continuing system, that system will reveal a *practical duplicity* or contradiction, more or less reflected in theoretical equivocations. This duplicity of structure expresses itself in the form of *commutability* between poles, i.e. the reversibility of intra-systemic operations, and of *equilibrating inversions*. Thus we have seen the transition operation in the grid preserving categories and exchanging predicates, and the fetish or isomorphising operation preserving predicates and exchanging categories. Categorial error has determinate and differentiable form. Fourth, the plasticity of ideological thought is consistent with both fixed or relatively enduring structures and typical or dominant outcomes; but because the system is formally internally inconsistent, external constraints need to be imposed on it to explain the determinate outcomes which result.

P's epistemic function is a fundamentalist one; more particularly, it is a *naturalising justificationist* one. For, if the general project of First Philosophy is to afford natural, human or spiritual grounds for (normally current) knowledge as a bedrock for it, in P's problem-field this project must be realised in a way which conforms with the interpretation of substantive scientific knowledge already fixed by the cognitive function. Its philosophy function, encapsulating the positivistic illusion, is designed to effect the disappearance of the discourse within which P's work is done, as we have seen; the overt burden of the epistemic function thus falls on P's objectivistic normalising function, systematically repudiating the IA of consciousness.

The task of fundamentalist epistemology here is to find an 'X' which will carry over into the world, so satisfying P's cognitive function (its conception of knowledge). For this X must be an *ungrounded grounder*, a moment of self-certifying certainty, which ensures its own validity and can at the same time pass for being. What is required here is thus the closing of any gap between belief and knowledge in the self-validation of a moment of belief, fusing validity (IA) and credibility (EA), exactly parallel to the closing of the gap between knowledge and being in the self-realisation of a moment of knowledge, fusing world (ID) and knowledge (TD). And of course this moment in which validity is guaranteed by the fact of its credibility, the moment of semblance, just is the subjective moment in which the world is exhausted, and so finally caught, in our apprehension of it in sense-consciousness. In P's foundational moment validity and credibility (fundamentalist fusion) and being and knowledge (anthroporealist fusion) are intertwined, fused and interdefined, so as at once to prescribe and naturalise the given (in a descriptivist prescriptivism and empirical realism respectively).

Formally the reductionist fusion of normativity to objectivity is manifest in the systematic descriptive-normative ambiguity in phenomenalism and material object empiricism (as indicated in Diagram 3.6 on p. 264 and noted more generally in Chapter 1.4). Practically it results in internal contradictions, compromise formations, duplicities, commutabilities and inversions parallel to those resulting from the reductionist fusion of being to knowledge. And its ideological meaning appears the same: objectivism at level [2] transmutes, at level [1], into a theoretical solipsism and the subjective redefinition of being, and at level [3], into the prescription of the given (i.e. for the reproduction of the made) and the celebration of the free individual, the supposedly autonomous agent (subject to every determination of the world); just as the epistemologisation of being, in the epistemic fallacy, at [2], oversees the ontological determination of knowledge by being, at [1], and its simple ontologisation or naturalisation at [3]. Hypernaturalism covers, complements and camouflages supernaturalism. If the epistemic fallacy undermines intransitivity in the ID and the ontic fallacy sociality in the TD, and the naturalistic fallacy undermines the possibility of rationality in the IA, what is the effect of the implicit mistake in the EA? It acts so as to undermine ($\alpha$)

objectivity in general, (β) historicity in particular. Both require some attention. There are three plain senses in which objectivity is vitiated in P. In the collapse of the ID, the objectivity of the intransitive objects of knowledge (structures, generative mechanisms and so forth) is lost. In the collapse of the extrinsic or historical aspect of the transitive dimension of science, the EA, the objectivity of knowledge as a social product irreducible to individual moments of decision, or more generally individual predicates, is relinquished. And in the collapse of the intrinsic or normative aspect of the transitive dimension of science, the IA, the groundability of decisions and judgements in objectively (in both the former senses) validatable considerations is forfeited. In respect of the loss of historicity, fundamentalism, atomism (in its social, epistemic and ontic forms) and actualism are all profoundly anti-historical. The fusion of being, knowing, believing and validating in P's foundational moment is sufficient to relay an anti-historical impetus in one part of the system everywhere else. Thus when normative and descriptive forms of ahistorical epistemological essentialism are naturalistically combined in what I characterised in 1.4 as the genetic fallacy, the denegation of historicity typically takes the form of the prescriptive transhistorical projection (and so universalisation) of the present. Where the projection fails, an epistemological CP clause, a $\lambda\mu$ transform, is invoked. Likewise where the present fails, as measured against the ahistorical, universal standard. Needless to say, such apparent disengagement of norm and actuality cannot be overtly rationalised in the system. For the collapse of real to epistemic possibility, of structure to event, in actualism entails the impossibility of transhistorical and contemporary criticism alike. With the extinction of real possibility goes the ground of human freedom, with the decomposition of structure the project of human emancipation. Diagram 3.27 schematises the constitution of P's problem-field.

If the thrust of my argument from § 3 on is correct, P satisfies the classical Marxian criterion for the characterisation of a belief system as 'ideological', viz. as a system of explicitly categorially false consciousness, outlined in § 2 above). A full explanatory critique of P would, however, consist in a critical explanation of its origins, development, reformations, displacements, recondensations, self-modulation and transformation over time. Obviously nothing of this scope has been attempted here. However it is worth noting that such a critique would still

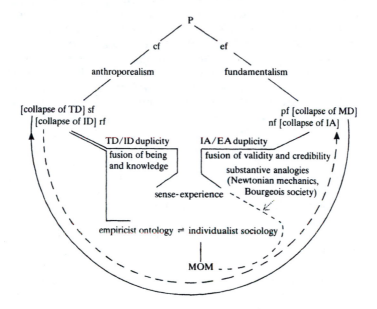

Diagram 3.27

N.B. cf = cognitive function; ef = epistemic function; sf = social function; rf = realist function; pf = philosophy funtion; nf = normalising function. MOM = underlying behaviourist-utilitarian model of (tacitly gendered) man.

require supplementation and reworking in the light of specific studies of historical contexts, episodes and individuals at what I called level [4] (see p. 234 above) of analysis of specific ideologies (and their critiques), viz. the level of concrete historical mediations, about which nothing has been said, though naturally much has been presupposed, here. A theoretical crique will inevitably remain partial, insofar as there are conditions presupposed, contextually implicated or contingently necessary but undiscussed, and incomplete, in virtue of the multiple determination of its particular historical instances. These are not deficiencies, but inevitabilities, in theory; they differentiate it precisely from applied concrete historiographical work. But it is misleading to think of the concrete as 'richer' in some absolute sense: it may be richer in detail but it is poorer in possibility. There is no question of overriding epistemological priority here: both are indispensable, and interdependent, moments of social science. Moreover while description of a structure takes logical priority to descriptions of changes (transformations) in it, and while the theoretical level is onto- logically prior to any particular agency which will sustain or transform it, what is reproduced or transformed at that level — that is, the content of the structure — may consist in systematic tendencies to transformation, dissipation, displacement or other types of change. In principle every structure may contain self- transformative tendencies and every instantiation of a structural form may be more or less uniquely conjuncturally co- determined and circumscribed. But in practice phenomena such as historical periodisation, systemic binding, routinsation, quasi- functional overdetermination, institutional regimentation and reinforcement and ideological rationalisation predispose us to focus on the short dramatic episode rather than the long cumulative build-up, the self-conscious alteration in human agency rather than the gradual unreflected modulation of practice, on the stimulus rather than the enabling conditions, as the source of change. This is a mistake. But it is an under- standable and perhaps inevitable one, given our spontaneous interest in our present states and ourselves rather than our con- ditions and consequences.

I have designated postivism by 'P' to draw attention to the abstract, although really transfactually efficacious, character of the cognitive structure I have been discussing, and to remind the reader that its precise historical forms and historical effects will always require mediation at much more concrete orders of ana- lysis. Moreover my proto-explanatory critique is as yet incom- plete, insofar as I have barely touched on the self-reflexive criterion viz. (6) (on p. 244). Among the most significant con- siderations here, to focus once more merely on conditions within the cognitive sphere, for realism seem to have been: (1) the rapid development of the 'material forces of enquiry' over the last century or so; (2) the collapse of the Newtonian *Weltanschauung*; (3) the development of historical materialism and the crisis of the human sciences; and (4) the failure of logicist and formalist programmes in the philosophy of mathe- matics and science. It is (1), permitting the identification of second, third and fourth tiers of structure which makes scientific realism seem, in its 'vertical' aspect, more than just an attractive hypothesis[48] and reverses the effective normalisation and domestication of the first modern scientific revolution of Kepler, Galileo and Newton within the structures of empirical realism. For an empiricist and/or idealist account of science is far less plausible when scientists are engaged with the effects of forces of forces and can smash atoms of atoms. And when bacteria or viruses can actually be seen under the microscope, then instrumentalist or fictionalist interpretations of scientific theory begin to seem, to say the least, strained and far-fetched. (2) The implications of the experience of the refutation and breakdown of the Newtonian system, if consistently pursued, include not only the recognition of the need for the sociality of our knowledge and the historicity, diversity and epistemic relativity of its forms, but for the transcendental reality and transfactual efficacy of its objects. And it relegates any isomorphising knowledge/world fusion to the status of an anthroporealist dream. (3) points towards a conception of the duality of structure and practice as irreducible aspects of the transformative and transformational historical process, ultimately grounded in our biological being and the geo-historical ecology of our globe. (4) Research indicating the inadequacy of closed, syntactical and purely extensionalist conceptions of cognitive structures, indicates a way of building on the best insights of Deweyan pragmatics, Wittgensteinian contextualism, phenomenology and structuralism, towards a conception of the production and reproduction of cognitive structures *in use.*

This standpoint approaches that of Marx in his critique of political economy, although it lacks Marx's concept of history, the peculiar emphasis of his materialism and of course his 'dialectic'.[49] It is from the standpoint of Marx's critique, with which I have been exploiting analogies, that I have been conceiving P as a mode of production in its own right, just as the sciences themselves are. More specifically, I have been treating P as a mode of production of ideology, producing characteristic and an in principle indefinite number of, as well as, when the

---

48. It will be recalled that I argued in 1.4 that when 'vertical' is combined with 'horizontal' realism, it becomes not just attractive, but transcendentally necessary.

49. For some preliminary thoughts on this, see my entries on 'Dialectic', 'Knowledge, Theory of', 'Materialism' and 'Science' in *A Dictionary of Marxist Thought*, ed. T. Bottomore et al, Oxford 1983.

occasion demands (operating κ, μ, λ and ρ transform on its structure), opportunistically transmutable, effects, tightly intricated into the mode of reproduction of normal science and the existing social order. It secures these effects, primarily at the level of spontaneous consciousness and apologetic theory (through the atomisation, naturalisation, simplification, routinisation and normalisation of being, including social being including knowledge (including of course knowledge of natural being)). In this way it accomplishes the destratification, undifferentiation and dehistoricisation of all reality and the derealisation, detotalisation and canonisation of contemporary specifically social reality.

We have seen that P has a quotient of necessity in the TD in that it reflects a seemingly inevitable moment of epistemic consciousness in any conceivable discursive life, but that in the ID it constitutes sheer mystification. While the properties P typically ascribes to knowledge congratulate and contain science, limned as sure and safe, the properties it ascribes to being reinforce and echo more general social ideologies. P is, as I have stressed, only the kernel of a very plastic system S. But it is the *dominant* ideologies that establish the vectors determining the form of P, the postivist account of science.

The pliability of ideological thought must not be confused with the underdetermination of theory of experience by evidence or the lability intrinsic to any developing scientific research programme. I have used a very restrictive definition of ideology as explicitly categorially false consciousness. On the basis of this definition, ideology appears differentiated from science not only negatively, by the absence of characteristically scientific procedures, but positively, by the presence of certain characteristic strategems of its own. It should be noted that the structure of the explanatory critique employed here is not simply that P, in representing the social world as natural in fetishism or in reducing the real to the actual in actualism or in reconstructing the individual as autonomous in atomism, is categorially confused. But *also* that the very forms in which the socialised world presents itself to experience — in epistemic perception in the fact form and in certain historically determinate forms of society in characteristically bourgeois ideological forms[50] — are categorially confused. Hence categorially false consciousness figures in the explanatory critique of P at two levels — both as *explanandum* and as *explanans*. Categorial error of the former sort is constitutive of P, but it is categorial error of the latter sort which explains its continuing efficacy as a system of thought which is reproduced in a serious and practical state; that is, believed and acted upon. This means, in the first place, that, if P is real in its own right, we are dealing with two orders of categorical error (and 'Colletti-contradiction') here. And in the second that, understood as the spontaneous philosophy of a self-understood world, any explanatory critique of P has implications for, and no explanatory critique of P can ultimately succeed without, a transformed transformative historical praxis.

The importance of positivism lies partly in the fact that almost all post-Humean, post-Kantian philosophies stand in certain critical logical and historical relations to it; partly in the fact that it is the philosophy of *das Bestehende*, of commonsense and uncommon nonsense par excellence; partly in the fact that it is intimately associated, on the one hand, with the most successful scientific system hitherto seen, viz. Newtonian mechanics, and, on the other, with the most powerful socio-economic order hitherto known, namely capitalism; partly in the fact that it continues to structure contemporary philosophy of science and social science, even where these are formally opposed to it; and partly in the fact that it continues to inform the nocturnal reflective consciousness of probably most natural scientists and the diurnal practice of many human scientists, albeit in perhaps modified and somewhat refined forms. Elsewhere I have attempted to reconstruct the genealogy of contem-

---

50. For instance, 'The sphere of circulation or commodity exchange, within whose boundaries the sale and purchase of labour-power goes on, is in fact a very Eden of the innate rights of man. It is the exclusive realm of Freedom, Equality, Property and Bentham ... Freedom, because both buyer and seller ... are determined by their own free will .... Equality, because ... they exchange equivalent for equivalent. Property, because each disposes of what is his own. And Bentham, becaue each looks only to his own advantage'. (K. Marx, *Capital Vol, 1*, Harmondsworth 1976, p. 280.) Or we could refer to the interpellation of individuals as free agents in their constitution as subjects (see L. Althusser, 'Ideology and Ideological State Apparatuses', *Lenin and Philosophy*, London 1971, pp. 160 ff.); or to the rationalisation of authoritarian/elitist (bureaucratic, managerial) and instrumentalist-manipulative social forms and practices (see, e.g., J. Habermas, *Towards a Rational Society*, London 1971, chapter 6). However both Althusser and habermas, perhaps the two most influential recent Marxist philosophers writing on ideology, diverge from Marx in regarding the ideological figures they highlight as necessary (Althusser) or at least grounded in a universal and necessary interest (Habermas).

porary anti-monist philosophy of science, as comprising in effect voluntaristic, sceptical and sociologistic recondensations of epistemologically displaced positivist themes,[51] and to show how hermeneuticist and neo-Kantian philosophies of social science tacitly presuppose positivism — first in their acceptance of it as the essentially unquestiond truth about the world known by natural science; second in their reproduction (in transposed forms) of characteristically positivist philosophical positions in their accounts of knowledge of the social world.[52]

These historical developments cannot be reduced to the simple synchronic transformations of P discussed in § 5; they introduce new terms and relations and command an assertoric content irreducible to that of P. But underpinning them is P and behind the structure of P lies its problem-field. And this problem-field is structured by anthroporealism and fundamentalism. It is *this* structure from which contemporary philosophy has not broken. These historical displacements of P cannot be interpreted simply as repetitions or inversions, complements or duals of P. But they do almost always repeat, invert, complement or dualise (or contain repetitions, inversions, complements or duals of) the constituents of P's underlying problem-field, appropriately redescribed in terms of an explanatory critical metatheory. And within this problem-field, as it has been historically developing from the seventeenth century, P has been, at least since the mid-nineteenth century and probably still is, the dominant structure in respect of our understanding of knowledge and science.

It is important not to regard P as a mere effect of the conditions which explain its reproduction and efficacy. For if we may pass it a back-handed compliment from Marx: 'It is in reality much easier to discover the earthly kernel of the misty creations than ... to develop from the critical, given relations of life the forms in which they have been apotheosized'.[53] This is the special trick of P. For we have seen that the generation of P in philosophical theory is the task of a special site, the grid, which must produce, in response to the play of its problem-field, a product that will not only satisfy its demands as

51. See my 'Feyerabend and Bachelard', *New Left Review* 94, 1975, pp. 31-55.
52. See my *The Possibility of Naturalism*, especially chapter 4.
53. K. Marx, *Capital Vol. 1*, Harmondsworth 1976, p. 494 n.

expressed in a (fundamentalist) epistemic function of scientistic and objectivistic bent, and pass muster as an account of science fulfilling particular (empirical) realist and (individualist) social functions, but *in so doing* — herein lies the achievement — produce a product which will lend itself immediately to the propagation of those overt and resonance effects which distinguish P from any of a dozen or more categorially confused and axiologically inconsistent accounts of science. This is no mean achievement. For who normally listens to philosophers? Who reads Bergson or Holbach? P even manages the feat of producing a norm of scientific objectivity, together with a model of human subjectivity, which is most rigorously applied where — if I can shade this cow in the Hegelian night — its philosophy is most grotesquely, absurdly inapplicable. The premise of this tentative investigation, provisionally concluded, is that system P is a living ideology; that this must be explained at least primarily in terms of the way it meets cognitive requirements and practical needs outside philosophy; and that it is in terms of these that the vectors defining its internal constitution must be explained. 'This', Marx continues, 'is the only materialistic and therefore the only scientific method.'[54]

It is worth emphasising the limits of a proto-explanatory critique of this type. No-one who is a positivist will be convinced by it, nor should anyone who is a materialist overestimate the power of ideas to change ideas. But under certain conditions, ideas can change the world. One such idea is that of Marxism, which acts in a totality in which discursive and non-discursive elements are interlaced. In this totality philosophy decides nothing, but it forms a final court of procedural appeal (metaphysics $\alpha$) as well as the medium for the articulation and critique of basic conceptual *Gestalten* (metaphysics $\beta$) for the lower level, substantive courts and assemblies in which the fates of practical, class and other struggles, of individual lives and of the forms of social relations and activity are daily decided. The established order some time ago sat in judgement on science. And its verdict: *positivism*, together with its various internal transforms and capacities for historical displacement and reformation, still rests. With good reason — for positivism at once naturalises and normalises things and reflects in an endless hall

---

54. *Loc cit.*

of mirrors the self-image of Bourgeois Man. It is, one might say, the house-philosophy of the bourgeoisie. Those who would rationally change the world need to re-open the case at all levels, in every science, in each practice, lest they be caught in a trap spun by a spider who knows the web of its problem-field well, knows that another name by which system P goes is that of vulgar (that is, unthinking) materialism.

# Index

Page numbers in *italics* refer to figures.